Globalization and Egalitarian Redistribution

OTHER BOOKS FROM THE PERSISTENT INEQUALITY PROJECT

Samuel Bowles, Herbert Gintis, and Melissa Osborne Groves, eds. 2005. *Unequal Chances: Family Background and Economic Success.* Princeton and New York: Princeton University Press and Russell Sage Foundation.

Samuel Bowles, Steven N. Durlauf, and Karla Hoff, eds. 2006. *Poverty Traps.* Princeton and New York: Princeton University Press and Russell Sage Foundation.

Jean-Marie Baland, Pranab Bardhan, and Samuel Bowles, eds. 2006. *Inequality, Cooperation, and Environmental Sustainability.* Princeton and New York: Princeton University Press and Russell Sage Foundation.

Globalization and Egalitarian Redistribution

Edited by Pranab Bardhan,
Samuel Bowles & Michael Wallerstein

RUSSELL SAGE FOUNDATION • NEW YORK

PRINCETON UNIVERSITY PRESS • PRINCETON AND OXFORD

Copyright © 2006 by Russell Sage Foundation

Requests for permission to reproduce material from this work should be sent to Permissions, Princeton University Press

Published by Princeton University Press, 41 William Street, Princeton, New Jersey 08540

In the United Kingdom: Princeton University Press, 3 Market Place, Woodstock, Oxfordshire OX20 1SY

And the Russell Sage Foundation, 112 East 64th Street, New York, New York 10021

All Rights Reserved

Library of Congress Cataloging-in-Publication Data

Globalization and egalitarian redistribution / edited by Pranab Bardhan, Samuel Bowles, and Michael Wallerstein.
    p. cm.
   "Russell Sage Foundation, New York".
   Includes bibliographical references and index.
   ISBN-13: 978-0-691-12519-0 (alk. paper)
   ISBN-10: 0-691-12519-8 (alk. paper)
   1. International economic integration—Social aspects. 2. Income distribution. 3. Equality.
 I. Bardhan, Pranab K. II. Bowles, Samuel. III. Wallerstein, Michael, 1951–

HF1418.5.G581655 2006
337.1—dc22   2005049940

British Library Cataloging-in-Publication Data is available

This book has been composed in Adobe Garamond.

Printed on acid-free paper. ∞

pup.princeton.edu

Printed in the United States of America

10 9 8 7 6 5 4 3 2 1

Contents

Tables

Illustrations

Preface

SCHOLARLY INTEREST IN the relationship between globalization and inequality has burgeoned in recent years along with the growing economic integration of national economies into a global economic system. In the eyes of many—scholars, policymakers, and activists alike—globalization has provided a favorable environment for the political assault on the welfare state and on trade union bargaining, which gathered force in many advanced economies during the last two decades of the twentieth century. Critics of nationally based policies of social insurance and income redistribution to the less well off frequently invoke the imperatives of "global competitiveness." In this book we address a series of questions concerning the relationship between increased economic integration and the economic effectiveness and political viability of policies of national states and trade unions that are designed to enhance economic security and to redistribute economic opportunity and income to the less well off.

A grant from the Russell Sage Foundation to the Santa Fe Institute to study "Persistent Inequality in a Competitive World" allowed us to convene a workshop of the authors to discuss initial drafts of the papers. We are grateful to the foundation and especially to Eric Wanner and Suzanne Nichols for their support. Other projects funded by the Russell Sage Foundation grant to the Santa Fe Institute included studies of the role of inequality as a possible impediment to cooperation in the protection of local environmental commons; the poverty traps that contribute to persistent inequality among families, nations, and ethnic groups; and the transmission of economic status within families across generations. The following books resulted from these other studies in the "Persistent Inequality" project:

Samuel Bowles, Herbert Gintis, and Melissa Osborne Groves, eds. *Unequal Chances: Family Background and Economic Success.* Princeton and New York: Princeton University Press and Russell Sage Foundation.

Samuel Bowles, Steven N. Durlauf, and Karla Hoff, eds. 2006. *Poverty Traps.* Princeton and New York: Princeton University Press and Russell Sage Foundation.

Jean-Marie Baland, Pranab Bardhan, and Samuel Bowles, eds. 2006. *Inequality, Cooperation, and Environmental Sustainability.* Princeton and New York: Princeton University Press and Russell Sage Foundation.

We are grateful to Andi Sutherland, Tim Taylor, Margaret Alexander, Bae Smith, and others of the staff of the Santa Fe Institute for their contributions to this project. Amara Levy-Moore assisted in the preparation of the manuscript and we thank her as well. Alison Kalett and Tim Sullivan at Princeton University Press converted a complicated manuscript into a beautiful book. We are also grateful to the MacArthur Foundation for its generous support of the Research Network on the Effects of Inequality on Economic Performance. (Information about the Net-work can be found at http://globetrotter.berkeley.edu/macarthur/inequality/.) Much of what is presented here was developed as a part of the Network's ongoing research agenda. Finally, we thank the Behavioral Sciences Program of the Santa Fe Institute for its support of this project.

Pranab Bardhan, Samuel Bowles, and Michael Wallerstein
Santa Fe, New Mexico
August 2005

Contributors

KEITH BANTING, School of Policy Studies, Queen's University

PRANAB BARDHAN, Department of Economics, University of California, Berkeley

CARLES BOIX, Department of Political Science, University of Chicago

SAMUEL BOWLES, Behavioral Sciences Program, Santa Fe Institute and Department of Economics, University of Siena

MINSIK CHOI, Department of Economics, University of Massachusetts, Boston

RICHARD JOHNSTON, Department of Political Science, University of British Columbia

COVADONGA MESEGUER YEBRA, CIDE Center for Research and Teaching in Economics

KARL OVE MOENE, Department of Economics, University of Oslo

LAYNA MOSLEY, Department of Political Science, University of North Carolina, Chapel Hill

CLAUS OFFE, Department of Sociology, Humboldt University

UGO PAGANO, Department of Economics, University of Siena and Central European University

ADAM PRZEWORSKI, Department of Politics, New York University

KENNETH SCHEVE, Department of Political Science, University of Michigan

MATTHEW J. SLAUGHTER, Tuck School of Business, Dartmouth University

STUART SOROKA, Department of Political Science, McGill University

MICHAEL WALLERSTEIN, Department of Political Science, Yale University

Globalization and Egalitarian Redistribution

Introduction

Pranab Bardhan, Samuel Bowles & Michael Wallerstein

THE WORD "GLOBALIZATION" had not been coined in the early 1930s, but in a paper titled "National Self-Sufficiency" John Maynard Keynes sounded an alarm about its consequences that resonates today:

> We each have our own fancy. Not believing that we are saved already, we each should like to have a try at working out our own salvation. We do not wish, therefore, to be at the mercy of world forces working out, or trying to work out, some uniform equilibrium according to the ideal principles, if they can be called such, of *laissez-faire* capitalism. . . . We wish for the time at least . . . to be our own masters and to be as free as we can . . . to make our own favorite experiments towards the ideal social republic of the future. (Keynes 1932–33: 763, 768)

Few now remember Keynes's prescient advocacy of local self-determination and national policy experimentation; but the tension between global integration and national sovereignty has become a staple of the conventional wisdom, endorsed by scholars and diffused by the media. A leading mid-twentieth-century international trade economist, Charles Kindleberger, concluded,

> The nation-state is just about through as an economic unit. . . . It is too easy to get about. Two-hundred-thousand-ton tankers, . . . airbuses and the like will not permit the sovereign independence of the nation-state in economic affairs. (Kindleberger 1969:207)

If super tankers and airbuses—according to Kindleberger—would reduce the state to little more than a price-taking entity like the firm in neoclassical economics, the argument must hold with additional force in the contemporary "weightless economy" of instantaneous information transfer.

Many recently have advanced the position that global economic integration has sharply circumscribed the latitude for egalitarian redistribution and social insurance by national states. But is Kindleberger right?

• • •

For well-known reasons, a reduction of impediments to international flows of goods and factors of production may enhance allocative efficiency both globally and within national economies. The increased competition among national states associated with the freer movement of goods and factors is also widely thought to contribute to governmental accountability to its citizenry.

Economic integration, however, is also thought to raise the economic costs of programs by the nation-state that redistribute income to the poor and that provide economic security for their populations. Among the reasons is that some of the more internationally mobile factors of production—capital and professional labor—tend to be owned by the rich, and a nation-specific tax on a mobile factor induces national-output-reducing relocations of these factors. Similar reasoning demonstrates the high cost of attempting to alter the relative prices of factors of production, for example, through trade union bargaining aimed at raising the wage relative to the after-tax expected return to capital. Even Pareto-improving social insurance–based policies are compromised, as cross-border mobility of citizens allows the lucky to escape the tax costs of supporting the unlucky, thereby reintroducing the problem of adverse selection associated with private insurance and that public insurance was thought to avoid (Sinn 1997).

The result is a generalization of what Arthur Okun (1975) called redistribution in "leaky buckets": the net benefit to the recipient may fall considerably short of the loss to those paying the costs. Even the intended beneficiaries may suffer as a result. In a democracy, leaky buckets thus make it more difficult to secure electoral support for egalitarian redistribution, and thus compromise both the ethical appeal and the political viability of redistributive programs. By exacerbating the generalized leaky bucket problem, trade liberalization and other aspects of economic integration are thus thought to restrict the class of redistributive policies that are politically sustainable in democratic nation-states.

The chapters that follow address the following questions: *Does globalization raise the costs and compromise the political viability of national policies designed to redistribute income to the less well off and to insure people against economic risks? If so, are there alterations in the canonical social democratic, corporatist, or liberal welfare state policy packages that can address the challenges posed by globalization, effectively assisting the poor and the unlucky while securing durable electoral support?*

These are difficult questions, and the chapters that follow will disappoint the reader seeking simple answers. But we do not think that the task of reconciling global integration with economic security and distributive justice is insurmountable. Indeed, we suspect that adverse affects of globalization on the political viability of national-level redistributive institutions have been considerably exaggerated among policymakers and the public.

•   •   •

The term "globalization" has been used to refer to such distinct developments as the Americanization of popular cultures around the world, the increasing importance of the World Trade Organization and other supranational institutions, and the encroachments by markets and states on small-scale societies. Here (excepting the chapter by Bowles and Pagano) we adopt a more restrictive sense of the term. Globalization refers to the reduced impediments to the movement of goods, people, information, and finance across national boundaries. Two main contributors to globalization are a dramatic reduction in the cost of transportation and communication and a shift in national-level tariffs and other economic policies facilitating international exchange and investment. Historians recognize two globalization eras: one from the end of the Napoleonic Wars to World War One, and the other from the end of World War Two to the present. The period prior to 1815 and between the two world wars are termed by the economic historian Jeffrey Williamson (2003) as "anti-global."

Our concern here is not with the much-debated question, Does globalization increase economic inequality? We want to know, instead, how globalization affects policies designed to address inequality, whatever its source. But a brief review of the "does globalization increase inequality?" question will suggest some pitfalls to be avoided.

Reasons why globalization can work powerfully to reduce inequalities are familiar to economists. The freer flow of information, goods, and capital from the richer to poorer nations should raise productivity and increase the demand for labor in the labor-abundant and technologically lagging nations, inducing tendencies toward convergence of wage rates for equivalent labor throughout the world (along the lines of Paul Samuelson's factor price equalization theorem). Globalization might also induce more competitive product markets, reducing profit markups—the discrepancy between prices and marginal costs—and thus raising real wages. Finally, competition among nation-states and the ability of citizens to compare institutional performance across nations might also provide greater popular accountability for state and para-statal institutions often dominated by elites.

The historical record of inequality both between and within nations, however, suggests powerful forces counteracting these tendencies. Figure I.1 (from Bourguignon and Morrison 2002) gives an estimate of world inequality form 1820 to 1992. While the early data are the best currently available estimates, they are necessarily imprecise. The period covers the two globalization eras and the intervening anti-global era mentioned earlier. While within-country inequality has declined somewhat—most sharply during the "anti-global" period under the impact of the two world wars—between-country inequality increased, only recently reversed by the dramatic catch-up of China during the past two decades (not shown).[1]

Among these divergence-inducing tendencies are between-country differences in institutions. These effects of institutional differences might have been heightened by globalization but would have been at work even in its absence. Most notable in this regard is the emergence of capitalist economies in Western Europe and its offshoots and the persistence of institutional impediments to growth (in some cases under the auspices of colonial regimes) in much of the rest of the world.[2]

• • •

We do not conclude from figure I.1 that globalization contributed to inequality—that is far too grand a claim to be established by a single set of data. Rather, we

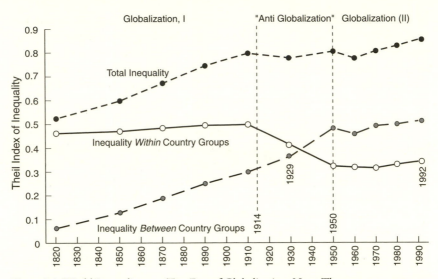

Figure I.1. World Inequality over Two Eras of Globalization. Note: The country groups are fifteen countries with high quality data and eighteen regional country groupings with similar levels of GDP per capita. Source: Bourguignon and Morrison (2002).

wish to emphasize that standard economic models might give a partial and hence misleading account of the dynamics of income distribution and its relationship to economic integration. This is especially the case in reasoning about the response of national states to the new incentives and constraints posed by a more integrated world economy. In the following chapters, therefore, we seek to provide carefully reasoned causal accounts of aspects of the relationship between globalization and egalitarian public policy.

An important part of this task is to isolate the dimensions of globalization that are pertinent to our question. A number of empirical studies beginning with Gordon (1988) have stressed that while cross-border flows of goods and investment have increased in recent years, the degree of openness as measured by the ratio of export, imports, and capital flows to total output is not substantially greater in recent decades than it was a century ago.[3]

These aggregate indices are poor measures of the degree of global economic integration for our concerns here, however. The reason is that the size of cross-border flows does not bear any simple (or even monotonic) relationship to the absence of impediments to trade: trade and investment flows may be absent where impediments are prohibitive, or where there are no impediments. Consider between-country net investment flows or labor migration. Capital or labor move from one country to the other in response to differences in the expected returns on these factors of production (taking account of risk, taxes, and all other influences affecting expected returns). But differences in expected returns are prima facie evidence of a *lack* of economic integration, namely a violation of the law of the single price according to which the expected returns to factors of production do not differ across nations (other than the effects of transportation costs). The global reallocation of labor and capital is one of the ways in which the law of the single price might come into force.

In the competitive equilibrium of a fully market-integrated world (were this ideal to occur), labor and capital would be distributed among countries in such a way as to equalize the rates of returns on these factors. For this reason, we would not observe net flows of either capital or labor. Thus the size of investment or of labor movements between countries is not monotonically related to the degree of economic integration. There may be little movement of factors of production either because there are impediments to movement—indicating a lack of global integration—or because there is no incentive to move because the law of the single price is observed, indicating the complete integration of global economies.

Cross-border flows of goods will occur for similar reasons. The level of the cross-border movements provide a measure of *both* the presence or absence of impediments to movement *and* the extent to which differing endowments of factors of production and economies of scale make specialization advantageous. Changes in the latter will induce changes in the level of aggregate trade flows even where there are no changes in the impediments to movement.

We focus here not on the size of the aggregate flows of investment, trade, and migration, but rather on the microeconomic effects of these flows. The reason is that the answer to our question depends on the incentives facing firms, voters, and others. For example, suppose we seek to understand the impact of globalization on a trade union that would like to promote both employment opportunities and higher wages for its members. The relevant indices should measure the impact of globalization on the demand curve for labor, and specifically on the effect that wage changes will have on the demand for labor The more competitive environment of an open economy may increase the employment losses associated with wage increases, and correspondingly raise the employment gains associated with lower wages. If opportunities for firms to relocate offered by globalization are sufficiently inviting, then a trade union or a social democratic government might prefer lower to higher wages. We would also like to know not only the size of investment flows, but also the effect of globalization on the responsiveness of national investment to own-country wage levels and tax rates relative to the rest of the world. There is little hard evidence that by these microeconomic measures openness has increased in recent years, but it seems plausible to think that it has, or at least will.

• • •

The questions addressed in this volume are multifaceted. The essays that follow address different aspects of the impact of globalization on the economics and politics of redistributive policies, using a variety of methods. It may be helpful, therefore, to begin with an overview of the book so that readers can see how the different chapters fit together.

Pranab Bardhan, in his essay "Globalization and the Limits to Poverty Alleviation," surveys the impact of globalization on poverty in poor and middle-income countries. Bardhan summarizes a variety of ways in which increasing economic integration affects the incidence of poverty in the Third World, both positively and negatively. While the set of connections between globalization and Third World poverty described by Bardhan is complex, his overall conclusion can be stated simply: Most of the economic constraints facing the poor in low and middle-income countries have little to do with globalization and much to do with domestic institutions. Insofar as globalization matters, the poor in the Third World often suffer from too little rather than too much. Eliminating the trade barriers and subsidies adopted by rich countries that discriminate against products produced in the Third World, Bardhan argues, would significantly improve the material welfare of the poor in the Third World.

From a European perspective, Claus Offe is less sanguine about the impact of globalization on the poor in rich countries. In his essay "Social Protection in a Supranational Context," Offe considers the recent experience of the European Union as an extreme example of economic integration at a supranational level. Offe questions whether the intricate system of social protections provided at the national level in Western Europe can survive the loss of national autonomy in key areas of economic policy. In Offe's account, the structure of social protection can be described as consisting of four tiers: (1) regulation of who can work (child labor laws), hours of work, and health and safety in the workplace; (2) social insurance policies that provide protection for those unable to work because of sickness, old age, or unemployment; (3) collective bargaining institutions that protect workers' income while working; and (4) macroeconomic policies to achieve and maintain full employment. Of the four tiers, Offe argues that only the first has been successfully transferred from the national level to the European Union. Offe considers three possible futures. In the first, the social insurance edifice is reconstructed at the level of the European Union. In the second, the national systems of social protection are gradually dismantled as countries struggle to keep expenditures within EU-imposed limits and to achieve full employment by enhancing the "flexibility" of their labor markets. Offe's final and darkest scenario is that the decline of social protections provokes a nationalist backlash promoting "illiberal forms of paternalistic protectionism."

Minsik Choi investigates the impact of capital mobility on collective bargaining outcomes in his essay "Threat Effects of Capital Mobility on Wage Bargaining." Choi observes that globalization can effect wages through two channels. The first and most studied channel is the effect of trade on the demand for different types of labor and, ultimately, the wages received by workers at different skill levels. The second channel is the impact of capital mobility on employers' ability to drive a harder bargain with labor and to obtain a larger share of the surplus. In an empirical study of wages in the United States, Choi finds evidence supporting both channels. In particular, Choi finds that capital mobility has significantly reduced unions' ability to obtain wage increases for lower-skilled union members. The implication of Choi's study is that globalization in general and capital mobility in particular is undermining the bargaining power of low-skilled workers in developed countries.

Taken together, the essays by Bardhan, Offe, and Choi suggest that globalization constrains redistributive policies in rich countries more than in poor countries. Layna Mosley, in her essay "Constraints, Opportunities, and Information: Financial Market–Government Relations around the World," argues that exactly the opposite is the case with respect to the relationship between governments and the global market for capital. Mosley relies on both interviews with bond traders and statistical analysis to study how the bond market reacts to national policy choices. Her fundamental finding is that the constraints imposed by the bond market on advanced industrial societies are "strong but narrow," while the constraints imposed on developing countries are "strong and broad." Because traders of bonds issued by rich countries are unconcerned about the possibility of default, the only economic indicators that concern these traders are the rate of inflation and the budget deficit. Changes of government or of policy that have no effect on the rate of inflation or the budget deficit are ignored by the bond market. In contrast, traders of bonds of developing countries are very concerned with the risk of default. As a consequence, traders of Third World bonds pay close attention to a wide variety of macro- and microeconomic policies, quickly raising the costs of funds to governments that take any action that might reduce the country's willingness or capacity to repay the debt in the future.

The essays by Offe, Choi, and Mosley provide evidence that the constraints imposed by globalization are important. Put most simply, globalization reduces the ability of governments to tax or to alter the return received by internationally mobile factors of production. Samuel Bowles, in his essay "Egalitarian Redistribution in Globally Integrated Economies," argues that globalization does not constrain other redistributive policies that raise efficiency. For example, a redistribution of assets may provide the poor with sufficient wealth to gain access to credit markets that were previously closed, enabling the poor to borrow and invest. The establishment of producer cooperatives may lower production costs by reducing or eliminating the need for external monitoring of work effort. The provision of public goods, such as roads or irrigation systems, can provide large gains in terms of both efficiency and poverty alleviation. While the cost of redistributive policies that reduce efficiency increases with increased economic integration, globalization does not diminish the feasibility of redistributive policies that enhance efficiency. If anything, Bowles argues, global economic integration increases the potential gains to producers from efficiency-promoting redistributive policies. If economic integration implies that mobile factors of production receive a given global rate of return, local productivity gains will be entirely captured by the owners of nonmobile factors of production, who are likely to be relatively poor.

Karl Ove Moene and Michael Wallerstein, in their essay "Social Democracy as a Development Strategy," make a similar argument with respect to the social democratic strategy of development successfully pursued in the Nordic countries. Moene and Wallerstein argue that the core of the social democratic development strategy was a policy of reducing the wage differential received by similar workers in different industries. Employing a simple model of development as the transition from traditional to modern activities, Moene and Wallerstein show that the reduction of wage differentials among similar workers may have a significant, positive impact on the growth of industry and the development of the economy. Noting that the social democrats opposed trade restrictions, Moene and Wallerstein argue that reducing wage inequality as a strategy of development is no less feasible in a world with few barriers to the movement of goods and capital than it was when it was adopted by the Nordic social democrats in the 1930s.

The central question raised but not answered in the essays by Bardhan, Bowles, and Moene and Wallerstein concerns the political feasibility of egalitarian redistributive policies. Potentially successful policies must be feasible politically as well as from an economic point of view. Global economic integration may affect redistributive policies by altering the political environment as much as by raising or lowering the economic costs and benefits of different policy choices.

Adam Przeworski and Covadonga Meseguer Yebra, in their essay "Globalization and Democracy," explore the consequences of globalization on the range of policy choices. In particular, they study the extent to which globalization forces all countries to adopt similar policies and the extent to which globalization forces all parties within individual countries to advocate similar policies. Przeworski and Meseguer argue that standard theories of globalization and democracy imply two opposing effects. To the extent that globalization leads to specialization that generates increasing cross-national differences in the distribution of income, the level of taxation and spending preferred by a majority of voters will diverge among countries. To the extent that globalization increases income inequality, party platforms will diverge within countries. To the extent that globalization increases the cost of taxation, however, globalization reduces policy differences both within and among countries. Przeworski and Meseguer argue that the net result of globalization on policy convergence is indeterminate in theory and unclear in terms of empirical evidence. Przeworski and Meseguer end by suggesting that policy differences among countries and among parties within countries may be as significant as ever. In their view, discontent with globalization stems not from the absence of choice, but from the fact that none of the feasible choices provide full compensation for the victims of globalization.

Samuel Bowles and Ugo Pagano, in their essay "Economic Integration, Cultural Standardization, and the Politics of Social Insurance," start by observing that, in key respects, globalization represents a continuation of the process of standardization of language and measures, specialized production, and increased mobility that began on a national scale with the rise of the nation-state. But where the nation-state provided protection against the insecurities inherent in economic specialization with an array of social insurance policies, no such protections are available at the supranational level. Bowles and Pagano speculate that globalization may create a new political cleavage between "cosmopolitans," who have skills and assets that allow them to adjust easily to changes in global markets, and "provincials," who are less mobile. On the one hand, increased specialization may lead to greater insecurity and greater demand for national policies of social protection from provincials. On the other hand, the growing political influence of cosmopolitans may undermine political support for such policies, leaving many exposed to the insecurity of global markets with less protection than before.

Stuart Soroka, Keith Banting, and Richard Johnston investigate the political consequences of immigration in their essay "Immigration and Redistribution in a Global Era." As indicated by the rise of right-wing anti-immigrant parties in Europe, immigration is potentially an explosive issue. In perhaps the first study of the impact of immigration on social insurance expenditures, Soroka, Banting, and Johnston find that greater change in the stock of immigrants is indeed associated with decreasing social insurance expenditures in advanced industrial societies in the period 1965–2000. Further, they show that the negative relationship remains, even after controlling for the ideology of the parties in government and measures of need. Thus, the fear expressed by many, including Offe in his contribution to this volume, that immigration undermines support for social insurance programs, perhaps by undercutting feelings of identification and solidarity with benefit recipients, appears to be well grounded.

Most of the chapters summarized so far study the impact of an exogenous increase in globalization, whether defined as lower trade barriers, increased capital mobility or immigration, or some facet of redistributive politics. But globalization itself is endogenous to the political system. The reduction of trade barriers, the elimination of capital controls and the expansion of legal immigration are all policy choices. The last two chapters to be summarized represent complementary approaches to studying globalization and redistribution as jointly determined political decisions.

Carles Boix, in his essay "Between Redistribution and Trade: The Political Economy of Protectionism and Domestic Compensation," approaches the topic historically by comparing two Australian states, Victoria and New South Wales, in the final decades of the nineteenth century, prior to the establishment of the federal government in Australia in 1901. The two states were similar in terms of most economic indicators. In both states, the major political divide was between a free trade party and a protectionist party, with labor in the pivotal position between the two. As Boix recounts, in Victoria the protectionist party joined with the unions to form a winning coalition based on a policy package of tariffs and wage regulation that guaranteed that the benefits of protection would be shared with industrial workers. In New South Wales, in contrast, the winning coalition united an independent labor party with the free trade party to enact a program of income taxes (instead of tariffs) and higher levels of social spending. The implication of Boix's study is that when labor is in a pivotal position, generous social insurance policies are a precondition for the adoption of free trade policies.

Kenneth Scheve and Matthew Slaughter reach a similar conclusion using a very different method in their essay, "Public Opinion, International Organization, and the Welfare State." Using a variety of cross-national public opinion data sets, Scheve and Slaughter draw on data from advanced industrial societies to study public support for free trade and immigration. The authors find that the respondent's skill level has a large impact on political preferences toward free trade and immigration in exactly the way suggested by the standard economic theory under the assumption that workers are mobile across industries. High-skilled workers are more supportive of globalization than low-skilled workers, whether or not the workers are employed in the traded goods sector or sheltered sector of the economy. Scheve and Slaughter also find that support for international openness is higher under conditions of full employment, and in countries with higher spending on unemployment insurance and active labor market policies. Comparing the support of free trade with or without increased aid for displaced workers provides further evidence of the linkage between preferences regarding free trade and those regarding social insurance policies. In the United States, as in most countries examined by Scheve and Slaughter, a majority opposes free trade when trade is mentioned in isolation. A majority of Americans, however, support free trade if free trade is combined with government assistance for those who might lose their jobs. In sum, Scheve and Slaughter find support in contemporary public opinion for the combination of free trade and social insurance that prevailed in New South Wales at the turn of the century. Far from being in conflict with globalization, the implementation of redistributive policies may be a precondition for sustaining policies of international openness under democratic conditions.

• • •

A brief summary cannot possibly capture the subtleties of the analysis and the richness of the observations contained in the essays that follow. Together, they provide a varied set of findings with respect to the impact of globalization on the feasibility of egalitarian redistributive policies. In spite of the complexity of the questions, the variety of methods employed, and the multiplicity of findings that are reported, there are general conclusions that emerge from the set of essays taken as a whole. This is the topic of the final chapter in the book.

Our conclusions are somewhat more optimistic than Keynes's alarm in 1932. Globalization need not place citizens, trade unionists, and community members, as he put it, "at the mercy of world forces working out . . . some uniform equilibrium according to the ideal principles . . . of laissez-faire capitalism." There are three reasons why Keynes's warning is at least overdrawn, if not entirely misplaced.

First, the institutions and policies that survive the competitive selection process of global competition need not be uniform across countries. The reasons for this go beyond the long shadow of history cast by the path-dependent nature of institutional evolution. As Bowles and Pagano point out, global specialization may actually promote institutional diversity, as it increases between-country differences in the mix of goods produced and thereby may support distinct systems of economic governance.

Second, even where tendencies for homogenization of institutions are strong, there is little reason to think that the result will be anything like laissez-faire capitalism, which exists today only on the blackboards of economics classrooms. Since the Great Depression and the late-twentieth-century emergence of environmental degradation as a major public concern, governments in all of the advanced economies have assumed major responsibilities in macroeconomic management, poverty alleviation, social insurance, and environmental protection. Contrary to the impression that many nations are experiencing a rollback of government activity over the past quarter-century, the size of the government sector (the ratio of government expenditures to gross domestic product) has increased in virtually all of the advanced economies (the United Kingdom and the United States being exceptions). If nations occasionally emulate those who are doing well by standard economic measures, the pressures of global competition are likely to favor mixed systems of competitive markets and active states, not laissez-faire.

Finally, as the chapters to follow amply demonstrate, there are little grounds for Keynes's fear that the freer movement of goods, people, information, and finance will preclude national experimentation in the pursuit of egalitarian objectives. Globalization does make some experimentation more costly, namely those that would lower the after-tax rate of return to capital. But dismantling the barriers to economic opportunity faced by the poor in credit markets, schooling, and access to health care, and making public bodies more responsive to the voices of the poor can enhance productivity. Where this is the case, global competition can favor egalitarian solutions.

NOTES

1. It appears likely that further reductions in between-country inequality will occur as if the second most populous nation, India, continues its recent course of relatively rapid growth.

2. See, especially, Sokoloff and Engerman (2000); Acemoglu, Johnson, and Robinson (2002); Pomeranz (2001); Jones (1987); Banerjee and Iyer (2002); and Quah 1996.

3. See also Taylor (2002); Glyn and Sutcliffe (1999); and the works cited there.

REFERENCES

Acemoglu, Daron, Simon Johnson, and J. A. Robinson. 2002. "Reversal of Fortune: Geography and Institutions in the Making of the Modern World Income Distribution." *Quarterly Journal of Economics* 117 (4): 1231–94.

Banerjee, Abhijit, and Lakshmi Iyer. 2002. "History, Institutions and Economic Performance: The Legacy of Colonial Land Tenure Systems in India." MIT Working Paper 02-27.

Bourguignon, F., and C. Morrison. 2002. "Inequality among World Citizens: 1820–1992." *American Economic Review* 92 (4): 727–44.

Glyn, A., and R. Sutcliffe. 1999. "Still Underwhelmed: Indicators of Globalization and their Misinterpretation." *Review of Radical Political Economy* 31 (1): 111–32.

Gordon, David. 1988. "The Global Economy: New Edifice or Crumbling Foundations?" *New Left Review* 68: 24–64.

Gordon, David, Samuel Bowles, and Thomas Weisskopf. 1998. "Power, Profits and Investment: An Institutionalist Explanation of the Stagnation of U.S. Net Investment after the Mid-1960's." In S. Bowles and T. Weisskopf (eds.), *Economics and Social Justice: Essays on Power, Labour and Institutional Change*. Cheltenham, U.K.: Edward Elgar.

Heintz, James, and Samuel Bowles. 1997. "Wages and Employment in the South African Economy." Manuscript, University of Massachusetts.

Jones, Eric. 1987. *The European Miracle: Environments, Economies, and Geopolitics in the History of Europe and Asia*. Cambridge: Cambridge University Press.

Keynes, J. M. 1932–33. "National Self-Sufficiency." *Yale Review* 22.

Kindleberger, Charles P. 1969. *American Business Abroad: Six Lectures on Direct Investment*. New Haven: Yale University Press.

Koechlin, Timothy. 1992. "The Responsiveness of Domestic Investment to Foreign Economic Conditions." *Journal of Post Keynesian Economics* 15 (1): 63–83.

Okun, Arthur. 1975. *Equality and Efficiency: The Big Trade-Off*. Washington, D.C.: Brookings Institution Press.

Pomeranz, Kenneth. 2001. *The Great Divergence: China, Europe, and the Making of the Modern World Economy*. Rev. ed. Princeton: Princeton University Press.

Quah, D. 1996. "Twin Peaks: Growth and Convergence in Models of Distribution Dynamics." *Economic Journal* 106 (437): 1045–55.

Sinn, H. W. 1997. "The Selection Principle and Market Failure in Systems Competition." *Journal of Public Economics* 66: 247–74.

Slaughter, M. 2001. "International Trade and Labour-Demand Elasticities." *Journal of International Economics* 54 (1): 27–56.

Sokoloff, K., and S. Engerman. 2000. "Institutions, Factor Endowments, and Paths of Development in the New World." *Journal of Economic Perspectives* 14 (3): 217–32.

Taylor, A. 2002. "A Century of Current Account Dynamics." *Journal of International Money and Finance* 21: 725–48.

Williamson, Jeffrey. 2003. "Globalization, Income Distribution and History." University of Siena International Summer School for Economic Research Background Papers.

CHAPTER 1

Globalization and the Limits to Poverty Alleviation

Pranab Bardhan

DIFFERENT MEANINGS OF GLOBALIZATION

A RAGING ISSUE of academic and public debate (that has spilled over into the streets in noisy demonstrations in recent years) concerns the impact of globalization on the well-being of the world's poor. Of course, different people mean different things by globalization: Some interpret it to mean the global reach of new technology and capital movements, some refer to outsourcing by domestic companies in rich countries, others protest against the tentacles of corporate capitalism. As I see it, a large part of the opposition to globalization relates to its three different aspects:

1. The fragility of valued local and indigenous cultures of masses of people in the world facing the onslaught of global mass production and cultural homogenization (through global brand-name products, movies, music, fast food, soft drinks, the Internet, etc.).
2. The devastation caused to fragile economies by billions of dollars of volatile short-term capital stampeding around the globe in herd-like movements.
3. The damage caused to jobs, wages, and incomes of poor people by the dislocations and competition of international trade and foreign investment and the weakening of the ability of the state to compensate for this damage and in general to alleviate poverty.

These three issues are interrelated: for example, ethnic handicrafts wiped out by imports of manufactures may be seen as both an economic and a cultural loss; when short-term speculative capital rushes out of a developing country it inevitably has adverse effects on its medium- to long-term investment climate as well. But these are conceptually separable issues. In this chapter I shall confine myself to a discussion of the third issue—in other words, I shall mainly interpret globalization to mean openness to foreign trade and long-term capital flows and try to understand the possible difficulties poverty alleviation policies in poor countries may face from such international economic integration. To achieve this understanding we need first to look at the processes by which globalization may affect the conditions of the poor, and then analyze the ways in which the policies meant to relieve those conditions are hemmed in by global constraints. In general I believe that globalization can cause many hardships for the poor but it also opens up opportunities that some countries can utilize and others do not, largely depending on their domestic political and economic institutions; and the net outcome is often quite complex and almost always context-dependent, belying the glib pronouncements for or against globalization made in the opposing camps.

For the record, let me say that on the important issues (1) and (2)—which are not addressed in the rest of the chapter—I am generally in favor of some modest restrictions on the full fury of globalization. On (1), I think that there are valid arguments for cultural protection that even an economist can make[1]: (a) preservation of cultural diversity, on the same lines as that for biodiversity and "option value" in environmental economics; (b) intertemporal externality in the form of "forgetting by not doing" in production of local varieties, on lines similar to the more familiar case of "learning by doing"; (c) endogenous preferences, when what we choose depends on the range of varieties available and also when these preferences may be molded by giant international firms selling some standardized products but with large advertisement budgets, etc. On issue (2), let me point out that much of the financial crisis in developing countries in recent years was initially caused by overexposure to foreign currency–denominated short-term debts. These, everybody now recognizes, are particularly crisis-prone financial instruments. In most cases there was too little discipline in borrowing before the crises and too much discipline afterward. Many international economists (even those who otherwise support free trade) now believe in the need for some form of control over short-term capital flows, particularly if domestic financial institutions and banking standards are weak—opinions differ, however, on the specific form such control should take and on the assessment of the effects of the rise in the cost of capital that this control might entail. I also think that it is imperative for the international community to work toward the creation and supervision of some international hedging and insurance institution against the impact of capital flow volatility.

I am also leaving out globalization in the form of international labor flows or more emigration of workers from poor to rich countries. If significant numbers of unskilled workers were allowed entry into rich countries, even in limited and regulated doses, a large dent could have been made in world poverty, many times what can possibly be brought about by other forms of international integration;[2] but very few people, even those who are concerned about the world's poor, seem prepared to entertain this "radical" idea.

GLOBAL PROCESSES AND THE WORKING POOR

One common cliché in the literature as well as in the streets is that globalization is making the rich richer and the poor poorer. While inequality may be increasing in many countries (on account of a whole host of factors, including globalization),[3] my focus in this chapter is on the conditions of those trapped in absolute poverty (measured by some bare minimum standard) in low-income countries. It is not at all clear that the poor are getting poorer everywhere in recent decades when large strides in international economic integration have taken place.[4] A quarter-century ago, most of the world's poorest people were concentrated in East, Southeast, and South Asia, sub-Saharan Africa, and Central America. Since then, poverty (percentage of people below some poverty line) has substantially declined in large parts of China, Indonesia, and South Asia, and there also have been significant improvements in other social indicators (like literacy or longevity) in most low-income countries, while poverty has remained stubbornly high in sub-Saharan Africa. But correlation does not imply causation: just as a large decline in poverty in China along with globalization does not necessarily mean a causal relation between them, the same may be the case for the nondecline in Africa. No one has convincingly shown that the massive decline in poverty in China is primarily due to globalization, and not, to a large extent, due to domestic agricultural reforms, improvements in infrastructure, or relaxation in the restrictions on rural to urban migration. Much of the persistence or even deterioration in poverty in Africa may have little to do with globalization and more to do with unstable or failed political regimes, wars, and civil conflicts, which afflicted several of those countries; if anything, such instability only reduced their extent of globalization, as it scared off many foreign investors and traders. One thus needs to spell out the causal mechanisms at work to make a convincing argument.

The causal processes through which international economic integration—of the type (3) of the first section—can affect poverty primarily involve the poor in their capacity as workers and as recipients of public services. Let us first take the case of poor workers. They are mainly either self-employed or wage earners. The self-employed work on their own tiny farms or as artisans and petty entrepreneurs in small shops and firms. The major constraints that they usually face are in credit, marketing, and insurance, in infrastructure (like roads, power, ports, and irrigation), and in government regulations (involving venal inspectors, insecure land rights, etc.). These often require substantive domestic policy changes, and foreign traders and investors are not directly to blame (in fact, they might sometimes help in relieving some of the bottlenecks in infrastructure and services and in essential parts, components, and equipment). If these changes are not made and the self-employed poor remain constrained, then, of course, it is difficult for them to withstand competition from large agribusiness or firms (foreign or domestic).

Less-constrained small farms or firms are sometimes more productive than their larger counterparts, and they are also sometimes more successful in export markets. Small producers are often heavily involved in exports (for example, coffee producers of Uganda, rice growers in Vietnam, garment producers in Bangladesh or Cambodia). In exports, however, the major hurdle they face is often due to not more globalization but less. Developed countries' protectionism and subsidization of farm and food products and simple manufactures (like textiles and clothing) severely restrict their export prospects for poor countries.[5] By estimates of the World Bank, the total losses incurred by exporters of textiles and garments on account of these trade barriers amount to more than $30 billion and the loss to poor countries from agricultural tariffs and subsidies in rich countries is estimated to be about $20 billion. I wish that the antiglobal protesters of rich countries turned their energies toward the vested interests in their own countries that prolong this protectionism and cripple the efforts of the poor of the world to climb out of their poverty. Pro-poor opponents of NAFTA point out how competition from U.S. agribusiness is destroying the livelihoods of small farmers in Mexico, without being equally vocal about the huge farm subsidies in the United States (now going to be even substantially larger under the new U.S. farm policy) that are largely responsible for this. U.S. wheat export prices are estimated to be 46 percent below cost of production, U.S. corn export prices are at 20 percent below cost, and so on.[6] The average cow in the European Union gets a government subsidy per year that is nearly twice the per capita income of India.

Another increasingly important barrier to trade that many small farmers of developing countries face in world markets is that rich countries now shut out many of these imports under a host of safety and sanitary regulations (sometimes imposed under pressure from lobbyists of import-competing farms in those countries). This actually increases the need for involving rich-country transnational companies in marketing poor-country products. These companies can deal with the regulatory and lobbying machinery in rich countries far better than the small producers of poor countries can and at the same time can provide consumers with credible guarantees of quality and safety. Of course, these companies will charge hefty fees for this marketing service (usually much larger than the total production cost), but the small farmers will usually be better off with them rather than without.

Similarly, it may be very difficult, costly, and time-consuming for small producers of manufactures or services in developing countries to establish brand name and reputation in the areas of quality and on-time delivery, which are absolutely crucial in marketing, particularly in international markets (much more so than comparative costs of production, which traditional trade theory emphasizes). This is where multinational marketing chains with global brand names, mediating between domestic suppliers and foreign buyers, can be very helpful for a long time, and so for small producers, paying the high marketing margin that these chains charge might sometimes be worth it. At the same time, coordinated attempts on the part of developing countries, with technical assistance from international organizations, to build international quality certification institutions for their products should be a high priority.

At the lower end of the value chain, more than fifty developing countries depend on three or fewer primary commodities for more than half of their export. Exports of such products are often a curse as well as a blessing for these countries, as their prices fluctuate wildly and as the economy is too dependent on them. As a result of recent cases of elimination of the erstwhile inefficiently run marketing boards and the dismantling of wasteful stabilization schemes, farmers in many African countries now receive a higher fraction of a more volatile (and, in some cases, lower) world market price. International commodity agreements among these countries to control their supply in the world market have not worked very well in the past. For reducing their economic vulnerability, developing countries probably have few alternatives than to diversify in production and skill-formation, and to move gradually up the supply chain toward activities with more added value for the same commodity, while arranging at an international level institutions of insurance for farmers in poor countries.

Turning to poor wage-earners, the theoretical literature on how international trade affects the absolute level of the real wage of unskilled workers is extremely small relative to the one on wage inequality (which, though an important issue, is not my concern here). I can think of seven types of theoretical mechanisms through which this effect might be significant in developing countries, and the outcomes can go either way.

1. The traditional Stolper-Samuelson mechanism applied to a simple two-country (rich-poor) two-factor (capital-labor) world suggests that the workers in the poor country, which presumably has abundant supplies of unskilled labor and therefore a comparative advantage in products intensive in unskilled labor, should benefit from trade liberalization. This is, of course, complicated by the fact that developing countries (say, Brazil, Mexico, or Turkey) may import labor-intensive products from even poorer countries (say, China, Indonesia, or Bangladesh), so that trade even in terms of this mechanism might lead to lower wages in the former set of developing countries.[7]

2. If some factors of production are intersectorally immobile, and some goods are non-traded, real wage of an unskilled worker in a poor country might not go up with trade liberalization even in an otherwise standard model of trade theory. Take a three-good model in a hypothetical African country: one is a nontradable good (say, a subsistence food crop) that is largely grown by women who for various social and economic reasons cannot move to other sectors; another good (say, an exportable tree crop) produced largely by men in a capital-intensive way (maybe simply because tree crops lock up capital for a long period); and the third good is an importable (say, processed food) that is somewhat substitutable in consumption for the subsistence food. In this three-sector model it is not difficult to show that the real wage of women might go down when the importable processed food is made cheaper by trade liberalization (under the condition that the elasticity of substitution in consumption of the two foods is sufficiently high). What we have said about poor African women here is equally true for other people anywhere who are mobility-constrained (old workers and people who do not have the collateral to raise capital to start new ventures or move to new sectors, etc.).

3. Take a two-period model where labor on a long-term contract is trained in the first period and this training bears fruit in the second period, when these long-contract workers are more productive than untrained short-contract casual laborers. If opening the economy increases the competition and the probability of going out of business, employers may go more for short-contract and less productive and lower-wage laborers, bringing down the average wage. By similar reasoning, a firm may have less incentive in an open economy to invest in developing a reputation for fairness in wage payments.

4. On the other hand, increased foreign competition might lead to the demise of old inefficient firms and the entry of new more efficient firms, or a better allocation of resources within existing firms, which might lead to a rise in average wages in industries that attain such productivity gains.[8]

5. If firms facing more foreign competition and pressure to reduce costs outsource activities to smaller firms or household enterprises in the informal sector,[9] the average wage (of those formerly employed in the formal sector) may go down, but this need not impoverish workers in general if the poorer informal workers get more employment this way.

6. If technical change in rich countries is biased against the services of unskilled labor (for which there is plenty of evidence) and if globalization means that its impact reaches remote corners of the world, then again employment and the wages of unskilled labor in poor countries will go down, as has been reportedly the case, for example, with global tenders to construction companies like Bechtel or Mitsui using labor-saving technology that left many construction workers unemployed in India.

7. As foreign competition (or even the threat of it) lowers profit margins, the old rent-sharing arrangements between employers and unionized workers come under pressure. Rents decline both for capital and labor, but labor may have to take a larger cut if, as has been argued, the increase in the (perceived) elasticity of demand in the product market (due to opening of the economy to trade and foreign investment) leads to an increase in the elasticity of demand for labor, lowering its bargaining power and generally weakening unions.[10] This may lead to lower wages and, sometimes more important, increased risk of unemployment. Scheve and Slaughter (2002) show how globalization of production through multinational enterprises in particular and related trade can make labor demand more elastic (through increased product market competition and substitution of foreign factors of production, including intermediate inputs for domestic factors) and thereby raise economic insecurity for workers.

Some Evidence

Now let us briefly discuss the empirical evidence on the effect of foreign trade and investment on the wages of unskilled labor in developing countries. The micro-evidence on this is rather limited. (I am ignoring the usual, flawed, cross-country regressions.) More often than not it reports data on correlations, not a careful empirical analysis of the causal process. For example, the critics of NAFTA will readily point to the decline in real wages of unskilled workers in Mexico in the few years immediately after NAFTA came into operation, overlooking the fact that much of the decline may be due to the peso crisis that engulfed Mexico in this period, which had very little to do with the opening of trade with North America. It is important to disentangle the effects on wages of trade reform from those flowing from macroeconomic policy changes or other ongoing deregulatory reforms and technological changes.

On the whole, the labor market effect of trade liberalization in developing countries on the basis of the few microeconometric studies is rather mixed and quantitatively small. Analyzing a set of twenty-five trade liberalization episodes in developing countries, using internationally comparable sectoral labor data, Seddon and Wacziarg (2002) come to the conclusion that trade liberalization has far smaller effects on intersectoral reallocation (even at the three-digit level within manufacturing) than is conventionally presumed. What is more likely is that much of the structural change is intrasectoral and that some of the potential changes are neutralized by policies like exchange rate depreciation, labor regulations, and sector-specific subsidies. The micro-studies of effects of trade reform in Mexico and Morocco by Revenga (1997), Feliciano (2001), and Currie and Harrison (1997) attribute the small effect on employment to labor regulations or to the firms adjusting to trade reform by reducing their formerly protected profit margins and raising productivity rather than laying off workers. But even when the net effect on employment is relatively small, there might be considerable amount of job reallocation and dislocation, as Levinsohn (1999) finds, using firm-level data in Chile. Comparing factories owned by multinational firms with domestic factories of the same size and efficiency in Indonesia, Bernard and Sjoholm (2003) find that the probability of closure was 20 percent higher for the former over a fifteen-year period.

Goldberg and Pavcnik (2001), on the basis of panel data from the Colombian National Household Survey over 1985–94, look at the effect of trade policy on industry wage premiums, that is, the aspect of wages that cannot be explained by worker or firm characteristics. They find that the two most protected sectors in Colombia were textiles and apparel, and wood and wood-product manufacturing, which are relatively unskilled labor–intensive sectors, and, with industry fixed effects, trade protection is found to increase industry wage premiums. This is quite consistent with traditional trade theory, particularly when one keeps in mind that such protection of labor-intensive industries in developing countries might be against imports from even more labor-abundant countries, as we noted earlier in our theoretical mechanism (1).

Even when poor unskilled workers lose from trade liberalization in such contexts, it may be possible to combine a policy of trade liberalization with a domestic policy of compensating the losers at low cost. Harrison, Rutherford, and Tarr

(2003) have used a computable general equilibrium model for Turkey to show with a numerical exercise that a direct income subsidy to the losers of trade reform, financed by a VAT, is quite cost effective. The main problem, of course, is that of credible commitment on the part of the ruling politicians that losers will be compensated. Recent history in many countries is full of governments' reneged promises to displaced workers. Obviously, this is a particularly important matter in poor countries where there is very little effective social protection available from the state. Rich countries have better social safety nets and some programs in place that help displaced workers to adjust (like the federal adjustment assistance program in the United States). International organizations that preach the benefits of free trade should take the responsibility of funding and facilitating such adjustment assistance programs in poor countries to help workers in coping with job losses and getting retrained and redeployed. Until issues of general economic security for poor workers in developing countries is satisfactorily resolved, globalization is bound to raise anxiety and hostility among workers worried about their job security. It is also not a coincidence that countries that have a better record in building institutions of conflict management and coordination have coped better with the dislocations brought about by international trade: the major example is the case of Scandinavian countries, where in spite of a strong tradition of organized labor movement and worker solidarity over many decades of the past century, the unions there in general have been in favor of an open economy.

Let us now briefly turn to the case of the poor as recipients of public services. In the low-income developing countries the poor, particularly those who are in the preponderant informal sector, do not receive much effective social protection from the state (which makes them particularly vulnerable in case of job displacement brought about by international competition), but the public sector is usually involved in basic services like education and health and public works programs. Cuts in public budgets on these basic services are often attributed to globalization, as the budget cuts aimed at reducing fiscal deficits often come as part of a package of macroeconomic stabilization prescribed by international agencies like the IMF. I agree with a common characterization of some of the IMF conditionalities on a crisis-affected country as analogous to medieval ways of trying to cure a patient by blood-letting. But one should keep in mind that the fiscal deficit in these poor countries are often brought about in the first place more by domestic profligacy in matters of subsidies to the rich, or by salaries for the bloated public sector or military extravaganza. Faced with mounting fiscal deficits, the governments often find it politically easier to cut the public expenditures for the voiceless poor, and that is primarily due to the domestic political clout of the rich who are disinclined to share in the necessary fiscal austerity, and it is always convenient to blame an external agency for a problem that is essentially domestic in origin.

The low quality and quantity of public services like education and health care in poor countries is not just due to their relatively low share in the public budget.

To a large extent, even the limited money allocated in the budget does not reach the poor because of all kinds of top-heavy administrative obstacles and bureaucratic and political corruption.[11] Again this is a domestic institutional failure, not largely an external problem. The major effort required here is to strengthen the domestic institutions of accountability.

Policy Issues

Finally, let us take up the general issue of possible loss of national policy options relevant for the poor that are brought about by a developing country's participation in international trade and investment. First of all, I agree with the antiglobal protesters that many of the international organizations that define the rules of this order are accountable more to the corporate and financial community of rich countries than to the poor, and that the decision-making processes in these organizations need to be much more transparent and responsive to the people whose lives their decisions crucially affect.[12] At the same time it should be pointed out that the protesters in rich countries often speak in the name of the world's poor but support policies that sometimes might actually harm them (more on this later).

Coming to the issue of a government's fiscal options in a global economy, many people think that the scope for taxing capital to raise revenue is severely limited by the threat of capital flight in the long run, even if we ignore the problem of short-term speculative capital flows. (In fact, capital itself does not have to flee the country; quite often accounting practices, through strategic bookkeeping adjustments, allow the base for capital taxes to migrate even when capital itself does not). While this limitation can be serious, one should not exaggerate its effects. Most countries collect only a small part of their revenues from capital taxation, even in relatively closed economies. In any case, there are strong arguments for funding redistributive policies through progressive consumption taxes (say, VAT) rather than taxes on capital or labor. Of course, there is a need for tax coordination across countries, and there is some evidence that capital taxation is declining and also converging across countries. But again, one should not overstate this. Even in the highly integrated European Union corporate tax rates have substantially converged not to zero, as some people anticipated, but to about 35 percent. In general between two equilibria, one with high taxes and high public goods provision and the other with low taxes and low public goods, capital need not choose the latter over the former.

Serious obstacles to redistributive policies are often domestic. At the microlevel of firms, farms, neighborhoods, and local communities there is scope for a great deal of efficiency-enhancing egalitarian measures that can help the poor and that are not primarily blocked by the forces of globalization. Various asset redistribution and poverty alleviation policies (like land reform, expansion of education and health facilities for the poor, guaranteed public works programs as a last resort for the unemployed, cooperative and peer-monitored credit and marketing for small firms and farms, formation of local community organizations to manage the local environmental resources, etc.) can improve productive efficiency and expand opportunities for the poor, and yet might be within the range of capability of domestic institutions of the community and the polity. The main hindrance in devoting substantial fiscal and organizational resources to these projects is the considerable opposition from domestic vested interests—landlords, corrupt and/ or inept politicians and bureaucrats, and the currently subsidized rich. Closing the economy does not reduce the power of these vested interests. If anything, the forces of competition unleashed by international integration might reduce their monopoly power.

An area where more empirical work needs to be done on poor countries is this question of comparative market structure with or without an open economy. On the one hand, an open economy is likely to be more "contestable" (with even monopoly sellers facing more threats of potential entry) than an economy where domestic sellers are sheltered from foreign competition. On the other hand, the giant transnational companies with deep pockets can afford to resort to predatory pricing vis-à-vis smaller domestic sellers, particularly in industries where economies of scale and other such entry barriers are important. One can only note that over the years competition among transnationals in international markets has increased. In general it is not clear if domestic consumers (and workers) always prefer domestic monopolists to foreign ones. Some might prefer to be exploited by Citibank rather than by the local loan shark.

It is true that the monopoly marketing chains, like those that we referred to earlier, eat up a large part of the gains from trade that form the staple of international economics textbooks. Just to cite one example, even today long after the infamous days of the reign of the United Fruit Company, the local producer in Ecuador gets only $2 or $3 for each 43 lb. box of bananas sold by the marketing chains in the United States or Europe for about $25. But the important question here is what the counterfactual is. The trade economists state that the alternative scenario of no trade is worse for the poor banana grower. The activist-protesters suggest that the monopolist transnational marketing company should keep lower margins. They should then agitate more for antitrust action, not anti-trade action. Otherwise their protests often end up merely strengthening the hands of protectionists in rich countries. Faced with this, the producers in poor countries have to ask themselves essentially the trade economists' counterfactual: yes, we know the world is unfair, but can we do any better by closing down our economy? But this also means that there should be energetic international attempts to certify codes against international restrictive business practices and to establish, as the Oxfam Report (referred to earlier) recommends, an antitrust investigation agency, possibly under WTO auspices.

Trade economists usually do not consider the possible impact of international operations on the domestic political equilibrium. Large transnational companies, working through the governments of rich countries and with their threats of financial withdrawal, can sometimes shift the political equilibrium particularly in small countries and weak states, although it has to be noted that crass manipulations and the "gunboat diplomacy" of the past are getting somewhat more difficult to perform than before. Others suggest that in countries with some established political and bureaucratic structures the internationally exposed sector, if it becomes better off, may undermine older alliances that might have retarded economic progress. We need more systematic empirical studies of how opening the economy might change the nature of politics in a developing country, controlling for other factors. There is some evidence that in Mexico the post-NAFTA exposure to international trade helped in bringing about the erosion of support for the long-dominant and corrupt ruling party (PRI).[13] The mechanisms that are involved—if they work at all—in forging political coalitions and institutions that might ultimately help the poor are likely to vary from one country to another.

While the transnational companies might have deeper pockets and larger political clout vis-à-vis the poor unskilled laborers of a country, there is very little evidence that the latter get lower wages and fewer jobs in the presence of those companies, compared to what they would get in their absence, other things remaining the same (see, for example, Aitken, Harrison, and Lipsey 1996; Harrison and Scorse 2003). Contrary to the impression created by the campaign in affluent countries against "sweatshops" run by transnational companies in poor countries, it can be pointed out that the poor are often banging at the gates of these sweatshops for a chance of entry, since their current alternative is much worse, in inferior occupations, work conditions, or unemployment.

Here again there is a clash of counterfactuals between the two sides of the debate. The protesters say (at least implicitly) that Nike wages may be higher than the wages earned in the vast hinterland from which streams of poor workers come, but they are lower than they would be if Nike's (monopsonist) profits were lower. Trade economists say that if there were no Nike, the wage would revert to the low hinterland wage, and some also implicitly deny the existence of the (local) monopsony, and so presume that the implementation of a minimum ("fair") wage would push some of the workers to the hinterland. Clearly there is a need here for good empirical projects to investigate the nature of the labor markets facing international firms like Nike in poor countries. In their absence, one wonders to what extent the standard argument for a minimum wage, as given by progressive labor economists and sociologists in the context of a monopsonist employer, applies to the current problem. The monopsony power of Nike would imply that if Nike tries to hire more workers from the hinterland, it will drive up the marginal cost of labor against itself. If one believes instead that there is an almost "unlimited" supply of hinterland labor "banging at the gates," then the marginal and average cost of hiring labor for Nike should not be very different, and so the usual argument that a minimum wage will not reduce employment under monopsony should not apply here.

Similarly, for those who complain about the exploitation of young women in the garment factories of transnational companies do not often appreciate the relative improvement in the conditions and status of these women (say, in the garment industry in Bangladesh or Mauritius) compared to the alternatives otherwise available to them. This is not an argument against efforts to improve their work conditions (and certainly not in favor of the totally indefensible cases of forced labor or hazardous or unsafe work conditions[14]), but it is an appeal for looking at the reality of the severely limited opportunities faced by the poor and the unintended consequences of trying to restrict rich-country imports of "sweatshop" products in terms of the harm it causes to the displaced poor workers.

A similar argument applies to the case of child labor. Simply banning imports of products that have used child labor is likely to send the children not to schools but to much inferior occupations in the usually much larger nontraded sector.[15] (In India, for example, an estimated 95 percent of child workers are in the nontraded sector anyway). In Vietnam a quarter of all children work in agriculture. From 1993 to 1997 the government gradually relaxed its rice export quota, which led to rice producers getting a better price. Using the Vietnam Living Standards Survey data for a panel of 4000 households in this period, Edmonds and Pavcnik (2001) estimate that this better price received for rice can account for almost half of the decline in child labor that took place in this period. Here is a case in which increased earning opportunities from participation in the international market with a product that is intensive in child labor led to the withdrawal of children from work. A policy of trade sanctions against Vietnamese rice, with the apparent good intention of reducing child labor in its production, could have the opposite effect.

Clearly, taking mainly a legal or regulatory approach (like simply banning child labor or boycotting their produce) to achieve an otherwise laudable social goal is the wrong way to go about it. Unintended consequences abound, and the solutions are often a little more complex than the simplistic remedies proposed by some activists. The widely noted program in Mexico, PROGRESA, of paying a subsidy to the mother conditional on her children's school attendance has made a significant dent on child labor. The program (now under a different name) has expanded substantially in Mexico, and neither NAFTA nor global integration has gotten in the way. It is also important to understand the need for coordinated action among the different parties involved. A good example is the Partners' Agreement to Eliminate Child Labor in the Soccer Ball Industry in Pakistan in the mid-1990s, by which the transnational sporting goods companies (located in the city of Sialkot in Pakistan and producing a large fraction of the world supply of soccer balls), the Pakistan Chamber of Commerce, International Labor Organization (ILO), and some nongovernmental organizations (NGOs) reached an agreement to eliminate child labor in that industry, provide scholarships to the displaced children, to arrange the school facilities needed, and to monitor the agreement (see IPEC 1999). Such coordination programs, if they can involve all the many relevant parties (including the small producers), rather than trade boy-cotts or exogenously imposed "codes of conduct," are likely to be much more ef-fective and equitable.

ENVIRONMENT AND INTELLECTUAL PROPERTY RIGHTS

Environmentalists argue that trade liberalization damages the poor by encourag-ing overexploitation of the fragile environmental resources (forestry, fishery, sur-face and groundwater irrigation, grazing lands, etc.) on which the daily liveli-hoods of the rural poor in particular depend. Here also the answers are actually complex, and mere trade restriction is not the solution. The environmental ef-fects of trade liberalization on the rural economy depend on the crop pattern and the methods of production. Take, for example, an African rural economy where the exportable product is a capital-intensive tree crop (like coffee or cocoa), the import-substitute is a land-intensive crop (like maize), and there is a labor-intensive subsistence (nontraded) crop (like roots and tubers). The economy may have a comparative advantage in tree crops. In this case, an increase in import substitu-tion leads to an expansion of cultivated land under the land-intensive crop as well as a shortening of the fallow period, leading to depletion of natural vegetation and biomass. Trade liberalization in this context, through encouraging the pro-duction of the less land-intensive tree crop, can significantly improve the natural biomass, as has been shown by Lopez (2000) for Côte d'Ivoire in the latter part of the 1980s, using the data from the Living Standards Survey and some remote sensing data from satellite images.

One reason why land-intensive crops may lead to overuse of land and deple-tion of natural vegetation (or that expansion of the agricultural frontier in general leads to deforestation) is the lack of well-defined property rights or lack of their enforcement in public or communal land. In such cases, the private cost of ex-panding production is less than the social cost and there is overuse and degrada-tion of environmental resources. If the country exports such resource-intensive products, foreign trade may make this misallocation worse. International trade theorists point out that trade restriction is not the first-best policy in this situation, correcting the property rights regime is. But the latter involves large changes in the legal-regulatory or community-institutional framework, which take a long time to implement, and given the threshold effects and irreversibilities in environmental degradation (a forest regeneration requires a minimum stock, for example), one may not afford to wait. In that case, some program of (time-bound) trade restric-tion coupled with serious attempts at the overhaul of the domestic institutional framework might be necessary. In other cases, domestic policy changes can be im-plemented much more quickly, and restricting trade is unnecessary and undesir-able. For example, administered underpricing of precious environmental resources (irrigation water in India, energy in Russia, timber concessions in Indonesia, etc.)

is a major cause of resource depletion, and correcting it should not take much time. Domestic vested interests, not globalization, are responsible for the prolongation of such socially damaging policies.

In the case of some resource-intensive exports, it is difficult for a country by itself to adopt environmental regulations if its international competitors do not adopt them at the same time and have the ability to undercut the former in international markets. Here again there is an obvious need for coordination in the environmental regulation policies of the countries concerned. Given the low elasticity of demand for many resource-intensive primary export commodities from developing countries in the world market, such coordinated policies, while raising prices and the terms of trade, need not lead to a decline in export revenue.

A common charge against multinational companies is that they flock to developing country "pollution havens" to take advantage of lax environmental standards. In one of the very few careful empirical studies on the question, Eskeland and Harrison (2003) examine the pattern of foreign investment in Mexico, Venezuela, Morocco, and Côte d'Ivoire. They find no evidence that foreign investment in these countries is related to pollution abatement costs in rich countries. They also find that within a given industry, foreign plants are significantly more energy-efficient and use cleaner types of energy compared to their local peers.

Finally, I largely agree with many protester/activists on the issue of TRIPs (trade-related intellectual property rights). This was brought within the WTO purview under considerable U.S. pressure, and developing countries reluctantly went along in exchange for the promise (partly and sometimes covertly defaulted on by now) of substantial reductions in protection of textiles and farm products by rich countries. A World Bank study estimates that the TRIPs arrangement will raise the revenue of six rich countries by about $40 billion. One can imagine the increased burden, for example, on private households and public health programs in poor countries as the protected drug prices rise under TRIPs. For many products the cited justification of patents in terms of keeping incentives alive for new research does not warrant the rapacious monopoly pricing for a prolonged period. (The patent life in the rest of the world was raised under TRIPS to the U.S. standard of twenty years.) Even when the original patent runs out, the transnational company holding the patent often has various ways of effectively extending it (by slightly changing the composition of ingredients in the product), bribing or intimidating the potential producers of the generic substitute, and, through high-pressure advertising, keeping many of the customers hooked on to the original brand. In some cases the patent holder privately appropriates the benefits of publicly funded research. In other cases private companies are patenting in rich countries plant genetic and other resources collected from poor countries, the uses for which have been part of the common knowledge pool of communities for centuries. It is also recognized now by many scientific researchers that existing patents often act as an obstacle to further research that tries to build on earlier findings. (In developing countries this includes research for adapting new technology to the special conditions there.)

The problem of international patents in life-saving drugs in poor countries recently caught public attention in connection with the controversies about the prices of anti-retroviral drugs for AIDS patients in Africa. That case showed how the transnational pharmaceutical companies kept on threatening action (until they had to relent under international public pressure) against poor countries even when the latter were only trying to adopt measures (like "compulsory licensing" and "parallel imports") that are deemed legitimate in national public health emergencies under existing WTO rules. The hypocrisy of the U.S. government on this issue became particularly blatant when, during the anthrax scare at the end of 2001, it announced that it would refuse to pay high prices to Bayer, the company that produces an anti-anthrax drug. The Trade Representative of the same government had threatened trade sanctions against developing countries for trying to do similar things in their medical emergencies.

The major problem in corporate drug research is that only a tiny fraction of what the companies spend on finding new diet pills or anti-wrinkle creams is spent on drugs or vaccines against the major killer diseases of the world, like malaria or TB. Since these diseases kill millions of people (many of them children) mainly in countries with low purchasing power, the transnational pharmaceutical companies are less interested. There are now the beginnings of some international attempts to arrange for a commitment on the part of international organizations like WHO and the World Bank in collaboration with NGOs like Medecins sans Frontières, private foundations (like the Gates Foundation) and donor agencies, and local governments to purchase vaccines to be developed by transnational companies against some of the killer diseases.[16] This is another major example of how international coordination and public-private partnerships can be vital in resolving complex international problems. For other diseases (like diabetes or cancer) that kill large numbers of people in both rich and poor countries, the incentive argument for enforcing patents in poor countries is weak, since that research will be carried out by the transnational drug companies in any case as the market in rich countries is large enough (provided resale can be limited).[17]

Conclusions

In general, while globalization in the sense of opening the economy to trade and long-term capital flows can constrain some policy options and wipe out some existing jobs and entrepreneurial opportunities for the poor and for small enterprises, in the medium to long run it need not make the poor much worse off if appropriate domestic policies and institutions are in place and if appropriate coordination among the involved parties can be organized. If the institutional prerequisites can be managed, globalization opens the door for some new opportunities even for the poor. Of course, domestic institutional reform is not easy and it requires political leadership, popular participation, and administrative capacity that are often lacking in poor countries. One can only say that if we keep the focus on agitating against transnational companies and international organizations like the WTO, attention in those countries often gets deflected from the domestic institutional vested interests, and the day of politically challenging them gets postponed. In fact, in some cases opening the economy might unleash forces for such a challenge.

As in the debates that flared up several decades ago around "dependency" theories, there is often a tendency to attribute many of the problems of underdevelopment to the inexorable forces of the international economic and political order, ignoring the sway of the domestic vested interests. In many countries, poverty alleviation in the form of expansion of credit and marketing facilities, land reform, public works programs for the unemployed, or provision of education and health need not be blocked by the forces of globalization. This, of course, requires a restructuring of existing budget priorities and a better and more accountable political and administrative framework, but the obstacles to these are often largely domestic (particularly in countries where there are some coherent governance structures in place). In other words, for these countries, globalization is often not the main cause of their problems, contrary to the claim of critics of globalization—just as globalization is often not the main solution to these problems, contrary to the claims of some gung-ho free traders.

All this, of course, does not absolve the responsibility of international organizations and entities in helping the poor of the world, by working toward a reduction of rich-country protection on goods produced by the poor, by energetic antitrust action to challenge the monopoly power of international (producing and trading) companies based in rich countries, by facilitating international partnerships in research and development of products (for example, drugs, vaccines, crops) suitable for the poor, and by organizing more substantial (and more effectively governed) financial and technology transfers and international adjustment assistance for displaced workers, and help in (legal and technical) capacity-building for poor countries in international negotiations and quality certification organizations. Globalization should not be allowed to be used, either by its critics or by its proponents, as an excuse for inaction on the domestic as well as the international front when it comes to the matter of relieving the poverty that oppresses the life of billions of people in the world.

NOTES

1. In Aubert, Bardhan, and Dayton-Johnson (2003) we have formalized some of these arguments in terms of theoretical models.

2. Walmsley and Winters (2002) have estimated that the global gains from allowing even temporary entry of both skilled and unskilled labor services equivalent to 3 percent of the workforce in OECD countries will amount to about one-and-a-half times the total gains from merchandise trade liberalization.

3. Whether world income distribution as a whole is getting more unequal is moot, as hundreds of millions of poor people in large countries like China, India, and Indonesia have improved their living standards in recent years.

4. For example, Chen and Ravallion (2004) estimate that in developing countries the proportion of the total population living in households with consumption expenditure per capita less than about $1 per day in 2001 (at 1993 purchasing power parity) was 21 percent (22.5 percent if one were to exclude China), compared to 40 percent in 1981 (31.7 percent if China is excluded). The total number of poor people measured this way was about 1.48 billion in 1981, and 1.09 billion in 2001. In sub-Saharan Africa in the same period, the percentage of poor people *increased* from 42 to 46 percent. All this is, of course, subject to many caveats about measuring poverty in terms of one common dollar standard of poverty for many different countries.

5. This is, of course, not to minimize the trade barriers imposed by developing countries on imports of other developing countries.

6. See, for example, the recent Oxfam Report, *Rigged Rules and Double Standards: Trade, Globalization, and the Fight against Poverty*, 2002.

7. See Wood (1997).

8. The positive link between trade liberalization and productivity has been found in Chile, Colombia, Côte d'Ivoire, Brazil, India, and South Korea. One of the most careful micro-studies on this question is by Pavcnik (2002), who finds that massive trade liberalization in Chile in the late 1970s and early 1980s led to growth of productivity at the plant level at the average rate to 3 to 10 percent. For the other country studies, see the references in Pavcnik (2002).

9. Attanasio, Goldberg, and Pavcnik (2004) find some evidence that the increase in the size of the informal sector in Colombia toward the end of the 1990s is related to increased foreign competition.

10. See Currie and Harrison (1997); Rodrik (1997); Leamer (1998); and Reddy (2001). The theoretical relation between product market demand elasticity and the elasticity of derived demand for labor is somewhat more complex than usual in the case of imperfect competition and is not always clear-cut. The empirical evidence in developing countries on the trade-induced changes in the elasticity of demand for labor is rather scanty. Fajnzylber, Maloney, and Ribeiro (2001), on the basis of plant-level data and taking both incumbent and exiting or entering firms into account, find in Chile and Colombia very ambiguous effects of trade liberalization on wage elasticities.

11. To give just one instance of a rough magnitude of the problem, the World Bank recently estimated that of the total nonsalary budget sanctioned by the central government in Uganda in the period 1991–1995 for schools, only about 13 percent actually reached them.

12. The protesters' demand for the abolition of the WTO is, however, misplaced. If the alternative to a multilateral organization like the WTO is for a developing country to face the United States in bilateral trade negotiations, the United States is likely to be much more dominant and arbitrary in such negotiations than in the dispensations of the WTO

(which in its arbitration decisions has sometimes ruled against the U.S. position). It is also to be noted that in the WTO each member country has one vote (the convention is to reach decisions by "consensus"), whereas in the Bretton Wood institutions (IMF and the World Bank) voting is dollar-weighted. But there is no denying the fact that the rich countries (and their large corporate lobbies) exercise a dominant effect on the agenda-setting and decision-making of the WTO, as with the Bretton Wood institutions. At the Doha meeting, and subsequently, there were some welcome signs of a slow opening of the process to the developing countries. But serious efforts are needed to strengthen the technical negotiation capacity of poor countries in international trade forums where they face the well-equipped and well-funded teams of lawyers and negotiators representing rich countries.

13. See A. Diaz-Cayers, B. Magaloni, and B. R. Weingast (2000).

14. Conceptually, one should distinguish between unsafe or hazardous work conditions and forced labor on the one hand and low-wage jobs on the other. Under capitalism, just as workers willing to sell themselves as serfs are not permitted to do so, unsafe work conditions that can cause bodily injury are to be strictly regulated. That is the reason why they are part of the ILO core labor standards that have been ratified by most countries. The case for stopping workers from accepting low-wage jobs, however, is much weaker.

15. In 1993, Senator Tom Harkins in the U.S. Congress brought a bill to ban imports of products using child labor. It was not passed, but almost immediately after the introduction of the bill, the garment industry in Bangladesh dismissed an estimated fifty thousand children. It was found by UNICEF (1997) that (with the concerted effort of some education NGOs) about ten thousand children did go back to school, but the rest went to much inferior occupations, including stone breaking and child prostitution. Later an agreement between the manufacturers in Bangladesh and UNICEF and ILO tried to provide better opportunities for some of the children.

16. For a discussion of the relevant incentive issues in vaccine research and ways of improving credibility of purchase commitment, see Kremer (2001).

17. Lanjouw (2002) has suggested a small change in the administration of patent laws in rich countries that forces pharmaceutical companies to choose between patent protection in rich countries and protection in a designated list of poor countries. This will make them give up protection in those poor countries for drugs against global diseases since the larger market is in rich countries, while preserving the vast majority of patent incentives.

REFERENCES

Aitken, B., A. Harrison, and R. Lipsey. 1996. "Wages and Foreign Ownership: A Comparative Study of Mexico, Venezuela, and the United States." *Journal of International Economics* 40 (3/4): 345–71.

Aubert, C., P. Bardhan, and J. Dayton-Johnson. 2003. "Artfilms, Handicrafts, and Other Cultural Goods: The Case for Subsidy." Working paper, Economics Department, University of California, Berkeley.

Attanasio, O., P. K. Goldberg, and N. Pavcnik. 2004. "Trade Reforms and Wage Inequality in Colombia." *Journal of Development Economics* 74 (2): 331–66.

Bernard, A., and F. Sjoholm. 2003. "Foreign Owners and Plant Survival." National Bureau of Economic Research, Working Paper no. 10039.

Chen, S., and M. Ravallion. 2004. "How Have the World's Poorest Fared since the Early 1980s." World Bank Policy Research Working Paper no. 3341.

Currie, J., and A. Harrison. 1997. "Sharing the Costs: The Impact of Trade Reform on Capital and Labor in Morocco." *Journal of Labor Economics* 15 (3): S44–S71.

Diaz-Cayers, A., B. Magaloni, and B. R. Weingast. 2000. "Democratization and the Economy in Mexico: Equilibrium (PRI) Hegemony and Its Demise." Manuscript, Stanford University and University of California, Los Angeles.

Edmonds, E., and N. Pavcnik. 2001. "Does Globalization Increase Child Labor? Evidence from Vietnam." Manuscript, Dartmouth College.

Eskeland, G., and A. Harrison. 2003. "Moving to Greener Pastures? Multinationals and the Pollution Haven Hypothesis." *Journal of Development Economics* 70 (1): 1–24.

Fajnzylber, P., W. F. Maloney, and E. Ribeiro. 2001. "Firm Entry and Exit, Labor Demand and Trade Reform: Evidence from Chile and Colombia." World Bank Policy Research Working Paper no. 2659, Washington, D.C.

Feliciano, Z. M. 2001. "Workers and Trade Liberalization: The Impact of Trade Reforms in Mexico on Wages and Employment." *Industrial and Labor Relations Review* 55 (1): 95–115.

Goldberg, P., and N. Pavcnik. 2001. "Trade Protection and Wages: Evidence from Colombian Trade Reform." Manuscript.

Harrison, A., and J. Scorse. 2003. "The Impact of Globalization on Compliance with Labor Standards: A Plant-Level Study." Manuscript, University of California, Berkeley.

Harrison, G. W., T. B. Rutherford, and D. G. Tarr. 2003. "Trade Liberalization, Poverty and Efficient Equity." *Journal of Development Economics* 1 (1): 97–128.

International Program on the Elimination of Child Labor (IPEC). 1999. *IPEC Action against Child Labor: Achievements, Lessons Learned, and Indications for the Future.* Geneva: ILO.

Kremer, M. 2001. "Creating Markets for New Vaccines." Pp. 35–118 in A. B. Jaffe, J. Lerner, and S. Stern (eds.), *Innovation Policy and the Economy.* Cambridge: MIT Press.

Lanjouw, J. O. 2002. "A Patent Policy for Global Diseases: U.S. and International Legal Issues." *Harvard Journal of Law and Technology* 16 (1): 85–124.

Leamer, E. E. 1998. "In Search of Stolper-Samuelson Linkages between International Trade and Lower Wages." Pp. 141–202 in S. M. Collins (ed.), *Imports, Exports, and the American Worker.* Washington, D.C.: Brookings Institution Press.

Levinsohn, J. 1999. "Employment Responses to International Liberalization in Chile." *Journal of International Economics* 47 (2): 321–44.

Lopez, R. 2000. "Trade Reform and Environmental Externalities in General Equilibrium: Analysis for an Archetype Poor Tropical Country." *Environment and Development Economics* 4 (4): 337–404.

Pavcnik, N. 2002. "Trade Liberalization, Exit and Productivity Improvements: Evidence from Chilean Plants." *Review of Economic Studies* 69 (1): 245–76.

Reddy, S. 2001. "Liberalization, Distribution and Political Economy." Manuscript, Barnard College, New York.

Revenga, A. 1997. "Employment and Wage Effects of Trade Liberalization: The Case of Mexican Manufacturing." *Journal of Labor Economics* 15 (3): S20–S43.

Rodrik, D. 1997. *Has Globalization Gone Too Far?* Washington, D.C.: Institute of International Economics.

Scheve, K. F., and M. J. Slaughter. 2002. "Economic Insecurity and Globalization of Production." National Bureau of Economic Research Working Paper no. 9339, Cambridge, Mass.

Seddon, J., and R. Wacziarg. 2002. "Trade Liberalization and Intersectoral Labor Movements." Manuscript, Stanford University.

UNICEF. 1997. *The State of the World's Children.* London: Oxford University Press.

Walmsley, T. and A. Winters. 2002. "Relaxing Restrictions on the Temporary Movement of Natural Persons: A Simulation Analysis." GTAP Resource Center Paper no. 949, Purdue University.

Wood, A. 1997. "Openness and Wage Inequality in Developing Countries: The Latin American Challenge to East Asian Conventional Wisdom." *World Bank Economic Review* 11 (1): 33–57.

CHAPTER 2

Social Protection in a Supranational Context

EUROPEAN INTEGRATION AND THE FATES
OF THE "EUROPEAN SOCIAL MODEL"

Claus Offe

THE THREE QUESTIONS I want to discuss here are as follows: (1) Is there such a thing as "European capitalism" or a specific "European" model of social order? Are there institutional and structural features that apply more or less to *all* European political economies and *only* to European political economies? How do European political economies and societies contrast if compared to their liberal counterparts of the Anglo-Saxon world? (2) If they exist, how can these distinctive similarities, or family affinities of European capitalisms, be explained in historical terms and justified in normative or functional terms? (3) What can we expect and predict concerning the impact of European integration upon the distinctive features of European "social capitalism"? Is it likely that European societies will converge in the process of integration on the distinctive European "social model," as represented by and inherited from European nation-states, or is there evidence of trends to the opposite? If the former, European integration would then undermine the "Europeanness" of the emerging political economy of the European Union.

"EUROPEAN" CAPITALISM?

As to the first of these questions, much of the historical and social science literature is preoccupied with an approach that has been labeled "methodological nationalism" (Smith 1979). The national state and society, not "Europe" as a whole, is the standard unit of analysis, and for good reasons. On the one hand, the nation-state must be conceived of as a self-contained and self-governing entity with distinctive centers of legitimate political rule and the enforcement capacity due to which it has effectively shaped the institutional structure of its society and economy. Also, until recently, most of the data that are available for social scientific analysis are gathered by national agencies, such as national statistical offices, according to national standards and definitions. Virtually all cross-sectional comparative literature compares countries, and much less so subnational units (such as regions) or supranational units (such as "families of nations"; cf. Castles 1993).

There are, however, a number of features that European societies are thought to have in common. Some of these features have remained distinctively European, while others have spread from Europe and its pioneering role to other parts of the globe. Instances of such historically rooted and distinctive features of "Europeanness" are Christianity, the legacies of the absolutist state (Ertman 1997; Anderson 1993), the modes in which this early modern form of political rule has been overcome, a history of vast interstate warfare, colonialism, doctrines and precepts of revolutionary liberation, the nation-state, the sciences, and capitalism itself. This list does, however, invite the objection that there are as many dissimilarities among European states and groups of states: Christianity is divided into Roman Catholicism and Orthodoxy in the fourteenth century and then again into the former and Protestantism in the sixteenth. Revolutionary liberation and nation-state building occurred in some countries, but not (or with much delay) in others. Some states acquired vast colonial empires, others did not. Some countries in Europe were capitalist pioneers, others latecomers. And so on. Nevertheless, historians (e.g., Kaelble 1987) and sociologists (e.g., Crouch 1999; Therborn 1995) have elaborated structural similarities that supposedly govern all (or, at any rate, most) European societies.

These similarities are either of a substantive or a procedural nature, manifesting themselves in distinctive structures or in institutionalized ways of "getting things done." As to the former, religious life, the family, the city, political parties and party cleavages, economic institutions, and artistic forms are cited as instances of shared features of all European societies. As to "procedural" similarities (and as an offshoot of the Weberian problem of "occidental rationalism," or "modernization," with its dialectic of liberating increments of bureaucratic, technological, etc. control and the concomitant loss of freedom within "iron cages"), "Europe" has been associated with the idea and practice of limiting, balancing, and managing diversity and conflict, and buffering the consequences of change, through the use of state power (see Crouch 1999: ch. 14).

The social, economic, and political contours of Europe are not easy to determine. Even if it comes to defining a subset of its features, such as the welfare state, we are bound to conclude that "the idea of a European welfare state model does not leap automatically from the data" (Baldwin 1996: 35). The rhetoric of the "European Social Model," as it was inaugurated by Jacques Delors in the 1980s and eventually canonized in the documents of the Barcelona European Council of 2002, may be criticized for representing more of a normative vision than a consolidated reality. Much of the academic literature points at the wide range of variation that can be European welfare states, economic institutions, and forms of democracy. Perhaps a reasonably clear and meaningful identity of "the" European model emerges only if Europe is contrasted to non-European global regions, such as East Asia, the underdeveloped global South, or North America (Münkler 1991). Moreover, (West) European history of the second half of the twentieth century is to a large extent shaped by the United States and its military, political, intellectual, economic, and aesthetic hegemony. What ties social actors together are links (such as mass air travel, global markets, the Internet) of a global, not a European, scope. Arguably, "Europeanness" is nothing that can be found in the shared histories of European societies but, to the contrary, something that is in the still-elusive state of "becoming," an artifact of European integration and its homogenizing impact. Also, in speaking of "European" society, authors often have in mind some features that characterize core Western European societies and that (partly) serve as a pole of attraction or a model for imitation to societies located in Europe's eastern and southern peripheries.

Yet in spite of these various caveats concerning the risks of reifying "Europeanness," modern European history is shaped, I submit, by what one might call a "logic of discontinuity." This discontinuity applies in time and space. It is a "logic" in that discontinuity poses challenges and calls for types of responses that exhibit some European elective affinity. Spatial discontinuity results from the ongoing contest over land borders and the need of all states to define and defend their contested territorial base against neighboring states, which historically happened most often in the form of international war, conquest, and separation.[1]

By discontinuity in time, I mean the relative frequency of regime changes in European history. There is no (Continental) European country that matches the United States in both the stability of its territorial shape (not to mention its territorial size) and the longevity of its constitution.[2] A third kind of discontinuity within European societies has to do with (territorial) religious divisions and divisions of social class, with both of them being crystallized in terms of formal representative organizations (such as political parties, churches, associations) as well as distinct universes of social intercourse. The conclusion to be drawn from these facts of territorialized fragmentation, historical discontinuity, and social divisions is that any "winner-takes-all strategy" does not possibly lead to stable and viable solutions. In both political and economic life, the weaker part is granted some measure of status and protection according to some universally perceived (after World War II, that is) need for "dialogue." Instead of the logic of "winner takes all," diversity must be recognized, represented, accommodated, managed, and reconciled through dialogue rather than being ruled out by majoritarian procedures or all-out market competition. Hence the many "co-concepts" that are being used by social scientists to capture the distinctive essentials of European political economies in the second half of the twentieth century, such as compromise, coalition governments, coordinated capitalism, corporatist bargaining, cooperation, and consociationalism.

People can flee unbearable threats and conflicts, and they have done so in the history of nineteenth- and twentieth-century Europe by the tens of millions, with most of them turning to the Americas. But entire societies and states cannot escape by relocating into insular situations or virgin lands. They are trapped in an environment of discontinuity and contest. Nor can they hope to cope with this environment of discontinuities (the most important of which come in terms of nations, social classes, and religious belief systems) by imposing upon it a lasting ("millenarian") and spatially all-inclusive ("imperial") order. The two "totalitarian" regimes that European history has seen in the twentieth century have served to demonstrate, through the disasters they have caused and the eventual defeat they have suffered, the validity of this impossibility theorem. If discontinuities, conflicts, and diversities (of interests, identities, ideas) can neither be escaped through "exit" nor repressed through state terror, the only remaining option is to institutionalize some viable form of coexistence of classes, states, and identities. In the European context, every regime of political and economic order has been challenged from three sides: from old and entrenched social forces, from ascending classes, and from foreign (as well as, in some countries, subnational) rival forces. These challenges must be overcome by structures that facilitate cooperation. Both the history and the territorial situation of Europe have put a high premium on learning this lesson ever since the Westphalian peace settlement—the lesson of bridging, regulating, and constraining domestic and international conflict while at the same time recognizing the legitimacy and inescapability of diversity. There is a European way in which "diversity itself is handled" and institutionally transformed into "ordered, limited, and structured diversity" (Crouch 1999: 404).

Status, Standards, Protection

The European method of handling and structuring diversity works through the provision of autonomies, privileges, and other kinds of protective status rights. There is a wealth of research conducted in the 1990s on comparative capitalism. By calling a political economy "capitalist" we refer essentially to the dominant economic role of private firms whose activities are steered by market prices, the competitive search for efficiency increases, methodical accounting, and expected profitability; decisions on all aspects of production are made on the basis of enforceable property rights, and a market for labor and labor contracts provide the key mechanism of income distribution. Taken together, these features of capitalism have come to be seen as an almost universally applicable and hence rather uninformative label. After all, and especially after the demise of state socialism, what else, other than "capitalism," can we expect to find as the organizing principles of economic life in developed, as well as in developing, economies? The emphasis has shifted to the plural: capitalisms instead of capitalism, and the distinguishing historical contexts, institutional features, and record of productive and distributive performance of those varieties of capitalism.

Thus "capitalism," once viewed as a single species of social and economic organization, is now rather being conceptualized as a zoo full of different species. One defining feature of (Continental) European capitalism and the social order resulting from it is the prominence of state-defined and state-protected status rights. By "status" I mean a positive and statutory (as opposed to merely tradition-based) bundle of rights and duties, standards, licenses, mandates, legally prescribed procedures, entitlements, subsidies, and privileges that are attached to virtually every participant in economic transaction and the collective actors representing and governing these participants and entering into "dialogue" with each other. Such a status order stands equally in contrast to a voluntaristic regime of free contracting as it stands in contrast to a regime of the discretionary exercise of political power. It is established and defended not just in terms of providing protection and security, but, at least to some extent, also in terms of furthering long-term productivity, collective economic interest, and stability through nonmarket and nonhierarchical modes of coordination. The measure of the strength of the status component of a capitalist economic system is the degree to which partners to contracts are endowed with nonnegotiable entitlements and duties.

This rule of voluntaristic contractual transactions being constrained by status categories applies to the entire range of economically relevant institutions in European societies, including banks and financial markets; trade unions, employers associations, and the practices of wage determination and income distribution; the regulation and protection of the commercial sector and small enterprise; agriculture; the networks of transportation, energy, and communication; vocational training and tertiary education; the role and mission of central banks; the professions; corporate governance; international trade, tariffs, and migration; the tax system; state-controlled and state-subsidized patterns of housing and the real estate market, as well as urban and regional development, including the conservation of physical resources; social security and other welfare state institutions; public sector employment; company-level labor relations; property rights, both in things and in ideas, and their adjudication; and the governance of research, development, and innovation.[3]

For instance, and as a rule of thumb, in the United States you get paid for what you *actually* do, while in Europe you get paid for what you *can* do according to some status-conferring certificate obtained through formal training. Similarly, in the United States your level of pay will most often be determined by individual or company-level contractual agreements, while in most European systems trade unions and employers associations are assigned the collective status right of determining an entire industry-wide pay regime through collective bargaining. In the latter case, the level and kind of rewards are tied to regulatory rules of training and licensing, which logically precede the market and are relatively immune from market forces. The individual pursuit of economic gain is "embedded" (this being one of the key terms of the comparative capitalism literature, a term dating back to Polanyi 1944) in a set of formal (i.e., legislated) and informal (moral and culture-bound) institutional patterns that constrain the permissible range of profit-seeking transactions as well as the types of participants in contractual interaction. The degree of embeddedness is the greater the more specific and constraining the rules are that limit the pursuit of individual gain in markets (beyond, that is, what general legal rules of criminal and civil law prohibit anyway). Embeddedness refers to the degree to which contractual relations are premised upon a nonnegotiable status order governing economic activity, akin to what has been termed "decommodification" by Esping-Andersen (1990) and others.

While constraining and distorting the short-term economic outcomes that would result from "free" markets, that is, markets exclusively driven by short term and individual cost and price considerations and voluntary contracts, embeddedness is designed, or at any rate invariably defended and justified, in terms of three standards of collective rationality. These supra-individual rationality standards are temporal, social, and functional; they emphasize future-and-past-regardingness, other-regardingness, and the attention to collectively beneficial, though often non-obvious, functions and side effects that they perform.

To illustrate, let us take the case of trade unionism. If trade unions are strong due to a strong status in wage determination assigned to them by law (or even constitutionally, as in article 9 of the German Basic Law), and if they represent the work force of entire sectors of industry rather than that of individual companies, chances are comparatively greater that they will adopt some awareness of and consideration for the consequences that their demands and strategies entail for the employment prospects of workers in general, as well as upon the rate of inflation and their industry's competitiveness. As a consequence of this organizational setup, they become more readily "*other-regarding*" than company unions, due to their narrow concern for the maximization of nominal wages of a small percentage of the industry's or nation's overall work force, could ever afford to be. Similarly, and in the *temporal dimension*, the institutionalization of a "skill rent" as a wage component that is being paid regardless of actual job requirements will encourage the acquisition and continuous upgrading of skills, thus creating, unlike the conditions prevailing in highly mobile "hire-and-fire" labor markets, a reservoir of skills that will economize on transactions costs and increase the duration of job tenure due to workers' enhanced flexibility. Thirdly, high wages and high skills will provide, as a desirable *functional side effect*, a powerful incentive to employers to utilize possibilities for labor-saving technical change, thus increasing the efficiency and competitiveness of production.

Taken together, economic status rights will not only *protect* economic actors (employees, farmers, artisans, small and medium-sized businesses, banks, professions, etc.) from adverse market impacts and thus institutionalize social and economic conflict; they can also *contribute* to overall and long-term (economic as well as noneconomic) outcomes that are held to be superior to pure market transaction with its blindness to the interests of others, to externalities, and to the past or future. If there is anything distinctive about the "European" model of capitalism, it is the insight, congealed in a myriad of economic institutions and regulatory arrangements, that the interest of "all of us" will be served well exactly if the pursuit of interest of "each of us" is to some extent constrained by categorical status rights.

There can be little doubt, however, that the relationship between a market-constraining, state-sponsored order of status and standards, on the one hand, and measures of economic performance (growth, employment, productivity, competitiveness, stability), on the other, is at best a curvilinear one. "Too little" regulation will turn out to be as counterproductive in its consequences as "too much." There is no valid presumption of "the more the better." This suggests the notion of an optimum level of nonmarket ingredients and status rights, with further increases of these ingredients beyond the optimum, leading to sclerosis and rigidity.

To illustrate: Workers' status rights are often intended to contribute to the labor market performance and economic growth. The status rights of young workers to acquire skills in a semipublic system of vocational training can enhance their overall employment prospects and help to avoid the marginalizing effects of youth unemployment, in addition to supplying the human capital upon which economic growth may critically depend.

But this notion of rationally optimizing an institutional arrangement by defining the best mix of state-sponsored status components and contractual voluntarism is clearly a "hyper-rationalist," and ultimately a meaningless, project. It is simply not self-evident who should be authorized to *define* that point of equilibrium, as conflicting values (e.g., security vs. efficiency) are involved and trade-offs are essentially contested. Who, after all, is competent enough to determine how much allocative inefficiency is "worth" how much gain in dynamic efficiency (see Streeck and Yamamura 2001: 4), with a compelling answer becoming even harder to find if the choice is not just between short-term and long-term efficiency, but between either of these and values such as security, equity, or social justice. Moreover, any "optimal" mix may be short-lived, as optimality is contingent upon changing conditions and competitive relations within the global economy. Furthermore, even if such equilibrium could be authoritatively defined, it is not clear how the blueprint could be *implemented* against the well-entrenched political resistance of those who stand to lose from even incremental change. The underlying claim that embedded and constrained versions of capitalism "work better" than their liberal and "pure" counterparts holds true in some cases and periods, but not in others. Sometimes (as in the 1980s), Continental European capitalisms have performed better than liberal ones; at other times (such as the latter part of the 1990s) the reverse applies. As there is thus not the slightest guarantee that the given "status component" of the social and economic order is "optimal" at any given point or can effectively be made optimal through continuous fine-tuning by enlightened elites, the question is how viable a given status order is when it faces challenges.

European Integration vs. Globalization

"Globalization" is often thought of as an anonymous process that is accounted for in terms of the relative growth of international trade, of foreign direct investment (FDI), and of financial transactions that can be observed as a persistent trend beginning in the 1980s and 1990s. It is the aggregate effect of the behavior of *economic* strategic actors. Also, the number of countries that are robustly able to stay out of the trend is in decline, and particularly so after the major "anti-globalizing" barrier, namely the Iron Curtain, became ineffective (with North Korea and very few others remaining the exception that proves the rule). While "globalization," or the disproportionate growth of international trade, foreign direct investment, and border-transcending financial transactions that we have experienced since the 1980s is an evolving system of factual power relations and (inter)dependencies with marginal and often contested elements of governance, the European Union is first and foremost a *politically* designed and legally defined project that is about to give itself a constitution. Nothing of that kind is going to happen to the global economy any time soon.

At any rate, the European Union is not an anonymous process that can be described and explained only in retrospect. Rather, it is a continually negotiated design in which *political* actors play the major role. It is in no way "global," but sharply delimited in its territorial extension. The relevance of borders for European economic development is not declining, but rather increasing—and intentionally so, as anyone who has to confront the European Union from the outside, such as Latin American politicians and business elites with their experience of facing a "Fortress Europe," will readily agree.

But EU integration and globalization are also interconnected in a number of ways. The former can be conceived of as a device to put European national economies in the favorable position of being able to defend themselves against unwelcome effects of "globalization" (such as the penetration of agricultural markets); at the same time, the Europe-wide integration of markets is expected to enhance Europe's productivity through economies of scale and specialization effects, global competitiveness, and capacity for innovation so as to allow Europeans to profit rather than suffer from globalization. But EU integration can also be seen as the opposite of globalization in that its capacity to govern and regulate the regional version of an international economy is arguably far greater (as it involves, among other things, more limited conflicts of interest and values) than is the case with attempts to regulate global trade and global economic transactions through governing mechanisms such as the WTO. After all, and even after Eastern Enlargement is completed in the new EU-25, the range of variation of GNP per capita among member states is far more limited than it is among the "participants" of the global process of growing economic (inter)dependence and interpenetration.

Yet it is still possible to draw parallels between economic globalization and European integration. The most important of these is the partial disempowerment of national governments. In either case, national governments see their agendas set by supra- or transnational forces that are largely beyond their control. This applies with particular force to issues of monetary, fiscal, trade, and labor market policy. Moreover, the policy instruments by which they are able to address the agenda, which is partly determined by external inputs, become severely limited.

Instruments such as taxation, subsidies, protective tariffs, and demand-side macro-economic management are blunted both by adverse reactions of mobile factors of production and by the ban that supranational authorities (WTO and IMF in the case of globalization; the Commission of the European Communities and the European Court of Justice in the case of European integration) impose upon the use of these instruments. Seen in this perspective, European integration can be analyzed as an atypically benign, prosperous, and well-regulated regional analogy to the encompassing dynamics of "globalization."

The European social model has evolved after the Second World War, roughly during the third quarter of the twentieth century, as a unique (in time and space) combination of social and economic policies, both of which were encapsulated in the same institutional arena, that of the nation-state. As far as social policies are concerned, the welfare state provides for the security of status of the national citizenry and sets the stage for social integration and dialogue among encompassing collective actors. It does so not in order to cope with exceptional economic crises (such as the New Deal programs of the 1930s) but as an institutional arrangement that is at the same time enhancing security and promoting growth and productivity and thus designed to contribute to the prosperity of the national economy. Security, integration, and institutionalized dialogue favor growth in three ways. First, they stabilize domestic demand. Second, they increase the cost of employment of labor and thus provide a powerful incentive for employers/investors to economize on costly labor resources by introducing labor-saving technical change, thereby also enhancing productivity and international competitiveness of the national economy. Third, social security and dialogue help to avoid much of the costs and frictions resulting from socioeconomic conflict. The economic growth thus promoted will then in turn yield a growth dividend that makes the maintenance of the welfare state (and even its continuous expansion) fiscally affordable. In this way, the welfare state and economic growth have been tied to each other in a beneficial loop of reciprocal facilitation. It is this tie, often referred to as the "unity" of social and economic policy, that has been broken by European integration: While economic growth can no longer be influenced by national fiscal, monetary, and trade policies in the open economies of the Common Market, social policies remain fixed to the arena of national policy-making.

The Challenge of European Integration

As noted above, the distinctive feature of European capitalisms has evolved under the impact of the "logic of discontinuity." This logic has necessitated the adoption of some state-sponsored status order that protects—according to precepts of a "social" market economy and "organized," "embedded," and "regulated" capitalism—economic agents from some of the impact of the "anarchy of the market," while (ideally) at the same time improving market outcomes. The various institutional patterns that I have mentioned are designed for (or can be justified in terms of) the accommodation of conflicting interests, cooperation, bargaining, consensus, the limitation of conflict, and sustainability.

European integration is a project and partial accomplishment that, in the light of these considerations, allows for two interpretations that are radically contradicting each other. On the one hand, it can be seen as (and was certainly envisioned by its early protagonists to eventually become) a framework of cooperation and regulation that completes at the transnational plane what had been accomplished at the level of member states, namely a regime of fair and peaceful competition that rules out not only international war in Europe, but also cutthroat economic rivalries, thus establishing, through "positive" integration, a Europe-wide and supranationally embedded political economy that evenly serves the interests of all member states involved. This is the vision associated with the name of Jacques Delors and the 1994 White Book on "Growth, Competitiveness, and Employment." But on the other hand, European integration can be seen as a strategy of institution-building and extensive as well as intensive market enlargement that involves not the transposition of the more benign aspects of European capitalisms to the transnational level but, to the contrary, and through the means of market-making and "negative" integration, its demolition at the *national* level. It can thus also be seen as a device that paves the way for the ultimate triumph of market liberalism on the European Continent by enforcing upon member states the adoption of regimes of privatization, deregulation, and fiscal austerity. According to this pessimistic reading of the impact of the new Europeanized political economy (as defined by the parameters of the Single Market, Economic and Monetary Union, and most recently Eastern Enlargement), member states will be deprived of their capacity to maintain the kind of protective arrangements and status order that each of them had built up in the course of their national history. This approach to integration is associated with New Labour's (as well as the 1997 Luxemburg EU Summit's) emphasis on recommodification through "activation." According to this latter reading of the integration process, the Europeanized political economy will significantly come to deviate from the type of European capitalism that prospered under the protection of national regimes (cf. Offe 2000; Aust et al. 2002).

It is too early to pass definitive judgment on which of these diametrically opposed interpretations/predictions/proposals will come closer to the truth. According to the first and optimistic reading, we would have to expect an effective supranational regime of social protection and status rights to be established at the European level. According to the pessimistic reading, we would expect social and economic insecurity to become more intense; the difference between integration winners and integration losers to widen across social classes, sectors of industry, and regions; social exclusion to become more common; the capacity of national governments to maintain their protective status arrangements to be rendered more limited and precarious, as intensified tax competition, dried-up fiscal re-sources, and the European Central Bank's strict stability regime penalizes budget deficits; nationalist and xenophobic anti-European reactions to play an increas-ing role in electoral politics; and the horizons of solidarity and cooperation shrinking to relatively small subnational (i.e., regional, sectoral, and corporate) units (Streeck 2000) rather than expanding to the inclusive level of an all-European polity and regime of social protection. In sum, and as Michael Dauderstädt, a leading expert of the Friedrich Ebert Foundation, the German Social Demo-cratic think tank, has put it in an unpublished memorandum: "Will European integration protect or destroy the 'European social model?' " And if the latter, he goes on to speculate that "it could . . . turn out to be political dynamite when important social groups perceive that their interests are endangered by European policies or rules." Similar concerns about the "social quality" of Europe, even more so than related ones about the European Union's "democratic deficit," rank very high on the research agenda of Europeanists (see Scharpf 2002) as well as in the normative debates on the future of the integration process. After market in-tegration has largely been accomplished, "social" integration will become the key issue.

Underlying the appeal for negative integration and a stronger role for market allocation is a polemic against the built-in egalitarianism of the European model of welfare capitalism, which supposedly strangles its competitiveness and effi-ciency. Yet contrary to a widely shared misunderstanding, the European welfare state does not have much to do with the egalitarian notion of "equality of out-comes," neither normatively nor positively. Not even "equality of opportunity" figures prominently among the welfare states' goals or accomplishments, at least to the extent that the major policy area which is capable of promoting that goal, namely education and training, is not thought of in Europe as belonging to the field of welfare state and social policy proper. Discourses on equality focus not on the equal endowment with material resources, but with equal rights, such as equal rights to labor market access and nondiscriminatory recruitment practices. Least of all is redistribution of income or, to the extent it actually occurs through welfare state programs, redistribution among *social classes*. Much more substantial is the redistribution that occurs across non-class divides, such as redistribution among generations, between gender categories, between the households of single persons and those of families, etc. Most importantly, there are *intra*-class redis-tributive effects within solidaristic social security arrangements. The guiding principle of the European welfare state is the security and protection of workers, not equality of outcomes such as income or wealth. This security consists in an (always partial) protection from market contingencies and (some of) the typical risks that occur in the human life course, such as illness, or lack of income due to old age or unemployment. These risks are covered by welfare state programs and institutions because they cannot, in typical cases, be compensated or provided for by workers' income or savings alone. Thus instead of providing for material equality, the welfare state aims at "including" the large majority of citizens in an arrangement of security and protection of relative status. Its ambition is to build a floor below which nobody is supposed to fall, with both the level of that floor and the universe of those to be protected in their absolute and relative status being essentially contested.

Yet on the other hand, and despite the absence of an egalitarian objective of the provision of status rights, there is in fact little doubt that some measure of outcome equality is an *indirect* effect of the status rights that workers and their families enjoy. For in the absence of such rights, they would have to accept inferior working conditions and levels of pay that reliance on these rights allows them to refuse. While the welfare state is in no way designed to achieve equality of outcomes, its mode of operation stands in the way of allowing for a downward stretching of the wage scale and working conditions by offering workers a comparatively comfortable "reservation wage."

In this sense, it can be said that the security provided by welfare state arrangements has the effect, now very much in the center of attention and debate, of compressing the wage scale by rendering obsolete the employment of labor with low skills and low productivity. Due to the welfare state's policies of building a floor of minimum conditions, workers are no longer forced to "accept any job"; instead, they enjoy the freedom to say "no." The flipside of this coin consists in the fact that labor force mobilization (measured as the product of the proportion of people in gainful employment and the number of hours they work per year) will be significantly lower in the presence of status rights than in its absence, as these rights condition limits to the extent that the wage scale can be stretched downward. The wider impact of this effect is ambiguous. On the one hand, it will deactivate a part of the labor force that otherwise would be available for low-skill and low-pay employment. On the other hand, it forces employers to strive for increases in labor productivity, as much as it protects employees from the competition of low-skill competitors on the supply side of the labor market. Also, and to the extent employers find low-wage workers elsewhere (e.g., in the new member states of Central East Europe) it is *their* turn to enjoy the freedom to say "no" to domestic and highly protected workers.

THE WELFARE STATE EDIFICE

The welfare state is an accumulation of rights that the worker does not have to earn, but which come as an original endowment of "social" citizenship. It can be visualized as an edifice that was erected over a period of more than one-and-a-half centuries in what is now the OECD world. Very schematically speaking, this structure of security has three floors and a roof. Each of the floors is—and always has been since its inception—the scene of a dynamic process of ongoing remodeling, expansion, partial demolition, reconstruction, and innovation, all of which accounts for significant variations across national welfare regimes and points in time. But the structure and function, as well as (almost) the historical sequence in which the floors were built, stay the same across welfare states. Each floor is designed to deal with a particular security concern of wage labor.

The ground floor contains provisions regulating access to labor markets and to jobs and issues of health and safety *at work*.[4] Time-related measures are probably the oldest components, namely the limitation of the work day, along with the prohibition of child labor. The regulation of unhealthy and unsafe work environments were further steps. The procedural regulation of working conditions— such as the speed of assembly lines and work schedules and overtime—through work councils and other forms of codetermination were later added to the structure of the first floor, as were on-the-job training programs and organizational innovations such as job rotation. Preventive health measures were also an important component of the work-related regime of safety and security, as were seniority rules and job tenure. All these measures were implemented through statutory law and a public machinery of factory inspectorates and labor courts, on the one hand, and legally mandated forms of codetermination and joint decision-making between management and workers, on the other. The common denominator of the myriad of regulations to be found here is the intention—shared to some extent by workers and their organizations, policymakers, and employers—to protect workers from some of the disutility and hazards of the labor process, thereby enhancing not just work motivation and productivity, but also the long-term physical integrity of the worker as a productive agent. This agent must be protected from conditions that would lead to the premature exhaustion and obsolescence of labor power, its physical condition, its loyalty and motivation, and its skills.

The second floor is the scene of provisions pertaining to the ("social") security of the wage worker *outside* of work and in the absence of income from currently earned wages. They consist in either transfer payments replacing wages or in social services, such as day care services. There are two classical standard conditions that cause the workers' inability to earn income: recognized *disability* (either due to chronic health conditions or to old age, whichever comes first) and *sickness* (including physical conditions resulting from work accidents). These are covered by social security arrangements, pioneered by the Bismarckian social reforms of the 1880s. They basically consist in a state-mandated and typically state-subsidized arrangement of forced savings that generates funds out of which wages of the disabled/pensioners can be partially replaced and health/ability to work can be restored through medical treatment. Alternatively, social security can be financed out of general taxes, with less immediate implications of changing employment and demographic conditions upon the (nonwage) cost of labor. After health insurance and pension insurance, and typically with considerable delay, comes the recognition of a third risk for which wage-replacement is granted, if only for a limited period of time and after a minimum time of preceding employment, namely *unemployment* (though not for failure to obtain a job in the first place!). A fourth "risk" pertains not to the inability to earn, but to the insufficiency of the income earned due to the presence in the worker's household of dependent children and the additional expenses incurred for their upbringing and the resulting loss of the household's earning capacity. *Family subsidies* are partly designed (in the form of tax allowances) as compensation for relative income loss (relative to households with no or fewer children and hence greater earning capacity), partly as a flat rate reward for parent-citizens and the service to the wider community they assumedly perform through the raising of their offspring.

On the third floor, the institutional devices are located, which are intended to deal with the decline of workers' capacity to *defend their income*, both in absolute terms of real income (to be defended against inflation) and in terms of relative income (to be defended against productivity increases, which shift the ratio of wages to profits in favor of the latter). The institutional pattern that serves these two purposes is trade unionism and the making of collective wage agreements, including its ultimate weapon of strike action. For unionism to become an "institutional" pattern (rather than a mere fact of labor walkouts and shop floor revolts), trade unions must be recognized by employers, as well as by the legal order in general, as legitimate representatives of employees' income interests. To gain such recognition, which typically have occurred under conditions of either international war or severe economic crisis, two obstacles must be effectively overcome. As trade unions are, from an economic point of view, nothing but supply-side cartels, recognizing them as legitimate representatives means exempting them from "antitrust" measures and the general ban of "combinations" that a strictly liberal market economy is premised upon. Furthermore, to enable them to wield the strike weapon, workers and unions must be exempt from the liability for the harm that they inflict by using that weapon against employers. Also, the stronger trade unions are and the more they operate at the multi-company level, the more they will be inclined to fight, apart from higher wages, for a more compressed wage scale to strengthen a sense of solidarity and commitment among their (potential) members and to boost union density. This effect of collective bargaining, which can be seen as the unions' complement to management's efficiency wage strategies, is today widely believed to interfere with the employment prospects of less productive workers. Continental European labor and industrial relations systems differ from country to country concerning the complex ways that have developed of endowing trade unions with these licenses and institutional status rights, in return for which unions are more or less strictly regulated concerning the procedures that must be observed in raising and settling industrial disputes on wages and conditions.

Finally, the roof of the building. As it is in the nature and purpose of a roof, it protects the integrity of the entire building and prevents its lower parts from damage. The roof metaphor serves here to summarize a set of policies that are designed to protect and safeguard the various status-conferring and security arrangements just described. These policies, epitomized by what used to be called the "Keynesian welfare state," include labor market and employment policies, together with the monetary, fiscal, trade, and other economic policies that are designed to promote and maintain "full" employment on which the security of the previously discussed three security arrangements critically depends. This dependency is due to the fact that in the absence of a condition of reasonably "full" employment, none of the three categories of status rights of workers—rights in the labor process, rights outside of work, and rights to defend distributive status through collective action of workers through unions—can be effectively maintained. In a severe and protracted labor-market imbalance with an excess supply of labor, the market will be flooded by employment-seeking workers willing, for lack of a better choice, to forego the protection at work; social security systems will break down under the imbalance of "too few" contributors and "too many" claimants; and trade unions will lack the organizational resources and bargaining power to raise real wages in proportion to productivity gains and redistributive goals or even defend current levels of real income.

So much seems uncontroversial among European social and economic policymakers, virtually all of whom agree that the employment situation is the key issue of social order and stability. What is controversial, however, is the logic by which security and (full) employment are tied to each other. The majority of European *social democrats* argues that in order to *preserve* the core components of the welfare state, full employment must be restored. As a corollary to this argument, it is claimed that all three components of the welfare state arrangement, at least if appropriately revised and "modernized" through carefully designed moves of retrenchment, will serve as effective *instruments* for the achievement of the goal of full employment through growth.

Market liberals take the opposite view by claiming that to restore "full" (or rather, to generate "more") employment in the open economies of the single market, most of the structure of protective and status-conferring institutional patterns of labor regulation, social security provisions, and unions' bargaining power are obstacles to full employment that must first be *largely demolished*, thereby forcing workers to adjust to market incentives and the imperatives of efficiency and competitiveness. Market liberals do not usually believe that welfare state institutions greatly contribute to the efficiency of production now that the "Fordist" pattern of mass production in relatively closed economies has largely become a matter of the past. Nor is there any reason, in their view, to fear that political instability will emerge as a result of the demolition of major parts of the welfare state, at least after leftist political radicalism has similarly become a matter of the past.

Also, a third voice, fortunately one with much less resonance, is making itself increasingly heard in European politics, a voice that claims that the social security of workers (as well as, incidentally, the protection of citizens from violent crime), on the one hand, and efficiency of production and competitiveness, on the other, can only be reconciled if national borders are sealed to the influx of foreign workers, foreign goods, and those praying to "foreign" gods. Since the mid-nineties, integrating Europe has seen the sometimes sudden and spectacular rise to electoral success of figures such as Pia Kjaersgaard (DK), Umberto Bossi and Gianfranco Fini (I), Pim Fortuyn (NL), with Jean-Marie Le Pen (F), Jörg Haider (A), and Carl Hagen (N) being among the pioneers of this new field of populist political entrepreneurship, all of whom share a strong anti-European orientation. Le Pen has described himself in the 2002 French electoral campaign as being a leftist in social affairs, a rightist in economic affairs, and a nationalist for everything else. This formula, which is designed to resolve the tension between liberal market freedom and welfare state status rights by ethno-nationalist, xenophobic, and anti-European appeals, is applied by his rightist populist colleagues as well. As to the welfare ingredients of this formula, the protection offered is not the one accomplished through strengthening the status, security, and bargaining power of the weaker participants in labor contracts, as in the social democratic tradition. It is through granting benefits and offering paternalistic redistribution to needy members of the national community, such as single mothers, low-income tenants, and family farmers. The emphasis is on the protection of life and property against crime, and particularly crime committed by non-nationals or facilitated by open borders (such as mandated by the Schengen Agreement). What rightist populist social policies invoke are the two quintessentially noncontractual, or "communal," forms of collective life: the family (as opposed to marriage) and the ethnic nation (as opposed to the republic or, for that matter, the nascent Europolity). In recent years, the electoral fortune of the populist right has been growing in inverse proportion to that of the social democratic left. In some places, the populist right has been able to accomplish the unlikely success of attracting both the support of prosperous libertarian middle-class "yuppies" (with their opposition to high taxes and social spending and a taste for tightening other people's belts) and frustrated working-class elements who have lost faith in leftist policies and promises.

It is the triangle of reluctant social democrats, aggressive market liberals, and more-or-less militant rightist populists that forms the ideological space of political contestation and policy debates in the EU-15, with a clear prospect that rightist anti-integrationist forces will gain from the transition to EU-25.

If, as a consequence of "globalization,"—that is, the increase of international flows of investment, goods, information, and people—the nation-state's sovereign governing capacity is declining, what happens to the welfare state and its components that were historically premised upon robust nation-states? Three familiar alternative trajectories can be envisaged, corresponding to the three types of political forces just mentioned. First, the architecture of security is gradually demolished, giving way to a version of the liberal equality of rights, including the uninhibited freedom to enter into border-crossing transactions. According to proponents of this perspective of market-making or *negative integration*, states must, due to their definitive loss of "border control" and in the face of increased factor mobility, lower the ambitions invested in the social security arrangement to gain and maintain advantages of international competitiveness. If they stick to inherited standards of status and protection, they will be punished by markets through the outflow of capital and the influx of labor, with the former by itself being the cause of likely increases of unemployment. Or, secondly, a populist backlash will be triggered by the repercussions of internationalization, resulting in potentially most illiberal forms of paternalistic protectionism of national borders—the option of *positive disintegration*. Thirdly, some functional equivalent of security-enhancing status rights will be transferred from the nation-state level to supranational forms of political organization, often referred to as *positive integration*.

According to this latter perspective, Europe is currently in need of, as well as in search of, policies and patterns of political decision-making that would denationalize the diverse welfare state arrangements that have evolved over many decades at the national levels and to transfer them, their regulation and mode of financing, to the European level. The motivation for this search stems not so much from lofty ambitions of social reform and European-wide social justice as it is driven by defensive considerations. The goal of denationalizing social protection, in other words, is being envisaged in terms of what to avoid, not what to achieve. What is to be avoided is either of the (polarized and mutually invigorating) extremes of a mere market-liberal *negative integration* and rightist-populist reactions that would amount to a backlash of *positive disintegration*. Yet the road "in between," that of "positive integration," leads through largely uncharted territory. "Social dumping," "race to the bottom," "beggar my neighbor," and the rise of the "competition state," that is, a fiscally starved state that is reduced to the status of a strategically impotent price-taker facing the uncontrollable dynamics of capital mobility, are some of the catchwords representing the fears that people associate with the "negative," mere market-making instead of market-regulating form of EU-integration, with additional threats of heightened factor mobility, or rather massive inflows of labor and outflows of capital, being associated with the new realities of Eastern Enlargement toward EU-25.

It is also widely felt by political elites that to maintain popular support for both the deepening of ("ever closer") European integration and the widening of its scope ("Eastern Enlargement"), Europe must present itself to its citizens as a credible project of social security and protection, and certainly not as a threat to established social status rights. At the very least, and after the European Union is still evidently deficient (relative to the member state polities) in terms of its democratic legitimacy, pro-European consensus and identification among non-elites is likely to dwindle, strengthening the forces of populist renationalization, in case a loss is perceived to take place not just in terms of democratic legitimacy, but also of social protection and security. Thus, and in order to hold together the component parts of integrating Europe and to pave the road toward wider and deeper future integration, European elites have every political reason to go beyond the negative integration of markets and proceed, visibly and credibly, toward a positive integration of a "social" Europe. The question is: Does Europe have the resources and institutional devices actually to do so?

Yet the transition from market-*making* negative integration through the abolition of tariffs and other hindrances and distortions of competition to market-*constraining* positive integration through the adoption of a Europe-wide regime of social protection and security is a process that, if anything, will take decades rather than years to conclude.[5] This is so because of the extraordinary obstacles and complexities involved. These can be summarized in seven points:

1. The scope and *level* of generosity of social protection as well as the status rights of collective actors (trade unions, employers' associations) differ from member state to member state. This implies that any conceivable supranational European social policy regime that represents an "average" between the high performers and the low performers would be vehemently opposed by either of them. It would be opposed by (e.g., the Scandinavian) high performers because the *political* objection would apply that some of "our" social achievements are being sacrificed on the altar of European integration. But it would also be opposed by the low social protection achievers (e.g., Portugal) for the *economic* reason that "Europe" forces "us" to become more generous, thus undercutting the competitive advantage that "we" enjoy due to our lower costs of labor. The only conceivable way to prevent this conflict from evolving was seen in preventing it to emerge at the European level, a preventive measure known under the euphemism of "subsidiarity" (Article 5, TEC), which leaves, as a *matter of European law*, the exclusive jurisdiction on social affairs to the member states. Yet the actual possibility of member states to design and implement autonomous policies of social protection has, as a *matter of fact*, been severely constrained by an EU-inaugurated EMU and Single Market regime with its effective ban on autonomous policies of setting exchange rates, interest rates, and fiscal debt, as well as controlling capital movements and movements of goods and services across national borders, all of which amount to considerations of social protection being trumped by those of the competitiveness of the national economy of member states.

2. The actual growth and labor market performance of European economies, as well as their overall level of economic development, varies by country and, in particular, by region within countries, with the better-off countries being typically the small and medium-sized ones in the West and North of the EU territory. According to Eurostat data, official unemployment rates range from 2 and 3 percent in Luxemburg and the Netherlands in 2001 to between 10 and 13 percent in Greece and Spain. GDP per person slightly exceeds the OECD average in Belgium and Denmark, while it lags

as far behind as 60 percent in Portugal or even 58 percent in Greece. This implies a corresponding difference in the urgency by which national governments will be prepared to make efforts to improve their employment situation as a means to maintain their level of social protection.

3. The *institutional structure* of both social security arrangements and industrial/labor relations systems differs widely among EU member states and their social policy regimes. Benefit levels vary as considerably as the modes of financing these benefits. The same applies to the institutional arrangements of wage determination. It is exactly because each of the member states has a highly developed institutional system in place on the second and third floor of our welfare state structure, and because each of these systems has generated its entrenched interests and peculiar expectations, that harmonization or convergence is so difficult to achieve as a political project and jointly adopted institutional design. Even those who agree that a "positively" integrated "Social Europe" must be created to compensate for the Common Market's corrosive effects upon national welfare states are unlikely to find it as easy to agree on any particular institutional blueprint according to which "Social Europe" is to be built. This difficulty does not preclude various kinds of "spontaneous" adjustments and convergences as they are necessitated by capital mobility and competitive pressures, as opposed to Europe-wide designed and formally adopted ones. A case in point is the corrosion of systems of multi-employer collective bargaining, which is being replaced by the practice of company-level concession bargaining and government-sponsored emergency measures ("social pacts"; Hassel 1998). Such phenomena of de-institutionalized ad hoc crisis responses are often summarily and in an alarmist tone referred to as a "race to the bottom."

4. At the same time, quantitative and qualitative regime divergences constitute not only robust obstacles to harmonization and "positive" integration, but also considerable *distortions of market competition*. For instance, the Bismarckian countries that finance their social security systems largely through fixed contributions of employers and employees suffer competitive disadvantages as compared to countries where social security expenditures are largely financed through general taxes. The presence of these distortions suggests the need for achieving a more unified welfare state regime in the interest of creating a level playing field for market integration itself, and not just in terms of some harmonized model of "Social Europe."

5. Such harmonization is also called for as severe fiscal imbalances within national systems of social security—which are all the more likely to occur as a result of persistent high levels of unemployment prevailing in some of the member states—will force national governments to adopt fiscal measures (i.e., budgetary deficits) that are in manifest violation of the Growth and Stability Pact, the fiscal and monetary regime adopted as a disciplinary device to sustain the EMU. If labor market and social protection policies are left entirely to the discretion of member states in the name of

"subsidiarity," national policy actors are likely to resort to measures (such as subsidies or budget deficits) that imply severe negative externalities (such as interest rate hikes, decline of the external value of the Euro) for other member states or for the EMU as a whole.

6. Thus what appears impossible for reasons 1 to 3 is widely seen as desirable and even necessary for reasons 4 and 5, as well as a further one, which derives from the consideration that some convergence and harmonization is also called for in terms of political integration itself. To maintain the permissive consensus supportive of "ever-closer integration" and to prevent the further spread of anti-European mobilization of the nationalist and populist-protectionist sort, national social security and collective status arrangements must be protected against the perception of being jeopardized by European market integration and threatened by "social dumping" and a "race to the bottom." The protagonists of market integration have always claimed that the single market, due to the economies of scale that it yields, the intensified competition that it generates, as well as the equalizing effects of funds spent on regional development and cohesion would lead all member states into a bright future of growth, employment, and prosperity. As this promise has not been credibly redeemed, at least for the time being, it seems all the more urgent for European policymakers to counteract the perception that the Single Market is the cause of job losses and the partial demolition of national systems of social protection.

7. While everything that belongs to the ground floor of the welfare state structure (the nondiscriminatory regulation of access to labor markets and jobs, the rules governing health and safety at work) is firmly established and equalized across the European Union by European law, it is also well understood by now that the affordability of the various national arrangements at the second and third floors (social security and wage determination) is entirely contingent upon the solidity of the "roof," that is, the labor market performance of member states. But lacking any governing capacity and fiscal authority of its own, Commission and Council do not enjoy the authority to boost overall European labor market performance, while member state governments maintain the exclusive responsibility for labor market and employment policy in the name of "subsidiarity"—a responsibility, however, that is largely rendered nominal by the unfettered mobility of both labor and capital, on the one hand, and the constraining EMU ("Maastricht") criteria, on the other. Thus member states have the nominal authority, yet not the effective means, at their disposal to do something about the employment situation, which in its turn determines the sustainability of the welfare state edifice. Could it be, then, that European institutions could avail themselves, even in the absence of the formal authority to do so, of the means to shape European-level labor market and employment policies, in the pursuit of which some "harmonization through the back door" would incrementally be introduced?

What the European Employment Strategy (EES) is designed to achieve is a rather precarious mix of market-making at the Community level with some preservation of status rights at the national level. As to the former, the clear emphasis is upon enhancing the employability of labor through human capital formation, increasing labor's flexibility, and mobilizing those social categories for (increased) employment who have been marginalized, discriminated against, or excluded from the labor market. The European Union's official target figures for employment of the population ages 15 to 64 to be reached by 2010 are 70 percent of the entire population, 60 percent of working-age women, and 50 percent of the elderly (ages 55+). This ambitious set of goals is argued for in terms of securing the sustainability of national social insurance systems, that is, of breaking the vicious circle (made worse by the demographic composition of aging societies) of increasing unemployment or inactivity rates → generous allowances for early retirement and other forms of wage replacement as a policy response → increase of non-wage social security contributions to public pension systems → increase of non-wage labor costs → increasing unemployment. The ambitiousness of these targets, which are set for all of the EU-25, is evident from the fact that in 2003 only three member states (Sweden, Denmark, Great Britain) had reached all of them, with member states such as France, Germany, Italy, and Poland lagging more or less far behind in all of them. How these goals are to be reached remains the responsibility of the member states' governments. What EES guidelines call for, however, is the use of "incentives" for labor market participation, which is a euphemism for both the lowering and the increased targeting of reservation wages.

I will not concern myself any further with the substantive developments and accomplishments that the European Union has achieved so far or is likely to achieve. Rather, I will focus for the rest of this chapter on new methods of "coordinating" policy-making by which European policymakers have tried to accomplish what "cannot" be done (due to reasons 1, 2, and 3) yet still "must" be done (due to reasons 4 to 6 and under the challenges of 7), if without the ordinary machinery of "direct effect" rulings and other means of authoritative making and implementing of supranational European Union policy.

"Stateless" Policy-Formation?

There is by now a ten-year history of the European Union's attempts to cope with this configuration of constraints and challenges. It starts with Jacques Delors's White Book on *Growth, Competitiveness, and Employment* (1994), which reflects the member states' great difficulties in addressing unemployment and sets the stage for addressing the issue at a European level. It calls for greater coordination and convergence of employment policy. At the 1994 Essen Council, the first contours of an European Employment Strategy were worked out. These were then incorporated in the "employment chapter" (articles 125–130) of the Amsterdam Treaty on the European Communities (TEC), signed in October of 1997 and coming into force in May 1999. The policy instruments provided for in this chapter are of a characteristically "soft" nature: annual review of the EU employment situation at the Council level, formulation of "guidelines" to be taken into account by member states, annual reports to be submitted by member states on their employment policies, policy recommendations addressed to member states, exchange of information on "best practices" among member states, creation of an "employment committee" advising the Council of Ministers. Immediately following the Amsterdam conference, the Luxemburg "job summit" of 1997 worked out these policy instruments in more detail and included the obligation of member states to submit "national action plans" that are subject to "multilateral surveillance." The development of this set of policy devices was continued at the Council meetings of Cardiff (1998), Cologne (1999), and, most significantly, Lisbon (2000), where the "Open Method of Coordination" (OMC) that comprises these procedures was defined for the first time.[6] As a result, the scope of policy areas to which OMC was to be applied was significantly broadened so as to include issues of "social inclusion," research policy, the formation of an "information society," "entrepreneurial policy," health and pension policy (Stockholm 2001), education, Eastern Enlargement, immigration policy, and "sustainable development." Procedures for all these policy areas, however, are still considerably less elaborate and specific than those applying to EES. (For the current analysis and debate on these policy methods, see de la Porte and Pochet 2002; Goetschy 2001; Hodson and Maher 2001; and Trubek and Mosher 2001.)

The European Union has no direct way of addressing issues of wage determination and the distribution of incomes. These remain entirely a matter of national policy-making and institutions. There are, however, indirect methods of getting hold of these two strategic variables, and these have recently been explored and developed, beginning with the Lisbon summit (2000). In model terms, wage levels and the wage structure interact with (a) the quantity of *labor supply*, that is, the activity rate, and, in particular, the employment rate, within the population ages 15 to 64; and (b) the *skills of labor*, with upgrading skills having a positive effect upon both individual income and employment security of workers and the overall volume of employable labor.

The European priorities, as promulgated at the Luxemburg, Lisbon, and Stockholm summits, concentrate on two dimensions of labor supply: quantity and skills. They do so in the name of a new normative concept (or rhetoric), that of "cohesion," the promotion of "inclusion," and the fighting of "discrimination." The analysis behind this strategy is roughly this. If labor market participation rates lag behind those actually achieved in other advanced societies, parts of Europe's growth potential will be wasted, and transfer budgets will be strained. Nonparticipation must be due to either of two causes: people are *prevented* from participation, which amounts to "discrimination," or they are not motivated or *capable* to participate, in which case "unemployability" or excessively generous reservation wages is taken to be the cause. Both of them add up to the pathology of economic and social "exclusion," which must be fought by strategies of "inclusion," thus strengthening social "cohesion." Inclusion refers to fighting discrimination by race, ethnicity, and nationality, as well as physical handicaps, but most importantly by gender (Article 3 (2) TEC) and by age. Integrating the underutilized supply of female labor and 55+ labor into gainful activity is therefore a key component of all EU policy documents issued by the Commissions' Directorate-General for Employment and Social Affairs and various Council directives (such as 2000/43 and 2000/78). This antidiscrimination agenda has the dual attractiveness of (a) being "egalitarian" in terms of rights and opportunities, without redistributive expenditures attached, and (b) being instrumental, if implemented, for the viability and sustainability of member states' public pension systems (as emphasized by the Stockholm summit, March 2001) as well as, less explicitly, inducing wage restraint and a downward stretching of the wage scale through the mobilization of additional labor supply at the lower range of the skill and wage spectrum.

Nothing, however, is mandatory, binding, or authoritative in this iterative annual process of formulating supranational guidelines and monitoring their implementation. Hence compliance on the part of member states is entirely voluntary, concerning both the kind of their policy priorities and the degree of effort with which they are being pursued. While it is too early to assess the effects of this mode of policy-making and to attribute causally any success to the OMC, two underlying assumptions of this method of policy-making are fairly clear. One of them is cognitive, the other motivational.

Knowledge, Motivation, and Policy Learning

One of the key mechanisms on which the OMC is assumed to operate is cognitive (see Jacobson 2002). The key phrases are "best practice," "benchmarking," and "management by objectives," "peer control," and "temporal standardization and disciplining." The rather technocratic background intuition is that "we" can benefit from learning from how others have managed to succeed, with the implication being that policy failure must be due to inadequate learning capacity. For the purpose of facilitating cross-national policy learning, a substantial fund of € 100 million has been set up to conduct research on discriminatory practices and to promote the exchange among member states on how to fight them (Council decision 2000/750). But it is far from obvious which practices are to be recognized as "best," given the multitude of evaluative criteria and the trade-offs that apply to them. To illustrate, extensive use of part-time employment might be the best way to create jobs and reduce unemployment, as the Dutch example suggests. But it might be far from best in stabilizing household income over the life course. Even if some standard of success is unequivocal, chances are that success is not easily attributed to individual measures and programs that are always embedded

into—and whose effectiveness is contingent upon—the entire ensemble of institutions of a member state and its policy regime with its built-in priorities and
constraints. For instance, some member states have a statutory minimum wage,
some don't; some have a big tax component in financing their pension system,
some rely almost exclusively on contributory schemes. Should the latter be required to imitate the "best practice" of the former? If so, successful policy learning would not just require them to adopt new "practices," but also to "unlearn"
and partially demolish entrenched institutional patterns (such as the trade unions',
as opposed to the legislature's, jurisdiction over wage determination in the case of
minimum wages or working time).

Such "unlearning" may in fact be the main purpose of the OMC, or its hidden
curriculum. The main purpose of this method of policy-making seems to be that
of bringing home to member states' political elites and constituencies the need for
"modernization" and "recalibration" of their hitherto adopted arrangements of social security, industrial relations, and labor market policies. The negative message is
that "nothing can stay as it is" and that we need to find out, on the basis of the experience of others, about more efficient and effective ways to achieve policy goals.
Thus OMC increases the pressure to suspect existing arrangements as potentially
obsolete, to experiment, revise, and innovate. As the national welfare state can no
longer constrain the market and impose a regime of partial decommodification
upon the labor market, it is now being left to the comparative study of market outcomes to decide which arrangements are in fact affordable and employment-
enhancing, and which ones must be dropped as a competitive liability.

What tends to get forgotten, however, within this learning approach to policy-
making is the fact that policies and political institutions are not just valued for
what they accomplish in terms of outcomes, but also in terms of the normative
standards of justice and appropriateness that they represent and the trust that
they generate. The question is: Are national electorates actually ready to see major
segments of their welfare states being sacrificed to the imperatives of international
competitiveness and the labor force mobilization goals of the EES? In other
words, policies will never enjoy democratic legitimacy in terms of the output they
generate alone, or their quality of functioning (at least in the long run) "*for* the
people." In addition, input-legitimacy—that is, some procedurally regulated
popular approval of the policies to be adopted and of the policy elites adopting
them—is also called for, their quality of being "*by* the people." Even in the manifest absence of a "European people" or "European nationhood" as the consolidated
demos authorizing policies, input legitimacy and the opportunity provided to the
constituent parts of the Euro-polity to hold policies and rulers accountable are by
no means superfluous. It is only by adding the source of input legitimacy that a
valid collective judgment can be passed as to whether the outputs a policy achieves
are worth achieving, and the costs for that output worth paying, both of which
questions are ultimately not the mandate of policymakers to answer. Needless to
say, there is nothing wrong with learning from others, with experimentation,

innovation, and institutional change—in principle, that is, and as long as learning yields demonstrably superior *and* fairly distributed outcomes, as opposed to being a euphemism for a power relation in which one side is in a position to dictate to others what to learn and unlearn. As long as the opaque discourses of policy experts involved in OMC harmonization efforts, as well as the results emerging from these discourses, remain detached from democratic channels through which they can be held accountable, the latter alternative cannot credibly be excluded, as these experts have neither the mandate to make public policy nor the institutional means to implement the results of their soft and informal coordinating activities.

The vision of promoting policy convergence at the European level by such "soft" means is highly ambitious indeed, given the very "hard" facts of national institutional differences and policy priorities. The European Commission itself, in its White Paper on "European Governance," relativizes the role to be played by OMC in that "it adds value at a European level where there is little scope for legislative solutions." Neither can it equal in its bindingness formal European law nor can it change the *aquis* of European law. To enhance its steering capacity and its potential for promoting convergence, the OMC would have to be complemented and "hardened" by legislative devices, now commonly referred to as "framework directives," which would attach some bindingness to the terms and procedures of coordination (Commission 2001). In the presence of authoritative framework directives, "national policy makers could no longer afford to ignore the policy discourses of Open Coordination" (Scharpf 2002: 16–17), which in the absence of such framework directives and in the name of subsidiarity they are left perfectly free to do. Thus Scharpf urges the "search for solutions [in the social policy field] which must have the character of European law in order to establish constitutional parity with the rules of European economic integration" (18). Yet it is exactly the unfeasibility of such directive policies that gave rise to the semiformal and para-legislative OMC approach in the first place.

Thus the thought of endowing OMC-generated rules with quasi-governmental force clearly amounts to a bootstrapping act of presupposing as given something that, if everything goes well and member state governments opt for voluntary compliance, will be only the outcome of the dynamics of OMC, namely some supranational European coordination. For the time being, OMC outcomes are neither formally binding (as they cannot be enforced against the will of member states' governments) nor can they replace or alter existing *acquis* regulations. The basic question for political theorists, the answer to which is at the same time of immense practical significance, is this: How can voluntary horizontal cooperation generate outcomes that are equivalent in its substantive effect to vertical control through constituted legislative and administrative authority? How can "soft law" be hardened so as to achieve the same degree of bindingness as formal directives?

The answer envisaged by OMC proponents is this: Multilateral information exchange, as orchestrated and supervised by the Commission, will lead to "policy learning" on the part of member states' governments. This convergent learning process will be propelled by mechanisms such as the definition of "best practices," the call for national action plans, specific recommendations, benchmarking, peer review, blaming and shaming, and the use of agreed-upon indicators of performance.

Yet as long as compliance on the part of national governments remains voluntary, the question remains: What are there incentives and *motives* to cooperate? For instance, the mechanism of "shaming" will be viable only to the extent that national constituencies will actually adopt the standard of the Commission's guidelines as a yardstick of evaluating their governments' performance. The rather heroic assumption is that national political constituencies will actually hold their governments accountable for complying with the guidelines of the Commission and the Summit. This presupposes that European standards, recommendations, and benchmarks are not only known to national electorates but, beyond that, are adopted as yardsticks of good policy. Why should "blame avoidance," the desire to escape being exposed as a poor performer or a laggard in "policy learning" according to the Commission's standards, become an overriding objective of voters within member states, given the perceived (economic as well as political) costliness of compliance? As long as "benchmarks" and standards of "good practice" are being perceived (if they are perceived at all) within national public spheres as little more than cloudy and ceremonial exhortations issued by remote Eurocrats, their role as operative standards of "good policy" remains at best dubious. This objection applies all the more as national governments usually have a rich supply of reasons and excuses ("subterfuge") to invoke as to why conditions beyond their control have hindered them to achieve better, in terms of labor market performance or social security finance, than they actually have. Often enough, their scope for action is constrained by national policy networks, configurations of veto players, entrenched interests, as well as the perceived national competitive advantage of noncooperation. It is thus only if the goal of overcoming social exclusion, social protection, and employment problems at the *European* level were firmly embraced by electorates, collective actors, and political elites at the *national* level that the "policy learning" dynamic and its motivational underpinnings envisaged by OMC would be likely to bear fruit.

For national elites and constituencies to approve of coordinated policy instruments, conditions within member states would have to be fairly similar in the first place. There can be little doubt, however, that there is a still-increasing divergence of labor market outcomes by country and, in particular, by region throughout Europe, a condition that will be exacerbated in the wake of Eastern Enlargement. Swank (2001) has convincingly argued that the impact of market integration upon the growth and employment performance of EU member states, as well as on the need for welfare state retrenchment, varies greatly among member states, as some of them are much less vulnerable to international pressures and challenges than others. The author argues that "the welfare state pressures

generated by . . . the economic and political logics of globalization will be fundamentally conditioned and shaped by national configurations of democratic political institutions" (205). In other words, some are better buffered against adverse
impacts of capital mobility than others, and some can afford a steeper learning
curve than their neighbors. The peculiarities and path dependencies of national
labor market and employment policies, as well as structural and institutional conditions within member countries, have generated vast differences across countries
and regions in terms of their labor market performance (e.g., in terms of labor
market participation rates, levels of unemployment, and average individual duration of unemployment), both within the OECD world in general and within the
European Union in particular (Scharpf 2000). Dissimilarities are evident not only
if we compare countries and regions within EU-15, but even more so if we compare policy areas. The supranational EU regime has been amazingly successful in
homogenizing across the European Union's monetary and fiscal conditions, but
not so the conditions of employment and social protection. The homogenization
of the latter has been lagging way behind, in spite of the vast expenditures
invested for many years into structural and regional subsidies. As Fritz Scharpf
observes, "Efforts to promote employment and social policy at the level of the
European Community have come . . . late and seem feeble in comparison to the
success stories of the Single Market and the Monetary Union" (2002: 2). This difference is to be attributed to the fact that the former policies (monetary and fiscal) are of a *regulatory* nature and can be effectively enforced by the Commission
and the ECB within the framework of the treaty, whereas the latter policies are
(re)distributive and thus depend for their success on the preparedness of member
state governments not only to sacrifice much of the national autonomy that they
enjoy according to the "subsidiarity" rule but also, at least on the part of the better employment performers, to pay with national resources for costly European
harmonization initiatives and to forego potential competitive advantages of their
national economies. Evidently and unsurprisingly, there is neither the willingness
of member states to do so nor the institutional capacity of European authorities
to force them to do so.

It is for this diversity of national policy priorities that, technically, the term
"coordination" as used by the OMC is a misnomer anyway. What the method is
intended to lead to is *cooperation*, which is much harder to achieve than coordination among actors with divergent interests. In the (rare) tabula rasa case of pure
coordination, all participants are interested in having a rule ("convention") in
place, whatever the rule may be. The typical case of cooperation, however, is one
in which preferences differ as to what the rule should be, and also the costs and
efforts required for complying with that rule are not the same for all players involved, as some may have to make more painful adjustments than others.

The making of the internal market through competition law, monetary
union, and fiscal constraints triumphs over the "embedding" of this market in
European policies of social protection and the promotion of employment. Nor

is this disparity coincidental. For it is exactly the rapid success of "negative" integration that has caused both the still-growing discrepancy of national and regional labor market outcomes and the incapacity of national governments to cope with them. To make market integration socially compatible, the voluntary adoption of policies according to OMC is not enough. " 'Social Europe' would stand on safer legal grounds if the Court and the Commission could be required to apply a . . . balancing test to potential conflicts between European internal-market and competition law and national policies promoting employment and social protection." (Scharpf 2002: 13) Yet the "would" in this sentence is logically as compelling as it remains a counterfactual in terms of its practical feasibility.

NOTES

The author has received helpful comments from Robert E. Goodin and Göran Therborn; particularly helpful was the reasearch assistance of Milena Buechs. The present paper draws upon and develops further parts of my essay "The European Model of 'Social' Capitalism: Can It Survive European Integration?" *Journal of Political Philosophy* 11, n. 4 (2003): 437–69.

1. A rather trivial reminder: There is a minority of countries in Europe, as well as a small minority of spaces within these countries, where the following rule does *not* apply: You cannot travel 200 miles (half a day of travel, by modern standards) in any direction without ending up in a different country (with its different history, language, etc.), or, for that matter, in salt water. Exceptions to this rule are only to be found, within EU-27 Europe, in France, Germany, and a tiny fraction of Spain.

2. Symptomatically, Switzerland, arguably the least Europeanized of European polities, seems to come closest to the United States in these respects among all European countries; this applies also to its being among the few European countries having escaped a land war on its own territory throughout the nineteen and twentieth centuries.

3. A linguistic reflection of the pervasive role of status categories in Continental European capitalism is the ubiquitous presence of collectivist and organicist nouns that most often do not have an equivalent in the English language. They refer to collectivities that are endowed with status rights and the members of which recognize themselves and each other as partaking in these rights and socioeconomic identities. Examples from the French and other Romance languages include the terms with the suffix "-at" (or Spanish "-ado", as in *salariat, artisanat,* and *patronat,* not to forget *proletariat*). In German there is the suffix "schaft" (etimologically akin to the suffix in citizen*ship*) being widely and frequently attached to virtually every socioeconomic role and collective unit. Examples include *Studentenschaft* (student body), *Wirtschaft* (the collectivity of employers/investors), *Ortschaft* (municipality), *Bauernschaft* (the farming community), *Belegschaft* (the work force of a company), *Beamtenschaft* (the civil service), *Gewerkschaft* (trade union), and numerous others, most famously *Gesellschaft* and *Gemeinschaft*. The use of this suffix suggests the internal coherence and external recognition of pre-given, supra-individual, and noncontractual properties of all members of the group as a corporate unit, comparable to the suggestion evoked by the ending of brother-*hood* (as used in the early North American trade union movement). While the German "-schaft" always denotes a collectivity of the bearers of some status, the English

equivalent "-ship" denotes individual instances of belonging or sharing in group properties, as in citizenship, scholarship, craftsmanship, or membership. To be sure, there is another "collectivizing" suffix in the English language, namely "-ry" (as in citizenry, yeomanry, soldiery, judiciary, etc.). But it connotes just the belonging of individuals to a social category, without implying some (self-)recognition as a collective body with ascribed status rights.

4. Underneath the ground floor, there is also a "basement" where the nonworking poor are dealt with through programs of welfare and poverty relief; this part of the building can be ignored for the purpose of the current discussion.

5. Any speculation on whether the conclusion of this process will still come soon enough to provide European citizens with reasons to support, rather than to fear and oppose, further integration and thus the Union as a whole with a measure of political legitimacy, is beyond the scope of the present essay.

6. The OMC mode of policy-making proceeds as follows, according to the Luxemburg process and based upon Article 128 TEC. First, the summit (European Council) adopts guidelines for employment policy to be observed by member states. These guidelines focus upon the prevention of exclusion, the activation of the unemployed, the promotion of "entrepreneurial spirit" and start-up enterprises, flexibility, and nondiscrimination. Second, each member state adopts an annual National Action Plan (NAP) specifying the overall guidelines for the particular context of national policy. Third, an annual report on employment, jointly authorized by Council and Commission, is submitted to the summit of the subsequent year as a feedback, eventually leading to the revision of guidelines and NAPs and potentially including specific recommendations concerning the policies and performance of individual countries.

References

Albert, Michel. 1991. *Capitalisme contre Capitalisme.* Paris: Éditions du Seuil.

Anderson, Perry. 1993. *Lineages of the absolutist state.* London: Verso.

Aust, Andreas, Sigrid Leitner, and Stephan Lessenich. 2002. "Konjunktur und Krise des Europäischen Sozialmodells. Ein Beitrag zur politischen Präexplantations-diagnostik." *Politische Vierteljahresschrift* 43 (2): 272–301.

Baldwin, Peter. 1996. "Can We Define a European Welfare State Model?" In Bent Greve (ed.), *Comparative Welfare Systems.* London: Macmillan.

Castles, Francis. 1993. *Families of Nations. Patterns of Public Policy in Western Democracies.* Aldershot, U.K.: Dartmouth.

Cecchini, P. 1988. *The European Challenge 1992: The benefits of a single market.* Aldershot, U.K.: Wildwood House.

Commission of the European Communities. 1993. *Growth, Competitiveness, Employment. The challenges and Ways Forward into the 21st Century.* White Book, KOM (93) 700. Luxemburg: Office for Official Publications of the European Communities.

———. 2001. *European Governance. A White Paper.* Brussels: COM. Available at http://europa.eu.int/eur-lex/en/com/cnc/2001/com2001_0428en01.pdf.

Council of the European Union. 2000a. "Implementing the Principle of Equal Treatment between Persons Irrespective of Racial or Ethnic Origin." Directive 2000/43/EC. *Official Journal of European Communities,* L180, 22–26.

————. 2000b. "Establishing a Community Action Programme to Combat Discrimination." Council Decision 2000/750/EC. *Official Journal of European Communities,* L303, 23–28.

Crouch, Colin. 1999. *Social Change in Western Europe.* Oxford: Oxford University Press.

de la Porte, Caroline, and Philippe Pochet, eds. 2002. *Building Social Europe Through the Open Method of Coordination.* Brussels: Peter Lang.

Ertman, Thomas. 1997. *Birth of the Leviathan.* Cambridge: Harvard University Press.

Esping-Andersen, Gøsta. 1990. *Three Worlds of Welfare Capitalism.* Princeton: Princeton University Press.

————, ed. 1996. *Welfare States in Transition.* London: Sage.

————. 1999. *Social Foundations of Postindustrial Economies.* Oxford: Oxford University Press.

————, ed. 2002. *Why We Need a New Welfare State.* Oxford: Oxford University Press.

Goetschy, Janine. 2001. "The European Employment Strategy from Amsterdam to Stockholm: Has It Reached Its Cruising Speed?" *Industrial Relations Journal* 32 (5): 401–18.

Hassel, Anke. 1998. "Soziale Pakte in Europa." *Gewerkschaftliche Monatshefte* 10: 626–37.

Hicks, Alexander. 1999. *Social Democracy and Welfare Capitalism. A Century of Income Security Politics.* Ithaca: Cornell University Press.

Hodson, Dermot, and Imelda Maher. 2001. "The Open Method as a New Mode of Governance: The Case of Soft Economic Policy Co-ordination." *Journal of Common Market Studies* 39 (4): 719–46.

Jacobson, Kerstin. 2002. "Soft Regulation and the Subtle Transformation of States. The Case of EU Employment Strategy." In Bengt Jacobson and Kerstin Sahlin-Andersson (eds.), *Transnational Regulation and the Transformation of States.* Forthcoming.

Kaelble, H. 2000. "Wie kam es zum Europäischen Sozialmodell?" *Jahrbuch für Europa- und Nordamerika-Studien* 4: 39–53.

Kaelble, Hartmut. 1987. *Auf dem Weg zu einer europäischen Gesellschaft : eine Sozialgeschichte Westeuropas 1880–1980.* Munich: Beck.

Kohli, Martin, ed. 2001. *Will Europe Work? Integration, Employment and the Social Order.* London: Routledge.

Münkler, Herfried. 1991. "Europa als politische Idee," *Leviathan* 19 (4): 521–41.

Offe, Claus. 2000. "The Democratic Welfare State in an Integrating Europe." Pp. 63–89 in Michael Th. Greven and Louis W. Pauly (eds.), *Democracy beyond the State? The European Dilemma and the Emerging Global Order.* Boston: Rowman and Littlefield.

Pierson, Paul, ed. 2001. *The New Politics of the Welfare State.* Oxford and New York: Oxford University Press.

Polanyi, Karl. [1944] 1980. *The Great Transformation. The Political and Economic Origins of Our Time.* Boston: Beacon.

Rhodes, Martin. 1997. "The Welfare State: Internal Challenges, External Constraints." Pp. 57–74 in M. Rhodes, P. Heywood, and V. Wright (eds.), *Developments in West European Politics.* London: Macmillan.

Schaefer, Armin. 2002. "Vier Perspektiven zur Entstehung und Entwicklung der 'Europäischen Beschäftigungspolitik.'" MPIfG Discussion Paper 02/9.

Scharpf, Fritz W. 1999. *Governing in Europe. Effective and Democratic?* Oxford: Oxford University Press.

———. 2000a. "Economic Changes, Vulnerabilities, and Institutional Capabilities." Pp. 21–124 in Fritz W. Scharpf and Vivien A. Schmidt (eds.), *Welfare and Work in the Open Economy. From Vulnerability to Competitiveness*, vol. I. Oxford: Oxford University Press.

———. 2000b. "The Viability of Advanced Welfare States in the International Economy: Vulnerabilities and Options." *Journal of European Public Policy* 7 (2): 190–228.

———. 2002. "The European Social Model: Coping with the Challenges of Diversity." MPIfG Working Paper 02/8. Cologne: Max-Planck-Institut für Gesellschaftsforschung.

Smith, Anthony D. 1979. *Nationalism in the Twentieth Century.* Oxford: Robertson.

Streeck, W. 1998, Vom Binnenmarkt zum Bundesstaat? Überlegungen zur politischen Ökonomie der europäischen Sozialpolitik. Pp. 369–422 in S. Leibfried and P. Pierson (eds.), *Standort Europa. Europäische Sozialpolitik,* Frankfurt am Main: Suhrkamp.

Streeck, Wolfgang. 2000. "Competitive Solidarity: Rethinking the 'European Social Model.'" Pp. 245–61 in Hinrichs, Karl, Herbert Kitschelt, Helmut Wiesenthal (eds.), *Kontingenz und Krise,* Frankfurt: Campus.

Streeck, Wolfgang, and Kozo Yamamura, eds. 2001. *The Origins of Nonliberal Capitalism.* Ithaca: Cornell University Press.

Swank, Duane. 2001. "Political Institutions and Welfare State Restructuring. The Impact of Institutions on Social Policy Change in Developed Democracies." In Paul Pierson (ed.), *The New Politics of the Welfare State.* Oxford: Oxford University Press.

———. 2002. *Global Capital, Political Institutions, and Policy Change in Developed Welfare States.* Cambridge: Cambridge University Press.

Teague, P. 1998. "Monetary Union and Social Europe." *Journal of European Social Policy* 8 (2): 117–37.

Therborn, Göran. 1995. *European Modernity and Beyond: The Trajectory of European Societies, 1945–2000.* London: Sage.

Trubek, David M., and James S. Mosher. 2001. "New Governance, EU Employment Policy, and the European Social Model." In Christian Joerges, Yves Mény, and J.H.H. Weiler (eds.), *Mountain or Molehill? A Critical Appraisal of the Commission White Paper on Governance.* Jean Monnet Working Paper No. 6/01, Florence, 95–117.

CHAPTER 3

Threat Effects of Capital Mobility on Wage Bargaining

Minsik Choi

THE PAST FEW DECADES have witnessed a rise in global economic integration. Most measures of national economic openness such as the share of import and exports in the GDP and the share of foreign capital in the domestic capital market have dramatically increased in both developed and developing countries. A growing number of studies investigating the impact of the recent globalization process on economic welfare of individual nations have drawn attention to labor market distortions, with an extensive focus on deepening wage inequality between skilled and less skilled workers in the United States, and on increasing unemployment in advanced European economies. These studies concentrate on whether the relative labor demand for skilled workers has been increased because of increasing internationalization, especially international trade (for recent surveys, see Borjas and Ramey 1995; Cline 1997; Feenstra 2000; Slaughter 2001).

The theoretical basis for these studies is mostly provided by Stolper-Samuelson's factor price equalization theorem. The theorem predicts the decline in wages of less-skilled workers in developed countries because of the decrease in the relative demand for less-skilled labor as a result of trade with developing countries where such labor is more abundant. The consensus on much of the empirical work that attempts to find a decrease in demand for unskilled labor in developed countries is that the price changes caused by trade have not been large enough to account for the trend of wage inequality (for a survey, see Slaughter 1999 and Baldwin 1995; Wood [1995, 1998], however, has found larger effects).

Fear of the possible negative impact of globalization on the economy of developed countries, such as job insecurity of the current work force, has been increasing among the public. Even though a majority of American workers acknowledge the gains and benefits from international trade, many workers, according to recent studies on the perceptions of American workers regarding globalization (Scheve and Slaughter 2001, this volume), are still concerned with the adverse labor market impacts of international transactions. Consequently, many tend to weigh the costs more heavily than the benefits.

Several researchers have suggested the need for a new perspective to investigate the impact of global economic integration. They argue that previous studies have attempted mainly to find a decreased relative demand for less-skilled workers directly and have overlooked the impact of change in the elasticity of the relative labor demand. The elasticity of the labor demand can change substantially when the nature of the bargaining relationship between workers and employers is affected.[1] Wages in their analysis are seen as bargaining outcomes rather than as simple market-clearing competitive wages, based on rent-sharing wage determination theory. They emphasize the enhanced capital mobility among other globalization features as the key factor underlying the secular trend in the bargaining relationship between workers and employers. The impact of globalization on the recent trend in wage inequality, therefore, should be understood in conjunction with its impact on the bargaining relationship between workers and employers. The new perspective can be referred to as "threat effect"—this suggests that the threat by firms to move production abroad, or the threat to outsource, may have important consequences on wages and profits even in the absence of large price or quantity changes (see Crotty, Epstein, and Kelly 1998; Rodrik 1997, 1999).[2] Reddy (2000) refers to this effect as the "bargaining channel." The threat effect is well described in Freeman (1995):

> It isn't necessary that the West import the toys. The threat to import them or to move plants to less-developed countries to produce the toys may suffice to force low-skilled westerners to take a cut in pay to maintain employment. In this situation, the open economy can cause lower pay for low-skilled westerners even without trade; to save my job, I accept Chinese-level pay, and that prevents imports. The invisible hand would have done its job, with proper invisibility.

Several theoretical studies explain the effect of foreign direct investment (FDI) as the major form of capital flight on wage and employment both in the host and the home countries.[3] By using the Nash-Bargaining framework they examine FDI in the context of the strategic bargaining relationship between an employer and workers (union; see Bughin and Vannini 1999; Naylor and Santoni 1999; Reddy 2000; Rodrik 1997, 1999; Zhao 1995, 1998). In the Nash-Bargaining framework outward FDI is formalized as the outside option that a firm could rely on when bargaining with its employees (or union) in the home country breaks down. Most of these studies, in general, illustrate how an increase in outside options facing the firm can lower workers' wages and increase firm profits. In this model, contrary to the standard Stolper-Samuelson model, no changes in prices or investment need occur for these changes in factor prices to result. This framework is more relevant to a situation where there are one-way investment flows—say, between a high-wage "North" and a low-wage "South." Most FDI, however, occurs as two-way flows between the more developed countries of the North. The analyses in these studies are applied to such two-way flows in more complicated settings and with two-way flows of investment between similar countries. The simple result of the single-country Nash framework usually holds: an increase in firms' outside options due to foreign direct investment lowers workers' wages for every level of employment, and increase corporations' level of profits.[4]

Despite the theoretical findings that capital flight can have a significant impact on workers' welfare, the question of how capital flight can affect workers' welfare has not received much attention in empirical studies. One possible reason is simply that appropriate data are not available for a firm-level analysis that is dictated by theoretical models. Another reason is that it is not clear how to measure the threat effects (or bargaining channel) at the empirical level. A few studies try to relate outward FDI to the U.S. labor market. These studies attempt to find direct impact of FDI on the relative demand for less-skilled workers, but their results are not conclusive. Feenstra and Hanson (1996) find that the change in outsourcing is positively associated with the change in the skilled wage share for the period of 1979–90. There is some evidence that outsourcing might have also had negative impacts on equality in U.K. manufacturing (Anderton and Brenton 1999).[5]

Slaughter (2000) focuses on the effect of multinational enterprises (MNEs) activity on the wage differential between production (less-skilled) and nonproduction (skilled) workers to test the hypothesis that MNE transfers have contributed to skill-upgrading within U.S. industries. He found, however, that most of his measures of MNE transfers have small and imprecisely estimated effects on the U.S. relative labor demand. Another study by Slaughter (2001) indirectly bears on the issue of threat effects. Slaughter exploits the idea that increased capital mobility and associated threat effects can increase the wage elasticity of demand for labor. Moreover, in his econometric work, Slaughter finds that this increase in elasticity seems to be associated with globalization variables, such as outsourcing, foreign affiliate share of U.S. MNE assets, and foreign affiliate share of U.S. MNE employment. When Slaughter puts a time dummy into the equation, however, these significant results mostly disappear. Slaughter notes that attempting better to understand the possible importance of threats might help to find what this time dummy is picking up, but he is skeptical about the prospects for directly identifying the impact of threat effects.

In a study of union wage sensitivity to trade and protection, Gaston and Trefler (1995) also include the foreign affiliates' employment, that is, employment outside the United States hired by U.S. multinationals from their foreign affiliates as an alternative proxy for the firm's bargaining strength. They find that foreign affiliates' employment has a negative but not significant impact on the wage premium in the union sample. Their analysis, however, looks at a one-time cross-section variation.[6]

The goal of this chapter is to provide a new approach to assess the impact of enhanced capital mobility on wages by focusing on the threat effect of foreign direct investment as the key factor in capital mobility. It attempts to fill in the gap between the theoretical and empirical work on the threat effect by suggesting one way to assess the validity of a threat effect and measure its impact empirically. It focuses on whether or not changes in industry union-wage premiums have been associated with the trend of outward FDI in U.S. manufacturing industries for the period from 1983 to 1996. The study will exploit variation within industries to examine how FDI as a measure of capital mobility relates to changes in the wage structure, using a unique industry-level panel dataset. The use of combined industry-level data is dictated by the lack of firm-level data that could provide appropriate information for the present study. All variables are broken down by industries and periods so that the analysis can be done in a fixed effects framework to control for unobserved heterogeneity.

To test the hypothesis that changes in industry-specific capital mobility are associated with the bargaining outcome, based on the threat effect theory, the study chooses union wage premium as the dependent variable instead of wages. This study is based on the idea that the employers' capital mobility impacts workers' welfare by altering the bargaining relationship between employers and workers. In this context, it is more proper to look at bargaining outcomes.

In relation to the study of wage dispersion between skilled and less-skilled workers, this study looks further for the relevant factors that can affect the widening wage gap through a de-unionization process. Studies of union behavior provide evidence that unions have played an important role in narrowing the wage gap among different groups, and therefore de-unionization is an important factor in explaining the rise in wage inequality (see DiNardo, Fortin, and Lemieux 1996). Although this study does not attempt to link changes in capital mobility to changes in union membership directly, by investigating the impact of capital mobility on the union's bargaining outcome, and by examining whether or not union wage premiums for less-skilled workers move with their overall wage differentials to skilled workers, it is possible to offer one way to link globalization to de-unionization in most advanced countries.

To preview the results of this study, the evidence indicates a significant negative impact of FDI on union workers' bargaining outcomes. Among union members, workers with only high school education have been more severely affected by the increase in outward foreign direct investment.

This chapter proceeds as follows. Empirical implications are drawn from the theoretical considerations, and a model based on the Nash bargaining model presented in the next section. The third section describes the data collecting processes, and the following section presents the empirical model and findings. The chapter closes with some concluding remarks.

THEORETICAL CONSIDERATIONS OF THE THREAT EFFECT
IN A NASH BARGAINING MODEL

The main idea of threat effect of outward FDI is closely related to changes in the employers' likelihood of moving production facilities abroad and the resulting changes in the elasticity of labor demand rather than actual shifts in labor demands. It is reasonable to assume that the likelihood of moving abroad is positively associated with the degree of ease with which investments abroad can be carried out. The important determinants of degree of ease in capital flight are transportation and technological developments in telecommunications. It is also affected by institutional changes, such as the formation of NAFTA and the WTO, which facilitate international transactions. If these factors contribute to employers' mobility unequally, an employer can use the disparity to enhance its own bargaining outcome. Further, if there are differences in mobility among workers it is the less mobile workers who will be more affected by increased capital mobility. Several studies have found that more educated workers (skilled workers) are more mobile than less-skilled workers (see Magnani 1997).

To examine the implications of the threat effect in the Nash bargaining framework; let's consider a bargaining game between the labor union and firm-owner.[7] Wages and employment are determined only through the bargaining process in the organized labor market and unilaterally by the firm-owner in the competitive labor market.[8] The wage level determined in the competitive market is considered to be the reservation wage level, w^*, for workers in the organized market. Let ϕ and $1 - \phi$ be the bargaining power of the labor union and the employer, respectively, and π^* stand for the profit level that the employer could attain by operating somewhere else, that is, the potential profit level attained by operating production facilities abroad or outsourcing. It is π^* that is affected by the firm's accessibility of overseas investment, which is positively associated with the degree of ease with which relocation or investment can be carried out. Therefore the potential profit from relocations π^* increases as the firm has greater access to overseas investment. π^* also increases when trade barriers are lower and transportation and communication costs decrease so that the mobility of production is enhanced. The maximization problem in the Nash bargaining model can be written in the following way:

$$\max_{w, n} \phi \log[(u(w) - u(w^*))n] + (1 - \phi) \log(\pi - \pi^*) \tag{1}$$

Where n is the number of employees in the union. Conventional assumptions hold for the utility function of the labor union, that is, $u'(w) > 0$ and $u''(w) < 0$. The concavity of the production function is also assumed and the profit function is defined as $f(n) - wn$.

The first-order conditions from the maximization problem are:

$$w : \frac{\phi \cdot u'(w)}{u(w) - u(w^*)} - \frac{(1 - \phi)n}{\pi - \pi^*} = 0 \tag{2}$$

$$n : \frac{\phi}{n} - (1 - \phi) \frac{f'(n) - w}{\pi - \pi^*} = 0. \tag{3}$$

Following Blanchflower, Oswald, and Sanfey (1996), I use the first-order approximation:

$$u(w^*) \cong u(w) + (w^* - w)u'(w). \tag{4}$$

Substituting this into the equation (2), the following equation can be obtained:

$$w \cong w^* + \frac{\phi}{1-\phi}\left(\frac{\pi - \pi^*}{n}\right). \tag{5}$$

The wage is determined by the reservation wage available outside the organized market in the event of a breakdown in bargaining, the relative bargaining power of the two sides, and the profit level per employee.

Equation (5) implies that:

$$\frac{\partial w}{\partial \pi^*} < 0 \tag{6}$$

The equilibrium bargaining wage must fall if the firm has more outside options. The empirical implication of this model is that the more FDI the firm has, the less the wage differential above the competitive wage level that the workers will receive. Stated differently, having more stock of FDI within a firm (or an affiliated industry) will signify the firm's increased outside option to the labor union at the bargaining table, and labor unions bargaining with such firms will make more wage concessions than labor unions facing firms with less investments abroad. Since all variables are broken into industry level in this study, the following interpretation of the model is more proper for empirical implications: if an industry has a relatively large share of foreign affiliates of production workers in this industry perceive that their employer is more likely to invest abroad than the other employers in industries that have lower share of production abroad. When they come to the bargaining table labor unions representing workers in the industry with high FDI foreign affiliates' share are more likely to accept a wage cut. The rent they enjoy from the monopoly power of their labor union, therefore, will be negatively affected.[9]

To sum up, the hypothesis to be tested in this study is that, all else being equal, a union representing workers in a firm whose affiliated industry has more outside options—as represented by their stock of foreign direct investment abroad—is more likely to concede in wage bargaining, and, accordingly, members will receive a smaller union wage premium.

WAGE STRUCTURE AND FOREIGN DIRECT INVESTMENT

To investigate the effect of outward FDI on union wage premiums, one can hope to get an ideal dataset that has individual firms' information, including foreign investments, as well as collective bargaining outcomes. Since there is no available data source of this kind, however, mainly three different sources of data are combined unavoidably to construct a unique industry-level panel dataset:[10] (1) Data on wages and other worker characteristics by education and industry are drawn from the 1983–96 Annual Merged Outgoing Rotation Group (MORG) of the Current Population Survey (CPS); (2) data on FDI are drawn from the *U.S. Direct*

Investment Abroad data collected by the Bureau of Economic Analysis (BEA); and (3) the National Bureau of Economic Research (NBER) Manufacturing Productivity Database provides information on U.S. manufacturing industries.[11]

Following data-merging practices that have been widely used in the labor economics field, three different datasets are merged by matching industry codes. The matching process can be easily done because each dataset reports the conversion rule to Standard Industrial Classification (SIC) categories from its own classification category. As a result of the matching process, the complete dataset for this study includes 31 manufacturing industries for the period 1983 to 1996.[12]

In this study, relative wages and the structure of wages across manufacturing industries are examined to determine whether they are correlated with the difference in the average industry capital mobility. To calculate measures of union premiums and relative wages across manufacturing industries, I first estimate the interindustry wage regression model. This regression approach is proposed by Dickens and Katz (1987) and Krueger and Summers (1988) in their studies of interindustry wage differentials. In such studies, differentials wages are assumed to be above the market-clearing wage level. As analyzed in the previous section, a market can reach a non-clearing wage equilibrium due to a number of institutional reasons, including collective action through union employers' rent-sharing wage-setting mechanisms, or gift-exchange wage-setting mechanisms.

In the actual regression, the natural logarithm of individual hourly wages in the calendar year prior to the survey are regressed on individual characteristic variables and socioeconomic variables with mutually exclusive industry dummies to calculate different measures of wage premiums. Three wage premiums are estimated by using different regression models:[13] (1) interindustry wage differentials by pooling union and non-union members, (2) interindustry wage differentials by using only union members, and (3) interindustry union wage differentials by including the interaction terms between industry dummies and union status in the wage equation. Two different measures of the union wage premium are used to check the sensitivity of the FDI variable to the different specifications.[14] Since the union wage premium is more appropriate than industry wage differentials to the bargaining model, which is the central idea of this study, the focus will be on the union wage premium. All interindustry differentials in this study are weighted by the industry's employment shares and normalized to compare with the average worker's wage level.[15] The estimation is restricted to workers ages 16 to 76 who satisfy sample-selection rules: (1) the individual is employed in the private sector; (2) the individual works for pay more than one hour a week; (3) the individual earns more than a dollar and less than 250 dollars an hour; (4) the individual is employed in a manufacturing sector except the petroleum industry.[16]

To examine relative wage differentials between skilled workers and less-skilled workers for the sample period, the various mean log wage gaps among different groups of workers sorted by their educational attainments are calculated by using 1983–1996 CPS MORG, reported in table 3.1. Table 3.1 shows that wage dis-

TABLE 3.1.
Logarithm Hourly Wages Differentials in U.S. Manufacturing, 1983–96

Wage Differentials	'83	'84	'85	'86	'87	'88	'89	'90	'91	'92	'93	'94	'95	'96
Union–Non-Union Members	0.11	0.12	0.12	0.12	0.12	0.12	0.1	0.09	0.08	0.1	0.11	0.13	0.1	0.1
Union–Non-Union Members with School 0–11	0.32	0.34	0.35	0.36	0.35	0.35	0.34	0.33	0.28	0.32	0.3	0.29	0.29	0.29
School 12+–School 0–11	0.31	0.31	0.33	0.34	0.35	0.33	0.35	0.38	0.39	0.39	0.4	0.44	0.46	0.44
School college–School 0–11	0.44	0.44	0.46	0.48	0.5	0.47	0.5	0.53	0.53	0.51	0.52	0.54	0.56	0.55
School college+–School 0–11	0.79	0.83	0.84	0.85	0.87	0.81	0.91	0.95	0.95	1.01	1.02	1.08	1.04	1.01

Note: Calculations made by author by using 1983–96 CPS MORG.

persion between less-educated workers and more-educated workers increased during the sample years and supports findings from previous studies. The difference in log hourly wages between workers with a high school diploma and workers with less than a high school diploma increased to .46 in 1995 from .31 in 1983. At the same time, the wage gap between workers covered by collective bargaining and workers without collective bargaining decreased. Especially among workers without a high school diploma, the gap in mean log wages between workers with collective bargaining and workers without bargaining decreased from .36 in 1986 to .29 in 1996. This evidence suggests that a decrease in collective bargaining outcomes contributes to an increase in wage dispersion between less-educated workers and more-educated workers during sample periods. The mean log wage dispersion, however, can be correlated with an individual's socioeconomic characteristics.

The interindustry union wage differentials are estimated by using the regression equation (A-1) and (A-2) in appendix A. The explanatory power of this model in terms of R-square values stays between 0.51 and 0.53 throughout the period from 1983 to 1993 and declined to 0.47 for the last three years. The number of observation also declined to less than 29,000 for these last three years. The statistical significance of these interindustry union wage coefficients are consistently at the 5 percent level except for several years in some industry categories: Drugs; Soap, Cleaners and Toilet Goods; Agricultural Chemicals; Other Chemical Goods; Office and Computing Machines. According to the regression results, for example, if a union member worker is employed in a firm in the beverages industry (industry category 2), she will earn 28.4 percent more than a worker who has exactly the same observed socioeconomic characteristics but is affiliated with the omitted industries (dairy and meat industries) in 1983.[17]

The FDI variable is measured by the employment share of Majority Owned Affiliates (MOFA) in U.S. employment. The average employment share has steadily increased from 20.6 percent in 1983 to 22.4 percent in 1996. Industries that have relatively high MOFA employments' share are Drugs (industry category 5), Soap, Cleaners, and Toilet Goods (6), Motor Vehicles and Equipment (19), and Tobacco (21).

Figure 3.1 illustrates a simple negative relationship between growth in the industry's FDI measured by the employment share and change in industry union wage premium. As shown in the figure, regression estimates are consistent with these graphical results. Details about the other variables used in the second step regression are reported in appendix A.

To sum up, the analysis in this section reconfirms results from previous studies on interindustry wage differentials that there is considerable variation in the wage structure over time within industries in the U.S. manufacturing sector.[18] Preliminary data analysis also suggests a correlation between wage differentials and outward FDI. The next empirical step is to examine several ways of estimating how changes in FDI could cause variation in wage structure.

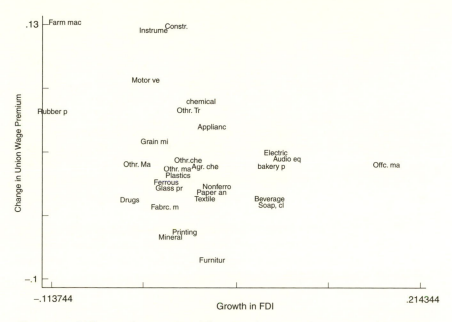

Figure 3.1. Differences between First Three Years' Averages (1983–85) and Last Three Years' Averages (1994–96). Note: The industry names are abbreviated. The full names are listed in appendix B.

EMPIRICAL MODEL AND RESULTS

In the next empirical step, the vector of regression coefficients from various wage equations are regressed on several industry-characteristic variables including the FDI variable.[19] These coefficients from the wage equation model are interpreted as the wage premiums that are not explained by individuals' characteristics and are attributed to their affiliation in the industry. The following regression model is estimated:

$$w_{jt}^{**} = \alpha + \beta_p P_{jt} + \beta_f F_{jt} + v_j + \mu_t + \varepsilon_{jt}. \tag{7}$$

Where w_{jt}^{**} is the wage premium in industry j in year t, P_{jt} is the vector of control variables for industry characteristics: unionization, rent, capital-labor ratio, unskilled labor share, average education level of the employee, and average establishment size as well as import penetration and proxy for technological change; F_{jt} is the outside option for the industry j measured either by the foreign affiliate's employment share or the capital stock share of U.S. industry-wide activity; v_j is an industry fixed effect; μ_t is a period fixed effect; and the disturbance ε_{jt} is assumed to be uncorrelated with the other variables in the model.

TABLE 3.2.
Wage Premium Regressions Results

Dependent Variable	Union Wage Premium I[a]		Union Wage Premium II[b]		Interindustry Wage Premium
	OLS (1)	IV (2)	OLS (3)	IV (4)	OLS (5)
Share of the U.S. FDI abroad	−0.148** (0.064)	−0.296** (0.115)	−0.278** (0.072)	−0.364** (0.114)	0.022 (0.037)
Imports	−0.011 (0.036)	−0.054 (0.051)	0.006 (0.041)	−0.019 (0.050)	−0.041* (0.022)
Technology	0.208 (0.156)	0.098 (0.203)	0.240 (0.177)	0.176 (0.199)	0.065 (0.093)
Unionization	0.229** (0.080)	1.367** (0.660)	0.208** (0.092)	0.867 (0.648)	0.156** (0.049)
Rent	0.0004 (0.0007)	0.0006 (0.0008)	−0.0001 (0.0407)	0.0001 (0.0008)	0.0003 (0.0004)
Capital/Labor Ratio	−0.003 (0.018)	−0.010 (0.022)	−0.009 (0.020)	−0.014 (0.022)	−0.003 (0.011)
Unskilled Labor Share	−0.441** (0.131)	−0.547** (0.172)	−0.098 (0.149)	−0.159 (0.169)	−0.278** (0.097)
Schooling	0.005 (0.014)	0.053 (0.033)	−0.032** (0.016)	−0.004 (0.032)	0.022** (0.008)
Average Establishment Size	−0.067** (0.029)	−0.0007** (0.0003)	−0.102** (0.033)	−0.0007* (0.0002)	0.021 (0.017)
Intercept	−0.014 (0.211)	−0.905 (0.573)	0.0637 (0.240)	0.121 (0.562)	−0.251 (0.168)
R^2	0.87	0.81	0.74	0.70	0.93

Note: The regressions have 334 observations. The observations are weighted by the inverse of the sampling variance of the dependent variable.

*Interindustry wage differentials among union members.

**Coefficients of interaction terms between industry dummies and union status dummy in log wage equations.

[a] Estimated by two-way-fixed effect model (i.e., with industry fixed effect and period fixed effect).

[b] Coefficients with * and ** are statistically significant at the 10 percent and 5 percent levels respectively. Standard errors are in parentheses.

Table 3.2 reports results from the regression model (7). Estimates of OLS and Instrumental variables method (IV) estimates of equation (7) are reported for union wage premium specifications.[20] The same regressors are included in all specifications. I use both ordinary least squares and instrumental variables method to address the potential endogeneity of industry unionization. For the instrumental variable, I compute a composite of union hospitality by weighting the Service sector union membership rate by the number of employees of each industry in fifty-one different locations (fifty states and Washington, D.C.). For instance, if the Motor Vehicles and Equipment sector has more employees in midwest states than anywhere else, and if the Service sector union membership in these states are higher than anywhere else, then the composite of the union hospitality of the Motor Vehicles and Equipment sector will be relatively high.

The estimates from OLS are similar to those of IV in all specifications. The first and second columns present the OLS and IV method results from the regression of union wage premium using interindustry wage differentials among union members. The union wage premium using the estimates of the interactions terms between union status and industry dummies are used as dependent variables in columns (3) and (4). The estimates of FDI in all specifications indicate that higher ratios of the affiliates' employment share of U.S. industry-wide employment are significantly associated with lower union wage premiums. Import penetration ratios, however, are not statistically significant at any conventional level. Estimates of the proxy for technological change are all positive but not significantly different from zero. In the case of interindustry wage differentials using a pooled sample (see column 5), the coefficients of FDI and technology from OLS are positive but not significant. The significantly negative coefficients (at the 5 percent level) of import penetration ratio suggest that the firm that is affiliated with an industry, where the import penetration level is relatively high, tends to pay lower wages to its employees than its counterparts in the industry with a low import penetration ratio. Further, the FDI variable is statistically significant in both OLS and IV methods in the case of union wage premium specifications, which indicates that the FDI effect is not sensitive to changes in the specification.

In the specification of interindustry wage differentials among union members, the results suggest that, assuming all employees are covered by collective bargaining, a union member affiliated with an industry with a higher level of FDI is paid less than a union member affiliated with an industry with a low level of FDI; as is predicted by the bargaining model in the previous section. The size of the FDI coefficient can also be interpreted by performing the following thought experiment: assume that a unionized worker is shifted from an industry with an average level of FDI abroad (21 percent) to an industry with no FDI. The estimated coefficients in the union wage premium specifications (columns 1–4) imply that the worker's union wage premium will show an increase that may range from 3.1 to 7.6 percent (21 percent times the coefficients). In those industries with the highest levels of FDI such as Soap, Cleaners, and Toilet Goods, the FDI threat effect is significant. For instance, these industries have an average FDI level of 50.7 percent and organized workers in these industries earn 18.4 percent ($50.7\% \times -0.36$) less than workers with the same observable characteristics in industries with no FDI. The elasticity of the union wage premium with respect to FDI ranges from 0.33 to 0.80.

As for the other control variables, the findings from this study are not very different from those of previous ones.[21] The coefficients of unionization in the union wage premium specifications are significantly positive. Since, the elasticity of demand for organized workers tends to be lower as unionization increases the employer will have to pay more to organized labor (Dickens and Katz 1987). The interindustry differentials are also higher in more unionized industries, which supports the so-called union threat effect. The firm will pay more to its employees in highly unionized industries to prevent their employees from being organized (Dickens and Katz 1987).

The positive coefficient of average schooling of employees in the industry in the case of the interindustry wage specification suggests that a firm paying higher wages attracts better qualified workers even though higher wages are not set explicitly to compensate them for their socioeconomic characteristics (Dickens and Katz 1987). The negative coefficient of unskilled labor share measured by occupation category at the industry level suggests that the firm affiliated with an industry where unskilled jobs are relatively greater has stronger bargaining power so that it can keep wages relatively lower.

Although the coefficients of the average establishment-size variable in every union wage premium specification are significant at the conventional level, they are close to zero. Previous studies (e.g., Bloch and Kuskin 1978 and Podgursky 1986) have shown that the union wage premium decreases with establishment size.[22]

To see the varying impact of employers' mobility on different groups of workers, who are divided according to their union membership and education level, additional regressions are conducted separately for the different groups. Results are reported in table 3.3. Among all workers in manufacturing sectors (pooled sample in table 3.3), higher import penetration is significantly associated with lower wage level for workers with 12 years schooling (up to high school diploma), while technological change is positively and significantly associated with a higher wage level. The estimate of the FDI variable is not statistically significant at any level in the pooled sample specifications.

The estimate of the FDI variable, however, becomes significantly negative in union sample specifications. In particular, workers with only twelve years of schooling suffer from a decreased bargaining outcome that are significantly associated with the higher outward FDI level while bargaining outcomes for unionized workers with more than a high school education are not influenced by the employers' increased mobility. The import penetration ratio is also an important factor in reduced union worker's bargaining outcomes.

The estimation method used in this study assumes that an industry's outward FDI levels are randomly distributed and that changes in stock of FDI are independent of industry characteristics such as union wage premium. This exogeneity is a strict assumption. To identify the coefficient of FDI variable in the regression equation (7), the effect of FDI on wages must be separated from the effect of other industry characteristic variables on wages. If the change in FDI over time is correlated with other industry variables, then the estimated coefficient will be biased. To assess the validity of this assumption I regress changes in outward FDI on previous growth of union wage premium and other industry characteristics. Results are reported in table 3.4. Results from the regression suggest that an

TABLE 3.3.
Wage Premium among Different Groups

Dependent Variable	Pooled Sample			Union Sample[a]		
	All	0–12 Years Schooling	12+ Schooling	All	0–12 Years Schooling	12+ Schooling
Share of the U.S. FDI abroad	0.022 (0.037)	0.038 (0.047)	0.040 (0.051)	−0.296** (0.115)	−0.439** (0.176)	0.006 (0.223)
Imports	−0.041* (0.022)	−0.087** (0.028)	−0.030 (0.030)	−0.054 (0.051)	−0.239** (0.085)	0.049 (0.109)
Technology	0.065 (0.093)	0.043 (0.117)	0.271** (0.128)	0.098 (0.203)	0.364 (0.281)	0.190 (0.356)
Unionization	0.156** (0.049)	0.060 (0.059)	−0.002 (0.064)	1.367** (0.660)	2.447** (1.107)	−0.972 (1.407)
Rent	0.0003 (0.0004)	−0.0005 (0.0005)	0.001** (0.0005)	0.0006 (0.0008)	−0.0002 (0.001)	0.003* (0.0016)
Capital/Labor Ratio	−0.003 (0.011)	−0.006 (0.014)	0.008 (0.015)	−0.010 (0.022)	−0.035 (0.039)	0.01 (0.043)
Unskilled Labor Share	−0.278** (0.097)	—	—	−0.547** (0.172)	—	—
Schooling	0.022** (0.008)	—	—	0.053 (0.033)	—	—
Average Establishment Size	0.021 (0.017)	0.019 (0.022)	0.025 (0.024)	−0.0007** (0.0003)	−0.001** (0.0005)	−0.0003* (0.0006)
Intercept	−0.251 (0.168)	−0.099 (0.117)	−0.160 (0.128)	−0.905 (0.573)	0.544 (0.371)	−0.250 (0.471)
R^2	0.93	0.86	0.83	0.81	0.60	0.56

Note: The regressions have 334 observations. The observations are weighted by the inverse of the sampling variance of the dependent variables. Regressions are run at the industry-year level. Coefficients with * and ** are statistically significant at the 10 percent and 5 percent levels respectively. Standard errors are in parentheses.

[a]IV method is used for union sample.

TABLE 3.4.
Regression of Change in Outward FDI on Union Wage Premium Growth

Dependent Variable	Change in FDI		
Union Wage Premium Growth	−0.027 (0.020)		−0.026 (0.020)
Initial Union Wage Premiums		0.028 (0.019)	0.027 (0.019)
Constant	−0.010 (0.007)	−0.010 (0.007)	−0.010 (0.007)
R^2	0.11	0.12	0.12
Observations	403	403	403

Note: Industry and year dummies are included in all specifications. Standard errors are in parentheses.

industry's outward FDI is not significantly motivated by previous growth of wage premium of union members.

Conclusion

The threat effects theory argues that enhanced capital mobility can have an impact on wages and profits even in the absence of large price or quantity changes. The threat effects have an impact on wages and profits by changing bargaining relationships between workers and employers.

Along with the findings from a previous study by Slaughter (2000), results from this empirical study support the threat effects theory. Slaughter (2000) fails to find that outward FDI has an impact on shifting the labor demand for workers in the home country. This study finds that while import penetration has a negative impact on both interindustry wage differentials and union wage premiums, FDI has a negative impact only on union wage premiums. This difference implies that outward FDI influences workers' wage levels through the bargaining channel as the threat effect model suggests; while import does the same through the demand and supply processes as well as through the bargaining channel.

This study demonstrates that the increased outward investment by U.S. manufacturing industries has been negatively associated with the wage premium that union members shared during the period from 1983 to 1996. Unlike previous studies of the impact of FDI on workers' welfare, this study attempts to understand the implicit threat effect of FDI by looking at the bargaining outcome instead of investigating the change in relative demand. Many studies on wage inequality have focused on underlying changes in U.S. labor demand in favor of skilled labor and have linked them to changes in international trade, outsourcing, and technology. We may fail to detect important changes in the welfare of less-skilled workers if we narrow our search to such channels. The abundance of anecdotes about the actual displacement of traditional jobs and workers' ever-growing sense of job insecurity calls for an identification of the right channels for analysis.

The threat effects theory may lead us to the right channel. The present study focuses on the manufacturing sector since blue-collar and less-educated workers are overrepresented in this sector.[23] This study also investigates workers who are covered by collective bargaining to understand the explicit impact of globalization on the bargaining outcome, since workers' fear, if any, must affect their success at the bargaining table. As the threat effect theory suggests, this study finds that firms' enhanced locational mobility as a result of the globalization process (e.g., the recent launches of NAFTA and WTO) is effective in pressuring workers who fear losing their jobs to concede at the bargaining table and accept a lower share of the rent.

APPENDIX A: DESCRIPTION OF VARIABLES AND DATA SOURCES
USED IN THE PAPER

• The *union wage premium* data are calculated in three different ways as follows: The natural logarithm of individual hourly wages is regressed on the socioeconomic variables, demographic variables, and industry dummies to get the first two wage premiums: (1) the industry wage premium from pooled data of union and non-union members, (2) the union wage premium from only union members. Estimated coefficients of industry dummies represent the wage differentials due to an individual's industry affiliation in both cases.

$$\log(w_{ij}) = \alpha + \beta_h H_i + \beta_j D_j + \varepsilon_{ij}, \quad i = 1, \ldots, I, \ j = 1, \ldots, J, \quad \text{(A-1)}$$

where w_{ij} is the hourly wage of individual i in industry j, H_i is a vector of individual characteristics and demographic variables, D_j is a vector of mutually exclusive dummy variables indicating industry of affiliation, and ε_{ij} is a random error with mean zero and variance σ^2.

The extension of equation (A-1) attempts to calculate the third wage premium, which is interpreted as the "union rent" (for instance, Cebula and Nair-Reichert 2000). The estimated coefficients of interaction terms between the union status dummy and industry dummies in the cross-section regression are interpreted as the wage differential based on a worker's union status and her industry affiliation. In other words, estimated coefficients are the wage differences earned by a worker who is covered by a union contract and employed in an industry relative to the workers in an omitted industry in the manufacturing sector:

$$\log(w_{ij}) = \alpha + \beta_h H_i + \beta_j D_j + w_j^{**}(D_j^* U_i) + \varepsilon_{ij}, \quad i = 1, \ldots, I, \ j = 1, \ldots, J \quad \text{(A-2)}$$

where U_i is the union dummy, and everything else is the same as equation (A-1).
• The *unionization* data are calculated by using Freeman and Medoff's (1979) method. Union membership percentage is calculated as:

$$U_j = \frac{\sum_i A_{ij} W_{ij}}{\sum_i W_{ij}} \cdot 100 \quad \text{(A-3)}$$

where U_j is the percentage of workers in industry j who are unionized, $A_{ij} = 1$ if worker i is employed and in a union, and is zero otherwise, W_{ij} is the CPS sampling weight. The MORG of CPS data are used for the computation.
• The *foreign direct investment* (FDI) data are derived by using *U.S. Direct Investment Abroad* data from the Bureau of Economic Analysis (BEA) and National Bureau of Economic Research (NBER) manufacturing industry productivity data. The BEA has collected the information about U.S. multinational enterprises through censuses and surveys. The BEA aggregates parents and affiliates into 32 different industries in

manufacturing sector for its publicly released data. Some are individual three-digit SIC industries; others are the sum of several three-digit or two-digit SIC industries. NBER manufacturing productivity data include four-digit SIC industries. The actual FDI data are calculated either as the employment share of majority-owned non-bank foreign affiliates of non-bank U.S. parents (MOFA)[24] in the U.S. industry-wide employment, or as the capital stock share of MOFA in the U.S. industry-wide capital stock. Thirty-one manufacturing industry categories are used in this study.

- The *import penetration* data are calculated by using the United Nation's Trade Data. The import penetration is defined as $(imports_j / (gdp_j + imports_j + exports_j))$, where $imports_j$ refers to imports in industry j, gdp_j refers to domestic output of industry j, and $exports_j$ refers to exports of industry j.

- The *rent* is measured by rent residual based on the method of Leamer et al. (2000) by using NBER manufacturing industry productivity data:

$$\frac{VA_i - w \cdot EMP_i}{EMP_i} = \alpha + \beta \cdot \frac{Capital}{EMP} + \varepsilon_i, \qquad (A\text{-}4)$$

where VA_i is the value added in industry i, EMP_i is the size of the employment in industry i, the coefficient α represents the per-worker cost of non-wage benefits plus average rents, β represents the capital-rental costs, and ε is the rent residuals. Since it is impossible to separate from the constant that part which represents average rents, I use only the estimated rent residuals.

- The *capital labor ratio* data are computed by using NBER manufacturing industry productivity data.

- The *unskilled labor share* data are derived as

$$S_j = \frac{\sum_i B_{ij} W_{ij}}{\sum_i W_{ij}} \cdot 100, \qquad (A\text{-}5)$$

where S_j is the percentage of workers in industry j who are unskilled labor; $B_{ij} = 1$ if worker i is employed and unskilled labor and is zero otherwise; W_{ij} is the CPS sampling weight. "Unskilled worker" is defined according to his/her occupation by using the CPS occupation classification. CPS occupation classifications 403–469, 499, and 863–889 are used as the unskilled occupations. The MORG of CPS data are used for the computation. This method of classifications is used in Gaston and Trefler (1994).

- The share of engineers and scientists in each industry measures *technological change*; I used the CPS MORG data to calculate this measure. Allen (2001) uses the share of engineers and scientists in each industry as proxies for technological change.

- *Size* is the establishment size defined as log of industry employment divided by the number of establishments. The NBER manufacturing industry productivity database and the Economic Census data are used for the number of establishments.

APPENDIX B: INDUSTRY CLASSIFICATION TABLE

TABLE 3.5.
Industry Classification

IC^a	Name of Industries (based on BEA classifications)	Constituent SIC
1	Grain mill and bakery products	204, 205
2	Beverages	208
3	Other bakery products	206, 207, 209
4	Industrial chemicals and synthetics	281, 282, 286
5	Drugs	283
6	Soap, cleaners, and toilet goods	284
7	Agricultural chemicals	287
8	Other chemical products	285, 289
9	Ferrous metal	331, 332, 339
10	Nonferrous metal	333, 334, 335, 336
11	Fabricated metal products	34
12	Farm and garden machinery	352
13	Construction, mining, and materials handling machinery	353
14	Office and computing machines	357
15	Other machinery	351, 354, 355, 356, 358, 359
16	Household appliances	363
17	Household audio and video, and communication equipment	365, 366
18	Other electrical machinery (including electronic components and accessories)	361, 362, 364, 367, 369
19	Motor vehicles and equipment	371
20	Other transportation equipment	372–376, 379
21	Tobacco manufactures	21
22	Textile products and apparel	22, 23
23	Lumber, wood, furniture, and fixtures	24, 25
24	Paper and allied products	26
25	Printing and publishing	27
26	Rubber products	301, 302, 305, 306
27	Miscellaneous plastics products	307
28	Glass products	321–323
29	Stone, clay, and other nonmetallic mineral products	324–329
30	Instruments and related products	38
31	Other manufactures	31, 39

[a] Industry Classifications used in this study.

NOTES

The author is grateful to Jerry Epstein for his support and help throughout the whole process of this study, and to Michael Ash, Lee Badgett, Sam Bowles, Mark Brenner, Jeannette Lim, Stephanie Luce, Michael Wallerstein, and all participants at the Political Economy Workshop at the University of Massachusetts, Amherst, for their comments and suggestions. Of course, I alone am responsible for all errors and omissions.

A data appendix and additional results used to generate the results presented in this paper are available upon request from Minsik Choi at University of Massachusetts Boston, 100 Morrissey Blvd., Boston, Mass. 02125.

1. The elasticity of relative labor demand also changes when the product market faces more intensified competition due to international economic integration. The increase in the elasticity of labor demand due to this feature of the globalization affects bargaining outcomes negatively.

2. Other authors who have mentioned threats as a potentially important feature in this field are Freeman (1995); Slaughter (2000); and Budd and Slaughter (2000).

3. To answer the question of why firms invest abroad itself is not the main purpose of this study. Since the threat effect results from the very fact that firms can go abroad more easily, it can be utilized no matter what the firms' purposes of foreign investment are. As to the question of why multinational firms go abroad, studies cite primarily two reasons: (1) access to the markets (horizontal FDI), and (2) looking for factor price differences (vertical FDI). Traditionally, horizontal FDI has been a major form of FDI among U.S. headquartered multinationals. A recent study finds that vertical FDI is more common and suggests that one should distinguish different types of FDI according to how multinationals' strategies respond to government policy (see Hanson et al. 2001).

4. I would like to point out that the new perspective does not entail that wages for less-skilled workers move in opposite directions in the North and South countries. Wages can stagnate (or drop) as long as there are threats of relocations by firms.

5. See Autor and Krueger (1997), however, for skepticism on the importance of outsourcing for changes in income distribution.

6. The present study is different from Gaston and Trefler (1995) in two respects: (1) MOFA (Majority-Owned Foreign Affiliates of U.S. Companies) employment share is treated as a proxy for the employer's bargaining power and in particular as a proxy for employer's outside option, and (2) this study investigates the within-industry variation by using panel data analysis.

7. The firm-owner represents shareholders, or management, who share the interest of maximizing profits. Employer, the firm-owner, and management are used interchangeably in this chapter.

8. In labor economics, there are two types of models that explain bargaining between employers and unions: (1) the right-to-manage model, and (2) the monopoly union model. In the right-to-manage model, while unions and employers bargain over wages, employers decide the employment level unilaterally. In the monopoly union model framework, wages and employment both are bargained. I take the monopoly union model to draw the empirical implications in this study. See Manning (1987) for a full survey of these two models.

9. The direction of the impact on employment, however, is not unambiguously determined and depends on the union's utility function, which reflects the union's policy on employment. Rodrik (1999), however, shows that employment goes down and firm profits go up with an increase in the availability of the firm's profits abroad.

10. I also used United Nations Trade Data to calculate the import penetration defined as $(imports_j / (gdp_j + imports_j + exports_j))$, where $imports_j$ refers to imports in industry j, gdp_j refers to domestic output of industry j, and $exports_j$ refers to exports of industry j.

11. CPS MORG data limits the beginning of the time period studied to 1983, because questions about union status were not included prior to that year. NBER data are available only up to 1996, and thus limit the end of the time period studied to 1996.

12. Details for the classification of the 31 manufacturing industries are in appendix A. The BEA has 32 manufacturing industry categories: International Surveys Industry (ISI) Categories. Other Electrical Machinery (SICs 361, 362, 364, 369) is merged with Electronic Components and Accessories (SIC 367) to match with CPS data in this study. The CPS industry classification (IND 80) does not distinguish Other Electrical Machinery from Electronic Components and Accessories. As for the procedure of matching three different datasets, Census Industry Codes (CIC) of MORG are first converted to Standard Industrial Classification Codes (SIC). BEA industry classifications (ISI categories) are also converted to SIC codes. NBER data are compiled by SIC.

13. The detailed estimation models are discussed in appendix A.

14. This measure of union wage differential has been used as a proxy for so-called union rent by Cebula and Nair-Reichert (2000). Details about the regression equation will be discussed later.

15. The wage differential estimation models are described in detail in appendix A.

16. The petroleum industry is not separated from the oil-producing industry in BEA public data, and so one cannot separate the data for the manufacturing sector from the mining industry. An individual employed in oil- or gas-related manufacturing industries from CPS data are also excluded in regression.

17. Workers employed in meat and dairy products are omitted in regressions.

18. See Allen (2001) for recent discussion on the interindustry wage structure in the United States.

19. Although it is tempting to include the FDI variable in the above individual earnings equation, it is well known that the resulting OLS standard errors are incorrect and exaggerate the significance of the included aggregate variables (Moulton 1986).

20. The disturbances in the second-step regressions are heteroscedastic because dependent variables in the second-step regression equations are estimated coefficients of the first-step regressions. I used GLS estimation with weights proportional to the covariance matrix of the estimated wage differentials from the first-step regressions. The GLS estimates are very similar to OLS and I report OLS estimates here.

21. Dickens and Katz (1987) provide a comprehensive review of all the existing studies of industries wages.

22. There are two approaches to explain why the union/non-union wage differential is affected by establishment size. First, the threat of unionization is greater in larger non-union firms, and so they might give higher compensation to their employees than smaller firms. Second, larger firms give high wages to enhance workers' effort level, reduce workers'

turnover, or to attract better employees. These two approaches predict that the union wage premium is smaller in larger establishments. Similar findings have been previously reported.

23. Twenty-three percent of those with not more than a high school education, as compared to 14 percent of those with a college education, were employed in the manufacturing sector as of 1987 (Berman et al. 1994).

24. Majority-owned affiliates (MOFA) are those in which parents hold at least a 50 percent ownership stake.

REFERENCES

Abowd, John, and Thomas Lemieux. 1991. "The Effects of International Trade on Collective Bargaining Outcomes: A Comparison of the United States and Canada." Pp. 343–67 in John Abowd and Richard Freeman (eds.), *Immigration, Trade, and the Labor Market.* Washington, D.C.: NBER.

Allen, Steven G. 2001. "Technology and the Wage Structure." *Journal of Labor Economics* 19 (2): 440–83.

Anderton, Bob, and Paul Brenton. 1999. "Did Outsourcing to Low Wage Countries Hurt Less Skilled Workers in the U.K.?" Pp. 147–66 in Paul Brenton and Jacques Pelkmans (eds.), *Global Trade and European Workers.* New York and London: St. Martin's and Macmillan.

Autor, D., L. Katz, and A. Krurger. 1997. "Computing Inequality: Have Computers Changed the Labor Market?" Princeton University Industrial Relations Working Paper No. 377.

Ashenfelter, Orley. 1978. "Union Relative Wage Effects: New Evidence and a Survey of Their Implications for Wage Inflation." In R. Stone and W. Peterson (eds.), *Econometric Contribution to Public Policy.* New York: St. Martin's.

Baldwin, Robert E. 1990. "Inferring Relative Factor Price Change form Quantitative Data." NBER Working Paper No. 7019.

Blanchflower, David G., Andrew Oswald, and Peter Sanfey. 1996. "Wages, Profits, and Rent-sharing." *Quarterly Journal of Economics* 3 (1): 227–51.

Bloch, Farrell E., and Mark S. Kuskin. 1978. "Wage Determination in the Union and Nonunion Sectors." *Industrial and Labor Relations Review* 31 (2): 183–92.

Borjas, George J. 1987. "Self-Selection and the Earnings of Immigrants." *American Economic Review* 77 (4): 531–53.

Borjas, George J., and Valerie A. Ramey. 1995. "Foreign Competition, Market Power, and Wage Inequality." *Quarterly Journal of Economics* 110 (4): 1075–110.

Budd, John W., and Matthew J. Slaughter. 2000. "Are Profits Shared Across Borders?" Mimeo, Dartmouth College.

Bughin, James, and Stefano Vannini. 1995. "Strategic Direct Investment under Unionized Oligopoly." *International Journal of Industrial Organization* 13: 127–45.

Card, David. 1996. "The Effect of Unions on the Structure of Wages: A Longitudinal Analysis." *Econometrica* 64 (4): 957–79.

Cebula, Richard, and Usha Nair-Reichert. 2000. "Union Rent Seeking and Import Competition in U.S. Manufacturing." *Journal of Labor Research* 21 (3): 478–87.

Cline, William R. 1997. *Trade and Income Distribution.* Washington, D.C.: Institute for International Economics.

Crotty, James, Gerald Epstein, and Patricia Kelly. 1998. "Multinational Corporations in the Neo-Liberal Regime." In Dean Baker, Gerald Epstein, and Robert Pollin (eds.), *Globalization and Progressive Economic Policy.* Cambridge: Cambridge University Press.

Dickens, William T., and Lawrence F. Katz. 1987. "Inter-Industry Wage Differences and Industry Characteristics." In Kevin Lang and Jonathan Leonard (eds.), *Unemployment and the Structure of Labor Markets.* London: Blackwell.

DiNardo, John, Nicole M. Fortin, and Thomas Lemieux. 1996. "Labor Market Institutions and the Distribution of Wages, 1973–1992: A Semiparametric Approach." *Econometrica* 64 (5): 1001–44.

Feenstra, Robert C., ed. 2000. *The Impact of International Trade on Wages.* Chicago: University of Chicago Press.

Feenstra, Robert C., and Gordon H. Hanson. 1996. "Globalization, Outsourcing, and Wage Inequality." *American Economic Review* 86 (2): 240–45.

Freeman, Richard B. 1995. "Are Your Wages Set in Beijing?" *Journal of Economic Perspectives* 9 (3): 15–32.

Freeman, Richard B., and Lawrence F. Katz. 1991. "Industrial Wage and Employment Determination in an Open Economy." Pp. 235–59 in John Abowd and Richard Freeman (eds.), *Immigration, Trade, and the Labor Market.* Washington, D.C.: NBER.

Freeman, Richard B., and James L. Medoff. 1979. "New Estimates of the Industrial Locus of Unionism in the U.S. NBER Working Paper Series No. 0273.

———. 1981. "The Impact of Collective Bargaining: Illusion or Reality?" Pp. 47–97 in Jack Steiber et al. (eds.), *U.S. Industrial Relations 1950–1980: A Critical Assessment.*

Gaston, Noel, and Daniel Trefler. 1994. "Protection, Trade, and Wages: Evidence from U.S. Manufacturing." *Industrial and Labor Relations Review* 47 (4): 574–93.

———. 1995. "Union Wage Sensitivity to Trade and Protection: Theory and Evidence." *Journal of International Economics* 39: 1–25.

Hanson, Gordon H., Raymond J. Mataloni, Jr., and Matthew J. Slaughter. 2001. "Expansion Strategies of U.S. Multinational Firms." NBER Working Paper No. 8433.

Katz, Lawrence F., and Lawrence H. Summers. 1989. "Can Inter-industry Wage Differentials Justify Strategic Trade Policy?" Pp. 85–116 in Robert Feenstra (ed.), *Trade Policies for International Competitiveness.* Chicago: University of Chicago Press.

Krueger, Alan B., and Lawrence H. Summers. 1988. "Efficiency Wages and the Inter-industry Wage Structure." *Econometrica* 56 (2): 259–93.

Lanot, Gauthier, and Ian Walker. 1998. "The Union/Non-union Wage Differential: An Application of Semi-Parametric Methods." *Journal of Econometrics* 84: 327–49.

Lawrence, Colin, and Robert Z. Lawrence. 1985. "Manufacturing Wage Dispersion: An End Game Interpretation." *Brookings Papers in Economic Activity* 16: 47–106.

Leamer, Edward. 2000. "Efforts and Wages: A New Look at the Interindustry Wage Differentials." Pp. 37–80 in Robert Feenstra (ed.), *The Impact of International Trade on Wages.* NBER Conference Report series. Chicago and London: University of Chicago Press.

Lemieux, Thomas. 1998. "Estimating the Effects of Unions on Wage Inequality in a Panel Data Model with Comparative Advantage and Nonrandom Selection." *Journal of Labor Economics* 16 (2): 261–91.

Macpherson, David A., and James B. Stewart. 1990. "The Effect of International Competition on Union and Nonunion Wages." *Industrial and Labor Relations Review* 43 (4): 434–46.

Magnani, Elisabetta. 1997. *Investment in Human Capital, Labor Mobility, and Inequality: Three Essays.* Ph.D. diss., Economics Department, Yale University.

Manning, Alan. 1987. "An Integration of Trade Union Models in a Sequential Bargaining Framework." *Economic Journal* 97: 121–39.

McDonald, Ian, and Robert Solow. 1981. "Wage Bargaining and Employment." *American Economic Review* 71: 896–908.

Moore, William J., and John Raisian. 1980. "Cyclical Sensitivity of Union-Nonunion Relative Wage Effects." *Journal of Labor Research* 1: 193–215.

Moulton, Brent R. 1986. "Random Group Effects and the Precision of Regression Estimates." *Journal of Econometrics* 32: 385–97.

Naylor, Robin. 1999. "Union Wage Strategies and International Trade." *Economic Journal* 109: 102–29.

Naylor, Robin, and Michele Santoni. 1999. "Foreign Direct Investment and Wage Bargaining." Centre for the Study of Globalization and Regionalization and Economic and Social Research Council, University of Warwick. Available at www.csgr.org.

Podgursky, Michael. 1986. "Unions, Establishment Size, and Intra-Industry Threat Effects." *Industrial and Labor Relations Review* 39 (2): 277–84.

Reddy, Sanjay. 2000. *Bargaining and Distribution: Essays on International Integration and National Regulation.* Ph.D. diss., Department of Economics, Harvard University.

Rodrik, Dani. 1997. *Has Globalization Gone Too Far?* Washington, D.C.: Institute for International Economics.

———. 1999, "Globalisation and Labour, or: If Globalisation Is a Bowl of Cherries, Why Are There So Many Glum Faces around the Table?" In R. Baldwin et al. (eds.), *Market Integration, Regionalism and the Global Economy.* Cambridge: Cambridge University Press.

Scheve, Kenneth F., and Mathew J. Slaughter. 2001. *Globalization and the Perceptions of American Workers.* Washington, D.C.: Institute for International Economics.

Slaughter, Matthew. 1999. "What Are the Results of Product-Price Studies and What Can We Learn From Their Difference?" Manuscript, Dartmouth College.

———. 2000, "Multinational Corporations, Outsourcing, and American Wage Divergence." *Journal of International Economics* 50: 449–72.

———. 2001. "International Trade and Labor-Demand Elasticities." *Journal of International Economics* 54 (1): 27–56.

Wood, Adrian. 1995. "How Trade Hurt Unskilled Workers." *Journal of Economic Perspectives* 9 (3, summer): 57–80.

———. 1998. "Globalisation and the Rise in Labour Market Inequalities." *Economic Journal* 108: 1463–82.

Zhao, Laixun. 1995. "Cross-Hauling Direct Foreign Investment and Unionized Oligopoly." *European Economic Review* 39: 1237–53.

———. 1998. "The Impact of Foreign Direct Investment on Wages and Employment," *Oxford Economic Papers* 50: 284–301.

CHAPTER 4

Constraints, Opportunities, and Information

FINANCIAL MARKET–GOVERNMENT RELATIONS
AROUND THE WORLD

Layna Mosley

> Politics are much more important [in developing markets] than in
> developed markets. Every aspect of policy/performance generates
> politically related concerns. [The question of] who governs matters in
> these markets. . . . It's hard to know what a government will do. . . .
> There are not necessarily clear priorities for these governments; there
> are so many issues, it's hard to know how they will prioritize. . . . The
> problems experienced in the developing world are totally nonexistent
> in the developed world.[1]

THIS CHAPTER EXAMINES the nature of financial market influences on government
policy-making. I focus specifically on the government bond market, which is a
most likely location for financial market pressures. I begin by exploring the factors that influence the nature of financial market pressures; this examination generates expectations about the relationship between policy outcomes and government bond rates in developed versus developing nations. Next, using qualitative
and quantitative data, I test these expectations. I argue that, as a result of their
concerns with default risk, financial market participants treat emerging markets
differently from developed ones. The chapter concludes with a discussion of how
financial market pressures interact with domestic political institutions, and of
how governments might seek to improve their autonomy vis-à-vis global capital
markets. There are also differences in the nature of financial market pressures over
time. For instance, we observe periods of high optimism regarding developing nations (as in the early 1990s, or prior to the Asian financial crisis), as well as periods of high skepticism (during and immediately after the Asian financial crisis).
In this chapter, however, I focus on variation across types of countries, rather than
over time.

NATIONAL POLITICS AND GLOBAL FINANCIAL MARKETS

In an era of capital mobility, electoral victories by left parties might send chills down the spines of international capital markets: left governments could preside over increased inflation, higher rates of corporate taxation, and larger public sectors. The extent to which elections create such worries for investors varies markedly, a fact illustrated by electoral victories of left parties in Brazil, Sweden, and Germany.

The October 2002 election in Brazil heralded the ascent to power of the leftist Workers' Party, led by Luis Inácio Lula da Silva ("Lula"). Financial markets had been nervous about the prospect of Lula's victory—and about Brazil's fiscal situation—for many months. In late September, in response to public opinion polls showing a widening lead for Lula, the currency fell 5 percent against the dollar, and the spread on interest rates between U.S. and Brazilian government bonds widened to over 22 percent (*Financial Times*, September 25, 2002). Credit ratings agencies downgraded Brazil's sovereign debt ratings, citing debt sustainability and economic stability in the face of a political transition. By late October, markets had priced Lula's victory into their assessments of credit and currency risk; the currency had fallen further (for a total decline of approximately 30 percent during 2002), and the substantial interest rate premium remained. Some analysts, however, began to suggest that Lula would moderate his positions once elected; the Bovespa stock index began to rally in the days preceding the election (*New York Times*, October 12, 2002).

Investors shifted their focus to whom Lula would appoint to his cabinet and the extent to which Lula would insist on hard-line Workers' Party economic policies. His initial statements appeared crafted to reassure financial markets, promising a balanced budget, low inflation, adherence to International Monetary Fund agreements, and continued debt payments, as well as job creation, social reform, and hunger relief (*New York Times*, January 19, 2003). The new government also was expected to increase the central bank's autonomy, and its choices for chief of staff and finance minister came from the moderate wing of the Workers' Party (*Economist*, January 4, 2003). These actions led to some improvements in financial markets, with a reduction of the risk premium to 17 percent in November, and to some improvements in the *real*'s value. At the same time, however, investors remained nervous about Brazil, and spreads hovered around 17 percent in early 2003. Investors continued to worry about how Lula would reconcile the demands of fiscal rectitude with his promises for social welfare, as well as about Brazil's continued ability to service and to roll over its public debt, which stood close to 60 percent of GDP (*Financial Times*, October 29, 2002).

In Germany and Sweden, elections in 2002 represented the continuation of left-party governments, and market responses were much less pronounced.[2] In Sweden's September 2002 poll, Goran Persson's Social Democrats increased their vote share from 36 to 40 percent, and Persson again moved to form an alliance with the Green and Left parties. In the two months prior to the election, the risk premium on Swedish government bonds (compared to U.S. benchmark bonds) varied from 0.7 to 1.1 percent, reaching 1.1 percent for much of the two weeks prior to the election.[3] On the day following the election, however, the Swedish krona gained in value, and long-term interest rates fell (*Financial Times*, September 17, 2002), signaling that financial markets were not worried about the fiscal and monetary policies of the incoming government. Although Persson had campaigned on a platform of providing generous welfare benefits, even if doing so resulted in higher taxes, market participants noted Persson's commitment to overall fiscal and monetary discipline (e.g., *Financial Times*, October 3, 2002).

Political uncertainty in the weeks following the election—namely, concerns over the Social Democrats' ability to garner support for a coalition with the Green and Left parties—contributed to the persistence of interest rate premia and to a decline in the krona's value (*Financial Times*, October 1, 2002). Again, however, the premia on government bonds never exceeded 1.35 percent and, by mid-November, they had fallen to less than 1 percent. The relatively small premium on Swedish debt, despite its leftist government and its generous social policies, might be explained by its fiscal discipline. In 2002, Sweden's surplus was 1.7 percent of GDP, and its debt was 53.6 percent of GDP, and falling. While the Social Democrats and other leftist parties called for more generous supply-side policies, they did not call for abandoning their independent central bank or for breaching the overall fiscal targets—and the Social Democrats supported Sweden's entry into the Economic and Monetary Union (EMU), promising a referendum in fall 2003.

In Germany, the September 22, 2002, election also had modest effects on financial market risk premia. Chancellor Gerhard Schroeder's narrow reelection led to short-term losses in the German equity market, as some investors expressed concerns about structural reform (*Financial Times*, September 23, 2002). Germany's fiscal situation, with a budget deficit of 3.75 percent of GDP, a debt of 61 percent of GDP, and an eventual warning from the European Union, may have given investors greater reason for concern. But, despite the Social Democratic victory and the fiscal situation, German interest rates remained low. In mid-August, German benchmark government bonds were at a 0.2 percent premium over U.S. government bonds. After the election, the premium reached 0.3 percent, and widened to 0.5 percent by early October. The market effects of the election, however, quickly receded, with the Germany-U.S. interest rate differential falling close to zero by late November. In part, markets may have hoped that the Green Party, which had a strong showing in the election and remained part of the governing coalition, would realize some of its proposals for fiscal reform (*New York Times*, September 24, 2002). But again, investors also appeared to realize that, no matter what its fiscal or structural difficulties, Germany remained a safe investment location.

We can contrast the European and the Brazilian cases along several dimensions: despite similar budgetary problems in Brazil and Germany (Brazil's deficit in 2002 was 5.2 percent of GDP; its inflation rate was higher at 8.8 percent), and similar debt levels in all three nations, the election of left-leaning governments evoked very different market reactions. All three nations saw increases in risk premia in the days leading up to and immediately after the elections. But in Sweden and Germany, these increases were small; and the increases quickly receded. By contrast, Brazil paid very large risk premia, perhaps greater than its shaky economic fundamentals suggested, and these premia persisted into 2003.[4]

The above contrast in financial market responses to electoral outcomes suggests heterogeneity in private investors' behavior. While investors may always be averse to left-leaning governments or expansionary public policies, they are more averse to these outcomes in developing nations. Additionally, because of their concerns about default, investors consider a wider range of policy variables when evaluating these nations. These governments, therefore, can expect to pay a higher financial market price for government partisanship, political instability, and fiscal expansion; and they can expect that a variety of policies—macro as well as supply-side—will generate financial market responses.

As a result, the impact of globalization on the feasibility of redistributive polices varies across countries. In nations with established political and economic systems and low risks of default, financial market pressures are "strong but narrow." Capital market openness allows investors to react swiftly and severely to changes in government policy outcomes; but investors consider only a small set of government policies when making asset allocation decisions. Governments that conform to capital market pressures in select macroeconomic areas, such as overall government budget deficits and rates of inflation, are relatively unconstrained in supply-side and microeconomic policy areas. But in emerging market nations, financial market pressures are both strong and broad: because of capital market openness, investors can easily punish governments, and their grounds for punishment include both macro- and supply-side policies, as well as political outcomes. Ultimately, then, those societies most in need of egalitarian redistribution may have, in terms of external financial market pressures, the most difficulty achieving it.

THEORY AND HYPOTHESES

Convergence, divergence, and economic globalization. During the past decade, scholars have devoted substantial attention to specifying the impact of economic globalization on national policy choices.[5] This theme has attracted interest not only in the academic realm but also within media and policy-making circles. Much of the popular literature on the subject offers grim prognoses for government policy-making autonomy. The academic literature falls into two broad groups—convergence and divergence. Predictions of convergence rely on the imperatives of cross-national competition and economic efficiency; the type of convergence predicted tends to be downward, rather than a common trend toward an intermediate position.[6] As races to the bottom ensue, governments lose the ability to provide goods and services to their citizens. Predictions of divergence, meanwhile, are based upon the continued diversity of national institutions and on domestic demands for compensation.[7]

In the realm of capital markets, the capacity for exit, and the political voice it confers on investors, is central to convergence-oriented accounts.[8] While capital market openness provides governments with greater access to capital,[9] it also subjects them to external discipline. Governments must sell their policies not only to domestic voters but also to international investors.[10] Because investors can respond swiftly and severely to actual or expected policy outcomes, governments must consider financial market participants' preferences when selecting policies.[11] Investors' credible threat of exit—assumed in the earlier structural dependence literature but guaranteed by international capital mobility—greatly increases their voice.

The alternative perspective, which predicts continued cross-national diversity in economic policies and institutions, relies on two arguments. First, national specialization is possible within globalization.[12] Firms and consumers have different preferences over taxation, services, and regulation; governments offer different combinations of these goods; and consumers and firms locate in the jurisdiction that best matches their preferences. Second, economic globalization serves to heighten, rather than to reduce, pressures for government intervention. This implies expanded or sustained domestic demands for government intervention. Governments have domestic political incentives to insulate individuals from externally generated insecurity and volatility; governments might pay an external economic price (in higher interest rates, for instance) for maintaining welfare state policies, but this price is offset by the internal political benefits of compensation.[13]

Recent empirical work assessing the validity of the convergence and divergence hypotheses, particularly in the advanced capitalist democracies, reveals a mixed pattern. Substantial cross-national diversity remains in areas such as government consumption spending, government transfer payments, public employment, and the public taxation,[14] but growing cross-national similarity characterizes aggregate monetary and fiscal policies. The latter is often associated positively with economic internationalization, while the former reveals the continued influence of domestic politics and institutions. Moreover, the impact of international capital markets on policy outcomes is contingent on earlier choices over exchange rate policies.[15] Under fixed exchange rates, leftist governments run larger budget deficits than right-leaning governments, and these governments use capital controls to reduce interest rate premia. Under floating rates, monetary—rather than fiscal—policy is the preferred partisan instrument: left-wing governments pursue looser monetary policies than do right-wing governments. In the developing world, economic globalization creates stronger pressures on governments, but some room for diversity in policies remains.[16]

This literature, although increasingly consistent in its empirical findings, does little to explore the causal mechanisms underpinning government policy choices. For instance, how do financial market participants evaluate government policy, and how do these evaluations generate the patterns of policy outcomes we observe?[17] To fill this lacuna, I specify a model of financial market operation, which describes the sources of cross-national and over-time variation in investors' influence.[18] I focus on the government bond market because it provides a *most likely* location for the operation of financial market pressures. Bonds are both an important source of financing for governments as well as a central part of large institutional investors' portfolios. The interest rates charged to governments for accessing the bond market also strongly influence the interest rates paid by other actors in the national economy. And higher public debt costs imply increased pressures in other areas of government policy.

My central argument is that the consideration of government policies by financial market actors varies markedly across groups of countries. This pattern is driven by variation in investors' certainty regarding governments' creditworthiness, as well as by the relative costs and benefits of employing information. In the advanced capitalist democracies, market participants consider key macroeconomic indicators, but not supply-side or micro-level policies. Market participants can charge high prices for certain government policies, but the range of policies used to set these prices is limited. In OECD nations, governments are pressured strongly to satisfy financial market preferences in terms of overall inflation and government budget deficit levels, but they retain domestic policy-making latitude in other areas. The result is a "strong but narrow" financial market constraint in the developed world. For developing nations, however, the scope of the financial market influence extends to cover both macro- and micro-policy areas. Market participants, concerned with default risk, consider many dimensions of government policy when making asset allocation decisions.[19] Domestic policy-making in these nations is more likely to conform to the convergence view, as the financial market constraint is both strong and broad.

Default risk, information, and financial market influences. Why do we expect differences in financial market behavior across groups of nations? The strength and scope of financial market influence depend on the level of international financial openness, on investors' incentives to collect and employ information, and on the extent to which investors focus on similar types of information. The level of financial openness and the use of similar information affect the magnitude (strength) of financial market influence, measured in terms of interest rate changes, while the incentives regarding the use of information establish the grounds (scope) for those changes.

To begin, the extent to which investors can move their holdings from one country to another determines the capacity of investors to punish governments. With no capital mobility—and no credible threat of exit—investors facing deteriorating conditions can wait and see, or convert their holdings to cash, but they cannot move their holdings to a different investment market. The strength of financial market pressures is reinforced by the structure of the investment management industry, which provides professional investors with incentives to rely on the same decision-making criteria. Because professional investors are evaluated in terms of their performance relative to that of other investors, contemporary government bond markets are, in fact, characterized by widespread reliance on similar indicators.[20] While the number of key indicators is central to determining the scope of the market constraint, the consensus among market actors on the identity of the key indicators is another important determinant of the *strength* of the financial market constraint.

The key actors are professional investors, that is, rational, wealth-maximizing decision-makers who face the challenge of distinguishing among sovereign borrowers. Investors have incomplete information regarding the credit worthiness of the countries whose bonds they are trading. The challenge to investors is to distinguish between good credit risks and poor credit risks, using government policy outcomes as signals of the government's type. But collecting and processing information regarding government policy outcomes—observing signals—is costly. Investors, therefore, actively decide whether or not to collect and use particular types of information, based on marginal costs and benefits.[21] Their decisions are based on two factors: first, on their prior beliefs regarding a government's type, based on the nation's level of economic development and, second, on a cost-benefit analysis of each piece of information.

When an investor has a strong prior belief that a government is of the "good credit risk" type, she will invest only a small amount in the collection of information. Identifying a government's type is a fairly simple task, one that usually can be done with a small amount of information, and at a low cost. When an investor does not have a strong prior belief regarding a government's type, she will invest a much larger amount in the collection of information. Here the marginal benefit of a piece of information exceeds its marginal cost, as it allows the investor to distinguish between types of borrowing governments. In these cases, market participants will devote their scarce attention and time resources to the information that provides the greatest marginal benefit.

The need to economize on the use of information is particularly strong when financial internationalization is high. If investment is confined to a single country or set of countries, investors are able to consider a wide range of information and to become very certain about the type of each government. But, when they are able to invest in a large number of nations, investors' information requirements are much greater.[22] For example, after investors diversify to twenty from five countries, investors who look at five indicators per country will have one hundred rather than twenty-five pieces of information to consider. Collecting and employing information about Country A prevents a market participant from collecting and employing information about Country B.[23]

Investment risk and economization. Investors may experience several types of investment risk: default risk, which results from a borrower failing to repay its obligation; inflation risk, which results when an asset's purchasing power declines; currency risk, which results from fluctuations in the value of local-currency denominated assets; and liquidity risk, where markets for an asset are thin and, therefore, transactions are difficult to execute.[24] When investors assign a high probability to governments being of the "good credit risk" type, default risk is minimal, and investors can focus their attention on assessing inflation risk. They need only look to broad measures of government policy outcomes as signals; provided that these signals confirm their prior beliefs, they will not dig deeper. Investors will reduce or eliminate the use of information relevant to default risk; they are willing to narrow their range of indicators because additional indicators are not relevant signals of the government's type. If salient investment risks (inflation risk and currency risk) can be evaluated on the basis of a small set of indicators, and if these indicators are high in quality, then the marginal benefit of employing additional information is quite small. Under these conditions, market actors will avoid the costs of additional information and will rely instead on a small set of indicators—"information shortcuts."[25] Therefore, when dealing with countries characterized by lower levels of default risk, market participants are likely to employ a narrow, less costly package of indicators. It is only when a "good credit risk" government does something out of character—rapidly increasing its level of public debt to a very high level, for example—that an investor would doubt its type.

But where governments are likely to be of the "bad credit risk" type, and investors cannot easily differentiate between types of borrowers, they must assess both inflation and default risk. They employ a wide risk of information to rebut or confirm their prior beliefs. In such cases, investors will use a wide range of information about a government's willingness *and* ability to pay in order to gauge the government's creditworthiness. In their efforts to assess default propensity, investors will consider macropolicy indicators (e.g., inflation, deficits, and debt) as well as supply-side policies, labor market regulation, and the composition of government spending. Small budget deficits and low inflation may indicate low future inflation risk, but they are insufficient to assess future default risk. Considering a wide range of indicators allows for a more accurate assessment of investment risk. In addition, when uncertainty about the quality of information and the implications of information for policy outcomes is high (e.g., when it is not clear if falling budget deficits indicate fiscal consolidation or merely "cheap talk"), market actors will gather more information. Employing a higher-cost package of indicators allows investors to come to more precise conclusions regarding governments' types.

In many cases, then, a broad range of information is not necessary to make correct assessments of investment risk. For instance, although a market participant who collects and evaluates every available piece of evidence about Sweden may generate a more accurate assessment of the future performance of Swedish government bonds, she will forego the opportunity to make accurate assessments regarding the future of Hungarian and Czech bonds. In doing so, she sacrifices the ability to make broadly accurate assessments of many assets in return for the ability to make a very accurate assessment of a single asset—hardly rational behavior in a geographically diversified capital market or in an environment where uncertainty regarding a government's type is low.

Developed versus developing nations.   The signaling framework suggests that financial market participants are most likely to rely on a narrow set of indicators when evaluating bonds issued by governments of developed democracies. Investors assign a high probability to the fact that OECD nations are of the "good credit risk" type. The label "developed democracy" provides a degree of confidence regarding government policy, a more narrow range of possible policies, and, therefore, reduced concerns about default risk. Although investors *are* concerned about government policy outcomes in these nations, and *are* aware of variation in outcomes among developed countries, they place a considerable amount of confidence in these governments. Market participants' overall confidence in government policies and in information quality leads them to consider only a small set of aggregate indicators. They view good performance on these aggregates—macro-indicators— as indicative of low inflation and exchange rate risk. At the same time, market participants see micro-indicators as largely unrelated to the government's type. And compliance with market pressures on macro-indicators does not necessitate particular changes in micro-indicators. Different mixes of micro-side policies characterize governments with small deficits and low inflation.[26] The result, then, is relatively narrow financial market influence.

On the other hand, almost by definition, emerging market economies lack well-developed domestic capital markets and sometimes experience difficulties repaying external loans. Investors assign significant probability to the possibility that emerging market economies are "bad credit risks." They have very uncertain prior beliefs regarding the type of emerging market borrowers. Some are creditworthy, while others are not, and a low-cost package of information does not allow investors to distinguish between the two. For instance, investors often do not assume that governing parties will uphold their debt servicing obligations. Recent defaults or near-defaults in Argentina (2001), Ecuador (1999), Indonesia (2002), Russia (1998), and Ukraine (1998), among others, are illustrative.[27] It is quite possible for a government to win domestic political favor by dealing harshly with foreign investors, or for political instability to generate a sovereign default.[28] Given the wide possible range of investment risks that financial market participants face in emerging markets, and investors' greater uncertainty regarding the salience of these risks in particular nations, investors must rely on a broad set of indicators. Doing so allows them to assess governments' willingness and ability to repay their debts.

Additionally, the borrowing strategies pursued by emerging market governments can exacerbate investors' concerns about the ability to pay. To access international capital markets (or to do so more cheaply), emerging market governments often issue foreign currency–denominated, short duration bonds. These issues not only alleviate risks for investors but also render default risk more salient.[29] Moreover, investors' desire to gather a wide swath of information is reinforced by the nature and availability of information in emerging markets: information may be of poor quality or simply unavailable. Rather than relying only on statistics from one official source, then, investors might collect fiscal policy information from several government ministries, the central bank, private industry, and intergovernmental organizations.[30]

As a result, the marginal benefits of additional information are great in emerging markets. Market participants will worry about the ways in which emerging market governments allocate spending, the supply-side policies employed by governments, and the implications of regional and national elections. They will assess investment risks using not only macroeconomic indicators (inflation, fiscal balances, current account deficits) but also a wide range of micro-side indicators (e.g., the breakdown of government spending across areas and the structure of tax systems) and the political climate. Expenditures for investment, for instance, are seen to increase repayment capacity, while expenditures for pure consumption do not.[31] Likewise, even among emerging market economies with similar levels of public investment expenditure, we might expect investors to examine the efficiency of these investments. These micro-side indicators serve as costly signals of developing nation governments' types: a good credit risk will allocate its budget in market-friendly or neoliberal ways, whereas a bad credit risk government will not. The costs of the signal are found in domestic politics: the rationalization of pensions and health care, to take an example, often hurts governments' public approval.[32]

This broad financial market constraint does not necessarily mean that market participants make more nuanced assessments of emerging market nations, or that they consider changes in one indicator in light of changes in many other indicators. Rather, it means that, for emerging market nations, there are more policy indicators that can elicit a financial market response.[33] For example, if there is no change in market expectations regarding Belgium's government deficit/GDP ratio or rate of inflation, there probably will be no change in Belgian government bond prices. Even if, however, there is no change in Peru's government budget deficit or inflation rate, bond prices may move in response to changes in the distribution of the government budget across spending categories.

In sum, the incentives facing professional investors suggest that the influence of international financial markets on the governments of developed countries is narrow in the sense that traders react to a small number of macroeconomic indicators, leaving governments wide latitude to pursue a variety of policy objectives. In contrast, the influence of international financial markets on emerging market governments with open capital accounts is both strong and broad. Market participants rely on a wide set of indicators and react sharply to changes that raise questions about a country's credit-worthiness.

EMPIRICAL ASSESSMENTS

Financial Market Influence in the Developed World

To what extent does investors' behavior conform to the above hypotheses? In previous work, I present evidence regarding financial market pressures in advanced industrial democracies.[34] I gathered several types of evidence: interviews of institutional investors and fund managers, conducted in London and Frankfurt in 1997 and 1998; surveys of financial market participants, carried out in 1999 and 2000, and cross-sectional time series analyses for the 1981–95 period. This evidence strongly supports the notion that financial market participants are concerned with developed country governments "getting the big numbers right," but they are much less concerned about the partisan affiliation or the micro-level policies of these governments. On the quantitative side, the strongest determinants of longer-term government bond rates are inflation and U.S. interest rates. Government fiscal balances, current account balances, and exchange rate levels also are significantly and somewhat strongly associated with government bond rates. Supply-side policies, on the other hand, generally do not have a strong and significant relationship with interest rates; and macro-policy outcomes are often uncorrelated with micro-policy and supply-side choices.

From these findings, it follows that governments of developed democracies are not constrained broadly by financial market pressures. Investors are interested principally in the aggregate economic outcomes of inflation and government budget deficits. The means by which governments achieve these outcomes, and the nature of government policies in other areas, do not concern financial market participants. Therefore, complying with financial market participants' preferences over particular aggregate outcomes leaves governments with "room to move." This finding provides a causal underpinning for the continued cross-national policy divergence frequently observed among OECD nations. It also is consistent with the notion that "stresses on contemporary welfare states would be there with or without globalization."[35]

Financial Market Influence in Emerging Markets

The situation is very different for governments of developing countries. Relatively open capital markets in middle-income developing nations allow for strong market responses to government policy changes.[36] Other factors can render these pressures even stronger: first, emerging market nations' reliance on foreign capital is greater than that in developed democracies; governments have fewer choices regarding how to access international capital markets. Additionally, emerging markets face the problem of greater capital flow volatility. Investment in emerging market economies often is driven by efforts at portfolio diversification and at high risk-adjusted returns, and often reacts to "push" factors in developed markets. In the 1990s, the volatility of returns on emerging market debt consistently and substantially exceeded that of returns in developed nation markets.[37] While emerging market governments may, as in the developed world, maintain divergent social and economic policies, doing so will be more costly (in terms of interest rate penalties and access to capital) in the developing world. Moreover, extant research on the relationship between default risk and interest rate premia in developing nations suggests that default risk *is* a central consideration.[38] For instance, a recent IMF review reports a relatively robust association between perceived default risk and levels of government debt.[39] And, as noted earlier, by borrowing at short maturities or in foreign currencies, emerging market governments often exacerbate default risk.

INTERVIEW AND SURVEY EVIDENCE: THE IMPORTANCE OF DEFAULT RISK

Interviews with professional investors.   The importance in the developing world of default risk and of gathering a wide set of information is reflected in my interviews with and surveys of professional investors.[40] These interviews, which were a followup to a 1997 survey that addressed developed nations, were conducted in late 1998 and focused on the constraints facing emerging market economies.[41] Interview subjects were London-based participants in fixed-income markets; such individuals tend to make longer-term recommendations regarding asset allocation and to deal with nations in a variety of geographic regions. Interviewees answered a set of open-ended questions regarding asset allocation in emerging market economies.

Recent defaults and near-defaults have raised the salience of default risks for market participants.[42] It is not surprising, therefore, that market participants are very concerned about governments' ability and willingness to pay. As in developed nations, market participants consider macro-outcomes, including the inflation rate and the deficit/GDP ratio. Additionally, because a government's ability to repay depends on its capacity to generate revenues, market participants also consider the sources of government revenue, the balance of payments position, existing government debt, and the structure of government borrowing. Because of the prevalence of foreign currency denomination, exchange rate considerations also are very important.

In contrast with developed-country asset allocation, market participants *also* look at micro-policy indicators. For instance, they consider not only a government's aggregate fiscal stance but also the components of its fiscal policy. They collect information regarding the sources of tax revenue and the government's capacity to collect taxes. On the expenditure side, market participants consider how resources are allocated across spending categories. Are public funds used for consumption or for [growth-enhancing] improvements in infrastructure? How is the pension system structured? What is the role of government subsidies in the economy? Furthermore, market participants consider a government's level of fiscal flexibility: in a crisis, is the government able to change or reallocate spending?

Moreover, professional investors point out that, in developing nations, unpredictable political climates affect governments' willingness to repay public debt.[43] In emerging market economies, market participants view the range of possible policy outcomes as relatively wide: some governments will pursue capital-friendly policies, but others may advocate policies hostile to international investors.[44] A change in government can have large implications for policy outcomes.[45] For instance, immediately following Hugo Chavez's strong electoral showing in 1998, the Venezuelan equity market index fell 8 percent. Market participants cited fears about Chavez's promises of radical political reform and his rejection of the "savage neo-liberal economic model."[46] The importance of politics to default makes country risk analysis an essential part of the asset allocation process; such analysis is essentially absent when investing in developed nations. Lastly, interviews suggest that the quality and availability of information are important considerations in emerging markets. Of those participants interviewed in October 1998, eleven of thirteen cited informational concerns as a factor in their emerging market asset allocation behavior, and eight of these eleven described information as a *very central* concern.[47]

Surveys of professional investors. A survey of mutual fund managers, conducted in mid-2000, provides similar evidence. The survey subjects for the first round were managers of the largest internationally oriented U.S. mutual funds, ranked according to assets under management.[48] This sample consisted of 178 individuals. The subjects for the second round of surveys were drawn from a database (Morningstar's Principia) that included mutual funds of all sizes; I selected those funds with substantial activity outside the United States.[49] This database generated a pool of 486 potential subjects. Each subject received a four-page questionnaire. Part I of the survey requested basic descriptive information, such as the number of and size of funds managed, the type of assets held, and the geographic allocation of capital. Part II asked respondents to rate the importance, on a scale of one to ten, of thirteen policies or political factors. A follow-up reminder regarding the survey was sent two weeks later.

A total of forty-seven surveys were returned. After eliminating those surveys that did not reach the intended recipients,[50] the resulting rate of response was approximately 8 percent. The very low response rate is not surprising, given the time demands faced by fund managers.[51] By comparing the characteristics of the respondents to those of the entire sample, however, we can increase our confidence that the bias generated by survey nonresponse is acceptable. Among respondents, the number of funds managed ranged from one to eighty-six, with four as the median number managed. Average fund assets under management were $17.5 billion in the May survey (reflecting the selection of participants based on fund size), $4.7 billion for the July respondents, and overall $8.9 billion. The median fund size was considerably smaller, at $1.5 billion.

To compare the respondents with the total potential pool of managers, the average fund size in the Principia database was $332 million. The average fund size for respondents—calculated by dividing total assets under management by the number of funds managed—was $1.1 billion.[52] Similarly, the median fund size is $34 million in the Principia database and $318 million in the May and July responses. The responses reported in the following paragraphs, then, are biased toward larger mutual funds. This may reflect the fact that the managers of smaller funds are less likely to devote time to responding to surveys. In any case, larger mutual funds are more able to impact the fortunes of emerging market nations, so a bias toward these funds is acceptable.

The overall asset allocation results from the survey indicate that, on average, 86.9 percent of fund managers' assets are invested in OECD, or advanced capitalist, nations, while the remaining 13.1 percent are invested in emerging market economies. On average, 34 percent of investment is in the Euro-11 area, 29 percent in North America, and 15 percent in Japan. Other investment locations include Latin America (6 percent), emerging Europe (2 percent), and the Middle East and Africa (2 percent). Again comparing this allocation with that of the wider Principia database, the allocations generally are similar.[53]

Survey respondents rated the importance of a series of policies and political factors to their asset allocation decisions. The rating scale ranged from one to ten, where lower values were denoted as "not at all important" and higher values as "very important." This evidence allows us to compare fund managers' treatment of emerging market and developed nations; if the strong and broad pattern holds in developing nations, we should observe marked differences in the importance of these factors, as well as a pronounced attention to default risk in emerging markets.

Table 4.1 reports these results. The first column lists the indicator, using the wording from the survey. The second column lists the overall average score. This column indicates that the most important indicators are the expected rate of inflation, and the ability and willingness of governments to repay debt. When we divide the sample based on geographic allocation, however, important differences appear. The third column reports the average for those fund managers with more than 25 percent of assets invested in emerging markets ($n = 7$); the fourth column reports averages for all others in the sample ($n = 40$). For all but one factor (tax policy), the importance of these factors is greater in emerging markets. In seven of thirteen cases, the difference between groups of respondents is statistically significant. Particularly large differences exist for the ability of governments to repay debt, monetary policy, fiscal policy, and expected changes in government. If we define emerging markets more loosely—as more than 10 percent of

TABLE 4.1.
The Importance of Policies and Political Factors to Asset Allocation

Factor	All Respondents	Emerging Markets (>25% assets)	All Other Respondents
Expected Rate of Inflation	6.93	8.5*	6.84
Political Independence of National Central Bank	6.15	7.8*	6.03
Expected Government Budget Deficit	5.73	7.0*	5.59
Political Independence/Insulation of Fiscal Policy-making Authorities	5.95	7.3*	5.89
Overall Level of Government Debt (e.g., Debt/GDP Ratio)	6.27	6.5	6.24
Total Size of Government Sector (e.g., Government Spending/GDP)	5.73	6.0	5.70
How Governments Allocate Spending Across Functional Categories (e.g., Public Investment Spending vs. Transfer Payments)	4.88	5.8	4.84
Tax Policy (e.g., Marginal Rates of Taxation)	6.39	5.8	6.59
Degree of Government Intervention in Labor Markets	6.07	7.0	6.08
Ability of Government to Repay Sovereign Debt	7.27	8.7*	7.14
Willingness of Government to Repay Sovereign Debt	7.46	8.3*	7.41
Partisan Orientation of Government (e.g., Social Democrats, Liberals, Christian Democrats)	4.98	5.33	4.97
Expected Changes in Government (e.g., Upcoming Elections)	6.29	7.67*	6.08

*Indicates a difference from "All other respondents" that is significant at a 90 percent or greater level of confidence.

assets in emerging markets—the differences between categories are similar, albeit with less statistical significance. The survey results, then, provide additional confirmation for our expectation that investors treat developed and emerging markets differently, and that default risk is more salient for emerging market investors. They also provide evidence that information quality and availability are more serious problems in emerging than in developed markets.[54]

Credit ratings. Lastly, evidence of investors' concern with default risk also occurs in the methodologies employed by sovereign credit ratings agencies. Some agencies, which include Standard and Poor's, Moody's, Duff and Phelps (DCR), and Fitch-IBCA, rate sovereign and corporate debt instruments. These agencies sell their ratings to institutional investors and other portfolio market investors. Other agencies, including Euromoney and Institutional Investor, provide country-risk ratings to a variety of private sector investors. The practices of these agencies reveal two things implied by the previous discussion: first, default risk is salient in emerging market economies but assumed to be nonexistent in developed economies. Second, greater uncertainty surrounds ratings in emerging market economies.

Although ratings agencies sometimes fail to anticipate major events, investors use them as a guidepost in the pricing of sovereign debt.[55] Additionally, because many institutional investors are required to hold assets of some minimum credit rating, ratings changes can generate substantial reallocations.[56] A review of ratings methodologies indicates that ratings agencies take for granted that default risk is very low in advanced industrial democracies, even when outstanding debt is high.[57] Variance among developed nations' ratings is very small, despite large differences in levels of public debt. Along these lines, Ul Haque et al.'s study of rating methodologies and outcomes finds that different groups of countries are treated differently by ratings agencies, above and beyond their objective economic characteristics.[58]

Ratings agencies devote the bulk of their attention to emerging market economies; there, they consider a wide range of economic policy outcomes and political attributes. They assume neither willingness nor ability to repay debt.[59] Rating agency assessments include aggregate fiscal outcomes as well as the breakdown of government spending, the structure of the tax system, and the nature of government regulation. For instance, Standard and Poor's considers the purposes of public sector borrowing as well as trends in inflation and public debt.[60] It also evaluates supply-side policies, including the tax code, domestic regulation, and national investment policies.[61] In light of recent financial crises, ratings agencies also have begun to place stronger emphases on the strength of domestic banking systems and on the degree of reliance on foreign capital inflows.[62]

Ratings outcomes highlight the creditworthiness of developed economies, as well as the investment community's difficulty in assessing investment risk in emerging markets. Credit ratings of OECD nations tend to be high, with little variance among countries, and a high correlation among different agencies' rat-ings. Emerging market nations (middle-income developing nations, classified as such by the World Bank) have lower ratings, on average; they also are character-ized by greater variance, both across countries and across ratings agencies. Inter-estingly, while low-income developing nations have lower average ratings than emerging market nations, they are characterized by less variance across countries and across ratings agencies. These outcomes suggest that uncertainty regarding information and politicoeconomic outcomes is highest among emerging market nations, generating greater variance across countries and less agreement across ratings agencies.[63]

QUANTITATIVE EVIDENCE

Variation in government policies. The "strong and broad" financial market constraint relies on investors' uncertainty regarding policy outcomes in develop-ing nations, as well as on higher levels of default risk in those nations. Evidence from the 1990s highlights the general pattern of policy variability in emerging markets. This variability, which is greater than in the developed world, renders investors less able to assume a constant level of risk across developing nations. Rather, they must look closely at each nation and its propensity for default.

Table 4.2 provides summary data for a variety of economic policy indicators, for a group of developed and developing nations.[64] These data suggest that eco-nomic fundamentals tend to be worse in developing nations, and perhaps more importantly, that these outcomes display more variation in developing nations. In each of the six categories listed, variance is greater in developing than in devel-oped nations. In all categories other than government debt and government con-sumption, policies also are "worse" in developing nations. Higher debt in the OECD likely reflects greater access to credit, while higher consumption reflects larger public sectors.

Correlates of interest rates. We also can use cross-sectional time series models to assess the extent to which economic policy outcomes and political factors are associated with government bond rates in the developing world. For the develop-ing world, macro-policy data are more readily available for recent years, and cross-nationally comparable data on micro-policy indicators are largely unavailable.[65] The results reported in this section rely on data for the developed and developing nations listed in the appendix, using annual data for the 1990 to 2000 period. Al-though cross-sectional time series estimation suffers from some problems for this sort of data, the results provide additional evidence of differences in the evalua-tions of developed and developing nations.

The strong and broad model of financial market influence on governments implies that, because of the salience of default risk, emerging market nations are treated differently from developed nations. That is, the constraint is broader, and perhaps stronger, not merely because governments of emerging market

TABLE 4.2.
Variance in Policy Outcomes, 1990–2000

Policy Indicator	Developed Nations: Mean	Developed Nations: Standard Deviation	Developing Nations: Mean	Developing Nations: Standard Deviation
Government Budget Balance/GDP	−1.96 ($n = 187$)	4.9	−2.65 ($n = 410$)	4.3
Inflation Rate[a]	2.76 ($n = 231$)	2.16	16.64 ($n = 445$)	19.87
Current Account Balance/GDP	1.05 ($n = 226$)	5.29	−2.58 ($n = 482$)	6.04
Government Debt/GNP	67.69 ($n = 175$)	25.91	52.05 ($n = 464$)	31.53
Government Consumption/GNP	19.78 ($n = 223$)	3.99	14.94 ($n = 513$)	5.67
Change in Real Effective Exchange Rate	−0.004 ($n = 231$)	0.050	0.015 ($n = 248$)	0.116

Note: n refers to the number of country-years. Calculations are based on data are from World Bank, *World Development Indicators* 2002, and *Global Development Finance* 2002. Debt data for developed nations also rely on the OECD *Economic Outlook*, December 2002.

[a] Excluded are the forty-eight country-years (in developing nations) in which annual inflation is greater than 100 percent. Excluding these nations serves to reduce cross-national variance.

economies pursue a different set of macro-policies than governments of developed economies, but also because emerging market governments are characterized by greater policy uncertainty, by less accurate information, and by higher levels of default risk. *Even when* emerging market economies have outcomes on macro-policy indicators that are similar to those of developed nations, they should pay higher interest rate premia.

The dependent variable in these analyses is the interest rate spread—the difference between the interest rate charged by banks on loans to prime customers (LIBOR, the London Interbank Offer Rate)[66] and the interest rate paid by banks for demand, time, or savings deposits. While all OECD nations issue comparable government securities, the pattern of issue varies widely across emerging market nations; data on the interest rate spread are cross-nationally comparable and more widely available. Where data on benchmark government bond or Treasury bill rates exist, they are highly correlated (bivariate correlations of 0.71 and 0.61, respectively) with the interest rate spread variable. Additionally, using an interest-rate-spread measure controls for changes over time in global credit conditions.

Table 4.3 reports results from several cross-sectional time series models, using annual data for the 1990–2000 period.[67] The independent variables include several macro-policy indicators—the rate of inflation, the current account/GDP ratio, the government budget balance/GDP, and government debt/GNP, as well as the exchange rate regime and the level of capital market openness.[68] To these basic economic variables, I add a dummy variable for elections, an interaction between elections and OECD nations (column 2); an indicator of the quality of economic data (column 3); and a dummy variable for OECD nations (column 4).

The models in table 4.3 suggest that, in both developed and developing nations, economic outcomes are important determinants of the interest rates paid by governments. Interest rates are associated significantly and positively with inflation, and significantly and negatively with current account balances.[69] Government budget balances are also associated negatively with interest rate spreads (larger deficits lead to higher spreads), but this association is statistically significant only in the last model. The government debt/GNP variable is always significant, but it is not in the expected direction: the estimate implies that nations with higher debt levels pay lower interest rates. This could reflect the fact that, where interest rates are very high, governments are less able to access international capital markets. Additionally, nations with floating exchange rate regimes and open capital markets tend to pay higher interest rates, all else being equal. When capital markets are opened, governments usually lose the ability to intervene in domestic financial markets, and interest rates rise closer to world levels.

To the basic model (1), model 2 adds an election dummy variable as well as an interaction term capturing the effects of elections in OECD nations (OECD*Election). The estimate on the election variable is positive and significant: during election years, interest rate spreads are higher, even after accounting for monetary and fiscal conditions. The interaction between OECD status and elections, however, is negative and significant; in general, elections result in higher interest rates, but in OECD nations, this effect disappears. While elections may matter for interest rates in developing nations, they do not in developed nations. Because investors are not concerned with default risk in developed nations, they do not need to consider the implications of political events for default when investing in the OECD. Other political variables, such as government fractionalization, are positively associated with interest rate levels (e.g., higher fractionalization associated with larger spreads); but these estimates are not statistically significant, and they reduce the number of observations.

Model 3 includes a dummy variable (subscription to SDDS, Special Data Dissemination Standard) to gauge the presence of informational concerns. The IMF launched the SDDS in 1996, with the aim of ensuring that developing countries provided timely and accurate economic information to the financial community. As of July 2005, sixty-one nations (developed and developing) subscribe to the data standard.[70] In the above model, subscription is associated significantly

TABLE 4.3.
Interest Rates in OECD and Developing Nations

Independent Variable	1 Economic Variables (Basic Model)	2 Basic Model plus Elections	3 Basic Model plus Elections and Data Standards	4 Basic Model plus Elections and OECD Member
Inflation Rate[a]	0.589*** (0.017)	0.586*** (0.017)	0.594*** (0.017)	0.575*** (0.017)
Current Account Balance/GDP	-0.494*** (0.096)	-0.531*** (0.094)	-0.541*** (0.094)	-0.376*** (0.108)
Government Budget Balance/GDP	-0.155 (0.119)	-0.108 (0.115)	-0.057 (0.117)	-0.408*** (0.124)
Government Debt/GNP	-0.026* (0.015)	-0.032** (0.014)	-0.029** (0.014)	-0.029* (0.017)
Capital Account Openness	0.372** (0.173)	0.477*** (0.161)	0.537*** (0.160)	1.504*** (0.317)
Exchange Rate Regime	0.572*** (0.097)	0.545*** (0.093)	0.591*** (0.094)	0.431*** (0.105)
Election Dummy Variable		2.581*** (0.678)	2.383*** (0.678)	1.898*** (0.739)

	Model 1	Model 2	Model 3
OECD*Election Interaction	−2.881*** (0.898)	−2.851*** (0.955)	−2.185** (0.908)
Subscription to SDDS		−1.356* (0.707)	
OECD Dummy Variable			−9.431*** (1.865)
Observations (N)	489	489	489
Countries	61	61	61
Wald Chi^2	1543.73	1734.27	1420.99

Note: Standard errors are in parentheses.
[a] All coefficients are rounded to three places.
*** $p < .01$; ** $p < .05$, * $p < .10$.

with lower interest rate spreads. Although there was no variance in this measure until 1996, it appears to have an impact on investor confidence in later years.

The final model (model 4) adds a "country category" variable, coded 1 for developed democracies (OECD nations), and zero for developing nations.[71] This variable gauges the extent to which, once macroeconomic outcomes are accounted for, developing nations *still* pay higher interest rates than developed nations. The negative and significant coefficient on this variable indicates that two nations, one developed and one developing, with similar macroeconomic fundamentals, are treated differently by financial market participants. The OECD variable likely serves as a proxy for financial market participants' concerns about the attributes of developing nations—for instance, high default risk, political uncertainty, and poor information quality.[72]

Lastly, when micro-policy variables (such as total government consumption, total tax revenue, government spending on subsidies, and health care spending) are added to the above models, they tend to be associated positively with interest rate spreads. In most cases, however, the estimates are statistically insignificant. The exception is expenditure on wages and salaries, which is associated significantly and positively with interest rate spreads. The wages measure, however, is correlated with country category; spending on wages tends to be much higher in frontier and emerging markets.[73] This effect, therefore, likely reflects an emerging markets vs. developed markets difference, rather than a general attention to micro-policy indicators.

In sum, because of concern with default risk and information quality, financial market pressures in developing nations are broader than those in developed nations. These broader constraints imply that, as developing nations open themselves to flows of short-term capital, they will experience both costs and benefits. The benefits will flow from a more efficient allocation of global investment and, presumably, higher rates of economic growth. The costs will come from greater constraints on policymaking autonomy, as well as from potential effects on equity and income distribution. If developing nation governments wish, for domestic political reasons, to maintain or create redistributive social policies that are viewed by investors as signaling a reduced commitment to repaying their foreign debt, they may well pay a high financial market price for doing so. Financial markets might reward redistributive policies that are growth promoting; this will depend on the extent to which investors consider longer-run outcomes rather than shorter-run budgetary effects.

Conclusions

This chapter explores the influences of global capital markets on government policy-making, with a specific focus on the government bond market. I suggest that, because of professional investors' incentives and information needs, financial market pressures will vary across groups of countries. In the advanced capitalist democracies, market participants consider key macroeconomic indicators, but not supply-side or micro-level policies. The result is a "strong but narrow" financial market constraint in the developed world. For developing nations, however, the scope of the financial market influence extends to cover both macro- and micro-policy areas. Market participants, concerned with default risk, consider many dimensions of government policy when making asset allocation decisions. Domestic policy-making in these nations is more likely to conform to the convergence view, as the financial market constraint is both strong and broad.

The empirical evidence presented in this chapter supports this view: as a result of their concerns with default risk, financial market participants treat emerging markets differently from—and more stringently than—developed ones. The consequences of strong and broad financial market influence for developing country governments are rather severe. Because the interest rates charged to governments are related directly to a wide range of economic policies, social policies, and institutional features, governments that want to please international market participants are highly constrained. We are likely to observe many instances of emerging market governments attempting to please pro-market constituents and international lenders rather than other domestic interest groups.

The implications of this conclusion for policy-making depend, however, on three sets of factors: (1) the interests and institutions that characterize domestic politics; (2) the role of push (global) versus pull (country-specific) factors in capital flows to emerging markets; and (3) the ability of developing countries to move between groups, emerging and developed. Each of these factors will mediate the ways in which financial market pressures ultimately influence redistributive policies, especially in a dynamic sense. By way of conclusion, I treat each in turn.

First, domestic interests and institutions vary across developing nations, and these will affect the ways in which governments respond to financial market pressures. In some cases, public opinion may push governments in exactly the same direction as global capital markets—toward monetary and fiscal restraint, and toward smaller public sectors. In other cases, the reverse will be true. In addition, domestic political institutions, such as electoral systems, coalition governments, and federalism, will affect the ways in which financial market pressures are interpreted domestically. Economic conditions—and the need to attract and retain capital—will also affect the extent to which governments will accede to or resist financial market pressures. Therefore, to understand fully the linkage between global capital and national governments, a second causal mechanism is necessary. We need to connect events in global capital markets with changes in government policy, and we must consider how various domestic institutions and ideologies mediate these changes. In other words, under what conditions do governments accede to financial market influence, resist this influence, or attempt to insulate themselves from it?[74]

Second, the account given in this chapter links country-specific ("pull") factors with capital market activity. While these pull factors are an important determinant of market activity in emerging markets, a second category of factors—"push factors"—also can be important. Under some circumstances, exogenous ("push") factors, rather than country-specific evaluations, drive activity in global capital markets.[75] These exogenous factors include investors' attitudes regarding risk, changes in U.S. interest rates, and savings/investment rates in wealthy nations. When push factors dominate, the link between capital flows and government policy outcomes is more tenuous. In such periods, market participants might seek the high returns available in emerging markets and be willing to charge risk premia that are lower than economic fundamentals imply. Governments will be less constrained. And in periods of flight from emerging markets, the risk premia charged to governments far exceed those implied by economic fundamentals. In these situations, governments can do little to attract foreign capital.

Thus, there is a second type of variation in financial market influence—variation over time, rather than across countries. Often, the global market environment is normal, and pull factors dominate; governments' costs of borrowing depends on their policies, as well as on their country category. In other periods, however, push factors dominate, and the global market environment is characterized by a mania (risk acceptance) or a panic (risk aversion). In these market environments, developing countries find their access to capital to be either very easy (mania) or very difficult (panic). In the former, even nations with poor policies can access capital at low rates, and constraints are meager; in the latter, even nations with good policies have difficult in attracting investment. Therefore, we should observe variation in policy that is correlated with variation in global market sentiment. For instance, when global liquidity is high, we should observe more cross-national diversity among developing-nation policies. Ultimately, if we want to understand the means by which emerging market economies might ameliorate the influence of global capital markets, we should seek out causal explanations for changes in global attitudes regarding emerging markets. It is also useful to realize that, under most conditions, a combination of push and pull factors drives capital flows. While the overall amount of flows depends on push factors, the division of flows among nations likely is due to pull factors.[76]

Third, how stable are the groups to which investors assign nations? That is, under what conditions might investors change their assessments of a nation from "emerging market" to "developed," with the attendant reduction in attention toward default risk and micro-policy outcomes? As investors update their country categorizations,[77] are some governments able to gain greater autonomy vis-à-vis global capital markets? It appears that, as a result of their longer-term policy and institutional choices, nations can move across categories, from "emerging market" to "emerged" to "developed democracies" (or in the opposite direction), and these moves bring changes in financial market pressures. Investors' concerns about default risk in Portugal, for instance, were likely much more severe in the late 1970s and early 1980s than they were in the late 1990s, when Portugal had democratized and was on the verge of joining EMU.[78] Likewise, barring the Asian and Mexican financial crises, the newer members of the OECD (e.g., Mexico, South

Korea) might well have climbed into the southern tier of the "developed" category in the late 1990s. Of course, moving across categories—which would bring a reduction in financial market pressures—may first require many policy choices (for instance, central bank independence) that serve to reduce governments' policy-making autonomy. Ultimately, there might not be a way for developing nations to avoid financial market constraints that are relatively strong and relatively broad.

APPENDIX: COUNTRY TABLE

TABLE 4.4.
Nations included in Tables 4.2 and 4.3

| | Developing Nations† | | |
OECD Nations	Emerging Markets	Frontier Markets	Others
Australia	Argentina	Botswana	Azerbaijan*
Belgium	Brazil	Bulgaria	Bolivia*
Canada	Chile	Croatia	Costa Rica
Denmark	China	Ecuador	Dominican Republic
Finland	Colombia	Estonia	El Salvador
France	Czech Republic	Jamaica	Georgia
Germany	Egypt	Kenya	Moldova*
Ireland	Greece	Latvia	Mongolia*
Italy	Hungary	Lithuania	Uruguay*
Japan	India	Mauritius	
Netherlands	Indonesia	Ukraine	
New Zealand	Jordan		
Norway	Korea		
Portugal	Malaysia		
Spain	Mexico		
Sweden	Morocco		
United Kingdom	Peru		
	Philippines		
	Poland		
	Russia		
	Slovakia		
	South Africa		
	Sri Lanka		
	Thailand		
	Zimbabwe		

†Additional developing nations are categorized as emerging and frontier but are excluded due to lack of data: Armenia, Bangladesh, Belize, Côte d'Ivoire, Ghana, Israel, Lebanon, Namibia, Pakistan, Romania, Slovenia, Taiwan, Trinidad and Tobago, Tunisia, Turkey, and Venezuela.

*Included in some IFC/S&P's indexing but not part of the frontier/emerging categories.

NOTES

I thank Michael Wallerstein for comments on an earlier version of this chapter, and Mariana Sousa for research assistance.

1. Interview with fund manager, October 1998, London.

2. The same can be said of the German and Swedish elections in 1998. See Mosley (2003a), ch. 3.

3. Data on German, Swedish, and U.S. benchmark bond rates are from Global Financial Data.

4. Interest rate spreads on Brazilian government bonds fell dramatically later in 2003; by early 2004, spreads were close to 4 percent. Investors attributed the fall to Lula's adherence to fiscal austerity and inflation control, as well as to general enthusiasm about Latin American emerging markets (*Economist*, February 4, 2004; *The Banker*, March 1, 2004).

5. For reviews of this literature, see Cohen (1996); Garrett (2001); and Mosley (2003a).

6. For examples and summaries of convergence arguments, see Andrews (1994); Garrett (1998); Garrett and Mitchell (2001); Germain (1997); and Strange (1996).

7. See Clayton and Pontusson (1998); Esping-Andersen (1996); Huber and Stephens (2001); Pierson (1994, 1996); and Tanzi and Schuknecht (2000).

8. Hirschman (1970). See also Cerny (1995); for similar views from policymakers, see James Carville, quoted in *Economist* (October 7, 1995, p. S3); and Reich (1997: p. 64).

9. Garrett (2000); Pierson (2001); and Quinn (1997).

10. Simmons (1999); Tanzi and Schuknecht (2000).

11. Obstfeld (1998). Likewise, Mueller (1998) suggests that, with international factor mobility, governments' ability to impose involuntary redistribution is curtailed sharply.

12. Tiebout (1956). Also see Hall and Soskice (2001); Huber and Stephens (2001); Kitschelt et al. (1999); Mueller (1998); and Pierson (2001).

13. See Adserá and Boix (2002); Garrett (1998); Garrett and Mitchell (2001); Mueller (1998); Notermans (2000); and Rodrik (1997).

14. Garrett and Mitchell (2001); Hallerberg and Basinger (1998); Huber and Stephens (2001); Oatley (1999); Quinn (1997); Scruggs and Lange (2002); and Swank (1998, 2002). Allan and Scruggs (2004) point out, however, that using programmatic qualities of welfare states (replacement rates, coverage ratios) rather than spending data paints a different picture. In their analyses, the welfare state is affected by global financial markets as well as by government partisanship, and some retrenchment has occurred.

15. Clark and Hallerberg (2000); Huber and Stephens (2001); and Oatley (1999).

16. On social security policies, see Brooks (2002). Rudra (2002) investigates the correlates of welfare spending in the developing world.

17. Also see Cohen (1996: 283–84).

18. For a more detailed discussion of this model, see Mosley (2003a).

19. See Mosley (2003a: ch. 4). For a classic treatment of default in economics, see Grossman and Stiglitz (1980).

20. The use of similar indicators also relates the propensity for herd behavior in international capital markets. See Mosley (2003a: chs. 2 and 3).

21. This concept of active acquisition of knowledge differs somewhat from a Bayesian approach, which would suggest that market participants passively receive information and then use the information to update their prior beliefs. See Lupia and McCubbins (1998); Eichengreen and Mody (2000); and Rubinstein (1998).

22. Erb et al. (1999). Calvo and Mendoza (2000a, 2000b) likewise note that international capital market openness increases the volume of available information, and therefore the costs of information processing.

23. Some claim that a reliance on a limited set of indicators also may lead to herd behavior, particularly when investors rely on news events or the behavior of other investors as information shortcuts.

24. Sobel (1999). On liquidity risk in emerging markets, see OECD (2002: 200–201).

25. Simon (1982).

26. See Mosley (2003a: ch. 3).

27. The *Financial Times* (September 24, 2002, p. 14) notes that the amount of sovereign defaults nearly doubled in (2002), and it is expected to increase again in (2003).

28. Sobel (1999). On the effects of regime instability on investment, see Przeworski et al. (2000).

29. See Mosley (2003a: ch. 6).

30. In addition, International Monetary Fund (IMF) programs can serve as "seals of approval" for private investors. The IMF, however, may not always enforce its programs, particularly when dealing with politically important borrowers (see Stone 2002). Another means by which investors can deal with informational concerns is to rely on international data standards (see Mosley 2003b).

31. IMF Survey (October 20, 1997, p. 328).

32. On costly signals and audience costs, see Fearon (1994) and Morrow (1994, 1999). See also Stokes (2001), who suggests that orthodox governments are more inclined than heterodox governments to switch to more market-friendly policies, as doing so sends a more credible signal to markets.

33. See also Calvo and Mendoza (2000b).

34. See Mosley (2000, 2003a).

35. Pierson (2001: 82). These stresses include the shift from manufacturing-oriented to service-oriented economies; changing demographic and family structures; and the maturation of welfare states. See also Garrett (1998); and Huber and Stephens (2001).

36. Armijo (1999); Garrett (2001).

37. IMF (1998: 23).

38. For example, Balkan (1992); Edwards (1986).

39. IMF (2001). Also see Min (1998).

40. Also see Armijo (1999); Grabel (1996); Haley (1999); Maxfield (1997); and Summers (2000).

41. This section draws on interviews with market participants conducted in London during October (1998). A full list of interview subjects' firms and dates of interviews is available from the author.

42. Also see *New York Times* (September 29, 1999, sect. C, p. 4).

43. Predictability is often more important than the form of government to market participants. Several point out that stability of policy is more important than the degree of democracy. See Armijo (1999); Mahon (1996).

44. Interviews 52, 53, 56, 57.

45. Interview 59.

46. *Financial Times* (November 24, 1998, p. 6; November 16, 1998, p. 28; November 10, 1998, p. 20).

47. Also see Summers (2000).

48. Ratings are based on data from CBS MarketWatch; several categories of mutual funds—including International, Global, and Emerging Market—were used to compile the survey pool.

49. Data are from the April 2000 release of the Principia CD-ROM. The fund categories of International Hybrid, Diversified Emerging Markets, Asia/Pacific Stock, Foreign Stock, World Stock, Latin America Stock, and Europe Stock were used.

50. This reduced the May sample size to 161 and the July sample size to 432.

51. On the general problem of survey nonresponse in political science, see Brehm (1993).

52. There is very little difference in fund size between the May and July survey groups; the average size for May respondents is $1.09 billion and the average for July respondents is $1.05 billion.

53. The categories used by Principia are slightly different than those used in the survey. The geographic breakdown is United States and Canada (10 percent), Europe (40 percent), Japan (15 percent), Asia-Pacific (16 percent), Latin America (6 percent), and others (3 percent). The breakdown between developed and emerging in Principia is 73 percent and 25 percent, with 2 percent of assets coded as "N/A."

54. For survey results that address information issues, see Mosley (2003b).

55. IMF (1998, 1999); World Bank (2000).

56. IMF (1998); Keefer and Knack (1997); and Sinclair (1994).

57. This discussion is based on the methodologies employed by Standard and Poor's, Institutional Investor, and Euromoney. For more detail, see Mosley (2003b: ch. 4) as well as Sobel (1999).

58. Ul Haque et al. (1997).

59. Interview, Director, IBCA (January 13, 1997); Sinclair (1994).

60. Standard and Poor's (March 27, 1995).

61. Standard and Poor's (August 1992).

62. IMF (1999); *IMF Survey* (August 17, 1998, pp. 259–60).

63. Information in this paragraph is based on credit ratings from Euromoney, Institutional Investor, and Standard and Poor's, for the mid- to late 1990s. Also see Calvo and Mendoza (2000b); Mosley (2003b); and Sobel (1999).

64. Country classifications rely on those generated by the International Finance Corporation's Emerging Markets Database, and are found in the appendix. See also www.spglobal/com/method.pdf.

65. *IMF Survey* (February 23, 1998, p. 52).

66. The LIBOR spread reflects the differences in risk between loans in national markets and low-risk interbank, dollar-denominated loans.

67. Cross-sectional time series models are estimated using generalized least squares, with a correction for AR(1) autocorrelation and heteroskedastic error variance across panels.

68. Data are taken from the World Development Indicators 2002. The exchange rate measure is from Reinhart and Rogoff (2002); it classifies exchange rates along a zero to fif-

teen scale, with zero connoting fully fixed, and fifteen assigned to fully floating regimes. The capital openness measure is taken from Brune et al. (2001); it ranges from zero (closed capital accounts) to nine (open capital accounts), and is an average measure for the 1990s.

69. Negative numbers indicate deficits, and so the negative coefficient implies higher rates with deficits, and lower rates with surpluses.

70. For a history of the SDDS and a discussion of its effectiveness, see Mosley (2003b).

71. Because of collinearity, model 4 does not include the SDDS subscription variable.

72. When the SDDS dummy variable is included in these models, the coefficient remains negative but is statistically insignificant.

73. For the 1990–2000 period, average spending on wages is 13.1 percent of expenditure in OECD nations, 19.9 percent of expenditure in emerging markets, and 22.7 percent of expenditure in frontier markets.

74. For a more detailed discussion of the domestic political side of financial market–government relations, see Mosley (2003a: ch. 5).

75. For example, Eichengreen and Mody (2000).

76. See also Mosley (2003a: ch. 4).

77. On Bayesian updating by investors, see Tomz (2001).

78. For a discussion of how EMU changes government-financial market relations, see Mosley (2004).

References

Adserá, Aliciá, and Carles Boix. 2002. "Trade, Democracy and the Size of the Public Sector: The Political Underpinnings of Openness." *International Organization* 56: 229–62.

Allan, James P., and Lyle Scruggs. 2004. "Political Partisanship and Welfare State Reform in Advanced Industrial Societies." *American Journal of Political Science* 48: 493–512.

Andrews, David M. 1994. "Capital Mobility and State Autonomy: Toward a Structural Theory of International Monetary Relations." *International Studies Quarterly* 38: 193–218.

Armijo, Leslie Ann, ed. 1999. *Financial Globalization and Democracy in Emerging Markets*. New York: St. Martin's.

Balkan, Errol M. 1992. "Political Instability, Country Risk and Probability of Default." *Applied Economics* 24: 999–1008.

Brehm, John. 1993. *The Phantom Respondents: Opinion Surveys and Political Representation*. Ann Arbor: University of Michigan Press.

Brooks, Sarah M. 2002. "Social Protection and Economic Integration: The Politics of Pension Reform in an Era of Capital Mobility." *Comparative Political Studies* 35 (5): 491–525.

Brune, Nancy, Geoffrey Garrett, Alexandra Guisinger, and Jason Sorens. 2001. "The Political Economy of Capital Account Liberalization." Paper prepared for the annual meeting of the American Political Science Association, San Francisco, August 30–September 2.

Calvo, Guillermo A., and Enrique G. Mendoza. 2000a. "Capital-Markets Crises and
    Economic Collapse in Emerging Markets: An Informational-Frictions Approach."
    American Economic Review 90: 59–64.
———. 2000b. "Rational Herd Behavior and the Globalization of Securities Markets,"
    Journal of International Economics 51 (1): 79–113.
Cerny, Philip G. 1995. "Globalization and the Changing Logic of Collective Action."
    International Organization 49: 595–626.
Clark, William Roberts, and Mark C. Hallerberg. 2000. "Mobile Capital, Domestic Insti-
    tutions and Electorally Induced Monetary and Fiscal Policy." *American Political Science
    Review* 94: 323–46.
Clayton, Richard, and Jonas Pontusson. 1998. "Welfare State Retrenchment Revisited:
    Entitlement Cuts, Public Sector Restructuring and Inegalitarian Trends in Advanced
    Capitalist Societies." *World Politics* 51: 67–98.
Cohen, Benjamin. 1996. "Phoenix Risen: The Resurrection of Global Finance." *World
    Politics* 48: 268–96.
Edwards, Sebastian. 1986. "The Pricing of Bonds and Bank Loans in International
    Markets." *European Economic Review* 30: 565–89.
Eichengreen, Barry, and Ashoka Mody. 2000. "What Explains Changing Spreads on
    Emerging-Market Debt: Fundamentals or Market Sentiment?" In Sebastian Edwards
    (ed.), *The Economics of International Capital Flows.* Chicago: University of Chicago
    Press.
Erb, Claude B., Campbell R. Harvey, and Tadas E. Viskanta. 1999. "A New
    Perspective on Emerging Market Bonds." *Journal of Portfolio Management,*
    pp. 83–92.
Esping-Andersen, Gøsta. 1996. *Welfare States in Transition: National Adaptations in
    Global Economies.* London: Sage, UN Research Institute for Social Development.
Fearon, James D. 1994. "Domestic Political Audiences and the Escalation of Interna-
    tional Disputes." *American Political Science Review* 88: 577–92.
Garrett, Geoffrey. 1998. *Partisan Politics in the Global Economy.* New York: Cambridge
    University Press.
———. 2000. "The Causes of Globalization." *Comparative Political Studies* 33: 941–91.
———. 2001. "Globalization and Government Spending Around the World." *Studies in
    Comparative International Development* 35 (4): 3–29.
Garrett, Geoffrey, and Deborah Mitchell. 2001. "Globalization and the Welfare State."
    European Journal of Political Research 39(2): 145–77.
Germain, Randall. 1997. *The International Organization of Credit: State and Global
    Finance in the World Economy.* Cambridge: Cambridge University Press.
Grabel, Ilene. 1996. "Marketing the Third World: Contradictions of Portfolio Investment
    in the Global Economy." *World Development* 24: 1761–76.
Grossman, Sanford J., and Joseph E. Stiglitz. 1980. "On the Impossibility of Informa-
    tionally Efficient Markets." *American Economic Review* 70: 393–408.
Haley, Mary Ann. 1999. "Emerging Market Makers: The Power of Institutional
    Investors." Pp. 74–89 in Leslie Ann Armijo (ed.), *Financial Globalization and
    Democracy in Emerging Markets.* New York: St. Martin's.
Hall, Peter, and David Soskice, eds. 2001. *Varieties of Capitalism: The Institutional
    Foundations of Comparative Advantage.* Oxford: Oxford University Press.

Hallerberg, Mark, and Scott Basinger. 1998. "Internationalization and Changes in Tax Policy in OECD Countries: The Importance of Domestic Veto Players." *Comparative Political Studies* 31: 321–53.

Hirschman, Albert. 1970. *Exit, Voice, and Loyalty.* Cambridge: MIT Press.

Huber, Evelyne, and John D. Stephens. 2001. *Development and Crisis of the Welfare State: Parties and Policies in Global Markets.* Chicago: University of Chicago Press.

International Monetary Fund (IMF). 1998. *International Capital Markets: Developments, Prospects, and Key Policy Issues* (September). Washington, D.C.: International Monetary Fund.

———. 1999. *International Capital Markets: Developments, Prospects, and Key Policy Issues* (September). Washington, D.C.: International Monetary Fund.

———. 2001. "Guidelines for Public Debt Management." Prepared by the staffs of the International Monetary Fund and the World Bank.

Keefer, Philip, and Stephen Knack. 1997. "Why Don't Poor Countries Catch Up? A Cross-National Test of an Institutional Explanation." *Economic Inquiry* 35: 590–602.

Kitschelt, Herbert, Peter Lange, Gary Marks, and John Stephens, eds. 1999. *Continuity and Change in Contemporary Capitalism.* Cambridge: Cambridge University Press.

Lupia, Arthur, and Mathew D. McCubbins. 1998. *The Democratic Dilemma: Can Citizens Learn What They Need to Know?* Cambridge: Cambridge University Press.

Mahon, James E., Jr. 1996. *Mobile Capital and Latin American Development.* University Park: Penn State University Press.

Maxfield, Sylvia. 1997. *Gatekeepers of Growth.* Princeton: Princeton University Press.

Min, Hong G. 1998. "Determinants of Emerging Market Bond Spread: Do Economic Fundamentals Matter?" World Bank Country Economics Department Paper no. 1899.

Morrow, James D. 1994. *Game Theory for Political Scientists.* Princeton: Princeton University Press.

———. 1999. "The Strategic Setting of Choices: Signaling, Commitment, and Negotiation in International Politics." Pp. 77–114 in David A. Lake and Robert Powell (eds), *Strategic Choice and International Relations.* Princeton: Princeton University Press.

Mosley, Layna. 2000. "Room to Move: International Financial Markets and National Welfare States." *International Organization* 54: 737–73.

———. 2003a. *Global Capital and National Governments.* Cambridge: Cambridge University Press.

———. 2003b. "Attempting Global Standards: National Governments, International Finance, and the IMF's Data Regime." *Review of International Political Economy* 10 (2): 332–63.

———. 2004. "Government-Financial Market Relations after EMU," *European Union Politics* 5 (2): 181–209.

Mueller, Dennis 1998. "Constitutional Constraints on Governments in a Global Economy." *Constitutional Political Economy* 9: 171–86.

Notermans, Ton. 2000. *Money, Markets and the State: Social Democratic Economic Policies since 1918.* Cambridge: Cambridge University Press.

Oatley, Thomas. 1999. "How Constraining Is Capital Mobility? The Partisan Hypothesis in an Open Economy." *American Journal of Political Science* 43: 1003–27.

Obstfeld, Maurice. 1998. "The Global Capital Market: Benefactor or Menace?" *Journal of Economic Perspectives* 12: 9–30.

OECD. 2002. *OECD Public Debt Markets: Trends and Recent Structural Changes.* Paris: OECD.

Pierson, Paul. 1994. *Dismantling the Welfare State? Reagan, Thatcher and the Politics of Retrenchment.* Cambridge: Cambridge University Press.

——. 1996. "The New Politics of the Welfare State." *World Politics* 48: 143–79.

——. 2001. *The New Politics of the Welfare State.* Oxford: Oxford University Press.

Przeworski, Adam, Michael Alvarez, Jose Antonio Cheibub, and Fernando Limongi. 2000. *Democracy and Development: Political Institutions and Well-Being in the World, 1950–1990.* Cambridge: Cambridge University Press.

Quinn, Dennis. 1997. "The Correlates of Change in International Financial Regulation." *American Political Science Review* 91: 531–51.

Reich, Robert B. 1997. *Locked in the Cabinet.* New York: Knopf.

Reinhart, Carmen, and Kenneth Rogoff. 2002. "The Modern History of Exchange Rate Arrangements: A Reinterpretation." NBER Working Paper no. 8963.

Rodrik, Dani. 1997. *Has Globalization Gone too Far?* Washington, D.C.: Institute for International Economics.

Rubinstein, Ariel. 1998. *Modeling Bounded Rationality.* Cambridge: MIT Press.

Rudra, Nita. 2002. "Globalization and the Decline of the Welfare State in Less Developed Countries." *International Organization* 56: 411–45.

Scruggs, Lyle, and Peter Lange. 2002. "Where Have All the Members Gone?: Globalization and National Labor Market Institutions." *Journal of Politics* 64: 126–53.

Simmons, Beth. 1999. "The Internationalization of Capital." Pp. 36–69 in Kitschelt et al. (eds.), *Continuity and Change in Contemporary Capitalism.* Cambridge: Cambridge University Press.

Simon, Herbert A. 1982. *Models of Bounded Rationality.* Cambridge: MIT Press.

Sinclair, Timothy. 1994. "Between State and Market: Hegemony and Institutions of Collective Action under Conditions of International Capital Mobility," *Policy Sciences* 27: 447–66.

Sobel, Andrew. 1999. *State Institutions, Private Incentives, Global Capital.* Ann Arbor: University of Michigan Press.

Stokes, Susan C. 2001. *Mandates and Democracy: Neoliberalism by Surprise in Latin America.* Cambridge: Cambridge University Press.

Stone, Randall. 2002. *Lending Credibility: The International Monetary Fund and the Post-Communist Transition.* Princeton: Princeton University Press.

Strange, Susan. 1996. *The Retreat of the State: The Diffusion of Power in the World Economy.* New York: Cambridge University Press.

Summers, Lawrence. 2000. "International Financial Crises: Causes, Prevention and Cures." *American Economic Review* 90: 1–16.

Swank, Duane. 1998. "Funding the Welfare State: Global Taxation of Business in Advanced Market Economies." *Political Studies* 46: 671–92.

——. 2002. *Global Capital, Political Institutions, and Policy Change in Developed Welfare States.* Cambridge: Cambridge University Press.

Tanzi, Vito, and Ludger Schuknecht. 2000. *Public Spending in the 20th Century: A Global Perspective.* Cambridge: Cambridge University Press.

Tiebout, C. 1956. "A Pure Theory of Local Expenditures." *Journal of Political Economy* 64: 416–24.

Tomz, Michael. 2001. "Sovereign Debt and International Cooperation: Reputational Reasons for Lending and Repayment." Ph.D. diss., Department of Government, Harvard University.

Ul Haque, Nadeem, Donald Mathieson, and Nelson Mark. 1997. "Rating the Raters of Country Creditworthiness." *Finance and Development*, pp. 10–13.

World Bank. 2000. *Global Development Finance.* Washington, D.C.: World Bank.

CHAPTER 5

Egalitarian Redistribution in Globally Integrated Economies

Samuel Bowles

A REDUCTION OF IMPEDIMENTS to international flows of goods, capital, and professional labor is widely thought to raise the economic costs of programs by the nation-state (and labor unions) to redistribute income to the poor and to provide economic security. Many think that globalization has made these policies at best ineffective and at worst counterproductive, leading to losses in employment and income among the least well off. Over the years, I have encountered these arguments in public and private *fora* among trade unionists (leaders and rank and file) in South Africa, Italy, Canada, and the United States, and in these countries and elsewhere among policymakers and political activists with egalitarian inclinations.

But are their fears misplaced? Some of the more politically and economically successful redistributive policies—for example Nordic social democracy and East Asian land reform—have been implemented in small open economies that would, according to this account, seem to provide a prohibitive environment for egalitarian interventions.[1] Other cases of open-economy egalitarianism include the Costa Rican welfare state, egalitarian distribution of health services and nutrition in Sri Lanka, wage compression in Singapore, and the public health policies' consequent dramatic reduction in infant mortality under the socialist government of the Seychelles Republic.[2]

Particularly striking are the cases of two Indian states, Kerala and West Bengal. Goods and factors of production move freely across their boundaries, and their state governments have limited control over the legal and fiscal environment of their state economies. But investments in health, schooling, and other human capacities in Kerala and land tenure reform in both states (especially West Bengal) have substantially redistributed income and improved the well-being of the poor. The leftist governments credited with these policies have been repeatedly returned to office in democratic elections.[3]

As even this brief description of cases of relatively successful egalitarian redistribution suggests, the reasons for the policies, as well as their design and the mechanisms by which they worked have differed substantially. Some owe their existence to electoral competition in polities with substantial majorities of poor voters; others have been implemented to forestall populist political successes. Each case exhibits serious shortcomings; but I will not dwell on these as my objective is not to elevate them as models. My point is more modest: unless the cases are entirely idiosyncratic, they suggest that the commonplace opposition between globalization and egalitarianism may be overdrawn.

In the following pages I present a model of globalization and redistribution seeking to answer this question: *in a globalized world economy, what programs of egalitarian redistribution and social insurance are implementable by democratic national states acting independently?*[4] An implementable program is one that is be economically and politically sustainable, that is, not likely to be undone either by the electorate or by private exchange.[5]

My response, drawing on recent work of many authors, is that in the absence of international coordination, globalization indeed makes it difficult for national states to affect the relative (after tax) prices of mobile goods and factors of production, and for this and other reasons it might limit the effectiveness of some conventional strategies of redistribution. But globalization does not rule out all egalitarian interventions. There remains a large class of governmental and other collective interventions leading to substantial improvements in the wages, employment prospects, and economic security of the less well off. Included are redistributions of assets that are productivity enhancing, namely those that provide efficient solutions to incentive problems arising in principal agent relationships such as wage employment, farm and residential tenancy, and the provision of environmental and social public goods in local commons situations.[6]

The model I develop shows that these policies remain implementable in the sense described earlier, even in what may be termed a hyper-globalized world, namely one in which investment responds instantaneously to between-country differences in the expected after-tax profit rate. This is not the world we live in, nor is it even a plausible approximation thereof (Bordo, Taylor, and Williamson 2003; Glyn and Sutcliffe 1999; Taylor 2002). But given the widespread view that these aspects of globalization will thwart attempts at egalitarian redistribution, it is worth finding out if this is indeed the case, under admittedly extreme globalization assumptions. Whether the model illuminates real (if very long-term) tendencies operating in the world or, alternatively, is a more hypothetical exercise (how the world would work if it *were* like that) cannot be determined on the basis of existing empirical information.

In the next section I present a highly abstract model of a national economy embedded in a globally competitive environment. The subsequent section addresses a range of conventional state and trade union policy measures. I then turn to asset redistributions before concluding with a discussion of policies and institutions.

GLOBALIZATION

The model presented below seeks to illuminate the opportunities for egalitarian redistribution in a national economy integrated into a world economy that is characterized by minimal impediments to capital mobility among nations. To focus on the contribution of globalization per se to the leaky bucket problem (and because the problems constituted by corruption and other forms of governmental malfeasance and unaccountability are well known) I will assume that governments are not self-serving leviathans (as in the public choice literature) but rather seek to improve the living standards of the less well off.

Redistribution takes the form of increases in the living standards of a homogeneous class of workers, either by raising their income or improving their prospects of being employed. Its focus is not on inequality per se but on labor market outcomes affecting two important aspects of workers' well-being, jobs and pay. It abstracts from differences among workers, and much else of importance, but seeks to explore the ramifications of two important empirical regularities. The first is that investment relocates globally in response to differences in expected after-tax profit rates, and the second is that under a wide range of institutional conditions real wages vary with the level of employment.[7]

The basic assumptions of the model follow. All markets are perfectly competitive, but labor (which is homogeneous within countries) is not mobile between countries. The global economy is thus modeled as if it were a national economy with a single capital market but segmented labor markets. The difference, of course, is that each labor market segment is represented by an autonomous government. There is a single good which is both consumed and used as capital (corn is eaten and planted as seed). At the end of each period, after the payment of wages, wealth holders (those who own the corn surplus, if it exists) may either consume corn or allocate it as an investment good among many national economies in response to national differences in expected after-tax profit rates.

Actors differ by wealth level: the wealthy are risk neutral while those without assets (workers, both employed and unemployed) are risk averse. Neither work effort nor the promise to repay a loan is contractible, and so the interactions between employers and workers and between lenders and borrowers are principal-agent relationships. Employers use monitoring and the threat of dismissal to induce workers to provide satisfactory levels of effort. For this reason (and perhaps others), the equilibrium of the labor market in each national economy is characterized by involuntary unemployment. Thus labor suppliers are quantity constrained in labor markets. Lacking wealth, they are unable provide collateral or other means of attenuating the incompleteness of the credit contract, and so they are also quantity constrained in credit markets.

The competitive equilibria of this model for the single global markets in capital goods (corn) and credit support a common rate of expected after-tax profit rate and rate of time preference globally (both equal to the risk-free interest rate). By contrast, nation-specific institutions and cultures concerning labor relations, government policies, and the degree of security of property rights give rise to national differences in equilibrium wages and employment. There are thus $n + 1$ prices in this model: each of n nations' real wage (price of an hour of labor relative to the price of corn) and the global risk-free interest rate (price of goods now relative to goods later). As I will investigate just a single national economy, I will not give national subscripts to the relevant variables.

Because firms in a given country use a single production function and are otherwise identical, we can analyze production and wage-setting as if it took place in a single (competitive) firm. Total labor effort is the average effort level per hour, e, of those employees not engaged in monitoring (whom I term the "directly productive" workers) multiplied by their hours of work, $h(1 - m)$, where h is the total (productive and monitoring) hours of work and m is the fraction of total work time accounted for by the monitors. Aggregate output, Q, is total labor effort times average output per unit of effort, y, with a fixed capital (seed) requirement k per hour of labor. So

$$Q = yeh(1 - m) \quad \text{for } K \geq kh(1 - m) \tag{1}$$

$$= 0 \qquad \text{for } K < kh(1 - m).$$

I normalize national labor supply at unity (given exogenously); so $h \in [0,1]$ is both the level of employment and the employment rate. Effort is determined by workers in response to the incentives and sanctions devised by the employer. As these include monitoring and the threat of job termination, the worker's optimal effort choice varies inversely with his or her fallback position. This is the expected utility if employment is terminated and it depends on the expected duration of a spell of unemployment and the level of support conditional on being unemployed, b. Suppose effort may be either 1 (imposing a disutility of $\underline{a}$ on the worker) or 0, and that the probability of termination if $e = 0$ is τ. Then, with suitable simplifying assumptions, the wage that will just induce workers to choose $e = 1$ equates the expected utility of the two effort choices, which gives

$$w^* = b + \underline{a}\tau/(1 - h) \tag{2}$$

as the "no shirking wage."[8] Of course τ and $\underline{a}$ depend on the institutional structure governing labor relations (the costs to the employer of firing a nonworking employee, the perceived fairness of the wage determination process, the degree of effectiveness of the monitoring system, and the like). Along with $e = 1$, which it insures, (2) implements both the firms' and the employees' first-order conditions, describing the feasible combinations of w, h, and e; it is thus the *labor supply equilibrium condition*.

The model underlying equation (2) is quite particular, but it gives a convenient analytical form to the much more general empirical regularity mentioned earlier, namely $w_h > 0$, the variation of wages and the employment level.[9] (For simplicity I assume monitors are paid the same wage as other employees and I do not address the problem of their incentives to work.) An artifact of the simplicity of this model is that because employees do not shirk, they are not fired, and so bear no risk. There is therefore a group of $1 - h$ permanently unemployed.

Labor demand (and hence the level of unemployment) depends on the allocation of the global capital stock among national economies in response to differences in the expected after-tax profit rate. Recalling that the capital good is an intermediate input, the profit rate before tax is just

$$r = \{(y - k)h(1 - m) - wh\}/kh(1 - m),$$

or, expressed in per hour of employment (by eliminating h from the above expression), the profit rate is net output per hour of labor minus the wage rate, divided by the capital input required to employ an hour of labor. Suppose that to finance its activities the national government levies a linear tax, t, on profits so that the after-tax profit rate is

$$\pi = r(1 - t) = (1 - t)[(y - k)(1 - m) - w]/[k(1 - m)]. \tag{3}$$

Wealth-holders finance a project if its expected return exceeds their rate of time preference, which I will assume is globally equal to the return on some risk-free instrument, ρ. Projects are exposed to a risk of "confiscation" or other unexpected reduction in their value, the probability of which, $c \in [0, 1]$, varies among countries, reflecting national differences in macroeconomic policy, political stability, criminality, and the like. Suppose if a confiscation takes place, the return is zero in the period of the confiscation: wages are paid, but the expected costs of contestation occasioned by the confiscation exactly exhaust the profits. The expected profit rate is thus $\hat{\pi} = \pi(1 - c)$. Writing the insecurity premium, $\mu = 1/(1 - c)$, the national economy's level of corn investment is stationary if expected after-tax profit rates are equated across nations and are jointly equal to the risk-free interest rate ($\pi = \rho$) or:

$$\pi = \rho\mu \tag{4}$$

Because r is monotonically declining in w, there is just one wage rate that will satisfy (4). Using (3) to rewrite (4), we find that this wage, $\underline{w}$, is given by

$$\underline{w} = (1 - m)[y - k(1 + \rho\mu)/(1 - t)] \tag{5}$$

When (5) obtains, the level of the capital stock and, hence, employment are stationary. Thus (5) is the *equilibrium labor demand equation* (conditional on $e = 1$).[10]

Because $w^*(h)$ is monotonic, there is just one h consistent with $\underline{w}$. The general equilibrium of the national economy (taking ρ as exogenous) is defined by

$$w^* = \underline{w}, \tag{6}$$

satisfying the condition for stationarity of both the employment rate and the wage rate.[11] Their determination may be described as follows: the nation's specific institutions that influence the net after-tax productivity of labor and the risk premium determine the national wage rate consistent with optimizing by the owners

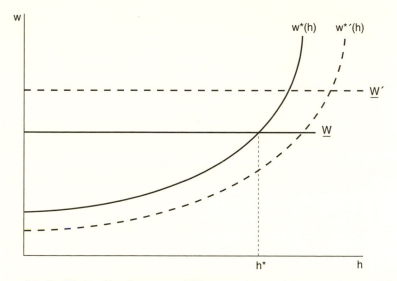

Figure 5.1. Equilibrium Employment and Wages in a National Economy. Note: $w^*(h)$ is the equilibrium labor supply function, while $\underline{w}$ is the equilibrium labor demand function. To the left of $w^*(h)$ wages fall, to the right of $w^*(h)$ wages rise. Above $\underline{w}$ the capital stock (and hence the demand for labor) increases; below $\underline{w}$ the capital stock decreases.

of mobile investment resources, and the nation's institutions concerning labor markets and work organization determine what national level of aggregate employment makes that wage consistent with individual optimizing by firms and workers. Figure 5.1 illustrates the equilibrium of this model for a given national economy. (Ignore the dashed lines for the moment.) Notice that for any wage less than w^*, $e = 0$, so $dh/dt < 0$ for $w < w^*$ or $w > \underline{w}$.

Finally, the global supply and demand for corn as an investment good together with the above conditions determine the risk-free interest rate, ρ. Suppose that in every country, production takes place according to the nationally specific versions of (6) and if, at the end of any given period, output net of wages, taxes, and confiscation losses is positive, then a given fraction of this sum is consumed by the wealthy. The remaining fraction, φ, is allocated to investment among national economies.[12] As capital (unlike labor) is not nationally specific, I assume φ is common across countries. At the end of each period, the corn output net of wages per unit invested is $[\pi(1 - c) + 1]$ and φ of this is supplied to the global stock of corn capital in the next period (by contrast, the supply of investment goods available in the country is infinitely elastic at the rate ρ). Call the amount $(\pi(1 - c) + 1)\varphi$ the corn surplus. Because in equilibrium $\pi(1 - c) = \rho$ in every country each country supplies an amount to next year's global capital stock equal to $[\rho + 1]\varphi$ for every unit of the current period's stock. The rate of growth of the world capital stock is thus $(\rho + 1)\varphi - 1$ or $\rho\varphi - (1 - \varphi)$.

The equilibrium global demand for investment goods is just the amount of corn necessary to provide the capital goods required by the employment of that fraction of each country's the labor force that is consistent with the zero profit condition—that given by (6). Thus market clearing (and stationarity of ρ) requires that the global corn surplus (the global supply of capital goods) grow at the same rate as the world labor supply, v. The ρ, which equates the growth rates of capital goods supply and labor supply, is given by

$$v = \rho\varphi - (1 - \varphi),$$

or

$$\rho = (v + 1)/\varphi - 1. \tag{7}$$

Countries with slower labor force growth will be permanent exporters of corn-capital and conversely. This is because excess supply of investment goods per unit of the current period capital stock (in a given country whose labor force is growing at the rate η) is

$$\Delta = \varphi(\pi(1 - c) + 1) - (1 + \eta). \tag{8}$$

The first term is the corn surplus available for investment per unit of the current period capital stock and the second is the increase in the capital stock required to sustain the equilibrium level of employment. Using (7) and the fact that $\pi(1 - c) = \rho$, we can see from (8) that $\Delta = v - \eta$. An implication is that when national labor forces all grow at the global average, in equilibrium all investment is domestically financed.[13]

To analyze the determination of global employment, notice that a common global ρ implies country-specific equilibrium labor demand functions, $\underline{w}_i(\rho)$, for each of the n national economies. Thus, given the n nation specific equilibrium labor supply functions, $w_i^*(h_i)$, the h_i's are determined as well. Express the dependence of each nation's employment level on the global risk-free interest rate as $h_i(\rho)$ with $h_i'(\rho) < 0$. So we may define global employment, $H(\rho)$, as the horizontal summation of the n nationally specific $h_i(\rho)$ functions, giving $H(\rho)$, with $H' < 0$, where the variation in world employment is simply that generated by varying ρ given the equilibrium condition (6).

Figure 5.2 illustrates the determination of global employment. In the following analysis of a single national economy, I treat ρ as exogenous.

INCREASING WAGES AND EMPLOYMENT

Where, as in figure 5.1, the equilibrium is unique and stable, the effect of country-specific policy interventions may be studied (as I will do presently) by a comparative static analysis of the displacement of the exogenous terms in $w^*(h)$ and $\underline{w}$. But the more complicated case of multiple equilibria (some of them un-

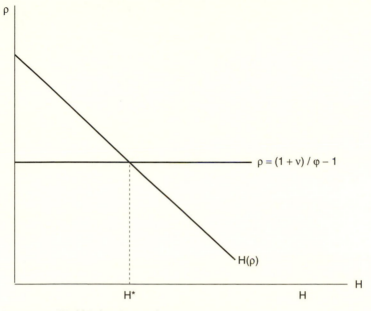

ρ

$\rho = (1 + v) / \varphi - 1$

H(ρ)

H*

H

H

Figure 5.2. World Labor Demand.

stable) cannot be ruled out, and they should be considered first. To see this, suppose that the confiscation probability c varies inversely with h—high levels of unemployment supporting a populist or criminal environment, for example—so $\mu = \mu(h)$ with $\mu' < 0$. Then $\underline{w}$ is increasing in h, which (because w^* is also increasing in h) means that there may exist many values of h equating the two.[14]

Figure 5.3. illustrates an upward-rising equilibrium labor demand function (ignore the dashed lines for the moment). There are two stable equilibria: a, the vicious circle of low employment, low wages, and high insecurity premium ("Nigeria") and a' the virtuous converse ("Taiwan"). The possibility of multiple stable equilibria enriches the policy analysis considerably, as it allows small one-time interventions to have permanent, non-marginal effects, and it provides a framework for analyzing possible divergent growth paths ("high road" vs. "low road" wage strategies, for example.) A one-time demand expansion, for example, pushing the employment level above the critical value h'' in figure 5.3 could permanently shift the equilibrium from the low wage/high insecurity poverty trap to its virtuous converse.

The impact of strategies to raise wages and employment may now be assessed through their curve-shifting effects in figures 5.1 or 5.3. For example, enhanced security of property rights, by reducing c (for any level of h), lowers μ, hence raises $\underline{w}$, and increases both h^* and w^*. This is illustrated by the dashed horizontal line in figure 5.1: its effect is an increase in both wages and employment. From

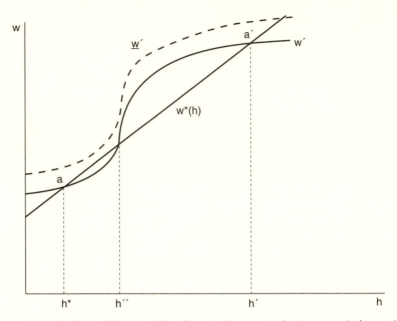

Figure 5.3. Multiple Equilibria Resulting from Endogenous Risk. Note: *a* and *a'* are stable equilibria.

figure 5.3, it can be seen that the upward shift in $\underline{w}(h)$ (the dashed line) might also eliminate the "low road" equilibrium, displacing a national economy previously entrapped there to a rapid transition to the "high road."

The effects of changes in labor relations and labor market structure are equally transparent. Efforts to protect workers from dismissal for cause by reducing τ through job protection strategies will shift the $w^*(h)$ function upward without affecting $\underline{w}$, leaving the wage rate unaffected but reducing employment. By contrast, reducing b, the magnitude of transfers whose availability is conditional on being out of work, has the opposite effect, indicated by the dashed $w^{*\prime}(h)$ function in figure 5.1. Unlike a reduction in τ, which reduces welfare, the welfare implications of an decrease in b are ambiguous, as it lowers the well-being of the least well off (the jobless), while reducing their numbers by increasing employment.

Trade unions may increase wages and/or employment in a number of ways, however (Bowles and Boyer 1990b). First, unions may draw on workers' private information concerning the performance of other workers to improve the disciplinary environment of the workplace (raising τ or lowering m). Second "union voice" effects (Freeman and Medoff 1984) may raise productivity and reduce the disutility of labor, (the latter would lower the $w(h)$ function, supporting a higher level of employment). Third, collective bargaining agreements to provide well-defined job ladders and security from cyclical job loss also provide greater incentives for firm-specific investments by workers (Pagano 1991.) Both union voice and specific investment effects shift $\underline{w}$ upwards and $w^*(h)$ to the right.[15] Fourth, negotiated incomes policies may lower or flatten the $w^*(h)$ function.[16] Finally, if $\underline{w}$ becomes accepted as a fairness norm—perhaps because it is the wage rate that will give the employer a rate of return equal to what other employers receive, or to the marginal disutility of foregoing current consumption—and if, as seems likely, perceived fairness is a determinant of work effort, the $w^*(h)$ function will flatten, thereby increasing the employment gains associated with upward shifts in $\underline{w}$ due to productivity gains. Because in equilibrium, no employee is working harder as a result of any of these changes, and because the unemployed prefer employment, the welfare gains associated with the implied trade union–induced increases in wages and or employment are unambiguous.

The effects of government expenditures and the efficiency of public service delivery may be explored in similar fashion. Suppose the productivity of a unit of effective labor y depends on λp, the effectiveness (λ) times the level (p) of public expenditure on productivity-enhancing complementary inputs (such as nutrition, health care, schooling, and infrastructure). Assume the government spends all of its tax revenues on some combination of p and b, the benefit paid to a worker when unemployed, giving the budget constraint (expressed as an equality).

$$b(1 - h) + p = th\{[(1 - m)y(\lambda p) - k] - w\} \tag{9}$$

From (9) it can be seen that the level of public expenditure p depends on the level of employment, for high levels of employment reduce tax revenues and increase the expenditures on unemployment benefits.

Thus for a given tax rate, there is a level of employment such that unemployment benefits exhaust the entire budget, and productivity per effective unit of labor is $y = y(0)$. Above this level of employment, productivity-enhancing public expenditures increase, which by (5) then require a higher wage to equilibrate the capital market, yielding the upward rising $\underline{w}$ function in figure 5.4. The also upward-rising $w^*(h)$ function (as drawn) intersects the equilibrium labor demand function twice, suggesting a possible high and low public investment divergence among nations.[17] Because for any level of h, $\underline{w}$ varies with λ and varies inversely with b, and because (as we have seen) decreasing b also shifts the $w^*(h)$ function to the right, it follows that reallocating expenditure from transfers conditioned on unemployment toward productivity-enhancing public investment will simultaneously raise the (stable) equilibrium wage and employment level.[18] It might appear that this change is unambiguously welfare enhancing, but a more realistic model in which the employed periodically lose their jobs would show that for sufficiently high levels of risk aversion among workers, the lost insurance would more than offset the higher expected wage.

Increases in productivity (y), whether due to public expenditure or exogenous technical change, shift $\underline{w}$ upward allowing increases in equilibrium employment. Differentiating (6) we see that the size of this employment effect depends criti-

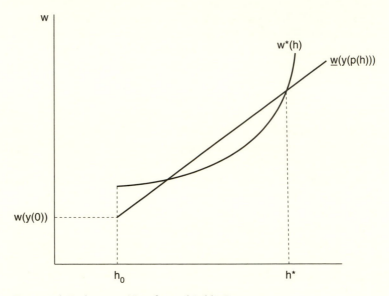

Figure 5.4. Endogenous Transfers and Public Investment.

cally on db/dy, the effect of the change in productivity on the fallback position of employed workers:

$$db/dy = \{(1 - m) - db/dy\}/w_b,$$ (10)

which has the same sign as its numerator, as we know that $w_b > 0$. Where productivity gains are shared with the unemployed through increases in b, and where monitoring levels are substantial, the upward shift in the equilibrium labor supply condition (2) entailed by the increased value of the unemployment benefit may even reverse the potential employment gains. There is thus a policy choice concerning the manner in which productivity increases should be shared with the unemployed: through expanding the number of jobs on the one hand, or by raising the average income of those remaining unemployed on the other.

As the examples in this section make clear, opportunities for raising wages and/or employment arise when allocative inefficiencies can be corrected either at minimal cost (as when union voice effects may attenuate the misalignment of incentives arising from the incomplete employment contract) or through expenditures on which the expected social rate of return exceeds ρ (as when credit constraints or other reasons induce workers to acquire inefficiently little schooling). The problems of credit constraints and incomplete contracts may also be addressed more directly by a redistribution of assets, or more precisely by a redistribution of the rights of residual claimancy and control commonly bundled with asset ownership, and by extending to the asset-poor the credit market and insurance opportunities of the wealthy.

Asset-Based Redistribution

Suppose at the beginning of each period, a national government borrows corn on the world market at the rate ρ, in turn lends it to teams of producers at the rate $\rho\mu$, who at the end of the period are equal residual claimants on the income of the team, after repaying the government an expected amount of $1 + \rho$ per unit of corn borrowed (accounting for confiscations occurring as before at the rate c.)[19] Assume that these co-ops adopt a labor discipline strategy similar to their erstwhile employers (dismissing nonperforming team mates). Co-ops are therefore constrained to offer members a level of income equivalent to $w^*(h)$ to deter shirking. (Because the producers now bear risk, the co-op must offer a certainty equivalent income equal to $w^*(h)$.) Work mates have private information on each others' work activities and, as residual claimants on the income of the team members, are motivated to participate in mutual monitoring, and so the monitoring costs of maintaining work effort will be reduced to $m^- < m$.[20] All other aspects of the model are as before.

The co-op's advantage of reduced monitoring may be more than offset by suboptimal risk-taking. The reason is that risk-averse members now control the production process and (relaxing the assumption of given production technologies) face a choice among production methods of varying risk and expected output. Recall that as employees, the producers bore no risk (they received a certain wage), but as residual claimants, they must bear risk, given that they are residual claimants on a stream of output which is subject to stochastic variation. For concreteness imagine that corn may be planted at various times, and the expected return and its variance depend on the planting date, with greater risk varying with higher expected returns over some range.

Suppose that expected output per hour of effective labor is $y(\sigma)$ where σ is the standard deviation of output and y is increasing and concave in its argument, reaching a maximum at σ^*. The risk-neutral employer of course selected σ^*, and so the analysis of the previous section assumed a level of expected productivity of $y = y(\sigma^*)$. Utility-maximizing risk-averse co-op members will select some level of $\sigma^- < \sigma^*$ and hence generate a level of expected income $y(\sigma^-) < y(\sigma^*)$. Co-op members are thus residual claimants on the lesser income stream generated by this lesser level of risk taking and, using (5), have an expected income of

$$\omega = (1 - m^-)\{y(\sigma) - k(1 + \rho\mu)/(1 - t)\} \tag{11}$$

Of course the expected value of their residual income $\omega(y(\sigma^-))$ may nonetheless exceed the $\underline{w}$ possible under wage employment, depending on the magnitude of the monitoring savings relative to the reduced expected income occasioned by suboptimal risk taking. But what matters for them is a comparison of the certain income $\underline{w}$ in wage employment with the certainty-equivalent income associated with the co-op's risky income stream, namely $\underline{\omega}(y(\sigma^-), \sigma^-)$.[21]

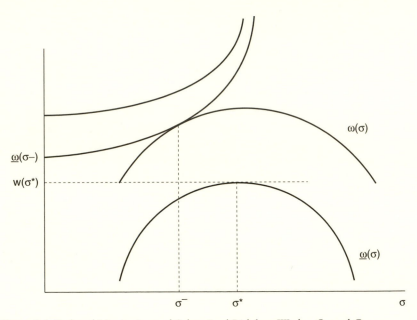

Figure 5.5. Reduced Monitoring and Suboptimal Risk by a Worker-Owned Co-op.

To define the members' certainty-equivalent income, I assume the disturbances in the income stream of the co-op are such that one can represent the utility function of the risk-averse members simply as

$$u = u(\omega, \sigma), \tag{12}$$

where ω is a "good" and σ is a "bad." Figure 5.5 illustrates two of the implied family of indifference loci.[22] The figure also indicates the capital-market clearing wage rate, $\underline{w}$ defined as before by (5), and the expected residual claim of the co-op member $\omega(\sigma)$; the latter, using (5) and (11), is given by

$$\omega(\sigma) = \underline{w}(\sigma)(1 - m^-)/(1 - m).$$

Risk-neutral indifference loci are flat of course, which is why the erstwhile employer selected σ^*. The vertical intercept of an indifference locus is the certainty equivalent of each point making up the locus, so $\hat{\omega}(y(\sigma^-), \sigma^-)$, for example, is the certainty equivalent income of the expected income and risk level resulting from the co-op's choice of σ^-.

For this example, $\hat{\omega}(\sigma^-) > \underline{w}(\sigma^*)$—producers' certainty equivalent income would be raised by the formation of co-ops—and for this reason co-ops would proliferate, and wage employment would be eliminated.

As figure 5.6 shows, the level of joblessness would fall as a result, though not more than h^- producers can belong to co-op work teams as the $1 - h^-$ jobless are

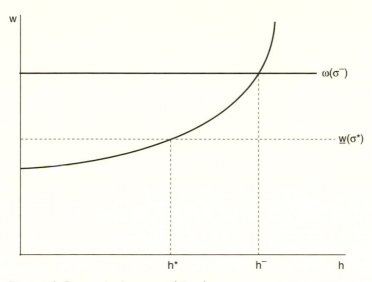

Figure 5.6. Cooperative Income and Employment.

required to sustain the no-shirking condition at the certainty-equivalent income consistent with the stationarity of the country's capital stock. If, by contrast, $\hat{\omega}(\sigma^-) < \underline{w}(\sigma^*)$, then of course producers would not accept the government loans, and co-ops would not form.

Suppose, however, that as in figure 5.5 the co-op is advantageous to the producers; why was the government's intervention required to allow their formation? The obvious answer—that the asset-less producers were precluded from borrowing at economically viable rates of interest—raises a more difficult question. If, as this answer implies, the wealthless producers' subjective cost of postponing current consumption exceeds $\rho\mu$, why would they not prefer to use the government loan for consumption purposes? They would; so a successful loan program would have to embody an enforceable provision restricting the use of the corn to planting rather than eating. But as we will see, this administrative difficulty is an artifact of the simplicity of the model.

Bardhan, Bowles, and Gintis (2000) show that a transfer of an asset (rather than a loan) mandated by the government may induce the producer to hold the asset and use it productively even in those cases in which the transfer of property rights could not have occurred through private contracting. This implies, of course, that both the ex ante and the ex post distribution of property rights are Nash equilibria. There are two reasons why this is possible. Both stem from the fact that the asset transfer alters the opportunities and constraints of the producer, with the ex post situation supporting use of the asset by the producer while the ex ante situation is precluding it.

First, changing the wealth status of the producer also changes his or her credit market status (and hence subjective cost of delaying consumption), increased wealth thus lowering the subjective cost of capital. And second, increased wealth may plausibly reduce the degree of risk aversion, so that while the choice of σ by a wealthless producer (say, renting the asset or using borrowed funds) might have precluded the project being viable, the (riskier and higher expected return) choice of the same producer with increased wealth (as owner of the asset) may be viable.[23] For this reason a one-time mandated redistribution of wealth—making the producers owners and residual claimants—may be sustainable in competitive equilibrium and thus have permanent effects.[24]

Whether the peer-monitoring advantages of the co-op will outweigh its risk avoidance will of course depend, among other things, on the policy environment. More adequate insurance may induce risk-averse producers to choose a higher level of σ (effectively rotating the indifference loci in figure 5.5 clockwise, (Bardhan, Bowles, and Gintis 2000). Such insurance policies may protect the producer against risk unassociated with the production process (health insurance, insurance against exogenous variation on housing wealth) or against those sources of variability in the income stream of the production process that are observable and not affected by the actions of the producer (for example, macroeconomic stabilization or weather-based crop insurance [Shiller 1993]. Because these insurance policies may be self-financing (fair), the gains to producers constitute Pareto-improvements and the range of egalitarian redistribution of residual claimancy and control of assets (through loans or outright transfers) that is consistent with global competitive equilibrium is expanded.

Egalitarian asset redistribution may have other productivity-enhancing effects, for example, in supporting more effective governance institutions in communities and firms, and at the national level, and in promoting a more growth-inducing structure of human capital accumulation.[25]

POLICIES

Of course, actual governments and trade unions may fail to implement efficient redistributions for a variety of well-known reasons. But on the basis of the above reasoning, there appears to be ample scope for the implementation of policies capable of raising wages, employment levels, and living standards of the less well-off owners of globally immobile factors of production, even in the empirically unlikely world of hyper-globalization posited in the model. It seems likely that substantial majorities of the relevant populations would benefit from these policies, and so the policies might be sustainable in democratic polities.

That these objectives can be furthered by nation-states acting singly is suggested by the dramatic national differences in real wage growth that have been sustained over long periods. Figure 5.7 presents data on real manufacturing wage

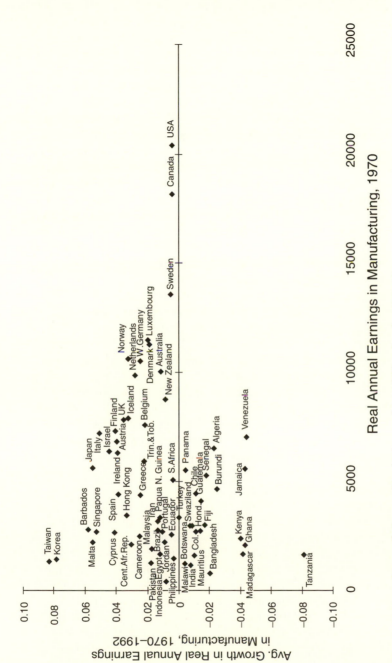

Figure 5.7. Annual Rate of Change of Real Wages and Initial Wage Levels, 1970–92.

growth over a twenty-two-year period.[26] Even taking account of the possible importance of productivity catch-up effects (by comparing national economies initially at the same wage level), one finds extraordinary differences: the *annual* rate
of change of real wage was 16 percentage points higher in Taiwan and S. Korea
than in Tanzania, and 10 percentage points higher in Barbados and Italy than in
Jamaica and Venezuela. Some of the high-wage growth economies have also experienced very rapid employment growth.

Figure 5.8 confirms what one would expect—that wage growth is closely tied
to productivity growth; but even for economies experiencing similar rates of increase in manufacturing value added per worker, the differences in wage growth
are substantial. Productivity in Indonesia grew at the same rate as in Italy, for example, but wages grew over 5 percent faster per annum in the latter. While many
of the differences are due to idiosyncratic events and circumstances—the differing impacts of the two oil shocks, for example—national contrasts of this magnitude suggest that institutional and policy choices do matter, even for small open
economies (this is consistent with the fact that economies in which wages exceeded $10,000 in 1972, and which shared broadly similar institutions, experi-
enced far less variability in subsequent wage growth).

We know remarkably little about which institutions and policies account for
the success stories. A common opinion in some policy circles is that strong
unions and substantial redistributive programs are counterproductive in attempting to raise living standards of the less well off. The reasoning behind this view is
that these institutions favor the egalitarian division of the pie, rather than more
promising long-term strategies of rapid growth in investment and average income. Examples confirming this reasoning are all too easy to produce.

But this view finds little support in the above data. Indeed a long historical
perspective suggests the opposite: as figure 5.9 shows, the golden age of the welfare state and of trade unionism in the advanced economies witnessed by far the
most rapid rates of growth of income per capita and investment in the history of
capitalism.[27] In most countries, the improvement of living standards of the less
well off was correspondingly rapid.

The model presented here and the empirical evidence suggests three ways that
egalitarian redistribution in open-economy settings may have succeeded. The first
is by increasing productivity (or certainty-equivalent income, where risk-bearing
is involved). Examples include the East Asian asset redistributions and the Nordic
(especially Swedish) and Singaporean policy of eliminating wage disparities
among similar workers, thus putting competitive pressure on low-productivity
firms and sectors and driving resources into higher-productivity uses.

The second is improving the labor discipline environment and thereby reducing
monitoring costs and shifting the equilibrium labor supply condition to the right.
Examples include the effect of wage increases on the disutility of effort (through
the fair wage effect), trade union and work team participation in monitoring, and
the effect of centralized wage bargaining on flattening the labor supply function.

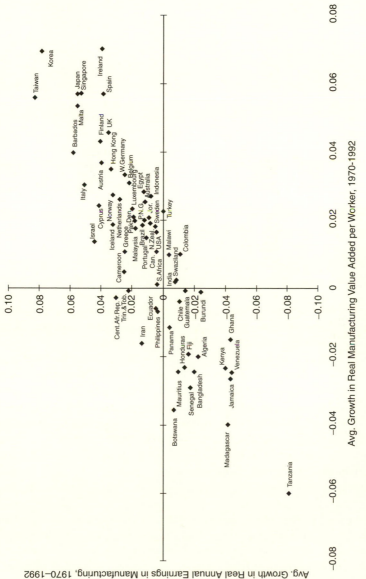

Figure 5.8. Rate of Change of Real Wages and Value Added per Worker, 1970–92.

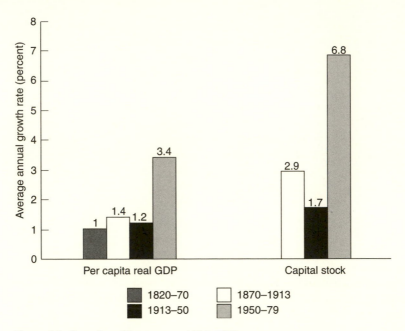

Figure 5.9. Growth and Investment, 1820–1979.

The fact that supervisory labor input is strikingly lower in countries with more egalitarian earnings distributions (Sweden, Japan) may reflect these and related effects (Gordon 1994).

The third strategy is simply to redistribute labor income in a more egalitarian manner without eroding effort incentives. Suppose, instead of providing income conditional on unemployment, the government gave all adult members of the population an unconditional grant β and financed the grant by a tax on wages supplemented by the general revenue savings occasioned by setting $b = 0$. Assume the government sought to do this while maintaining the status quo work incentive situation, as modeled in Bowles (1992). As $b = 0$, the equilibrium labor supply condition (no shirking condition) is now

$$w^* = a/\tau (1 - h); \tag{2'}$$

a flat tax on wage income of b would then restore equilibrium labor supply condition. As the labor demand equation has not been altered, the employment and (before-tax) wage level would thus remain at the status quo levels. The unconditional grant would be financed from tax revenues of hb plus savings on the elimination of the previous transfers of $(1 - h)b$. All adults would thus receive an unconditional grant of $\beta = bh/N$, where N is the adult population.

The effect would be a redistribution from the employed and the unemployed to those not in the labor force, obviously favoring the old, the young, women, and other groups sometimes called "excluded." It might be thought that the effects of the unconditional grant would be slight because family structure and other sharing arrangements allow income pooling. But this is not true: consider the empirically implausible case in which all of the differentially affected groups were paired in pooling arrangements (each employed worker coupled with a nonworker), so that the expected income of each household was unaffected by this policy. In this case dispersion of unconditional income claims to those who are unemployed or not in the labor force would predictably alter the intrafamily bargaining power and possibly also the credit market status of the previously relatively poor and powerless. This appears to be the case, for example of the quite generous transfers to the elderly in South Africa (Ardington and Lund 1995). Of course, the grant β need not take the form of a cash transfer but could rather be dedicated claims on health, education, recreation, and other services.

As this last example suggests, in the design and implementation of policies consistent with the supply-side egalitarian approach surveyed here, the heuristic distinction between the asset redistribution approach of the previous section and the wage and employment policies of the third section ("Increasing Wages and Employment") will lose some of its salience. Where labor contracts embody both job security and group- or firm-level gain-sharing, for example, employees may become defacto residual claimants on a substantial fraction of the income streams they generate. Trade union bargaining can thereby capture some of the peer monitoring advantages of outright asset distribution to co-ops. This is particularly likely to be the case where the monitoring labor effort by outsiders is ineffective (as in many information-based and other service activities), where firm-specific human resource investments are important, and where the capital required is either limited in amount or general (rather than transaction specific) and not subject to depreciation through misuse.

The land tenure reform in West Bengal mentioned at the outset embodied exactly this logic: the outright transfer of assets to farmers was precluded by the property clauses in the Indian constitution. Rather, the farmer's share of the crop was increased from a customary one-half to three-quarters, and tenants were given protection from eviction as long as they granted the landlord the stipulated reduced share. The result was a substantial increase in the rights of residual claimancy due not only to the increased share but also to the reduced threat of eviction, and hence the greater likelihood that the farmer would enjoy the future returns to land improvements and other investments.

CONCLUSION

Does globalization impede egalitarian redistribution?

What globalization does is to make it more costly and possibly politically infeasible to depress the expected after-tax rate of return to capital, or to alter the relative prices of tradeable goods and services. But while globalization—at least in the *hyper* form illustrated here—fixes the relative prices of some productive services, it precludes neither an egalitarian redistribution of the tangible and human assets from which those services flow, nor the enhancement of the assets currently owned by the less well off, nor the improvement of the institutionally determined flow of services from labor assets.

Thus, gain-seeking competition on a global scale does restrict the range of economically and politically sustainable relative prices, but it does not preclude egalitarian redistribution. The fundamental theorem of welfare economics defines conditions under which *any* technically feasible and Pareto optimal distribution of welfare can be attained by *some* redistribution of assets followed by competitive exchange. The theorem is not intended as a guide to policy, but it does underline an important truth: to the extent that globalization heightens competitive pressures it may reduce the attractiveness of redistributive approaches that rely on altering relative prices, but this hardly exhausts the set of egalitarian strategies.

An implication of the foregoing is that the traditional vehicles of egalitarian aspirations—trade unions and states—have a different but no less important role to play in a highly competitive world than in closed economies. The scope for conventional governmental and trade union measures that reduce the after-tax expected rate of profit is indeed restricted. But policies to implement Pareto-improving productivity gains may in some respects require a greater rather than lesser degree of collective interventions in atomistically competitive outcomes. Examples include an expanded role for publicly provided insurance to improve the trade-off between peer monitoring gains and suboptimal risk-taking losses entailed by more extensive residual claimancy and control of assets by the nonwealthy, and greater involvement of collective bargaining in more closely aligning the incentives of employers and employees with respect to both working and learning on the job.

A notable effect of globalization, unremarked thus far, is that (in the extreme form assumed here) it makes the nonwealthy members of a national population the residual claimants on the results of both their productive efforts and their success in solving productivity-dampening institutional failures. It thus inverts the more commonly assumed relationship in which the wealthy are the residual claimants on the income streams generated by the efforts of the less well off. While in competitive equilibrium the wealthy cannot get *less* than ρ, they also cannot get *more*, and so productivity improvements are fully captured by the nonwealthy. To the extent that conditions approximate those assumed in this model, then, the globalization may reduce the collective action problems confronting would-be coalitions of the nonwealthy seeking to enhance productivity by attenuating coordination failures.[28]

The theoretical results presented here, as well as the data in the previous section, suggest that efforts to raise the living standards of the less well off may succeed where they attenuate the incentive problems arising when property rights are ill defined or insecure, contracts are incomplete, and wealth is highly concentrated. The rationale for the egalitarian supply-side interventions summarized here—in contrast to policies restricted to pie-dividing or demand expansion—is dramatized by globalization, but it is no less compelling for closed economies.[29]

This is not to say that globalization makes no difference. Even in the very long-run perspective taken here, the effect of globalization on the out-of-equilibrium dynamics may be decisive. A one-time aggregate demand expansion may be crucial, for example, in permanently displacing an economy from a low road to a high road equilibrium of the type illustrated in figure 5.3, but the effectiveness of the necessary macroeconomic policies may be reduced by greater openness.

NOTES

Thanks for research assistance by Bridget Longridge, Yongjin Park, and Lawrance Evans, helpful contributions from Pranab Bardhan, Daniel Bromley, Helena De Letourdis, Steven Durlauf, Maurizio Franzini, David Lewis, Ugo Pagano, Fabio Petri, Eric Verhoogen, and Elisabeth Wood, and to the Russell Sage Foundation and the Behavioral Sciences Program of the Santa Fe Institute for financial support.

1. The nature of the openness that characterizes these cases (and those to follow) differs of course; all have relatively large trade flows while some have (or had) relatively restricted capital flows. See Moene (1998); Huber and Stephens (1998); Moene and Wallerstein (1993); Yang (1970); Putzel (2000); and Yager (1980).

2. Mesa-Lago (1989); Rosenberg (1981); Yashar (1995); Anand and Kanbur (1991); Isenman (1980); Lim (1984); and Republic of Seychelles (1999).

3. Ramachandran (1996); Sengupta and Gazdar (1996); Besley and Burgess (1998); and Banerjee, Gertler, and Ghatak (2002).

4. A program is implementable if its desired outcome is a stable Nash equilibrium of the appropriately defined game. More stringent requirements might be imposed, namely that the changes needed to enact the transition from the status quo to the desired program (not just the program itself) be implementable, or that the underlying preferences be stationary. I do not explore these problems here.

5. The cases of open economy egalitarianism cited earlier fail to meet some criteria of democracy over the relevant years (especially alternation of parties in power for South Korea, Taiwan, and Singapore), but none was an outright dictatorship, and most were exemplary democracies. See Przeworski, Alvarez, Cheibub, and Limongi (2000).

6. A review of these cases is provided in Bardhan, Bowles, and Gintis (2000). Asset-based redistribution is also stressed in Birdsall and Londono (1997). Franzini and Milone (1999) likewise view the constraints thought to be posed by globalization as exaggerated.

7. Econometric evidence of profit-led investment is presented in Catinat et al. (1988); Clark (1979); Kopcke (1985); Feldstein (1982); Bashkar and Glyn (1995); Bowles and Boyer (1990a); Bowles, Gordon, and Weisskopf (1989); and Gordon, Bowles, and Weisskopf (1998) and the works cited there. Evidence concerning the covariation of real wages and employment is found in Blanchflower and Oswald (1994) and Bowles (1991).

8. A bare bones model is this: Workers commit to a level of effort at the beginning of each period at which point with some probability they will be monitored and detected if they are shirking. The utility of providing effort is just $u(w) - a$, while for providing none

is $(1 - \tau)u(w) + \tau[(1 - h)u(b) + hu(w)]$, where the second term gives the consequences of termination, namely a probability $(1 - h)$ of remaining unemployed and receiving b, and a probability (h) of finding work at the going wage. The assumption that those who are terminated and then find work will not be monitored again until the beginning of the next period allows a particularly simple no-shirking condition: $u(w) - u(b) = a/\tau(1 - h)$; see Shapiro and Stiglitz (1984) and Bowles (1985). Bowles 1991 provides empirical estimates of the resulting wage function. The equation in the text lets $u(w) = w$ and $u(b) = b$, thus abstracting from workers' risk aversion. Endogenizing the employers' choice of the desired effort level and monitoring intensity would complicate the model but not alter the results.

9. An alternative formulation yielding similar qualitative results would make the wage level and effort level the outcome of a collective bargaining process, with the (Nash) bargain struck depending on the fallback position of the two parties, and labor's fallback rising with h.

10. Nothing of substance depends on the assumption that k is exogenous. Suppose the production function allows capital-labor substitution and exhibits constant returns. Firms then would chose an optimal level of k depending on the wage rate so that $k = k(w)$ with $k > 0$ and $y = y(k)$ with $y_k > 0$. The unique wage rate consistent with world capital market equilibrium (and independent of h) would exit as in (5) but with the production technology endogenous. Equation (5) would represent the wage satisfying both the firm's first order conditions for the choice of inputs and the global capital market equilibrium consistent with those inputs. This shows that making the dependence of y and k on w explicit does not alter the fact that there exists just one national wage rate consistent with equalized expected wage rates among nations. The invariance of $\underline{w}$ with respect to h results not from exogeneity of k but from the assumption that there are constant returns to scale at the national level and that no factors are in fixed supply.

11. The equilibrium exists as long as $w^*(0;b) < \underline{w} < w^*(1;b)$. The equilibrium is stable and unique under current assumptions, but as we will see presently, it need not be.

12. The invariance of φ with respect to ρ may be motivated in a number of ways. For example, it results from an intertemporal utility function of the wealthy of the form $u = ux^{1-\varphi}g^{\varphi}$ where x is this period's consumption and g is a bequest to the next generation equal to the returns on the invested corn, given next period. Nothing of substance would be altered if ρ and the investment share of the surplus were jointly determined.

13. Note that in this "hyper-globalized" economy with equal rates of labor force growth, there are no investment or trade flows in equilibrium, which underlines the importance of distinguishing between aggregate flow-based and microeconomic response-based measures of openness.

14. I here provide no reason to expect multiple equilibria—they are not difficult to imagine—but simply note that their possibility may help explain the pattern of divergence among apparently similar national economies. It may also illuminate what Quah (1996) calls the "twin peaks" pattern of divergence in income levels among countries.

15. In a multi-period context, a reduction in the probability of job loss for reasons other than insufficient effort (protection from cyclical layoffs, for example) reduces the no-shirking wage because it increases the value of not shirking.

16. Where, as in the Nordic social democratic countries and especially Sweden, collective bargaining explicitly sought to implement wages consistent with successful competition in global markets, the $w^*(h)$ function came to approximate the $\underline{w}$ function itself (the

latter defining the target wage in the above bargaining model), with firm- and industry-specific wage drift accounting for discrepancies between the two functions. Perhaps surprisingly, negotiated incomes policies can lower the labor supply equilibrium condition (for all values of h) even if $w^*(h)$ represents a conventional efficiency wage no-shirking condition; for the competitive equilibrium wage in that case will exceed that which would minimize the cost of an effective unit of labor if implemented by collusion among employers. The reason (explained in Bowles and Boyer 1988) is that each worker's fallback position includes the prospect of a job at *other* employers' wages, and so employers face a coordination problem resulting in their overpaying relative to their joint profit maximum. Thus there exists a lower wage that colluding employers would prefer and that might be implemented through negotiated incomes policies.

17. There is no "low road" equilibrium in this case, as h_o violates (6) while lower levels of employment violate the budget constraint.

18. The same is true for an increase in the effectiveness of public expenditures. For a given level of b, λ, and h, there exists a tax rate that maximizes $\underline{w}$ (and hence both employment and wages); for obvious reasons it varies inversely with b (if taxes were spent only on b, the optimal rate would be zero) and covaries with λ and h (where h is high, little tax revenue goes to unemployment benefits and more to productivity enhancement—so as long as the rate of return of public investment exceeds ρ, it raises $\underline{w}$.)

19. The simpler case in which individual producers use the corn to produce independently is transparent, but not empirically relevant where team production is required by economies of scale or for other reasons. I assume that there is no rental market in corn.

20. Bardhan, Bowles, and Gintis (2000) present a model of this process and point to a number of empirical cases in which reassigning residual claimancy to members of even very large teams has substantially increased output per worker hour.

21. To ensure that the loan is repaid with certainty, I must assume either that in those presumably rare cases where their realized residual claim is negative (realized gross income = $y^r < k(1 + \rho\mu)/(1 - t)$ co-op members have consumption-smoothing opportunities, or that these cases are sufficiently unlikely that they may be ignored.

22. A sufficient assumption is that risk is generated by a linear class of disturbances that would arise, for example, if the realized output level is defined by $y^r = \sigma z + y(\sigma)$, where z is a random variable with mean zero and standard deviation unity. This treatment draws on Bardhan, Bowles, and Gintis (2000) and the works by Sinn (1990) and Meyer (1987) cited there.

23. Evidence for an inverse relationship between wealth and risk aversion is presented in Saha, Shumway, and Talpaz (1994) and the studies cited there.

24. Technically, the distribution of wealth is governed by a non-ergodic dynamical process in which initial conditions (or one-time exogenous interventions) determine which of many possible equilibria will obtain. Galor and Zeira (1993) and others have shown that where credit constraints face the asset poor, and where there is a minimum economically viable project size (accounting for the necessity of team production in this case), the wealth distribution process may be non-ergodic.

25. Examples are given in Engerman and Sokoloff (1997); Engerman, Sokoloff, and Mariscal (1998); and Birdsall and Londono (1997).

26. The data from Verhoogen (1999) for this figure and the next are from the United Nations Industrial Development Organization Industrial Statistics Database. The wage

measure is average annual earnings in manufacturing. The productivity measure is value added per employee in manufacturing.

27. The data refer to thirteen economies comprising most of world output over the period covered and are from Glyn, Andrew, Hughes, Lipietz, and Singh (1990). The measure of capital accumulation is based on the tangible reproducible nonresidential fixed capital.

28. The argument is not that the nonwealthy have identical interests, but simply that the difficulty of securing mutually beneficial cooperative solutions with mobile wealth owners may be circumvented.

29. Abstracting from different national rates of population growth, equilibria of a closed economy version of this model are identical with the open economy version (though the out-of-equilibrium dynamics are quite different and may be critically important). To see why this is true, consider the supply of investment goods in a closed economy: the national surplus remaining after the consumption of the wealthy, in the open economy case, is the contribution of the nation to the global supply of investment goods; in the closed economy case this becomes the supply function for capital goods in that country (the open economy supply function is infinitely elastic at the rate ρ). Thus country-specific supply and demand for corn as an investment good are as indicated in equation (8) (supply is increasing in ρ as expected, while demand is invariant). If $\eta = v$, then there are no out-of-equilibrium flows of corn among countries. As before, there is a single interest rate $\rho = (1 + v)/\varphi - 1$ that clears the market in corn-for-investment, and (by the zero profit condition) this ρ determines w and therefore h. Thus the closed and open economy equilibria are identical. Of course, closed economies in which populations are growing more rapidly than the world average support higher equilibrium rates of expected profit and interest and thus experience lower wages and employment (because this year's workers must produce a larger surplus to employ a constant fraction (h^*) of the relatively more numerous workers of the next period.)

REFERENCES

Anand, S., and R. Kanbur. 1991. "Public Policy and Basic Needs Provision: Intervention and Achievement in Sri Lanka." In J. Dreze and A. Sen (eds.), *The Political Economy of Hunger: Vol III: Endemic Hunger*; Oxford: Clarendon.

Ardington, Elisabeth, and Frances Lund. 1995. "Pensions and Development: Social Security as Complementary to Programs of Reconstruction and Development." *Southern Africa* 12 (4): 557–77.

Banerjee, Abhijt, Paul J. Gertler, and Maitreesh Ghatak. 2002. "Empowerment and Efficiency: Tenancy Reform in West Bengal." *Journal of Political Economy* 110 (2): 239–80.

Bardhan, Pranab, S. Bowles, and H. Gintis. 2000. "Wealth Inequality, Credit Constraints, and Economic Performance." Pp. 541–603 in Anthony Atkinson and François Bourguignon (eds.), *Handbook of Income Distribution*. Dortrecht: North-Holland.

Bashkar, V., and A. Glyn eds. 1995. *Macroeconomic Policy after the Conservative Era: Research on Investment Savings and Finance*. Cambridge: Cambridge University Press.

Besley, T., and R. Burgess. 1998. "Land Reform, Poverty Reduction and Growth: Evidence From India." *Quarterly Journal of Economics* 115: 357–430.

Birdsall, N., and J. Londono. 1997. "Asset Inequality Matters: An Assessment of the World Bank's Approach to Poverty Reduction." *American Economic Review* 87 (2): 32–37.

Blanchflower, David G., and Andrew J. Oswald. 1994. *The Wage Curve.* Cambridge: MIT Press.

Bordo, A., A. Taylor, and Jeffrey Williamson, eds. 2003. *Globalization in Historical Perspective.* Chicago: University of Chicago Press.

Bowles, Samuel. 1985. "The Production Process in a Competitive Economy: Walrasian, Neo-Hobbesian, and Marxian Models." *American Economic Review* 75 (1): 16–36.

———. 1991. "The Reserve Army Effect on Wages in a Labour Discipline Model: U.S., 1954–1987." Pp. 383–406 in T. Mizoguchi (ed.), *Making Economies More Efficient and More Equitable: Factors Determining Income Distribution.* Oxford: Oxford University Press.

———. 1992. "Is Income Security Possible in a Capitalist Economy? An Agency Theoretic Analysis of an Unconditional Income Grant." *European Journal of Political Economy* 8: 557–78.

Bowles, Samuel, and Robert Boyer. 1988. "Labor Discipline and Aggregate Demand: A Microeconomic Model." *American Economic Review, Papers and Proceedings* 78: 2.

———. 1990a. "A Wage-led Employment Regime: Income Distribution, Labour Discipline, and Aggregate Demand in Welfare Capitalism." In S. Marglin and J. Schor (eds.), *The Golden Age of Capitalism; Reinterpreting the Postwar Experience.* Oxford: Clarendon.

———. 1990b. "Labor Market Flexibility and Decentralization as Barriers to High Employment? Notes on Employer Collusion, Centralized Wage Bargaining and Aggregate Employment." In Renato Brunetta and Carlo Dell'Aringa (eds.), *Labour Relations and Economic Performance.* London: Macmillan.

Bowles, Samuel, David M. Gordon, and Thomas E. Weisskopf. 1989. "Business Ascendancy and Economic Impasse." *Journal of Economic Perspectives* 3 (1): 107–34.

Catinat, M. et al. 1988. "Investment Behavior in Europe: A Comparative Analysis." *Recherches Economiques de Louvain* 54 (3): 277–324.

Clark, P. 1979. "Investment in the 1970s: Theory, Performance, and Prediction." *Brookings Papers on Economic Activity* 1: 73–113.

Engerman, S., K. Sokoloff, and E. Mariscal. 1998. "Schooling, Suffrage, and the Persistence of Inequality in the Americas, 1800–1945." Manuscript. University of California, Los Angeles.

Engerman, Stanley L., and Kenneth L. Sokoloff. 1997. "Factor Endowments, Institutions, and Differential Paths of Growth among New World Economies: A View from Economic Historians of the United States." In Stephen Haber (ed.), *How Latin America Fell Behind.* Palo Alto: Stanford University Press.

Feldstein, M. 1982. "Inflation, Tax Rules, and Investment: Some Econometric Evidence." *Econometrica* 50: 825–62.

Franzini, M., and L. Milone. 1999. "I dilemmi del welfare state nell'epoca della globalizzazione." In N. Acocella (ed.), *Globalizzazione e stato sociale.* Bologna: Il Mulino.

Freeman, R., and J. Medoff. 1984. *What Do Unions Do?* New York: Basic Books.

Galor, Oded, and Joseph Zeira. 1993. "Income Distribution and Macroeconomics." *Review of Economic Studies* 60 (1): 35-52.

Glyn, Andrew, and Robert Sutcliffe. 1999. "Still Underwhelmed: Indicators of Globalization and Their Misinterpretation." *Review of Radical Political Economy* 31 (1): 111–32.

Glyn, Andrew, Alan Hughes, Alain Lipietz, and Ajit Singh. 1990. "The Rise and Fall of the Golden Age." Pp. 39–125 in Stephen Marglin and Juliet B. Schor (eds.), *The Golden Age of Capitalism; Reinterpreting the Postwar Experience.* Oxford: Clarendon.

Gordon, D. 1994. "Bosses of Different Stripes: A Cross-National Perspective on Monitoring and Supervision." *American Economic Review* 84 (2): 375–79.

Gordon, D., S. Bowles, and T. Weisskopf. 1998. "Power, Profits and Investment: An Institutionalist Explanation of the Stagnation of U.S. Net Investment after the Mid-1960s." In S. Bowles and T. Weisskopf (eds.), *Economics and Social Justice: Essays on Power, Labour and Institutional Change.* Cheltenham: Edward Elgar.

Huber, E., and J. Stephens. 1998. "Internationalization and the Social Democratic Model." *Comparative Political Studies* 31 (3): 353–97.

Isenman, P. 1980. "Basic Needs: The Case of Sri Lanka." *World Development* 8 (3): 237–58.

Kopcke, R. 1985. "The Determinants of Investment Spending." *New England Economic Review,* pp. 19–35.

Lim, C. 1984. *Economic Structuring in Singapore.* Singapore: Federal Publications.

Mesa-Lago, C. 1989. "Costa Rica: A Latecomer Turned Boomer." In C. Mesa-Lago (ed.), *Ascent to Bankruptcy: Financing Social Security in Latin America.* Pittsburgh: University of Pittsburgh Press.

Meyer, Jack. 1987. "Two-Moment Decision Models and Expected Utility." *American Economic Review* 77 (3): 421–30.

Moene, K. O. 1998. "Feasibility of Social Democracy." Conference on Decentralised Development, Calcutta, University of Oslo.

Moene, K. O., and M. Wallerstein. 1993. "The Decline of Social Democracy." In K. G. Persson (ed.), *The Economic Development of Denmark and Norway since 1879.* Gloucester: Edward Elgar.

Pagano, U. 1991. "Property Rights, Asset Specificity, and the Division of Labour under Alternative Capitalist Relations." *Cambridge Journal of Economics* 15 (3): 315–42.

Przeworski, A, Michael E. Alvarez, José Antonio Cheibub, and Fernando Limongi. 2000. *Democracy and Development: Political Institutions and Well-being in the World, 1950–1990.* Cambridge: Cambridge University Press.

Putzel, J. 2000. "Land Reforms in Asia: Lessons from the Past for the 21st Century." London School of Economics Development Studies Institute Working Paper No. 004.

Quah, D. 1996. "Twin Peaks: Growth and Convergence in Models of Distribution Dynamics." *Economic Journal* 106 (437): 1045–55.

Ramachandran, V. K. 1996. "On Kerala's Development Achievements." In J. Dreze and A. Sen (eds.), *Indian Development: Selected Regional Perspectives.* Oxford: Oxford University Press.

Republic of Seychelles. 1999. *Statistical Abstract.* Victoria: Government Printer.

Rosenberg, M. 1981. "Social Reform in Costa Rica: Social Security and the Presidency of Rafael Angel Calderon." *Hispanic American Historical Review* 61 (2): 278–96.

Saha, Atanu, Richard C. Shumway, and Hovav Talpaz. 1994. "Joint Estimation of Risk Preference Structure and Technology Using Expo-Power Utility." *American Journal of Agricultural Economics* 76 (2): 173–84.

Sengupta, S., and H. Gazdar. 1996. "Agrarian Politics and Rural Development in West Bengal." In J. Dreze and A. Sen (eds.), *Indian Development: Selected Regional Perspectives*. Oxford: Oxford University Press.

Shapiro, Carl, and Joseph Stiglitz. 1984. "Unemployment as a Worker Discipline Device." *American Economic Review* 74 (3): 433–44.

Shiller, Robert J. 1993. *Macro Markets: Creating Institutions for Managing Society's Largest Economic Risks*. Oxford: Clarendon.

Sinn, H. W. 1990. "Expected Utility, Mu-Sigma Preferences, and Linear Distribution Classes: A Further Result." *Journal of Risk and Uncertainty* 3: 277–81.

Summers, R., and A. Heston. 1984. "Improved International Comparisons of Real Product and Its Composition, 1950–1980." *Review of Income and Wealth* 30: 207–71.

Taylor, A. 2002. "A Century of Current Account Dynamics." *Journal of International Money and Finance* 21: 725–48.

Verhoogen, E. 1999. "Trade Pressures and Wage Convergence." Manuscript, Brookings Institution.

Yager, J. 1980. *Transforming Agriculture in Taiwan: The Experience of the Joint Commission on Rural Reconstruction*. Ithaca and London: Cornell University Press.

Yang, M. 1970. *Socioeconomic Results of Land Reform in Taiwan*. Honolulu: East-West Center Press.

Yashar, D. J. 1995. "Civil War and Social Welfare: The Origins of Costa Rica's Competitive Party System." In S. Mainwaring and T. Scully (eds.), *Building Democratic Institutions: Party Systems in Latin America*. Stanford: Stanford University Press.

CHAPTER 6

Social Democracy as a Development Strategy

Karl Ove Moene & Michael Wallerstein

> "It is but equity besides, that they who feed cloath and lodge the whole body of the people, should have such a share of the produce of their own labour as to be themselves well fed, cloathed and lodged."
> —*Adam Smith* 1776

> "One has to understand that the ongoing crisis is not a crisis of real poverty, but an organizational crisis. The world is like a ship loaded with the goods of life, where the crew starves because it cannot figure out how the goods should be distributed."
> —*Ragnar Frisch* 1931

SOCIAL DEMOCRACY, it is often said, is nice but pricey. Whatever its merits in the rich countries of Western Europe, social democracy is frequently dismissed as an infeasible model for developing countries. Based on generosity toward the poor and protection against market competition, the argument goes, social democracy is only possible in consensual, homogeneous, and affluent societies with an extraordinary commitment to equality. In Third World countries that are conflict-ridden, heterogeneous, and poor, does the social democratic model have any relevance?

In this article we offer an agnostic view of the feasibility of the social democratic model of development in the Third World. First, we argue that consensus, homogeneity, and affluence are products of the social democratic model, not prerequisites. Second, we claim that the central social democratic policy in terms of economic development is the policy of wage compression attained through highly centralized wage-setting institutions. Third, we argue that the economic benefits of wage compression would be as significant in South Africa, Brazil, or India today as they were in the Nordic countries between 1935 and 1970. The political feasibility of a policy of wage compression, however, is open to doubt, hence our agnosticism regarding whether or not the social democratic road to affluence can be repeated.

In this chapter, we consider social democracy as a model of development rather than an end state. In particular, we will not enter into the debate regarding the future prospects of social democracy in Western Europe in the context of European economic integration, a common currency, an aging population, and the ever-increasing cost of providing the best health care that money can buy. The achievements of social democracy as a development strategy in terms of combining the socialist virtues of equality and security with the capitalist virtues of economic efficiency and technological dynamism are not seriously in dispute. What are disputed are the answers to the following questions: First, what was the contribution of specifically social democratic policies to the high level of affluence and equality in Northern Europe today? Second, would the policies that successfully promoted development in Northern Europe be equally effective and feasible in the Third World in the context of an increasingly integrated global economy?

NORDIC EXCEPTIONALISM

Social democracy in the Nordic countries can be characterized in multiple ways. In political terms, social democracy represented the mobilization of industrial workers such that workers' organizations exercised significant power in both the labor market and in government. Unions negotiated the terms of employment for most of the labor force and exerted a strong influence in politics through close connections to a social democratic party. The Social Democratic party was (and still is) the largest party in parliament and a frequent participant in government. In Norway and Sweden, in particular, the Social Democratic party enjoyed a long period of uninterrupted government (1933–76 in Sweden, and 1935–65 in Norway, not counting the five years of German occupation).[1] Institutionally, social democracy was distinguished by the growth of a large welfare state, the organization of encompassing and centralized trade unions, and the establishment of a system of routine consultation and cooperation among government, union, and employer representatives that has been given the label "corporatism" in political science.

In terms of social policy, social democracy in the Nordic countries was characterized by a wage policy of "solidaristic bargaining," that is, a commitment to the reduction of wage inequality, and by a welfare policy of providing basic goods and services to all as a right of citizenship. In trade policy, social democratic governments embraced free trade.[2] Protection was viewed as an ill-conceived subsidy to inefficient employers who did not deserve public support. Financial markets, however, were not open to international competition. In Norway, social democratic governments maintained extensive controls on the allocation of credit after the war. Swedish governments were more concerned with guiding the timing of investment rather than the allocation of credit among prospective borrowers. In neither country were financial markets deregulated until the 1980s. In sum, the Social Democrats, once in power, adopted the economics of Keynes and Frisch rather than of Marx. Quietly discarding the part of their political program that called for elimination of private concentrations of wealth, Social Democrats sought to construct a system of incentives that would lead private businesses to act in socially desirable ways without altering property rights.

In this chapter, we focus on the policy of solidaristic bargaining, that is, the policy of reducing wage inequality through centralized collective bargaining and, in Norway and Denmark, occasional government involvement. This is not because other social democratic policies, such as social insurance programs and free trade, are unimportant. Rather, the policy of solidaristic bargaining was the most innovative and most distinctive policy associated with social democracy.[3] A commitment to free trade was shared with liberal parties, while a commitment to social insurance was shared with all parties other than the liberal parties (Hicks 1999; Huber and Stephens 2001; Wilensky 2002). The nonsocialist governments in France intervened in credit markets as much or more than the social democratic governments in Northern Europe in the early postwar period. Only the Social Democrats, however, explicitly promoted the reduction of inequality among wage earners as a development strategy. Moreover, the commitment to greater wage equality was not merely rhetorical. Solidaristic bargaining was highly effective in compressing the wage distribution. By all measures, Scandinavia had the most egalitarian wage structure of any advanced industrial society by the 1970s (Freeman 1988, Wallerstein 1999).

How should the social democratic success in reducing inequality be explained? The most common explanations emphasize the importance of social homogeneity (Alesina, Glaeser, and Sacerdote 2001), a socialist (or Nordic) commitment to equality (Therborn 1986), a consensual model of decision-making (Wilensky 2002), and affluence. But conditions in Norway and Sweden in the period preceding the social democratic ascent to power were anything but consensual, egalitarian, and affluent.

In the 1920s and early 1930s, Norway and Sweden experienced the highest levels of industrial conflict in the world. In Norway the number of working days lost in strikes and lockouts in one year—1931—was three times larger than the total number of working days lost in industrial conflict over the twenty-five-year period 1945–70. In one of the first studies of comparative industrial conflict, Ingham (1974) contrasted the extraordinary militancy of Nordic workers with the relative docility of English workers during the interwar years. Moreover, employers were equally militant in defending their interests. More working days were lost in lockouts than in strikes. The consensus between employers and unions that characterized social democracy after the war was nowhere to be seen when the social democrats entered government in the 1930s.[4]

While the Nordic countries were relatively homogeneous in terms of religion and language, the working population was far from homogenous in terms of living conditions. In particular, the social and economic gap between rural and urban residents was huge. In Norway in 1934, average income per capita in rural municipalities was one third of the per capita incomes in urban municipalities. Referring to the difference in the average, however, understates the extent of regional inequality. Measured by income per capita, the gap between the poorest and richest rural municipality was 1 to 15, the gap between the poorest and richest city was 1 to 10, and the gap between the richest city and poorest rural municipality was 60 to 1 (Falch and Tovmo 2003). As in most poor countries today, the numbers exaggerate the real inequality because home production in subsistence farming and fishing is underreported. Nevertheless, Scandinavian Social Democrats came to power in societies no less economically divided than many poor countries of today.

As in developing countries today, there was significant underutilization of labor in Norway and Sweden in the interwar years. Surplus labor in the form of open unemployment was most evident. The rates of unemployed union members, the only official statistics available, were, in 1921, as high as 18 percent in Norway and 27 percent in Sweden. The rates fluctuated during the interwar period but never dropped below 9 to 10 percent. The peak of unemployment was reached in 1933 with 33 percent unemployed in Norway and 23 percent in Sweden. How representative these numbers are for the total rate of unemployment is debated.[5] Moreover, an unknown fraction of union members, upon losing their employment, returned to the countryside to work on family farms or on farms owned by relatives. While the exact numbers are in dispute, it is clear there was a large surplus of workers relative to the number of jobs even before the sharp decline of employment in the 1930s.

In addition, disguised unemployment in the countryside may have been as significant as open unemployment in the cities. Around half of the population in Norway lived in sparsely populated areas where most made a living from farming and fishing. Many of these workers lacked a job that offered steady income. The common practice of sharing work and income among family members in rural areas meant that remaining family members would work more if some members left for the cities. A withdrawal of part of the work force could, therefore, leave production unchanged. Thus, according to the production test of employment (Sen 1975), there was widespread disguised rural unemployment throughout the interwar years.

Finally, the economies that the Social Democrats inherited in the 1930s were far from affluent. As table 6.1 illustrates, the real per capita GDP of Sweden and Norway when the Social Democrats entered government (1933 in the case of

TABLE 6.1.
Real per capita GDP (1996 USD)

Norway 1935	4081
Sweden 1933	4535
Norway 1950	6598
Sweden 1951	7731
Brazil 1998	7103
South Africa 1998	7481

Sources: Center for International Comparisons (2002), Penn World Tables 6.0; Maddison (1964).

TABLE 6.2.
Share of GDP by Sector

	Agriculture and Fishing	Manufacturing, Mining, and Construction	Services
Norway 1930	16.7	30.4	52.9
Norway 1960	9.0	32.4	58.6
Brazil 2000	7.0	29.0	64.0
South Africa 2000	3.0	31.0	66.0

Sources: Statistics Norway (1995), World Bank (2002).

Sweden, 1935 in the case of Norway) was far below the current real per capita GDP of middle-income countries like Brazil or South Africa. Northern Europe became rich under social democratic government, not before. In fact, the per capita GDP of Brazil and South Africa today is comparable to the per capita GDP of Norway and Sweden in the 1950s. If Norway and Sweden could afford ambitious, egalitarian wage policies in the 1950s, so can Brazil and South Africa today.

Other economic and social indicators tell similar stories. Norway was less urbanized in the 1930s than are Brazil or South Africa today. The share of GDP generated by agriculture and fishing was greater in Norway in 1930 or in 1960 than in Brazil or South Africa today, as illustrated in table 6.2.

One potentially important difference is educational attainment.[6] Compulsory primary schooling was introduced in 1842 in Sweden and in 1860 in Norway (Olsson 1987, Bergsgård 1964). By 1960, virtually the entire adult population had at least a primary education in both Norway and Sweden, as compared with roughly a quarter of the adult population of South Africa and Brazil who had no schooling in 1990 (table 6.3). As table 6.3 reveals, however, the percentage of the adult population twenty-five years or older who had some secondary education was roughly the same in Norway in 1960 as in South Africa or Brazil today. In Norway in 1930, the share of the relevant age group who completed secondary school was only 2 percent for women and 4 percent for men (Statistics Norway 1995). The expansion of comprehensive primary and secondary education in Norway came after, not before, the social democrats came to power.

Social democratic governments that were formed in Sweden and Norway in the midst of the Great Depression were committed to reducing unemployment and alleviating poverty. The main slogan of the Social Democrats in the thirties was employment for everybody, which was a popular demand under the circumstances. Both governments increased government spending on policies such as unemployment benefits, public housing, and agricultural price supports. Most economic historians, however, think that the contribution of the relatively cau-

TABLE 6.3.
Educational Attainment of the Adult Population

	Percent of Adults 25 and Older with No Schooling	Percent of Adults 25 and Older with Primary Education Only or Less
South Africa 1990	25.9	73.1
Brazil 1990	22.4	88.2
Norway 1960	2.0	83.9
Sweden 1960	0.1	58.6

Source: Barro and Lee (1996).

tious Keynesian policies implemented by the social democratic governments to the subsequent recovery in Norway and Sweden was negligible (Hodne and Grytten 1992). The improvement of export markets due to the revival of the German economy was far more important in ending the depression in Scandinavia than any policy adopted by the social democratic governments. As table 6.4 shows, spending on social security, welfare, health, and education in Norway and Sweden in 1950, fifteen or more years after the Social Democrats came to power, was lower as a share of GDP than in Brazil today.

In retrospect, the key social democratic innovation in the 1930s was not the moderate increase in welfare spending but the institutional response to the problem that threatened the recovery program: What would keep the increased government spending from raising the wages of insiders in the labor market, rather than increasing employment? The problem came to a head in both countries in the construction industry.[7] Construction workers in Sweden and Norway were highly paid (although their work was seasonal), militant, and sheltered from foreign competition. When foreign demand collapsed in the 1930s, workers in the export sectors, such as metal workers, accepted large wage-reductions to stem the decline of employment. Construction workers came under no such pressure, in large part because of increased government spending on housing. Since construction workers were employed in the export sector as well as in home construction, higher construction wages raised labor costs in the export sector, threatening the

TABLE 6.4.
Spending on Social Security, Welfare, Health, and Education as a Share of GDP

Norway 1950	9.2
Sweden 1950	11.3
Brazil 1997	13.9

Sources: Huber and Stephens (2003), Olsson (1987), Kuhnle (1987).

jobs of metal workers. When construction unions called a strike in support of higher wages, the national confederation of unions intervened to force the strike to an early and, from the construction workers' point of view, unsuccessful conclusion.

The intervention of the national union confederation to end the strikes in construction was the initial step in a process of centralization of authority within the union movement in both Norway and Sweden, a process that was encouraged and supported by employers. "Basic agreements" between the national associations of unions and employers establishing rules for collective bargaining at the industry-level were reached in 1935 in Norway and 1938 in Sweden. In the 1950s, (1956 in Sweden, 1958 in Norway), bargaining at the industry level was replaced by direct negotiations over pay by the national associations of unions and employers. As white-collar and professional union confederations joined the centralized negotiations, the coverage of the central agreements expanded to include most of the working population in the private sector.[8]

The central agreements were necessarily general. The details of how the agreement were to be implemented was decided by subsequent bargaining at the industry and local level. The central agreements included an industrial peace obligation, however, that prohibited work stoppages once the central agreement was signed. After an agreement was reached at the central level, wage increases at the local level were limited to what could be obtained without the threat of a strike.

The centralized system of wage setting, which reached its zenith in the 1970s, had three important consequences. The first was the virtual elimination of industrial conflict. From the countries with the highest levels of strikes and lockouts in the world during the interwar years, Norway and Sweden became countries with some of the lowest levels of industrial conflict in the postwar period. The second consequence was to allow conditions in the export industries to determine aggregate wage growth. The centralized system of wage bargaining tied wage growth throughout the economy to the growth of wages in the export sector, since the unions in the export sector, those of the metal workers in particular, were the largest and most influential within the national confederations.

The third consequence of centralized wage setting was a gradual process of wage compression that, over time, generated the most egalitarian distribution of wages and salaries in the capitalist world. In the 1950s, wage compression was adopted as an explicit goal of the unions in both Norway and Sweden under the title of "solidaristic bargaining." But wage compression is closely associated with the centralization of wage setting in all advanced industrial societies, whether the centralization is achieved by centralized collective bargaining or by government intervention in the form of income policies, and whether or not wage compression is adopted as an explicit goal.[9]

While wage compression fit easily with the socialist heritage of the unions, the goals of solidaristic bargaining were defended more in terms of efficiency than in terms of equality. In the 1950s, two Swedish trade union economists, Gösta Rehn and Rudolf Meidner (Rehn 1952), argued that equalizing wages for workers with similar skills across Swedish firms and industries would promote economic development by raising wages in low-productivity firms or industries and restraining wages in high-productivity firms or industries. In a decentralized bargaining system, wages vary according to the productivity of the firm and the industry. In a centralized system, in contrast, wages are relatively insensitive to the profitability of the enterprise. On the one hand, centralized wage-setting implied that industries with low levels of productivity were prevented from paying low wages and were forced to reduce employment instead. On the other hand, workers in industries with high levels of productivity were prevented from sharing the profits generated by high levels of productivity in the form of higher wages. By reducing profits in low-productivity firms and increasing profits in high-productivity firms, labor and capital would be induced (or coerced) to move from low productive to highly productive activities, increasing aggregate efficiency as well as improving equality (Agell and Lommerud 1993; Moene and Wallerstein 1997).

Whatever the benefits of solidaristic bargaining in terms of efficiency—a study of productivity growth in Sweden by Hibbs and Locking (2000) finds evidence that the gain in efficiency was substantial—the cumulative impact on the distribution of wages and salaries was large. "Equal pay for equal work" is a common demand of unions, easily explained by unions' desire to reduce managerial discretion. Solidaristic bargaining extended the principle of "equal pay for equal work" from one industry to the entire economy, and then moved beyond the demand for "equal pay for equal work" toward the goal of "equal pay for all work." In Sweden between 1970, when comprehensive wage data on individuals began to be collected, and 1983, when the system of centralized bargaining collapsed, the variance of the log of hourly wages among private sector blue-collar workers declined by over 50 percent (Hibbs and Locking 2000). That dramatic decrease does not include the equally prominent reduction of the wage differential between blue-collar and white-collar workers. Hibbs and Locking (2000) estimate that a similar decline occurred during the 1960s as well, implying that the variance of log hourly wages in 1983 was only one quarter of what it was in 1960. In 1992, the ratio of the wage for a worker at the 90th percentile of the wage distribution to the wage for a worker at the 10th percentile was about 2 to 1 in Sweden, Norway, and Denmark, the lowest ratios of any country in the OECD (OECD 1996). In contrast, the 90 to 10 ratio was 5.4 to 1 in the United States in 1992.

Many other features of the Nordic model of social democracy follow from the policy of wage compression. Wage compression directly encouraged the movement of capital from less productive to more productive activities, but the effect on the incentives for workers to change occupations was mixed. While wage compression would increase job loss in industries with low productivity and job creation in industries with high productivity, employers in highly productive firms lost the ability to attract workers with offers of higher pay. The government, unions, and employers responded to the problem with an array of active labor market policies that subsidized the movement of workers from one industry to another with training programs and grants to cover moving expenses. To keep highly productive employers from undermining the policy of wage restraint by offering workers generous benefits (which were harder than wages to monitor at the central level), the Swedish employers' confederation lobbied the government to nationalize the provision of health care and pensions (Swenson 2002). Greater wage equality increased voters' willingness to support insurance-replacement policies such as social insurance against the loss of income due to unemployment, disability, sickness, and occupational injury.[10] The compression of wage differentials, in sum, had far-reaching economic and political consequences, one of which, we argue in the next section, was to increase the pace of economic development.

A SIMPLE MODEL OF DEVELOPMENT

To see the potential importance of wage compression for economic development, we present a simple model of a developing economy. The central aspect of development that the model incorporates is that the growth of a modern sector at the expense of traditional production depends on the size of the market for modern goods.[11] The model distinguishes between modern and traditional sectors depending on the technology they apply. While old technologies are assumed to have decreasing returns to scale, new technologies are assumed to have increasing returns. Increasing returns to scale imply that the profitability of modern plants depends on the size of the market. Foreign demand for the output of the modern sector, we assume, is exogenous. Domestic demand, in contrast, is assumed to be an increasing function of the size of the modern sector. The idea is that many consumers of modern sector goods are other modern sector firms or workers in the modern sector. The dependence of the growth of the modern sector on the size of the modern sector creates a feedback loop. The result may be a poverty trap, in which growth fails to occur, or sustained development in which initial growth of the modern sector encourages further modern sector growth until the traditional sector disappears. A central determinant of whether the economy develops or not that we emphasize in this model is the wage differential between modern and traditional sectors.

We start with the modern sector. Let x represent both the value of output and employment in a representative modern sector plant. We assume, in other words, that one unit of labor is required to produce one unit's worth of revenue for the enterprise. Labor is the only variable cost of production. In addition, we assume that there is a fixed cost of plant and equipment, c, associated with modern sector enterprises. Implicitly we have assumed that the minimum plant size is large enough to supply the domestic market. Note that we have assumed a form of increasing returns to scale in the modern sector, since the average cost of production declines as output increases. If workers in modern sector plants receive a wage of w, then profit per modern sector plant can be written as

$$\pi = (1 - w)x - c \tag{1}$$

Modern sector workers, we assume, are covered by collective agreements. If wage bargaining is decentralized, the wage agreement depends on the two sides' willingness to engage in industrial conflict. In the event of a work stoppage, we assume that modern sector workers receive an income roughly equivalent to what workers earn in the traditional sector, which we denote by q, while firms receive $- c$, since sunk costs are sunk. Applying the generalized Nash bargaining solution implies a modern sector wage of

$$w = q + \beta(1 - q), \tag{2}$$

where $\beta \in [0, 1]$ represents workers' share of the joint surplus in bargaining. Equation (3) implies that profits in the modern sector can be written as

$$\pi = (1 - \beta)(1 - q)x - c. \tag{3}$$

The demand for modern sector output depends on foreign demand and domestic demand. Domestic demand, in turn, depends on the size of the modern sector. In particular, we assume that a fixed proportion of modern sector income is spent on the output of domestic modern sector firms. It follows that the demand for modern sector output is an increasing, strictly convex function of the size of the modern sector, or $x = x(n)$ where n represents the share of modern commodities produced by domestic firms. (See the appendix for a full description of the mathematical details of the argument.) Implicit in our formulation is a view that development entails a process of import substitution as domestic modern sector firms replace foreign suppliers of modern commodities for the domestic market. In other words, we assume some degree of home market bias, such that domestic producers are preferred in the domestic market over imports. Imports may rise with development, however, as increasing income in the modern sector generates greater demand for the full range of modern sector commodities, including those that are not produced at home.

The fixed costs include normal returns on capital. Thus, negative profits imply disinvestment, while positive profits imply an above average rate of return that attracts increased investment in modern sector plants. This is captured by assuming that the change in the size of the modern sector over time, or dn/dt, is given by the equation

$$dn/dt = k\pi(x(n)), \tag{4}$$

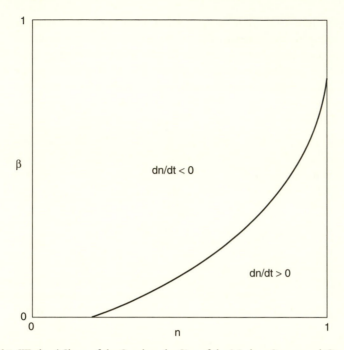

Figure 6.1. Workers' Share of the Surplus, the Size of the Modern Sector, and Growth.

where k is a positive constant. For a given wage, equations (2) and (4) imply that there is a minimum size, n^*, such that modern sector growth is positive. Indeed, if $n > n^*$, then the growth of the modern sector is an increasing, convex function of the size of the modern sector if there is sufficient excess labor in the traditional sector such that q remains constant. Alternatively, for a given size of the modern sector, n, equations (3) and (4) imply that there is a maximum wage differential $w - q = \beta(1 - q)$ such that modern sector growth is positive. A wage differential that is too large is incompatible with sustained development.

The impact of the wage differential between the modern and traditional sectors on the growth of the modern sector is illustrated in figure 6.1. The upward sloping curve represents the combinations of n and β such that profits are zero. If the initial pair (n, β) is below the curve, then profits are positive and the modern sector grows. If the initial pair (n, β) is above the curve, however, profits are negative and the modern sector declines.

The assumption that unions would push the modern sector into extinction if they could seems extreme. A reasonable modification would be that unions limit their wage demands to the level that is compatible with constant modern sector employment. The wage would then be given by whichever is less, $w = \beta + (1 - \beta)q$ or $w = 1 - (c/x)$. In this case, the alternative to sustained development is stagnation, not decline. The conditions for sustained development, however, are unchanged. A sufficiently high wage differential between modern and traditional sector workers blocks development.

To complete the model, we need to include the determination of earnings in the traditional sector and unemployment. Earnings in the traditional sector are assumed to be a declining function of the number of workers seeking traditional sector employment, $q = q(l)$, with $q'(l) \leq 0$, where l is the number of workers employed in the traditional sector. Production in the modern sector is typically geographically concentrated. To be available for modern sector employment, workers may have to leave the countryside and their source of traditional sector employment. Let u be the ratio of unemployed workers to modern sector workers so that un is the number of workers who are unemployed, and let $f(u)$ be the probability of obtaining a modern sector job, where $f(0) = 1$ and $f'(u) < 0$. With these assumptions, migration takes place until expected earnings are identical in the two sectors, that is until[12]

$$f(u)w = q(l) \tag{5}$$

As long as modern sector workers have bargaining power that is derived from their ability to shut down production, wages don't fall to clear the urban labor market.[13] Unemployment is involuntary in the sense that the unemployed would prefer to work at the wage that is offered by modern sector firms. Finally, the share of workers who are employed in modern enterprises, of unemployed workers, and of employed workers in traditional activities must equal the total labor force, L, or $nx + unx + l = L$. Thus, the model posits three groups of workers: modern sector workers, traditional sector workers in the countryside, and informal sector workers who are unemployed (or underemployed) in the cities.

The allocation of labor and the distribution of earnings for a given n are illustrated in figure 6.2, with employment on the horizontal axis and earnings on the vertical axis. Modern sector employment is represented by the distance from the left-hand vertical axis, while employment in the traditional sector is represented by the distance from the right hand vertical axis. Modern sector workers receive $w = \beta + (1 - \beta)q$, which does not depend on employment in the modern sector, while traditional sector workers receive q, which is a declining or constant function of employment in the traditional sector. The number of unemployed workers is determined by the intersection of the curve $f(u)w$ and $q(l)$ since migration is assumed to equalize expected earnings of traditional sector workers and the unemployed.

In figure 6.2, the curve $q(l)$ is drawn as flat until the number of workers in the traditional sector becomes sufficiently small. A flat $q(l)$ curve represents the case of a labor surplus economy where expansion of the modern sector has little effect on earnings in traditional activities, as postulated by Lewis (1954). If wage differential between the modern and traditional sectors is sufficiently low, then the modern sector will grow and the traditional sector will decline. Eventually, the share of workers in the traditional sector will fall enough such that $q(l)$ and w

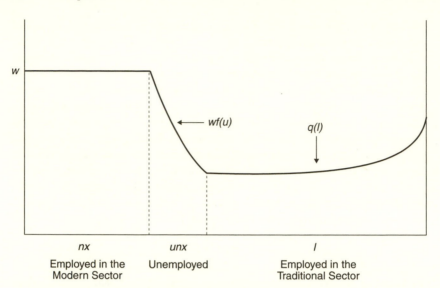

Figure 6.2. Wages and Employment with Surplus Labor.

will rise. But if the wage differential is too high, either the modern sector will stagnate or contract and development will not occur.

The model has Keynesian features in the sense that the level of demand determines modern sector output. A positive demand shock, such as an increase in exports, g, implies higher modern sector employment with a multiplier greater than one. Thus an increase in the demand for modern sector exports, such as occurred in the Nordic countries with the revival of the German economy in the 1930s, may create conditions of sustained development. Although we haven't included a government sector in the model, it is easy to show that increased government spending on modern sector output has the same impact as an increase in foreign demand.

The simple model we have described omits important considerations. In particular, the treatment of prices and foreign demand as exogenous, forces us to ignore the effect of wage demands on the competitiveness of exports, an important part of the Norwegian and Swedish story. But the model is sufficient for the purpose of demonstrating the potential importance of large wage-differences between the modern and traditional sectors in blocking economic growth. Adding a channel whereby modern sector wage setting would effect foreign demand, in addition to domestic demand, is to add further reasons why growth might be increased by a policy of reducing the wages earned in the most productive enterprises. Reducing the share of surplus received by relatively privileged workers, we suggest, was the essence of the social democratic development strategy. Essentially, centralization took wage setting out of the hands of the unions representing relatively high-paid workers and put wage setting in the hands of leaders of the labor movement as a whole.

In the end, the social democratic model of development owed more to Adam Smith than to Karl Marx. Both Adam Smith and the social democrats were ardent defenders of the poorest groups in society. Both saw modernization and expansion of markets as the key to escaping poverty. Both saw the primary task as being one of removing the obstacles to rapid modernization. Adam Smith viewed the primary obstacles to modernization as restrictions on the free movement of labor and capital, such as guild privileges and monopolies, that limited the size of the market and the extent of specialization. The Social Democrats, in effect, saw the primary obstacle to modernization as strong local unions whose wage premiums restricted the expansion of the most productive sectors. What distinguished the Social Democrats from more conservative followers of Adam Smith like Margaret Thatcher was their solution to the problem of restricting the power of local unions. While Thatcher's solution was to weaken unions as institutions, the social democratic approach was to strengthen unions as institutions and to structure collective bargaining in a highly centralized manner that reduced the influence of highly paid workers in the wage-setting process.

THE POLITICAL FEASIBILITY OF SOLIDARISTIC BARGAINING

Many economists, social democrats and non-social democrats alike, would accept the argument that development can be promoted by reducing the wage differential between modern sector and traditional sector workers. What makes the social democratic experience exceptional was that the policy of wage compression was voluntary, not coerced, and implemented by a union movement that included as members many of the high-wage workers whose wages would be restrained in the name of greater equality. Thus, the great challenge faced by those who would apply the lessons of social democracy in the Third World today is political. How can a democratic political movement with close ties to the unions implement a development strategy that centers on wage restraint?

It may be helpful to review the balance of political forces behind the implementation of solidaristic bargaining in the Nordic countries. Employers provided critical support for both centralized wage setting and solidaristic bargaining (Swenson 1989, 1991). While the Nordic countries are well known for the strength of unions, employers also achieved an extraordinary level of organization. Employers much preferred to bargain with the "sensible" leadership of the union confederations rather than with the militant union leadership on the shop floor. Solidaristic bargaining can increase aggregate profits relative to the wage schedule associated with decentralized bargaining by eliminating the rents that workers would otherwise obtain in local bargaining (Moene and Wallerstein 1997). Solidaristic bargaining can even increase aggregate profits relative to the wage schedule associated with a non-union labor market by limiting competition among employers for the workers (Swenson 2002, Moene and Wallerstein 2003b).

Another group that supported the policy of wage compression was the leadership of unions of low-wage workers. Since the union movement was encompassing, both unions representing low-wage workers and those representing high-wage workers had a voice in setting the union wage policy. While the policy of wage compression was controversial in unions of high-wage workers, it was enthusiastically supported by unions of low-wage workers. Thus, the political coalition that prevailed in the 1950s and established the pattern of centralized and solidaristic bargaining that was to last until the 1980s was comprised of the low-wage unions and employers. The unions with large numbers of low-wage members provided support for an egalitarian wage policy within the union confederations, while employers' preference for bargaining with the union confederation rather than with individual unions made it difficult for high-wage unions to bargaining separately. It is unlikely that the low-wage unions and the leadership of the union confederation would have been able to force the high-wage unions to accept an egalitarian wage policy without the backing of employers and the threat of lockouts against recalcitrant unions.[14]

In addition, we believe that the policy found support in the widespread preference of Nordic workers for a more egalitarian wage scale. We do not believe that Nordic workers are inherently more egalitarian than workers in other countries. Rather, our belief is that a preference for greater equality is widespread. The preference for greater equality, however, can be acted upon only to the extent that wages are set centrally. When wages are set at the plant level, wage compression can occur only within the plant. When wages are set at the industry level, wage compression occurs within the industry. When wages are set at the national level, wage compression occurs at the national level.

Social heterogeneity does not eliminate the preference for more egalitarian pay. Unions compress wages within the scope of the bargaining agreement even in racially and ethnically divided societies like the United States (Freeman and Medoff 1984). European countries divided by religion, such as the Netherlands and Germany, or by language, such as Belgium, have relatively centralized wage-setting institutions and relatively egalitarian wage distributions (Wallerstein 1999). It is possible, however, that the centralization of wage setting is easier to achieve in countries that are not divided by religion, language, or race. In addition, it is easier to centralize wage setting in countries with a small population.

The Nordic countries may have had another important advantage that countries in the Third World today do not. At the end of World War II, when solidaristic bargaining began to be implemented, the Nordic economies were operating at full employment. Full employment may seem like inauspicious circumstances to implement a policy of wage restraint, but it had an important advantage that is illustrated in figure 6.3. Figure 6.3 duplicates figure 6.2, except that the $q(l)$

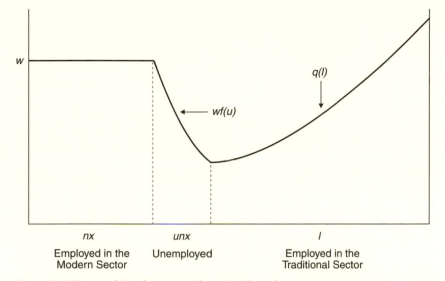

Figure 6.3. Wages and Employment without Surplus Labor.

curve is upward sloping throughout. Without surplus labor, any increase in modern sector employment will lead to an increase in the earnings of traditional sector workers. Since $w = \beta + (1 - \beta)q$, the rise in q generated by the reduction in β reduces the cost of solidaristic bargaining for modern sector workers. In addition, the increase in q implies that all traditional sector workers benefit from higher wages, not just those who move from traditional-sector to modern-sector jobs.

CONCLUSION

Is the social democratic model of development relevant in the contemporary world of economies increasingly integrated in global markets for goods and capital? The social democrats were committed to free trade but not the free flow of capital. We have de-emphasized, however, the importance of credit controls as an important part of the social democratic approach. The free flow of capital and of goods makes a policy of reducing wage differentials more, not less, effective as a strategy of development. Capital mobility implies that investment will be more responsive to policies, like solidaristic bargaining, that raise the return to capital. As the degree of international economic integration and capital mobility increases, so do the potential economic gains from reducing the wage differential between workers in the formal and in the traditional and informal sectors.

Is the social democratic model of development politically feasible in the Third World? This, it seems to us, is the critical question. The elements that appear to have been important in allowing wage differentials to be reduced through collective bargaining in Nordic countries were (a) well-organized employers, (b) encompassing trade unions that included the low-paid workers, and (c) immediate benefits of wage compression in terms of the earnings of those at the bottom. These conditions are not notably present in Africa, Asia, and Latin America today.

The Nordic countries had important advantages that enhanced the feasibility of the social democratic strategy of development, including universal primary education, which meant that traditional sector workers were literate; small size, which promoted the growth of encompassing unions and employers' associations (Wallerstein 1989); and luck in the form of booming export markets.[15] But we still understand little of the political dynamics that made wage compression possible in an environment with strong unions and a government that considered industrial workers to be its core constituents. Thus, we are reluctant to conclude that the social democratic experience cannot be repeated.

Appendix

In this section, we present the details of the model underlying figure 6.1 in the text. Let there be a continuum of measure one of modern commodities, all with prices fixed on the international market. Of these modern commodities, the fraction n is produced by local enterprises. For the sake of simplicity, we assume that each modern commodity is produced by one enterprise. As described in the text, output is linear in hours worked, with one unit of labor producing one unit of output. In addition, there are fixed costs of $c > 0$.

We assume that the fraction μ (with $\mu < 1$) of modern sector income $(x - c)n$ is spent on each of the modern commodities. Thus, the domestic demand for each modern sector enterprise is $\mu n (x - c)$. If we write foreign demand for each modern commodity produced locally as g, then output and employment in each modern sector enterprise is given by

$$x = \mu n(x - c) + g. \tag{6}$$

Equation (6) implies that production and employment in modern enterprises is an increasing, convex function of n

$$x(n) = \frac{g - \mu nc}{1 - \mu n},$$

provided $g > c$. If $g \leq c$, there is no wage low enough to make the first modern enterprise profitable. Note that the multiplier with respect to changes in the demand for export, that is the partial derivative of $x(n)$ with respect to g, is greater than one. The assumption that the domestic demand for modern commodities is unaffected by the income earned in the traditional sector can easily be relaxed without altering the way the model works. The central assumption is that the growth of the modern sector increases the demand for modern-sector output and higher output in the modern sector lowers the average costs of production.

Given a wage of $w = \beta + (1 - \beta)q$, the condition that profits are positive and the modern sector grows can be written in terms of the size of the modern sector:

$$\pi > 0 \Leftrightarrow n > \frac{c - (1 - \beta)(1 - q)g}{\mu c [1 - (1 - \beta)(1 - q)]} \equiv n^*.$$

Note that the minimum size compatible with sustained development, n^* is an increasing function of c, β, and q, and a decreasing function of μ and g.

Alternatively, we can write the condition that profits are positive in terms of the share of the joint surplus obtained by modern-sector workers:

$$\pi > 0 \Leftrightarrow \beta < \left(\frac{1}{1-q}\right)\left[\frac{g-c}{g-\mu cn} - q\right] \equiv \beta^*$$

The maximum share of the surplus compatible with sustained development, β^*, is an increasing, strictly convex function of n. This is the function drawn in figure 6.1 in the text.

NOTES

An earlier version of this chapter was presented at the Conference on Globalization and Egalitarian Redistribution, Santa Fe Institute, May 2002. We thank Pranab Bardhan, Sanjay Reddy, Asbjørn Rødseth, John Stephens and the participants at the conference for comments.

1. The Norwegian government flew to London in April 1940 and operated as a government in exile during the years of occupation, 1940–45.

2. Like many others, the Scandinavian countries introduced trade restrictions in the early 1930s. The trade restrictions were less heavy than in most other European countries, however, and they were introduced before the Social Democrats came to power. For several years after the war Norway maintained import restrictions, but more as an instrument of economic planning than of protection. For example, the import of private cars was prohibited, not to protect domestic car producers (Norway has none), but because private cars were not considered to be an essential commodity by the government.

3. Another policy innovation associated with social democracy that is much discussed is the development of active labor market policies, that is, policies that offer retraining to the unemployed in place of unemployment benefits. We emphasize solidaristic bargaining because we think it had far more important effects on both equality and growth.

4. One exception might be the Norwegian Labor Pact (Hovedavtalen) of 1935, an agreement between the employer association NAF and the unions in LO that stipulated negotiation procedures including rules for industrial conflicts. The Labor Pact, however, was highly controversial. A similar proposal was voted down by the LO members in 1934,

and the leaders of LO who favored the pact were replaced. A similar pact was signed in Sweden in 1938, after the Swedish Social Democrats came to power.

5. See Hodne and Grytten (1992) for a discussion.

6. We thank John Stephens for insisting on the importance of universal primary education in Scandinavia.

7. Swenson (1989, 1991) describes the events in Sweden. Bjørgum (1985) describes the events in Norway. The events leading to centralization are very similar in the two countries.

8. See Pontusson and Swenson (1996), Iversen (1996), and Wallerstein and Golden (1997) for contrasting studies of the rise and decline of centralized bargaining in Denmark, Norway, Sweden, and Finland.

9. For studies of the impact of centralized bargaining on the wage distribution, see Freeman (1988), Blau and Kahn (1996), Wallerstein (1999), Hibbs and Locking (2000), and Rueda and Pontusson (2000).

10. On the relationship between wage inequality and spending on social insurance policies, see Iversen and Soskice (2001) and Moene and Wallerstein (2001, 2003a).

11. The modern sector should not be equated with the industrial sector. Much of contemporary modern sector employment is in the service sector. For an empirical study that presents evidence in support of our assumption that growth is driven by the size of the internal market and exports demand, see Aides and Glaeser (1999).

12. This expression is just a variant of the Harris and Todaro (1970) mechanism for rural urban migration.

13. The presence of unions is not the only reason why wages in the modern sector might fail to fall to clear the urban labor market. Even if unions were absent, employers may not reduce wages until unemployment was eliminated for fear of the effect of wage reductions on workers' effort and turnover. See Weiss (1990) for a review of the literature.

14. In Norway, but not in Sweden, compulsory mediation and compulsory arbitration have frequently been used to force high-wage unions to accept wage moderation.

15. We do not include the absence of a politically powerful class of large landowners on our list. While the lack of a powerful landed elite may be an important part of the explanation for the political dominance of social democratic parties (Luebbert 1991), we do not think it had a direct bearing on the feasibility of the social democratic strategy of development. An egalitarian distribution of land can coexist with an inegalitarian distribution of wages and vice versa.

REFERENCES

Agell, Jonas, and Kjell Erik Lommerud. 1993. "Egalitarianism and Growth." *Scandinavian Journal of Economics* 95: 559–79.

Aides, Alberto F., and Edward L. Glaeser. 1999. "Evidence on Growth, Increasing Returns and the Extent of the Market." *Quarterly Journal of Economics* 114 (3): 1025–45.

Alesina, Alberto, Edward Glaeser, and Bruce Sacerdote. 2001. "Why Doesn't the U.S. Have a European-Style Welfare State?" Paper presented at the Brookings Panel on Economic Activity, Sept. 7, 2001, Washington, D.C.

Barro, Robert J., and Jong Wha Lee. 1996. "International Measures of Schooling Years and Schooling Quality." *American Economic Review* 86 (2): 218–28.

Bergsgård, Arne. 1964. *Norsk Historie, 1814–1880.* Oslo: Det Norsk Samlaget.

Bjørgum, Jorunn. 1985. "LO og NAF 1899–1940." *Tidsskrift for Arbeiderbevegelsens Historie* 2: 85–114.

Blau, Francine D., and Lawrence M. Kahn. 1996. "International Differences in Male Wage Inequality: Institutions versus Market Forces." *Journal of Political Economy* 104: 791–837.

Center for International Comparisons. 2002. *Penn World Tables 6.0.* University of Pennsylvania. Available at: www.pwt.econ.upenn.edu/.

Falch, Torben, and Per Tovmo. 2003. "Norwegian Local Public Finance in the 1930s and Beyond." *European Review of Economic History* 7: 127–54.

Freeman, Richard B. 1988. "Labour Market Institutions and Economic Performance." *Economic Policy* 3: 64–80.

Freeman, Richard B., and James L. Medoff. 1984. *What Do Unions Do?* New York: Basic Books.

Frisch, Ragnar. 1931. "Plan eller kaos." *Tidens Tegn*, November 5.

Harris, John R., and Michael P. Todaro. 1970. Migration, Unemployment and Development: A Two-Sector Analysis. *American Economic Review* 60: 126–42.

Hibbs, Douglas A., Jr., and Håkan Locking. 2000. "Wage Dispersion and Productive Efficiency: Evidence for Sweden." *Journal of Labor Economics* 18 (4): 755–82.

Hicks, Alexander. 1999. *Social Democracy and Welfare Capitalism: A Century of Income Security Politics.* Ithaca: Cornell University Press.

Hodne, Fritz, and Ola Honningdal Grytten. 1992. *Norsk Økonomi 1900–1990.* Oslo: Tano.

Huber, Evelyne, and John Stephens. 2001. *Development and Crisis of the Welfare State.* Chicago: University of Chicago Press.

Huber, Evelyne, and John Stephens. 2003. "Globalization and Social Policy." Paper prepared for the conference on "Globalization, the State and Society" at the School of Law, Washington University, in St. Louis, November 13–14.

Ingham, Geoffrey. 1974. *Strikes and Industrial Conflict: Britain and Scandinavia.* London: Macmillan.

Iversen, Torben. 1996. "Power, Flexibility and the Breakdown of Centralized Wage Bargaining: The Cases of Denmark and Sweden in Comparative Perspective." *Comparative Politics* 28: 399–436.

Iversen, Torben, and David Soskice. 2001. "An Asset Theory of Social Policy Preferences." *American Political Science Review* 95: 875–93.

Kuhnle, Stein. 1987. "Norway." In Peter Flora (ed.), *Growth to Limits*, vol. 4. Berlin: Walter de Gruyter.

Lewis, Arthur. 1954. "Economic Development with Unlimited supplies of Labour." *The Manchester School* 22: 139–91.

Luebbert, Gregory M. 1991. *Liberalism, Fascism or Social Democracy.* Oxford: Oxford University Press.

Maddison, Angus. 1964. *Economic Growth in the West.* New York: Norton.

Moene, Karl Ove, and Michael Wallerstein. 1997. "Pay Inequality." *Journal of Labor Economics* 15: 403–30.

———. 2001. "Inequality, Social Insurance and Redistribution." *American Political Science Review* 95 (4): 859–74.

————. 2003a. "Earnings Inequality and Welfare Spending: A Disaggregated Analysis." *World Politics* 55 (4): 485–516.

————. 2003b. "Does the Logic of Collective Action Explain the Logic of Corporatism?" *Journal of Theoretical Politics* 15: 271–97.

Olsson, Sven. 1987. "Sweden." In Peter Flora (ed.), *Growth to Limits*, vol. 4. Berlin: Walter de Gruyter.

Organization for Economic Cooperation and Development (OECD). 1996. *Employment Outlook, July*. Paris: OECD.

Pontusson, Jonas, and Peter Swenson. 1996. "Labor Markets, Production Strategies, and Wage Bargaining Institutions: The Swedish Employer Offensive in Comparative Perspective." *Comparative Political Studies* 29: 223–50.

Rehn, Gösta. 1952. "The Problem of Stability: An Analysis of Some Policy Proposals." In Ralph Turvey (ed.), *Wages Policy under Full Employment*. London: W. Hodge.

Rueda, David, and Jonas Pontusson. 2000. "Wage Inequality and Varieties of Capitalism." *World Politics* 52: 350–83.

Sen, Amartya. 1975. *Employment, Technology and Development*. Oxford: Clarendon.

Smith, Adam. 1976. *An Inquiry into the Nature and Causes of the Wealth of Nations*. Reprint. Chicago: University of Chicago Press.

Statistics Norway. 1995. *Historical Statistics*. Oslo: Central Bureau of Statistics.

Swenson, Peter. 1989. *Fair Shares: Unions, Pay and Politics in Sweden and West Germany*. Ithaca: Cornell University Press.

————. 1991. "Bringing Capital Back in, or Social Democracy." *World Politics* 43 (4): 513–44.

————. 2002. *Capitalists against Markets*. Oxford: Oxford University Press.

Therborn, Göran. 1986. *Why Some Peoples Are More Unemployed than Others*. London: Verso.

Wallerstein, Michael. 1989. "Union Organization in Advanced Industrial Democracies." *American Political Science Review* 83: 481–501.

————. 1999. "Wage-Setting Institutions and Pay Inequality in Advanced Industrial Societies." *American Journal of Political Science* 43: 649–80.

Wallerstein, Michael, and Miriam Golden. 1997. "The Fragmentation of the Bargaining Society: Wage-Setting in the Nordic Countries, 1950–1992." *Comparative Political Studies* 30 (6): 699–731.

Weiss, Andrew. 1990. *Efficiency Wages*. Princeton: Princeton University Press.

Wilensky, Harold. 2002. *Rich Democracies*. Berkeley: University of California Press.

World Bank. 2002. *World Development Indicators*. Washington, D.C.: World Bank.

CHAPTER 7

Globalization and Democracy

Adam Przeworski & Covadonga Meseguer Yebra

WE EXAMINE THE CLAIM that globalization narrows policy choices, thus depriving citizens of the ability to decide through the democratic process. By now a conventional story is that "globalization," whatever it is, sharply restricts the capacity of national governments to pursue policies preferred by citizens of their countries. Moreover, since the external constrains are overwhelming, parties representing different interests within each country are forced to propose the same policies or at least to pursue the same policies if elected. Hence, the democratic process is impotent. Here is how *The Economist* (27 September 2001) sees the current public opinion: "The institutions that in most people's eyes represent the global economy—the IMF, the World Bank and the World Trade Organization—are reviled far more widely than they are admired. . . . Governments, meanwhile, are accused of bowing down to business: globalisation leaves them no choice. Private capital moves across the planet unchecked. Wherever it goes, it bleeds democracy of content and puts 'profits before people.' "

Note that this claim is twofold. Globalization may push governments *in different countries* to follow similar policies. It may also compel parties representing different constituencies *within particular countries* to propose and implement similar policies. Another way to make this distinction is to think that globalization may reduce policy differences across economic conditions or may reduce partisan differences under the same conditions. These effects may operate in conjunction: if all governments have to pursue the same policy, then it makes no difference what parties propose in elections. They need not to, however: national governments may have a choice, but parties may still offer the same proposals. Moreover, the implications of these two effects for democracy are not the same.

To study the impact of globalization on the differences among politically sovereign countries, one can rely on the workhorse of political economy, the median voter model. Even if (two) parties within each country represent different interests, as long as they know the distribution of voter preferences, they converge to the ideal position of the voter with the median preference. With regard to policies that entail any kind of redistribution, this preference depends on income inequality and on the shadow cost of public funds. Hence, if each country autonomously chooses policies through the democratic process, the impact of globalization can be decomposed into its effect on income distribution and the effect on tax competition. This is, however, not the end of the story, since national policies can be coordinated voluntarily at the international scale or imposed from the outside independently of country-specific conditions. By forging a widespread opinion about best policies or by conditioning investment, loans, or aid on particular policies, foreign actors may either alter the preference of the decisive voter or insert a wedge between the preferences of less well-informed electorates and better-informed governments.

The impact of globalization on partisan differences within countries is much more difficult to determine. Clearly, if everyone knows that whichever party is elected will be subject to overwhelming external constraints, either parties will propose the same policies or their electoral proposals will not be credible. Suppose, however, that national governments have some margin in choosing policies. Does purely economic interdependence reduce the difference between policies of parties representing different interests?

To answer this question, we need to understand why parties would not converge to the same policies in politically sovereign countries, which is not obvious. Even if parties represent different interests, policies are constrained by incentive considerations originating from private decisions to save and to work, and these constraints may be sufficiently tight that in the end, as Clark (forthcoming) puts it in the title of his book, it may be "capitalism, not globalism" that forces different parties to adopt similar policies. Electoral constraints also push parties to converge: after all, to pursue policies, parties must win elections, and to win them they must receive support from the same group of marginal voters. Moreover, to the extent to which money influences political outcomes, political parties are more likely to win and to retain office if they pursue policies that generate financial support (Miliband 1970; Grossman and Helpman 2001). Hence, there are good reasons to expect that, even in completely isolated countries, parties with different ideological orientations would propose and implement similar policies. Indeed, a cursory glance at the history of economic policies in Western Europe shows that most of the time they did (Przeworski 2001). Hence, it is not easy to find something for globalization to restrict.

The chapter is organized as follows. First, we conjure a counterfactual of an autarkic, sovereign country and examine reasons why parties would converge to the same policies even under such conditions. To establish a benchmark, we introduce a model in which parties do not converge. Then we lift the assumption of economic autarky, by allowing commodity and capital flows, and examine their impact on cross-country and intracountry policy differences. Subsequently, we relax the assumption of political sovereignty, allowing policies to be coercively transmitted among countries through various mechanisms. We end by claiming that no conclusions about the impact of globalization on policy choice can be drawn, given the current state of knowledge, and then speculate about the impact of globalization on democracy.

BENCHMARK

The first difficulty is raised by the question "compared to what"? If globalization restricts the range of choices, we first need to know what this unrestricted range is. Hence, we need a benchmark.

Consider a world composed of countries in which governments are not subject to any external constraints: autarky in the economic realm and sovereignty in the political realm. No goods are traded, neither capital nor labor moves across borders, there are no international credit markets, no international organizations or agreements, and no pressures by external actors to influence policies of national governments. Since such a world never existed, this is obviously a counterfactual benchmark. But the exercise is illuminating, since it permits us to ask how large would have been the realm of choice under such conditions.

Economic and Political Constraints under Sovereign Autarky

To answer this question, we need to have some idea of how policies are chosen. One can give plausible rival answers to this question. Consider some candidates:

1. Assume that all politicians are utilitarian maximizers: all they want to do is to promote the public interest. For example, all parties seek to maximize the utility of a representative household in a linear economy with a CRRA utility function: this assumption is convenient since maximizing utility is then equivalent to maximizing the rate of economic growth (Barro 1990). Politicians may have different prior beliefs about the effectiveness of alternative policies, say, import substitution versus export promotion. If they are rational, however, they learn from experience both of their own and of other countries, perhaps taking into account the similarity of conditions (see later discussion). Parties choose policies $p \in P$, to maximize their objective. Letting γ stand for the rate of growth, their updated belief about the effectiveness of policy p will then be

$$E_{t+1}(\gamma \mid p) = \rho E_t(\gamma \mid p) + (1 - \rho)\bar{x}_t \mid p, \tag{1}$$

where ρ stands for the precision of their beliefs (inverse of variance) and $\bar{x}$ represents mean experience with policy p of countries facing similar conditions, including one's own. At each time, all parties compare their expectations with regard to different policies and choose the one with the highest value.

Now, unless politicians have a precise prior belief and the experience is noisy—a possibility to which we return—beliefs converge quickly, and soon everyone agrees that some policy p^* is superior to all other policies. New ideas may spring up from time to time independently of experience, but most of the time there will be no difference between political parties within each country and among governments across countries, at least countries facing similar conditions. Hence, there will be nothing for globalization to constrain.

2. Suppose that individuals are ordered by their incomes or by the shares of incomes they derive from return to capital, so that they have different preferences about growth versus redistribution. Say governments represent different interests, so that they are L and R. How much will they differ?

To answer this question, we need to tell a fuller story. One class of such stories—including Przeworski and Wallerstein (1988) and Bertola (1993)—is that governments maximize the present value of utility flows of either labor or capital (alternatively poor and rich) and that they choose tax instruments and tax rates to do so. If the instrument is a tax on incomes, the left government, even if it is a dictator, must consider incentive effects on investment. Then the optimal tax rate of a pure pro-labor government will not be very high. There will be a difference, but not large. In a linear economy, with output/capital ratio v, log utility function, market labor share m, and discount rate ρ, the optimal income tax rate of a dictator that represents homogeneous wage-earners is $\tau_L = (\rho/v - m)/(1 - m)$, which will be low however one calibrates the economy.

3. While economic constraints operate under any political regime, to focus on democracies, consider the effects of electoral competition. A static formulation will suffice (for a fully dynamic version, allowing for time inconsistency, see Persson and Tabellini 2000, chap. 12). Assume that individual incomes y_i are distributed log normally according to $y_i \sim LN(0,\sigma^2)$, where σ^2 is the variance of the log of incomes. The policy instrument is a proportional tax on incomes, τ.[1] Tax revenues are distributed under a balanced budget as uniform transfers, and they are consumed, so that tax rates uniquely determine the extent of redistribution. Let the shadow cost of public funds be λ. Then the post-fisc income or consumption of $i \in N$ will be

$$c_i = (1 - \tau)y_i + \tau y(1 - \lambda\tau), \qquad (2)$$

where y stands for average income. The amount of income redistributed to or from i is then

$$c_i - y_i = \tau[y(1 - \lambda\tau) - y_i]. \qquad (3)$$

There are two parties, L and R, each of which maximizes the expected consumption of its constituency, which consists of people with low incomes for the left part and people with high incomes for the right one. If parties know the distribution of voters' preferences, in the electoral equilibrium both parties converge to the peak preference of the voter with median income, which (in the interior) is

$$\tau^M = \frac{1 - y^M/y}{2\lambda} \equiv (1 - \Delta)/2\lambda, \qquad (4)$$

where y^M is the median income and $\Delta \equiv y^M/y = \exp(-\sigma^2/2)$. To get some sense of these numbers, here are illustrative values of τ^M.

The equilibrium tax rates increase in income inequality and decline in the deadweight costs. But in this model, parties converge to the same platform even if they represent different constituencies.

TABLE 7.1.
Illustrative Tax Rates as a Function of Inequality

	Poland 1986	*Mexico 1989*
λ	$\Delta \approx 0.82$	$\Delta \approx 0.59$
0.2	0.50	1.00
0.3	0.33	0.66

As the preceding discussion suggests, even if countries were completely autarkic economically and sovereign politically, the range of choice of governments in capitalist democracies would be limited by the constraints originating from private property and from electoral competition. Private property implies that decisions about the allocation of resources are made privately and that they are sensitive to relative rates of return. Since policies affect rates of return, governments must anticipate the effect of their policies on the rate of utilization and the allocation of resources. Electoral competition, in turn, forces parties to anticipate the effects of their proposals and of actual policies on their chances to be elected and reelected. If they share beliefs about the distribution of voters and about the effects of alternative policies—and they have ample opportunity to learn from experience— parties are pulled toward the same platforms and policies.

Choice under Sovereign Autarky

To examine the effects of globalization on the range of policy choices, one cannot begin on the assumption that in a non-globalized world parties would represent citizens who want different things, would propose different policies, and implement them if victorious. Parties may represent different constituencies, but they face constraints originating from their local economy and they must win elections to pursue policies. Moreover, if they learn from experience, most of the time politicians of different stripes hold the same beliefs. As a result, most of the time, they do the same while in office. Hence, even in a world of autarkic economies and sovereign states, we would expect to find only limited differences between parties within each country and, if learning transcends borders, only small differences among governments of different countries facing the same conditions.[2]

Given this conclusion, we might as well end the chapter right here, just with a rhetorical question: "What is there for globalization to narrow?" But since we would not have fulfilled our task, we need to investigate under what conditions parties would offer different proposals and pursue different policies in an autarkic, sovereign country. We know from Roemer (2001) that divergence is to be expected in an electoral equilibrium if parties represent different interests and if they are uncertain about something.[3] The former assumption is realistic, indeed, more plausible than the Downsian idea that parties care only about winning. The latter assumption is less persuasive, since parties have ample opportunity to learn over time. Suppose, however, that party leaders have strong experience and prior beliefs, about effects of alternative policies or about beliefs of voters, are noisy.

A relatively simple model of such situations is Roemer's (2001, section 5.2) Average-Member Nash Equilibrium, which captures a conception of a "perfectly representative democracy." We modify this model slightly to be able to derive comparative statics with regard to income inequality. The intuitive idea is the following: Take the assumptions of the median voter model introduced earlier, but assume that the left party believes that the shadow price of public funds is low, $\lambda = \underline{\lambda}$, while the right party believes it is high, $\lambda = \bar{\lambda}$. Neither party knows what the voters believe: all politicians know is that $\lambda \sim U[\underline{\lambda}, \bar{\lambda}]$. Each party maximizes expected average consumption of the people who vote for it. Party L proposes and implements τ_L; Party R offers and implements τ_R, $\tau_L \geq \tau_R$. In equilibrium, all individuals with incomes lower than some $\bar{y}(\tau_L, \tau_R; \lambda)$ vote for Party L and all those with incomes above it vote for Party R.

Armed with this model, we can calculate party platforms and the distance between them as a function of income inequality. The results are in table 7.2.

As in the case of certainty, higher inequality, as represented by Δ^{-1}, is associated with higher expected redistribution, $E(\tau)$, while higher expected deadweight losses reduce redistribution. As uncertainty increases, partisan proposals diverge.

TABLE 7.2.
Party Platforms and the Distance between Them as a Function of Inequality

Δ	τ^M	τ_L	τ_R	$E(\tau)$	$\tau_L - \tau_R$
		$\underline{\lambda} = 0.1$	$\bar{\lambda} = 0.3$		
0.90	0.25	0.30	0.14	0.26	0.16
0.80	0.50	0.55	0.27	0.46	0.28
0.60	1.00	1.00	0.62	0.88	0.38
		$\underline{\lambda} = 0.0$	$\bar{\lambda} = 0.4$		
0.90	0.25	0.27	0.09	0.23	0.18
0.80	0.50	0.51	0.17	0.41	0.34
0.60	1.00	0.95	0.39	0.75	0.56
		$\underline{\lambda} = 0.1$	$\bar{\lambda} = 0.5$		
0.90	0.17	0.20	0.07	0.17	0.13
0.80	0.33	0.31	0.13	0.29	0.18
0.60	0.67	0.64	0.29	0.55	0.25

More directly for our question, these simulations indicate that higher inequality is associated with larger policy difference between parties.

These are the results that we will use as the benchmark to study the impact of globalization on partisan differences.

GLOBALIZATION

Globalization may work in two ways: indirectly on conditions and directly on policies. Through trade and capital flows, globalization affects economic conditions in each country, so that even if policies are locally determined, they are affected by globalization. When countries lose some of their political sovereignty, national policies are directly influenced by some outside agents, whether or not they reflect national conditions. We consider these mechanisms in turn, first lifting the assumption of economic autarky and then of political sovereignty.

Economic Interdependence

INTERCOUNTRY DIFFERENCES

Let us begin again in a world in which all countries are economically autarkic and politically sovereign. All countries have identical distributions of income, so that the median voter dictates the same redistribution policy in all countries. Now lift the assumption of economic autarky, assuming that all countries open their borders to flows of commodities and of capital. Suppose that trade increases inequality in some countries (more developed or less developed: whichever you prefer), thus generating intercountry differences in income distribution. By the median voter mechanism, one expects a higher degree of redistribution in a country that became more unequal. But tax competition, arising from capital mobility,[4] increases the costs of redistributing incomes, thus driving down the electorally optimal rates of redistribution in all countries. The combined effect of trade and capital openness will thus cause policies to diverge (via the inequality-redistribution path), while the net effect on the rate of redistribution in the now less-equal country will depend on the relative magnitude of these two effects. Figure 7.1 shows how a story of two countries might look.

In the autarkic world, income distribution in the two countries is the same and so is the policy dictated by the median voter, τ^M. As inequality in country k increases, and so does τ_k^M. But the impact of tax competition is to reduce τ in both countries. Under the combined impact of trade and capital mobility, policies diverge, $\tau_k^M > \tau_j^M$, the tax rate in j falls, so that $\tau_j^M < \tau^M$, while the direction of policy change in k is indeterminate. Hence, *if the effect of openness is to increase income inequality in the already more-unequal countries*, then policies

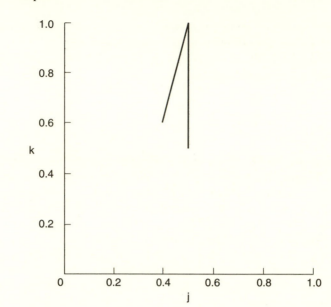

Figure 7.1. The Impact of Increased Inequality and of Capital Mobility on Tax Rates.

chosen by sovereign countries will diverge from one another, while the rates of redistribution may or may not decline everywhere. We later study other possibilities.

This argument is based on the assumption that capital mobility causes an additional deadweight loss if the tax rate in a country exceeds that of its closest competitor. Given the tax rate τ_k in the competing country k, the post-fisc income of individual i in country j is now

$$c_{ij} = (1 - \tau_j)y_{ij} + \tau_j y_j[(1 - \lambda\tau_j - \lambda(\tau_j - \tau_k)], \tag{5}$$

so that the median voter opts for and parties converge to

$$\tau_j^M(\tau_k) = (1 - \Delta_j)/4\lambda + \tau_k/4. \tag{6}$$

Solving for the Nash equilibrium yields

$$\tau_j^* = [4(1 - \Delta_j) + (1 - \Delta_k)]/15\lambda, \tag{6a}$$

$$\tau_k^* = [4(1 - \Delta_k) + (1 - \Delta_j)]/15\lambda. \tag{6b}$$

Table 7.3 shows some illustrative values (for $\lambda = 0.2$):[5]

We can now parametrize figure 7.1. Suppose that in the autarkic world both countries had $\Delta = 0.8$, so that their tax rates were $\tau^M = 0.5$. As an effect of trade, inequality in k increased to $\Delta = 0.6$. Poland, with $\Delta \approx 0.82$ in 1986 and $\Delta \approx 0.62$ in 1995 would be an illustration. If k had not opened its capital account, its tax

TABLE 7.3.
Illustrative Tax Rates in Open Economies as a Function of Inequality

Δ_j	Δ_k	τ_j	τ_k
0.8	—	0.50	—
—	0.6	—	1.00
0.8	0.8	0.33	0.33
0.8	0.6	0.40	0.60
0.6	0.6	0.66	0.66

rate would have been 1.00: this is the effect of inequality. Tax competition, in turn, brings the tax rate in k down to 0.6, which is still higher than under autarky, while reducing the tax rate in j from 0.5 to 0.4. Hence, as two autarkic countries with $\Delta = 0.8$ open to trade and capital flows, tax rates diverge, decreasing in the country where income distribution remained the same and increasing in the country where inequality increased. Note that if inequality had not changed in either country, tax competition would have the effect of lowering tax rates in both.[6] If openness had increased inequality in both countries, however, tax rates would have been higher in both in spite of tax competition.

Unless one introduces more assumptions than those found in Chinese astrology manuals, no conclusions follow. All one can say is that things are not as simple as they may appear. Economic openness may uniformly increase the rates of redistribution if its effect on inequality is universal and stronger than the effect of tax competition; openness may increase the variance if its effects on income distribution vary across countries; finally, openness may uniformly decrease redistribution if it has no effect on income distribution but it induces tax competition.

When theory is a poor guide, looking at data is sometimes of help. The average tax rate in the world increased somewhat and the variance did even more between 1975 and 1995. As Obstfeld (1998: 20) observes, "Looking at the effects of international tax competition so far, it is hard to argue that we see anything close to equivalent overall capital tax rates across countries, or equivalent levels of social spending." Eichengreen (1990), however, found that across-states tax variability in the United States, while far from zero, was much lower than within Europe. Hence, the verdict may not be yet in.

Estimates of the impact of economic openness on the degree of redistribution generate divergent results. Cameron (1978), Rodrik (1997), and Garrett (1998) argue that openness to trade increases economic volatility and creates demand for insurance via the public sector, but Iversen and Cusack (2000) disagree, providing evidence from the OECD countries.[7] International financial integration depresses the spending levels of governments in Cusack (1997) and in Garrett and Mitchell (2000), but these results are not robust. Note that capital mobility may have contradictory effects on the tax rates: by increasing income inequality (Mundell 1957), it should lead to higher tax rates, but to the extent it induces tax competition, it should depress them. Another complication is that capital mobility may not influence the aggregate tax levels but just shift the burden from capital onto labor. Yet here again, econometric results are strangely diverse: while Rodrik (1997) found such an effect, Quinn (1997), Swank (1998), Garrett (2000), and Garrett and Mitchell (2000) discovered that capital taxation is either unchanged or even higher in countries with open capital accounts. This may be true again if capital openness at the same time increases inequality and induces tax competition and the two effects counteract one another. In the end, we are not sure what to believe.

TRADE AND CAPITAL MOBILITY: INTRACOUNTRY DIFFERENCES

To study the effect of trade and tax competition on partisan differences within countries, we now apply the model with uncertainty to an open economy. Everything is the same as in the autarkic country in which parties are not certain about λ, except that now only post-fisc incomes are now given by (5). We do not solve for an equilibrium of tax competition, since all the necessary results can be shown without it. Hence, we take the tax rates τ_k as given and study partisan proposals in country j as a function of income inequality, for $\lambda \in (0.1, 0.3)$.

The rows where τ_k is not given repeat the benchmark results for a closed country. As we see, tax competition invariably reduces partisan differences within each country. These differences seem not to depend on the actual tax rate in the foreign country (they are within rounding errors of about ∓ 0.03). In the more equal country, partisan differences are reduced by about one-half, in the less equal country by about one-third. Increasing uncertainty to $\lambda \in (0.0, 0.4)$ without changing the expected value seems not to affect the distance between parties (the distance in the more equal country is still about 0.14 for all tax rates in k).

Why would tax competition not only reduce the expected tax rates but also the partisan differences? The Right party wants taxes to be low even in a closed economy; if it offers positive tax rates, it is only because it is then more likely to win an election and implement less redistribution than the Left party would have. The Left party wants more redistribution. But when a country faces tax competition, redistribution becomes additionally costly. Given that the marginal cost of redistribution increases in the tax rates, the trade-off becomes steeper for the Left party and it reduces its proposed rates by more than the Right one. Hence, the proposals converge.

Consider the following scenario. Under autarky, both countries have relatively low inequality, $\Delta = 0.8$. As a result of opening, income inequality in k increases sharply, to $\Delta = 0.6$, and tax competition emerges. Then the expected tax rate in j falls from 0.46 to 0.33 and the partisan difference is halved, while the expected tax rate in k increases somewhat, from 0.46 to 0.54, and partisan differences re-

TABLE 7.4.
Party Platforms and the Distance between Them as a Function of Inequality in Open
Economies

τ_k	τ_j^M	τ_L	τ_R	$E(\tau)$	$\tau_L - \tau_R$
		$\Delta = 0.8$			
none	0.50	0.55	0.27	0.46	0.28
0.33	0.33	0.35	0.20	0.33	0.15
0.66	0.42	0.41	0.27	0.40	0.14
1.00	0.50	0.50	0.37	0.48	0.13
		$\Delta = 0.6$			
none	1.00	1.00	0.62	0.88	0.38
0.33	0.58	0.60	0.32	0.54	0.28
0.66	0.66	0.67	0.41	0.61	0.26
1.00	0.75	0.81	0.52	0.71	0.29

main the same. Hence, even in politically sovereign countries, globalization will have reduced partisan differences in the country in which income distribution was not affected and will have increased the expected tax rate in the country that became more unequal.

Political Interdependence

Policies may spread from country to country through several, not mutually exclusive, mechanisms. One we already mentioned, namely, rational (Bayesian) learning. The second possibility is that everyone is doing what others are doing, either by coordinating policies or by pure emulation. The third is coercion, as typified by explicit conditionality of loans, grants, or aid. Finally, it is also possible that good ideas are so obvious that they spread like fire: once discovered or invented, they are instantaneously recognized as superior by almost everyone. If any of these mechanisms operate, policies converge across countries, almost instantaneously when they reflect a discovery of a superior idea, gradually when they entail learning or emulation, and conditionally when they involve coercion.

Meseguer (2002) examined the diffusion of four policies between 1950 and 1990: export orientation, privatization, participation in IMF programs, and central bank independence, the last not reported here.[8] She studied first whether policy diffusion resulted from a Bayesian learning process. In her model, governments start with some prior beliefs about the effectiveness of alternative policies, $p = \{A,B\}$. In each period, t, governments observe the average growth rates associated with these policies as well as their variability.[9] In the view of experience, governments update their beliefs about the average and about variability of outcomes. Policy choices at t are based on posterior beliefs, which become priors at $t+1$. The updating process proceeds sequentially. At $t+1$, new information is observed, beliefs are updated, and a new choice is made. Policy choice is a comparative exercise: governments choose the policy that, according to their posterior beliefs, will yield the best outcome with the least or most variability.[10]

As distinct from rational learning, emulation does not entail an understanding of the links between policies and outcomes (Rose 1991; Bennett 1991; May 1992). The number of other countries engaged in a particular policy during a particular year is a proxy for the general climate of opinion regarding that policy realm (Broz 1999). Governments may tie their hands or emulate policies pursued elsewhere for electoral reasons: if these policies are domestically unpopular, the political costs of adopting them are lower when many other countries are pursuing them (Vreeland 2000). They may also subject themselves, however, to common policy prescriptions or emulate policies of other countries because they believe that these policies are preferred by foreign investors and international financial institutions (Simmons and Elkins 2000; Weyland 2004). Emulation may thus be a way of self-imposing or anticipating external constraints.

Finally, it may be that governments do not choose but are forced to accept policies imposed by third parties. Coercion captures this idea and conditionality epitomizes it. Governments need loans, aid, or private investment, and they adopt policies preferred by foreign agents in exchange for them.[11]

To test these hypotheses, Meseguer (2002) estimated a Markov chain model in which transition probabilities depend on policy results, the number of other countries that pursue them, and the participation in IMF programs. The results concerning the probabilities of switching to export-orientation, to privatizing, and to participating in IMF programs are shown in figure 7.5. Experience is structured at three levels: one's country, the region a country belongs to, and the world. Hence, there are three sources of learning. Since conditions are likely to differ in the region and even more in the world, the hypothesis is that governments learn more from their own country's experience than from region and world experience (Robinson 1998). In turn, due to similarity in conditions, the experience of neighboring countries will be more informative than the experience in the world. The number of other countries under each of the policies (emulation) and participation in IMF programs (coercion) complete the model (t-values in parentheses).

In general, it seems that some rational learning, whether about the average performance or about the risks involved, is an inherent mechanism of international diffusion of policies. Governments learn either from the experience of their own countries or from those of their region and the rest of world. They exhibit different risk postures with regard to different policies. Yet with regard to some policies, they also emulate blindly or respond to direct pressures, as epito-

TABLE 7.5.
International Determinants of National Policies

Policy	Trade	Privatization	IMF
LaggedPolicy	−4.99***	−2.70***	−1.19***
	(−5.96)	(−5.67)	(−8.61)
	Own	Experience	
Average	0.02	0.16**	0.02**
	(0.53)	(2.23)	(3.08)
Variability	−0.07	−0.28	−0.02
	(−1.17)	(−0.58)	(−0.79)
	Regional	Experience	
Average	0.32**	0.23*	−0.02
	(1.98)	(1.65)	(−0.98)
Variability	−0.29	0.26	0.05*
	(−1.53)	(0.70)	(1.72)
	World	Experience	
Average	0.002	0.22*	0.21***
	(0.01)	(1.72)	(2.66)
Variability	−0.68***	−0.12	0.19***
	(−2.15)	(−0.77)	(3.21)
#Others	0.63***	0.75***	0.0005
	(3.95)	(3.89)	(0.012)
IMF	0.46**	0.19	
	(2.22)	(0.66)	
N	1171	586	3488

*p < .10
**p < .05
***p < .01

mized by IMF conditionality. Finally, note that since patterns of diffusion are gradual, there is little room for an explanation based on an uncontested superiority of new ideas.

The most salient result originates from the contrast between the switch to export orientation and the decision to begin privatizing. While privatization entails emulation, it is driven by rational learning: governments decide to privatize because they see that privatization increases growth rates. In contrast, the decisions to pursue export-oriented policies take into account only the performance within a particular region and exhibit strong risk aversion when governments look at the rest of the world. They are driven primarily by policy coordination (or emulation), and they are adopted when countries participate in IMF programs.

Presumably, even sovereign governments would learn from the experience of other countries. They might also emulate fashionable policies, even if one can suspect that increased international interactions make emulation easier. But to the extent that the number of other countries that pursue a particular policy indicates policy coordination or an anticipation of the policy preferences of donors and investors, emulation constitutes evidence of foreign influence over domestic policies. The impact of IMF, finally, is a piece of hard evidence that countries open themselves to trade under external pressures.

CONCLUSIONS, OR ABSENCE THEREOF

First, a summary:

1. There are reasons to expect that redistributive policies would differ little between similar countries and between parties representing different constituencies even if the world consisted of autarkic and sovereign countries.

2. The effect of economic openness on policy differences between and within countries depends on its impact on income distribution and on tax competition. If inequality increases in the more unequal countries, tax rates diverge; otherwise, they converge. Tax competition dampens redistribution everywhere. When parties represent different constituencies and are uncertain about something, rising inequality increases partisan differences but tax competition reduces them.

3. Direct external influences on national policies—whether in the form of a general opinion climate or explicit conditionality—seem to be highly policy-specific. Policies concerning central banks' independence are not transmitted across borders by learning, emulation, or conditionality. On the other hand, trade policies entail all three mechanisms. There are reasons to believe that international pressure forced some countries to trade; as more countries traded, keeping trade barriers became more costly; and governments learned from experience that lowering trade barriers is superior for growth.

This entire analysis is based on two assumptions: (1) that the relative income of the decisive voter—her percentile in income distribution—does not depend on income inequality and (2) that this voter demands more redistribution in more unequal societies. Given these assumptions, conclusions concerning the impact of globalization on policy choice are contingent on economics: the impact of openness on inequality.

Unfortunately, the conclusions should be even more contingent. Both statistical analyses of the OECD countries and anecdotal evidence from less developed ones show that more unequal countries may in fact redistribute less, rather than more. The decisive voter may be relatively more affluent in more unequal countries, either because relatively or absolutely poor people do not vote or because the relatively richer people have more influence over politics (Benabou 1996, 2001). Hence, even if demand for redistribution increases as the decisive voter becomes relatively poorer, the decisive voter may have higher relative income in more unequal countries. In turn, there are several arguments to the effect that the decisive voter may want more redistribution in more equal societies. Moene and Wallerstein (2001) argue that the demand for redistribution depends on the design of the redistributive policies, specifically, that demand for income insurance declines as inequality increases. Perotti (1996) initiated a line of analyses in which the effect of income distribution is different depending on per capita income. Benabou (2001) shows that if redistribution is productive, it is U-shaped with regard to inequality. Hence, it is at least equally plausible that via a combination of these mechanisms, rising inequality reduces rather than, as we have been assuming, increases the demand for redistribution in electoral equilibria.

While we have not replicated all the analyses, intuitively one would expect the following:

Effect of Inequality on Redistribution	Openness Increases Inequality in Countries that Are		
	More Unequal	Less Unequal	Everywhere
Increases	Taxes increase divergence	Taxes increase convergence	Taxes increase ???
U-shaped	Taxes increase divergence	Taxes decrease convergence	??? ???
Decreases	Taxes decrease convergence	Taxes decrease divergence	Taxes decrease ???

As we see, given our current state of knowledge, both about economic and political mechanisms, everything is possible.

GLOBALIZATION AND DEMOCRACY

Prima facie observation indicates that people around the world perceive a growing "democratic deficit" and that they associate their dissatisfaction with democracy to globalization. But what is it that they object against? Do they object against having no choice or against having bad choices?

It is not obvious that democrats should value having choice in itself. Our search—by the nature of things incomplete—found only one democratic theorist who requires democracy to offer distinct alternatives to citizens: Bobbio, whose *minimal* definition of democracy contains a condition that "those called upon to take decisions, or to elect those who are to take decisions, must be offered real alternatives" (1987: 25).[12] Yet whenever different parties propose or pursue similar policies, bells toll alarms about the functioning of democracy and about the legitimacy of electoral institutions. Elections are seen as pointless: "Tweedledum and Tweedledee," *"bonnet blanc et blanc bonnet."* When parties propose the same policies, there is nothing to choose; when they follow the same policies in office, electoral choices are inconsequential. Democracy is anemic. Observing democratic governments in Western Europe since World War I, one is struck by how old this complaint is:

1. During a 1922 budgetary debate in the Swedish parliament, the Liberal leader, Eden, observed that the Social Democratic government was "bourgeois to an unexpectedly high degree," to which Hjalmar Branting, the Prime Minister replied, "I believe that amongst the Swedish labouring masses who have given their votes to our party there exists a high political training and an insight into the exigencies of the situation. I think that in relying upon this we have dared to put into practice a policy that is (to quote Herr Eden) as 'bourgeois' as it could possibly be, in accordance with his own description." (Tingsten, 1973: 251). Leftist analyses of the MacDonald government as well as of the Front Populaire blamed them for not breaking with the standard economic wisdom of the time, accused them of "selling out," and questioned whether elections can make a difference in a capitalist economy (Miliband 1959, Lefranc 1965, Greene 1969).

2. The "Keynesian welfare state" evoked the same reaction, which exploded in 1968. The Cohn-Bendit brothers (1968) saw electoral competition as a choice between "gin and tonic and tonic and gin." The complaint that parties make no difference was passionate: "The working class is lost in administering its imaginary bastions. Comrades disguised as notables occupy themselves with municipal garbage dumps and school cafeterias. Or are these notables disguised as comrades? I no longer know." (Konopnicki 1979: 53)

3. Now again, the perception that choices facing all governments follow similar policies is widespread. Even *The Economist* (2 May 1995) triumphantly observed that "the differences between New Labour and watered-down Thatcherism are far more of style than of substance." The diagnosis is shared by critics of globalization: "Two things tend to happen: your economy grows and your politics shrinks. . . . The Golden Straitjacket narrows the political and economic choices of those now in power to relatively tight parameters. . . . Once your country puts on the Golden Straitjacket, its political choices get reduced to Pepsi or Coke" (Friedman 2001).

Is globalization responsible for the withering away of democratic choices? To the extent that national policies are directly influenced by outside actors— say, governments follow an IMF request to reduce spending in the face of glaring inequality—the inability of citizens to determine national policies through a democratic process is apparent. Even if a unique policy is optimal for everyone given the external constraints, citizens have no say in the determination of policies. If not joining the WTO or not obeying the dictates of a Washington "consensus" subjects a country to stiff economic or political sanctions, all governments will find it in the best, albeit constrained, interest of their country to join and obey. True, citizens may vote out of office a government that pursues this policy. But if the incumbent government adopted this policy because it had to, then all governments will do the same. Hence, the political processes within each country will be just inconsequential. No matter what parties propose and who gets elected, policies will be the same (Stokes 2001). While the democratic process is internal to each country, the real locus of decision-making is external. At most, citizens will be able to decide which party would best implement the same policy. Conditionality often breeds riots, emulation generates the perception that local policymakers blindly imitate wisdom of foreign origin.[13] When the policy advice is accompanied by a dose of hypocrisy—"do as we say," rather than "do as we do"—these perceptions turn bitter. The only way to empower national citizens would be to subject international relations to direct democratic control, a doubtful possibility according to Dahl (1999).

Globalization may also provide an excuse for the Left to escape its constituency. Claiming that redistribution is costly advances the interests of constituencies of right-wing parties. In turn, once right-wing parties proclaim that governments are limited in what they can do, the best response of left-wing parties is to say the same. Otherwise, the Left would be setting for itself a higher bar than the Right. Hence, there may exist some kind of collusive electoral equilibria (Harrington 1993) in which parties plead impotence in the face of globalization. As Rodrik (1997–98: 16) puts it, "Employers are doing so because it is in their interest, at least in the short run; politicians are doing so because it is convenient to plead helplessness in the face of the global economy." Forced to choose between globalization and the irresponsibility of the Left, *The Economist* (27 September 2001) predictably opts for the latter. In an article entitled "A crisis of legitimacy: People are fed up with politics. Do not blame globalisation for that," the writer observes, "In all kinds of ways, again and again, governments and their political opponents have used the supposed demands of globalisation to deny responsibility. If you tell people you are helpless often enough, they will start to believe you." The Left is the culprit:

One of the principal themes in western politics of the past ten or 15 years has been the "modernisation" of the left. Ex-socialist and moderate left-of-center parties alike have moved to the centre, and in some cases past it. . . . "The world has changed," Tony Blair tells his traditional party supporters, "but our values have not." In other words, if we only could, we would still like to do all the things leftist parties have traditionally done. We cannot, because the world now follows different rules. . . . We have to sound more like our conservative opponents—and the reason is globalisation.

But democracy may offer choices and it may work in a perfectly representative way under the constraints, and people may still object against globalization and, correctly, see democracy as impotent. Consider a country (with $E(\lambda) = 0.2$) that experiences increased inequality as a result of globalization (c_j is the post-fisc income of the median voter under different proposals; see table 7.6).

The partisan difference remains the same, so that voters have as much choice as before. The proposed tax rates increase. But these taxes will not compensate one half of the population for the increased inequality. However policy is determined and whoever wins, at least half of the voters will be worse off under globalization, even if democracy works perfectly: parties offer distinct proposals, every citizen is represented by a party, everyone votes, and the winner is decided by majority vote.

The median voter will not be worse off under globalization if economic openness increases average income by at least 10 percent. Whether globalization has this effect, we do not know: our bet is that if one were Bayesian about it, no effect would lie smack in the middle of the 95 percent confidence interval. But we know that, à la Besley and Coate (1997), the median voter would not have opted for opening commodity and capital markets unless she expected average income to increase by at least this amount. If the median voter in the isolated world could be assured that she would benefit from opening the economy even if the average income increased less than 10 percent, she would have opted for the efficient, income-increasing, policy. But commitment is not possible: once the country is open, inequality increases, and democratically determined policy will leave the median voter worse off.[14]

The fact seems to be that voters are rarely consulted with regard to decisions to lower tariffs or to abolish capital controls. These are "technical" decisions, presumably made by competent people with an eye on efficiency. Voters are left to cope with their distributional consequences. Once these decisions are made, however, the losers, even if they constitute a majority, are unable to overcome their

TABLE 7.6.
Consumption Level of the Median Voter in an Open Economy

Δ	τ^M	τ_L	τ_R	c_M	c_L	c_R
0.8	0.50	0.55	0.27	$0.85y$	$0.86y$	$0.84y$
0.6	0.66	0.67	0.41	$0.77y$	$0.77y$	$0.73y$

consequences even when parties continue to represent them, policies are decided by majority rule, and parties implement their electoral mandates.

The story may thus be the following. Under foreign influence—emulation or conditionality—governments plunge into an open world without a democratic consultation. Democracy continues to function after the economy is open. But once a country enters the global world, the constraints shift, and once they shift, the electoral process cannot compensate the losers. Democracy is impotent against the constraints imposed by economic openness. Here is Dunn's (2000: 152) analysis of the United Kingdom:

> In retrospect Mrs. Thatcher's most decisive political act was the complete dismantling, at the very beginning of her first term of office as Prime Minister, of all controls over capital movements into and out of the economy. What this did was to establish a space of political competition between capital and organized labour in which, in the end, the latter could only lose, and in which it was relatively simple to present its predestined loss as unequivocally in the interest of the population at large.

Now, if you think that Mrs. Thatcher was, as she never tired to emphasize, elected to do whatever she wanted, then the fact that redistribution of income ceased to be an option is not a bad limitation on choices. Voters gave Mrs. Thatcher a mandate to do whatever she thought was best; after she did it, some people did not like the choices they had: too bad. If you think, however, that people faced with the option of dismantling capital controls would have rejected it, anticipating the opportunity they would face as the result, then the meagerness of options induced by globalization is a bad limitation. If people bind themselves knowingly, they should not complain even if they do not like their bounds; but if they are bound involuntarily, they have every right to be mad.

In the end, what is not clear is whether the dissatisfaction with democracy arises from the erosion of partisan differences or from policies enclosed within the partisan spectrum. Do citizens feel politically impotent because there is little room between the walls or because the walls are in a bad place? Do they object against not having the freedom to choose or against the policies they can choose?

NOTES

1. All throughout we consider only income, rather than consumption taxes. The reason is that while consumption taxes are investment neutral in a closed eocomy, they would be neutral in an open economy only if exiting capital were taxed at the same rate as consumption (Wallerstein and Przeworski 1995). Abolishing capital controls eliminates this possibility.

2. Testing whether partisan control over the government affects policies and their outcomes is an industry that dates back to Hibbs (1977). This is not the place to summarize

the results: our general conclusion is that they are highly unstable, depending on the policy realm, model specification, the treatment of econometric difficulties, and samples (all of which, by the way, are limited to the OECD countries).

3. Divergence should be also expected if the incumbent is satisfied with the status quo policy, while challengers innovate (Bendor, Mookherjee, and Ray 2001).

4. Note that capital mobility may increase as a result of liberalizing the capital account but also as a result of increased trade, invention of new financial instruments, and developments in information technology.

5. Note that even though we keep λ the same as in the autarkic world, the deadweight loss of taxation in country j is now larger as long as $\tau_j > \tau_k/2$.

6. As Persson and Tabelini (2000: 329) observe, "Tax competition does not pay: it simply distorts governments' incentives."

7. We find that the standard deviation of growth rates declines systematically in openness to trade (4538 annual observations from wherever the data are available), ranging from 12.54 in countries with OPEN < 0.25, to 7.83 in countries with OPEN > 1.00.

8. The database for trade liberalization focused on fifty-one developing countries; the privatization database referred to thirty-seven Latin American and industrial countries, and for IMF, models were run on 135 developed and developing countries. Central Bank Independence is not reported since in most countries banks were independent at the first observation.

9. If results are very noisy, average economic performance conveys little information about the effectiveness of policies.

10. Depending on risk postures.

11. The caveats to this story are abundant. Recent research has shown that governments may seek conditionality in an attempt to curb opposition to policies that they want to implement (Vreeland 2000). In quite a few cases, conditionality helped nudge governments in the direction of adopting particular policies, but politicians were already inclined to move (Stallings 1992; Kahler 1992; Haggard and Williamson 1994).

12. Elsewhere, he argues that "to pass a judgement today on the development of democracy in a given country the question must be asked, not 'Who votes?' but 'On what issues can one vote?'" (1989: 157).

13. See Bresser Pereira (2002) for the claim that Brazilian economic policymakers naïvely accept theoretical wisdom originating from outside instead of thinking autonomously about what is in the best national interest.

14. This is why arguments that globalization increases efficiency or total output and reduces governmental rent-seeking (see Vanberg 2000) are irrelevant. Potential Pareto superiority (compensation criterion) is neither here nor there if the promise of compensation is not credible.

REFERENCES

Bannerjee, A., and E. Duflo. 2000. "Inequality and Growth: What Can Data Say?"
Mimeo, Department of Economics, MIT, June.
Barro, R. J. 1990. "Government Spending in a Simple Model of Endogenous Growth."
Journal of Political Economy 98: S103–S126.

Benabou, R. 1996. "Inequality and Growth." *NBER Macroeconomics Annual.* (Cambridge: MIT Press) 11: 74.

———. 2000. "Unequal Societies: Income Distribution and the Social Contract." *American Economic Review* 90: 96–129.

———. 2001. "Mobility as Progressivity, Ranking Income Processes According to Equality of Opportunity. NBER Working Paper No. 8431.

Bendor, J., D. Mookherjee, and D. Ray. 2001. "Reinforcement Learning in Repeated Interaction Games." *Advances in Theoretical Economics* 1 (1): article 3.

Bennett, C. 1991. "What Is Policy Convergence and What Causes It?" *British Journal of Political Science* 21: 215–33.

Bertola, G. 1993. "Factor Shares and Savings in Endogenous Growth." *American Economic Review* 83: 1184–198.

Besley, T., and S. Coate. 1998. "Sources of Inefficiency in Representative Democracy: A Dynamic Analysis." *American Economic Review* 88: 139–56.

Bobbio, N. 1987. *The Future of Democracy. A Defense of the Rules of the Game.* Minneapolis: University of Minnessota Press.

———. 1989. *Democracy and Dictatorship.* Minneapolis: University of Minnesota Press.

Bourgignon, F., and T. Verdier. 2000. "Oligarchy, Democracy, Inequality, and Growth." *Journal of Development Economics* 62: 285–313.

Bresser Pereira, L. C. 2002. "Latin America's Quasi-Stagnation." Forthcoming in Paul Davidson (ed.), *A Post Keynesian Perspective in 21st Century Economic Problems.* London: Edward Elgar.

Broz, L. 1999. "Political Institutions and the Transparency of Monetary Policy Committee." Manuscript, New York University.

Cameron, D. 1978. "The Expansion of the Public Economy: A Comparative Analysis." *American Political Science Review* 72: 1243–61.

Clark, W. R. Forthcoming. *Capitalism, Not Globalism: Capital Mobility, Central Bank Independence, and the Political Control of the Economy.* Ann Arbor: University of Michigan Press.

Cohn-Bendit Brothers. 1968. *Obsolete Communism: The Left-wing Alternative.* New York: McGraw-Hill.

Cusack T. R. 1997. "Partisan Politics and Public Finance: Changes in Public Spending in the Industrialized Democracies, 1955–1989." *Public Choice* 91: 375–95.

Dahl, R. 1999. "Prospects for Democracy." *Social Research* 66 (3)(Fall): 709–958.

Dunn, J. 2000. *The Cunning of Unreason: Making Sense of Politics.* London: Harper Collins.

Eichengreen, B. 1990. "One Money for Europe? Lessons from the U.S. Currency Union." *Economic Policy* 10: 118–87.

———. 2001. "Capital Account Liberalization: What Do Cross-Country Studies Tell Us?" *The World Bank Economic Review* 15: 341–66.

Feenstra, R. C. 1998. "Integration of Trade and Disintegration of Production in the Global Economy." *Journal of Economic Perspectives* 12: 31–50.

Friedman, T. 2001. *The Lexus and the Olive Tree: Understanding Globalization.* New York: Anchor.

Garrett, G. 1998. *Partisan Politics in the Global Economy.* New York: Cambridge University Press.

————. 2000. "Capital Mobility, Exchange Rates and Fiscal Policy in the Global Economy." *Review of International Political Economy* 7: 15–70.

Garrett, G., and D. Mitchell. 2000. "Globalization, Government Spending, and Taxation in the OECD." *European Journal of Political Research* 39 (2): 145–77.

Greene, N. 1969. *Crisis and Decline: The French Socialist Party in the Popular Front Era.* Ithaca: Cornell University Press.

Grossman, G. M., and E. Helpman. 2001. *Special Interest Politics.* Cambridge: MIT Press.

Haggard, S., and J. Williamson. 1994. "The Political Conditions for Economic Reform." Pp. 525–96 in John Williamson (ed.), *The Political Economy of Policy Reform.* Washington, D.C.: Institute for International Economics.

Harrington, J. E., Jr. 1993. "The Impact of Reelection Pressures on the Fulfillment of Campaign Promises." *Games and Economic Behavior* 5: 71–97.

Hibbs, D. A. 1977. "Political Parties and Macroeconomic Policy." *American Political Science Review* 71: 467–87.

Iversen, T and T. Cusack. 2000. "The Causes of Welfare State Expansion: Deindustrialization or Globalization?" *World Politics* 52 (3): 313–49.

Kahler, M. 1992. "External Influence, Conditionality, and the Politics of Adjustment." Pp. 89–138 in Stephan Haggard and Robert Kauffman (eds.), *The Politics of Economic Adjustment.* Princeton: Princeton University Press.

Konopnicki, G. 1979. *Vive le centenaire du P.C.F.* Paris: CERF.

Lefranc, G. 1965. *Histoire du Front Populaire.* Paris: Payot.

May, P. 1992. "Policy Learning and Failure." *Journal of Public Policy* 12: 331–54.

Meseguer, C. 2002. *Bayesian Learning About Policies.* Madrid: Instituto Juan March de Estudios e Investigaciones.

Miliband, R. 1959. *The State in Capitalist Society: The Analysis of the Western System of Power.* London: Weidenfeld and Nicolson.

————. 1970. "The Capitalist State: Reply to Nicos Roulantzas." *New Left Review* 59: 53–60.

————. 1972. *Parliamentary Socialism: A Study in the Politics of Labour.* 2nd ed. London: Merlin.

Moene, K., and M. Wallerstein. 2001. "Inequality, Social Insurance, and Redistribution." *American Political Science Review* 95: 859–73.

Mundell, R. A. 1957. "International Trade and Factor Mobility." *American Economic Review* 47: 321–35.

Obstfeld, M. 1998. "The Global Capital Market: Benefactor of Menace?" *Journal of Economic Perspectives* 12: 9–30.

Perotti, R. 1996. "Income Distribution, Democracy and Growth. What the Data Say." *Journal of Economic Growth* 1: 149–87.

Persson, T., and G. Tabellini. 2000. *Political Economics: Explaining Economic Policy.* Cambridge: MIT Press.

Przeworski, A. 2001. "How Many Ways Can Be Third?" In Andrew Glyn (ed.), *Social Democracy in Neoliberal Times: The Left and Economic Policy since 1980.* Oxford: Oxford University Press.

Przeworski, A., and M. Wallerstein. 1988. "Structural Dependence of the State on Capital." *American Political Science Review* 83: 1184–98.

Quinn, D. P. 1997. "The Correlates of Changes in International Financial Regulation." *American Political Science Review* 91: 531–51.

Robinson, J. 1998. "Theories of Bad Policy." *Policy Reform* 1: 1–14.

Rodrik, D. 1997. *Has Globalization Gone too Far?* Washington, D.C.: Institute for International Economics.

———. 1997–98. "Hard Tasks." *Boston Review of Books.* 22 (6): 15–16.

Roemer, J. E. 2001. *Political Competition: Theory and Applications.* Cambridge: Harvard University Press.

Rose, R. 1991. "What Is Lesson-Drawing?" *Journal of Public Policy* 2: 3–30.

Simmons, B., and Z. Elkins. 2000. "Globalization and Policy Diffusion: Explaining Three Decades of Liberalization." Mimeo, Department of Politics, University of California, Berkeley.

Stallings, B. 1992. "Internal Influence on Economic Policy: Debt, Stabilization, and Structural Reform." Pp. 41–88 in S. Haggard and R. Kauffman (eds.), *The Politics of Economic Adjustment.* Princeton: Princeton University Press.

Stokes, S. C. 2001. *Neoliberalism by Surprise.* New York: Cambridge University Press.

Swank, D. 1998. "Funding the Welfare State: Globalization and the Taxation of Business in Advanced Market Economies." *Political Studies* 45: 671–92.

Tingsten, H. 1973. *The Swedish Social Democrats.* Totowa, N.J.: Bedminster.

Vanberg, V. 2000. "Globalization, Democracy, and Citizens' Sovereignty: Can Competition among Governments Enhance Democracy?" *Constitutional Political Economy* 11: 87–112.

Vreeland, J. R. 2000. *Causes and Consequences of IMF Agreements.* Ph.D. diss., New York University.

Wallerstein, M., and A. Przeworski. 1995. "Capital Taxation with Open Borders." *Review of International Political Economy* 2 (3): 425–45.

Weil-Raynal, E. 1956. "Les obstacles économiques à l expérience Blum." *La Revue Socialiste* 98.

Weyland, K. 2004. "Conclusions." In K. Weyland (ed.), *Learning from Foreign Models in Latin American Policy Reform.* Washington, D.C.: Woodrow Wilson Center.

CHAPTER 8

Between Redistribution and Trade

THE POLITICAL ECONOMY OF PROTECTIONISM AND DOMESTIC COMPENSATION

Carles Boix

A CONSIDERABLE NUMBER of works in comparative political economy have attributed to economic openness an important role in explaining cross-national variation in the size of the public sector. In a path-breaking article based on a sample of advanced democracies, Cameron (1978) showed that public spending was positively correlated with the level of trade. This result, which Katzenstein (1985) examined through qualitative work, was then extended to the whole sample of world nations by Rodrik (1998). Yet, strikingly enough, this scholarly literature has so far neglected the importance of political conflict in explaining the strong and positive correlation found between trade openness and the size of the public sector in two ways. On the one hand, it has taken the level of economic openness as exogenous to political decisions—a strange claim given how substantial the literature on the political determinants of tariffs has become in the past two decades (Alt and Gilligan 1994; Alt et al. 1996). On the other hand, it has treated fiscal policy as an automatic response to trade openness—again an odd assumption in the light of the literature on welfare state formation and expansion (Esping-Andersen 1990).

The choice of the level of economic openness involves adjudicating between different economic factors or sectors that are differently positioned in the international economy in terms of their competitive advantage, and the types of risks imposed by external demand and the world business cycle. Those domestic sectors that are hurt by low tariffs or threatened by high income volatility (due to sudden shocks in the terms of trade) are likely to lobby for substantial trade barriers—unless the state compensates them directly in the event of an economic downturn. Thus, for example, workers in industries that are highly exposed to foreign competition or to very cyclical patterns of foreign demand may acquiesce to openness only in exchange for unemployment insurance. This implies that the choice of tariffs and taxes often consists in a simultaneous decision over fiscal and trade policy that depends on the redistributive effects of both public spending and trade openness.

The joint choice over openness and compensatory policies generally leads to one of the following fiscal regimes. On the one hand, unless a solid majority systematically and permanently benefits from free trade, governments open the economy to trade only if they are willing to and capable of establishing compensatory or insurance mechanisms to soften the impact of changes in external demand or the sudden emergence of foreign competitors. Conversely, whenever these compensatory mechanisms (such as unemployment insurance or vocational training schemes) are politically or economically unfeasible, countries will establish a regime that isolates them from external conditions and in which policymakers can fine-tune the domestic cycle to minimize unemployment and welfare losses.

The economic strategy eventually pursued by policymakers depends in part on the strength of different sectors (defined by their trade interests and fiscal capabilities). But it particularly hinges on whether political elites structure a coalition in which free traders credibly commit to compensate the losers of openness or whether, unable or opposed to making such compensatory promises, they embrace a protectionist strategy with no increase in public insurance or transfer programs. As shown in this chapter, the outcome depends on the agenda-setting powers of political leadership and on the latter's organizational capacity to sustain one of the two outcomes. To put it differently, in situations characterized by an identical array of interests and even political cleavages, the trade and fiscal strategy being adopted could differ completely depending on how politicians craft the decision-making process.

The contemporary theoretical and policy implications of the chapter are straightforward. Theories that predict the level of openness based on the distribution of interests disregard the possibility that policymakers may change the dimension of political conflict in a way that those that, according to strict calculations about their comparative advantage in world markets, would oppose the reduction of tariffs end up accepting free trade. This in fact explains why the strategies of "embedded liberalism" pursued in postwar Europe in general and that of free-trade social democracy in particular have been quite effective at building up generalized popular support for economic integration in most advanced countries. It also suggests that current debates framing globalization in terms of a dilemma between embracing free trade (while disarming the state) and protecting markets (to sustain the autonomy of governments and welfare levels at home) are misleading. In democratic states free trade has often been the quid pro quo of public compensation.

The chapter is organized as follows. The first section summarizes the body of literature that shows that public compensation and free trade are positively correlated. The second then discusses the limitations of that work and examines why we should consider trade and fiscal policy as jointly determined. The next section explores empirically the choice of different tax-tariff equilibria. Notice that to show the politically contingent nature of any trade regime, that is, to show that different trade regimes are political deals around certain coalitions hammered out by different sets of politicians, we cannot rely on econometric estimations. Gathering and then torturing a big dataset may give us strong correlations. But it will not shed any new light upon the mechanisms that underlie a trade deal. As pointed out before, scholars have already supplied us with that kind of statistical work: they have shown that openness and compensation are correlated. We are still at a loss, however, about the causes of that correlation. The only solution lies in engaging in historical work in which we observe the strategies of different parties and the types of political deals they reach. Nonetheless, to meet the requirements of scientific validity, this historical research must have two characteristics: it should be comparative; and the cases under examination, which vary on the dependent variable, should be identical in all their traits except for the explanatory variable of interest. Interestingly enough, the Australian colonies of Victoria and New South Wales (in the last decades of the nineteenth century) satisfy these criteria. Both of them were practically identical in population, the weight of the rural sector, the proportion of primary and manufacturing sectors in the economy, level of wealth, and political institutions. Yet whereas New South Wales maintained minimal tariffs, Victoria embraced a highly protectionist regime (which was the regime ultimately adopted by the Australian Commonwealth around 1906–08). The outcome was a function of the underlying political coalitions that crystallized in the 1880s and particularly in the 1890s. In Victoria, Protectionists articulated a coalition of manufacturing businesses, primary industries, and the urban working class around high tariffs and minimum wages for workers in protected industries. In New South Wales, the Free Trade party, strong in Sydney and its adjacent districts, attracted the lower-middle and working classes (directly and through a deal with the Labor party once this was organized) through the introduction of land and income taxes, arbitration mechanisms and generous public spending (about a fourth higher than Victoria in per capita terms). After the examination of both cases in this section, the next sections extend the analysis to fully sovereign countries: the fourth section shows how the Victorian "fiscal" model was transferred to Australia after the creation of a federal state in 1901; the fifth section examines, in turn, how the free trade and tax compensation triumphed, instead, in Britain and Scandinavia in the twentieth century. A conclusion follows.

FREE TRADE AND COMPENSATION

In exploring the consequences that the international economy has on the domestic political arena, a growing literature has shown in the past two decades that higher levels of trade systematically lead to a larger public sector across both developed and developing nations. In a path-breaking article, Cameron (1978) observed that the best predictor of an increase on the size of the public sector as a share of GDP in the period 1960–75 was the degree of economic openness (as the sum of exports and imports over GDP) in 1960 among OECD countries, with a correlation of 0.78. More recently, Rodrik (1998) has corroborated this association for the advanced world and has extended it to the level of government consumption and trade openness for the world sample.

Although recent econometric work has confirmed the robustness of this relationship (Garrett 2001; Adserà and Boix 2001), the actual theoretical mechanisms that underlie that statistical relationship are still the object of considerable theoretical debate. Broadly speaking, there are two types of theoretical explanations for the correlation between trade and openness. On the one hand, for scholars such as Cameron (1978), trade openness shapes the structure of the economy in a way that facilitates the formation of organizations and interests that impose high redistributive demands on the state. On the other hand, higher levels of trade integration (coupled with a high level of sectoral concentration in the economy) are seen as leading to growing risks associated with the international business cycle, which in turn put pressure on policymakers to develop publicly financed compensatory programs in favor of the exposed sectors.

In Cameron (1978), small, open economies are characterized by a high degree of industrial concentration—with a small number of large firms holding a substantial share of production and employment. As a result of having a small domestic market and fierce competition in exports, export-based countries specialize in a reduced number of sectors, led by companies large enough to contend with the fluctuations in the world market. High levels of industrial concentration facilitate, in turn, the formation of employers' associations and labor unions. Moreover, the labor force, somewhat less differentiated in occupation and skill, and hence less fragmented than in larger economies, organizes in rather centralized unions. A high degree of unionization and a relatively centralized union system then expand the public sector in two ways. First, they contribute to the formation of strong social democratic and labor parties, which in turn pursue aggressive redistributive agendas based on the expansion of the welfare state. Second, they lead to a structure of centralized wage bargaining at the national level. Strongly centralized union movements were particularly able to strike corporatist deals with national governments in the 1960s and the 1970s. In those corporatist arrangements, usually based on nationwide pacts among government, unions, and employers, unions offered wage moderation in exchange for expansionary policies geared toward full employment and an expansion of public expenditure, in areas such as unemployment benefits, health, or pensions.[1]

Cameron's work was then followed by Katzenstein's (1985) analysis of the structure of small, corporatist European countries. Although Katzenstein's work also connects domestic compensation to the level of economic openness, he traces the growth of the public sector to a broader set of incentives than Cameron's. In Katzenstein, small states are characterized by constraining economies of scale, a small number of economic sectors, and, in particular, considerable dependency on the fluctuations of the world business cycle. As a result, policymakers develop, generally through extensive consultation with all social agents institutionalized in widely cooperative bodies and practices, policy instruments that minimize the risks of being small. Unions and employers strike deals to secure wage moderation and flexible procedures to adapt to changes in world demand. States compensate the losers through generous unemployment coverage and public aid to failing industries. The public sector develops full-fledged public programs, in the form of human and physical capital formation, to secure the competitiveness of the country.

Katzenstein's insistence on the risks confronted by small, open economies has been taken up and extended by Rodrik (1998) in a formal setting. According to Rodrik, since more open economies have higher exposure to the risks derived from turbulent world markets, public expenditure, set by a state purely conceived as a social planner, grows to stabilize aggregate income and deliver social peace and political stability.[2] The model works as follows. First, greater openness increases rather than reduces domestic volatility and risk. Although the world market is less volatile than any domestic economy, particularly one of a small country, openness to trade normally implies specialization in production due to the law of comparative advantage. Accordingly, holding all other things constant, small, open economies are less diversified than large economies. Second, assuming than an economy cannot purchase insurance from the rest of the world, domestic welfare varies with fluctuations in domestic production.[3] Third, any economy has three sectors—a private tradables sector, a private nontradables sector, and the government—whose income streams feed into a representative household. The government sector is a "safe" sector from the international economy, that is, its employment and income levels are uncorrelated with world-driven shocks. As result, if the policymakers have as one of their objectives minimizing the risk borne by the household as a result of external shocks, we should expect an expansion of the public sector correlated with higher levels of trade openness. The strength of Rodrik's theoretical standpoint seems to be born out by the empirical evidence. First, external risk, measured in the form of fluctuations in the terms of trade, is positively associated with income volatility, measured through fluctuations in real GDP: a 10 percent increase in external risk comes with a 1.0 to 1.6 percent increase in the latter.[4] Second, openness and the volatility related to trade openness are related to a bigger public sector. For the world sample in the mid 1980s and late 1990s, an increase in trade openness (imports and exports of GDP) of 10 percent is associated with a 2 percent increase in government consumption in GDP. Similarly, the volatility of terms of trade and a high concentration in type of exports (which should increase risk) are correlated with a bigger share of government consumption in GDP.

These findings have been confirmed by more recent and sophisticated empirical analysis. Garrett (1998, 2001) has shown that trade openness is associated with higher levels of government consumption and overall spending for world cross-sections in the mid-1980s and the mid-1990s.[5] Similarly, Adserà and Boix (2001) show, employing a panel data of around sixty-five developing and developed nations for the period 1950–90, that the share of public revenues as a share of GDP is strongly and significantly correlated with trade openness. Controlling for economic development and political institutions, public revenue goes up from around 23 percent of GDP in a closed economy (where exports and imports equal 10 percent of GDP) to almost 30 percent of GDP (if trade openness equals 50 percent of GDP) and up to almost 35 percent when openness is very high (around 150 percent of GDP).

THE SIMULTANEOUS CHOICE OF TRADE AND FISCAL POLICIES

The current literature on the relationship between trade openness and public domestic compensation presents two limitations. First, the level of trade openness is (implicitly) attributed to parameters exogenous to the political decisions of domestic actors—this is striking given that political economists have to date developed several, very influential political-economic models of trade policy relating the level of openness to both the strategic interaction of states and the domestic distribution of interests. Second, the growth of the public sector has been merely thought of as an automatic, and in some cases a *functional*, requirement of having a free trade regime.[6]

Consider, for example, Rodrik (1998). In his model, households do not differ on the sources of income and the government sector, completely unlinked from the external economy, can expand as much as necessary (with the only constraint imposed by the distortionary effects of taxes) to minimize the volatility inherent to trade openness. This description of the economy is, however, unrealistic. Economic agents differ in their assets, both in terms of their abundance vis-à-vis the international economy and in terms of their position on the income ladder in the economy, and therefore in their preferences over taxes and levels of trade protection. With interest heterogeneity, different policies imply different distributional effects, and governments are affected, so to speak, by a politically determined budget constraint.

Accordingly, we need to think about the choice of the level of trade openness and the determination of the size of the public sector as two *political decisions* that are *simultaneously* taken by political agents in response to the same dilemma: how to cope with the distributional effects of increasing trade integration.

The response of policymakers leads to (at least) two different policy regimes. On the one hand, to insulate domestic actors from internationally induced changes in relative prices, national policymakers may choose to close the domestic economy. Once domestic actors are relatively isolated from external competition as well as from the variability of the world business cycle, there are no incentives to resort to higher levels of public expenditure to compensate voters for (temporary or permanent) employment losses.[7] As a result, economic insulation should be expected, *ceteris paribus*, to depress the level of public expenditure.

On the other hand, the sectors that gain from trade may set up public pro-grams to compensate trade losers to get the latter's political support for an open economy. Accordingly, the expansion of the public sector is not a mere deriva-tion of trade openness—as assumed in most of the current literature—but a truly political pre-condition needed to secure the liberalization of the economy. Once free trade policies are embraced, and, given that Keynesian demand man-agement is hardly available to open economies (Alt 1985), policymakers can only ensure high levels of social welfare (and therefore the support required to govern) by expanding the public sector to shore up declining economic sectors.

As small European nations democratized at the turn of the twentieth century, pressure from tradeable sectors to establish welfare systems grew steadily. It was mostly in response to the economic shock of the 1930s, however, when political elites employed welfare and investment spending to structure a pro–free trade coalition in small European states. That solution contrasted with the decision to set up protectionist policies as a way of steadying relative prices at home without having to raise taxes and redistributive income through the public sector in Latin America (and in New Zealand and Australia to some extent too) by that same period of time.[8]

Which redistributive strategy is eventually adopted (in response to the dilem-mas posed by growing trade flows) may in part be a function of the distribution of interests in the domestic economy—with import-competing and export sec-tors aligned in favor of different solutions (and with their relative size and organ-izational clout determining their capacity to impose their most favorable outcome). Ultimately, however, the policy regime in place is conditional on the structure of political institutions in each country and on the ability of free traders to commit, in a credible manner, to a compensation package. If free traders offer a compensa-tory package to lure part of the losing sectors, then a free trade solution will be imposed. Conversely, if they do not offer it or their offer is not credible, the los-ing sectors will reject the deal and protectionism will ensue. In short, the choice of trade regime hinges on the strategic capacity of politicians to organize a partic-ular coalition around one of two equally feasible outcomes.

The Australian Case: Victoria versus New South Wales

Tariffs in the Second Half of the Nineteenth Century

Before London granted self-government, which included control over tariff pol-icy, to five of the six Australian colonies between 1855 and 1859, the influence of domestic interests on tariffs was minimal. Import duties, concentrated on alco-hol, tea, tobacco, and luxury goods, only had a revenue-raising function. More-over, differences in tariffs were minor across colonies. In 1856, tariffs in New South Wales and Victoria amounted to 8.6 percent and 8.4 percent of the value of imports respectively.[9]

TABLE 8.1.
Custom Revenues as a Share of the Value of Imports in Victoria and New South Wales, 1856–80

	New South Wales	Victoria
1856	8.6	8.4
1861	8.9	n.a.
1865	6.0	n.a.
1870–71	9.5	11
1875	7.1	10
1880	8.6	10

Source: For 1856 and for New South Wales, calculated from data in Patterson (1968). For Victoria from 1870 onward, taken from Andersen and Garlaut (1987: 41).

The concession of self-governing institutions coincided with a major expansion of the Australian economy. After the discovery of gold mines, population multiplied by four from about 400,000 in 1851 to about 1,650,000 inhabitants twenty years later. As the gold reserves depleted, however, unemployment rose substantially. This in turn prompted the first debates over the role of fiscal policy, particularly tariffs, in the colonies.

In response to the economic crisis of the early 1860s, tariff policy started to differ across colonies. In Victoria a Tariff League was already in place in 1859, and several protectionist candidates ran in that year's election. The appointment of a select committee in 1860, heavily lobbied by the domestic manufacturers, led to the first parliamentary discussion of protectionist measures. By the mid-1860s the government explicitly admitted its adherence to protectionism and the strategic goal of employing commercial barriers. At first the espousal of protectionist convictions was mostly rhetorical: tariffs continued to be concentrated on alcohol, tobacco, and associated commodities, and were employed to cover the public deficit. But by the late 1860s, the Victorian government extended duties to most imported articles and gradually increased the tariff. As shown in table 8.1, in two decades Victorian custom revenues increased by about a fourth to 10 to 11 percent of the value of imports in the 1870s.

In New South Wales the growth of unemployment in 1858 also led to the formation of a parliamentary committee to "investigate the state of the Sydney working class" (Patterson 1968: 24). Like its Victorian counterpart, it too recommended the introduction of higher duties, of 10 to 15 percent, to correct "social evils." In the midst of considerable agitation over trade policy, the government resisted the notion of higher tariffs for several years until a straight five-year row of budget deficits led to the imposition of new import duties. Those measures, which were approved in 1866 as a temporary solution, were relatively moderate. The status quo of 1866 did not change in the following years. Several

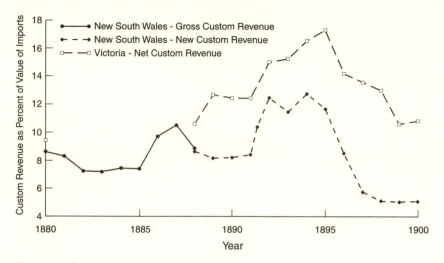

Figure 8.1. Custom Revenue, 1880–1900.

attempts at raising tariffs were defeated in the 1870s, and some duties were actually reduced in 1873–74. By the mid-1880s, custom revenues stood, as a percentage of imports, at the same level as that of the 1850s—at around 8 percent. In short, in contrast with the case of Victoria, protectionism as a permanent policy geared toward the defense of domestic industries was defeated and tariffs only fluctuated with the economic cycle and the revenue needs of the colony's government.

As shown in figure 8.1, differences between New South Wales and Victoria became much sharper in the late 1880s. Marking a substantial break with the stability of the previous decade, the Victorian parliament voted a steep increase in import duties in 1889—the overall tariff rate went up by about 2 points to 12.7 percent of the value of all imports. Since there was no fiscal imbalance at that point, tariffs were probably raised in direct response to growing foreign competition: imports had grown by about 38 percent in the previous six years. A sharp economic downturn from 1890 to 1893 triggered an abrupt fall in revenue. This was followed by the decision to raise duties again. The average tariff escalated to over 17 percent in 1895. At the recommendation of a special tariff commission in 1894–95, which followed protests about the incoherence of the new duties, parliament passed new legislation to drive tariffs back to their pre-1892 levels. Those measures and economic recovery combined to reduce the level of protection. Still, the overall tariff averaged around 12 percent in the last years of the century.

New South Wales responded in a markedly different way to the strains of economic recession and public deficits. After the victory of free traders in 1887, and in spite of a widening fiscal imbalance, the government substituted new excise duties and heavy borrowing for some moderate tariffs introduced two years before. Then a new cabinet led by the protectionist politician Dibbs passed, in the midst of the recession, a relatively heavy tariff packet, with an ad valorem duty of 15 percent on luxury goods and an ad valorem duty of 10 percent on a relatively broad list of goods. The average tariff level shot up to above 12 percent in the following years. Nevertheless, a victory by the free trader party in 1894 resulted in the overhaul of the tariff system. The overall tariff fell to 5 percent and did not change even after the return of the protectionist party to power in the 1899 election.

It is important to notice that differences in trade regimes were not limited to the overall level of protection but to the internal distribution of protection as well. In New South Wales, 83 percent of the custom revenue came from alcohol and spirits in 1899. In Victoria, only 37 percent did—the rest came from duties on manufacturing goods.

Domestic Interests and Constitutional Structure

To explore why Victoria and New South Wales followed such divergent policy paths, especially after 1890, table 8.2 compares their demographic and economic structures. What is striking is how similar the two of them were at the end of the nineteenth century. In both cases population was roughly over one million and distributed in very similar proportions between rural and metropolitan districts. Social conditions and economic welfare, measured through birth and death rates, factory wages, weekly housing rents, and living standards (ratio of wage to housing rent) were also extremely similar. Again, the employment profile was similar. Approximately the same percentage of men worked in primary occupations (agriculture, pastoral occupations, and mining). Victoria had slightly larger manufacturing and commercial sectors—but the difference seems too tiny to account for their opposite tariff policies. As noted by Andersen and Garnaut, "the port of Sydney played something of an entrepot role in relation to other Australian and southwest Pacific colonies, a situation that would have increased the voice of internationalists in New South Wales politics" (1987: 42). But this explanation is not very convincing. Already in 1871 Victoria made legal provisions to ensure, through special facilities and so-called drawbacks, that the entrepot trade of Melbourne was not jeopardized by the colony's tariffs. Victorian tariffs were mostly aimed at defending the interests of domestic manufacturers.

Land size is the only significant difference among the two colonies. New South Wales is about three-and-a-half times larger than Victoria. As argued by Patterson (1968), having a vast territory gave the colonial government in Sydney a clear fiscal advantage since it could draw upon the sale of land to finance its expenditure with-

TABLE 8.2.
Basic Traits of New South Wales and Victoria

	NSW	Victoria
Area (Sq. Miles)	310,700	87,884
Population (1899)	1,348,400	1,162,900
Birth Rate (per 1000 pop)	27	27
Death Rate (per 1000 pop)	12	14
Percentage Population in Capital	32.5	41.1
Percentage Employed in[a]:		
Professional	6.0	5.1
Domestic	4.4	3.3
Commercial	14.8	16.3
Transport	9.5	7.6
Manufacturing	18.9	22.0
Construction	8.2	6.9
Agriculture. Pastoral	28.7	27.7
Mining	8.4	7.9
Estimated Factory Wage (1900) (pounds)	73.5	66.4
Weekly Rent per House (1901) (shillings)	10.4	8.8
Factory Wage / House Rent (shillings)	142	151
Imports (pounds per head)	18.98	15.44
Exports (pounds per head)	21.10	15.97
Tariffs in 1900	5.22	10.61
(net revenue from duties as % of imports)		
Total Revenue (per person)	7.4	6.41
Total Expenditure (per person)	7.28	6.29

[a] From census of 1901.

out having to resort to high import duties. Figure 8.2 displays the revenues from land sales and leases as a percentage of total revenues in both colonies. It is true that the New South Wales Treasury benefited from an extraordinary revenue flow due to land sales in the 1870s. In 1875 and 1876, for example, over 50 percent of its resources came from land. This probably eased any pressure to rely on tariffs in the last decade. By the mid 1880s, however, land sales had tapered off and had become a minor part of the total budget. Moreover, the absence (presence) of land revenues cannot explain why tariffs were employed as protectionist tools in Victoria (and resisted in New South Wales as distortionary of the economy). It cannot explain either why the New South Wales consciously chose to introduce progressive land and income taxes in the mid-1890s to make up for lost revenue from lower tariffs instead of trying to boost its land sales.

The structure of the constitutional system in each colony does not seem to explain tariff policy either. Established as self-governing colonies at about the same

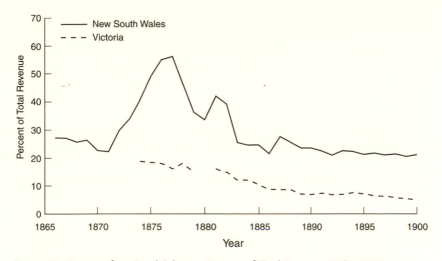

Figure 8.2. Revenue from Land Sales as a Percent of Total Revenue, 1865–1900.

time, both New South Wales and Victoria were parliamentarian democracies with similar institutional structures. Both of them were ruled by a two-chamber parliament. The upper house, or Legislative Council, represented the propertied elements. The lower house, or Legislative Assembly, was elected through male universal suffrage, mildly tempered by plural voting, since the 1860s. The appointment of members to the Legislative Council differed across colonies, and this difference ought to have skewed tariff policy in favor of free trade in Victoria. In both colonies the upper house was dominated by the squatters, that is, by the big pastoral interests, who favored low tariffs. Whereas in Victoria the members of the Legislative Council were elected by a limited, propertied electorate, in New South Wales, however, they were nominated by the governor. The latter system made the Legislative Council rather vulnerable to the executive threat of packing an unruly council with liberal members—a strategy used by the Reid government in 1894–95. By contrast, the Victorian system should have made and indeed did make the council a more effective instrument to oppose the lower house (Gollan 1960).

District apportionment in the lower house also varied across the two states. In New South Wales an electoral reform in 1893 ensured a very tight ratio between votes and seats. Victorian rural districts, which were actually favorable to high tariffs (a point to which I return later), were overrepresented: they had about 60 percent of the seats and 45 percent of the population. This may have aided protectionist interests in Victoria, but the distortion was not extraordinary and the Victorian coalition behind protectionism was large and mostly centered in the cities.[10]

Trade Policy as a Political Deal

The emergence of two distinct policy regimes in otherwise very similar regions can be traced back to the type of political coalitions that formed in each colony. In New South Wales, the free trade government established a political alliance with the lower-middle and urban working class (mainly represented by the Labor party after 1891) by which low tariffs were sustained in exchange for the introduction of land and income taxes and progressive industrial legislation. In Victoria, instead, protectionism was equated with progressive liberalism. Protectionist sentiments were already predominant within Victorian trade unions by the 1860s (Gollan 1960). Nonetheless, the upsurge of labor unrest in the early 1890s pushed the protectionist cabinet of Turner to establish institutional mechanisms (wage boards) in 1895–96 to pass on to workers the benefits of protection and thus strengthen their electoral support. To wit, both fiscal regimes were eminently redistributive and had the same goals: they were geared to satisfy the interests of a strongly mobilized working class. But the instruments they employed differed sharply. In Victoria tariffs were employed to raise workers' wages directly. In New South Wales imported consumer goods were cheaper, direct taxes higher, and, as shown in figures 8.3 and 8.4, public expenditure and revenue were higher (by about a fourth in per capita terms) and more stable (that is, more counter-cyclical).

The Case of New South Wales

In the 1890s New South Wales's politics was governed by three relatively disciplined political parties: Free Trade, Protectionist, and Labor. With no party in control of a majority, Labor successively allied with the Free Trade party, the Protectionists, and then finally with Free Trade. It was in this last round of negotiations, in 1894, than the New South Wales regime of free trade and compensation emerged as a stable political and economic strategy until the advent of the Australian federation.

The election of 1887 ushered in the creation of central councils to coordinate the free trade and the protectionist factions into relatively tight electoral and parliamentary organizations. Still, both parties were internally divided in their positions toward the redistributive role of the state. Within the Free Trade party, positions ranged from strict laissez-faire politicians concerned only with tariffs, such as Parkes, to radical liberals pushing for social programs to better the conditions of the working class. Similarly, the Protectionist party housed both pastoralists and farmers, who saw protection as a source of revenue that made direct taxes unnecessary, and pro-labor parliamentarians who played with the idea of creating a Protectionist Labor Party in 1890–91.

The creation of a progressive protectionist party was frustrated, however, by the formation of an independent Labor party in the election of 1891. After several

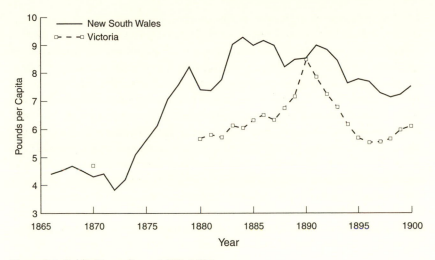

Figure 8.3. Public Expenditure, 1866–1900.

massive strikes ended up with the defeat of the union movement, the New South Trades Hall Council decided to launch, with notable success, its own political party. In a hanged parliament, in which Free Traders controlled forty-seven seats and Protectionists fifty-one, Labor became the king-maker with thirty-five members.

As a result, the New South Wales parliament of 1891–94 suffered considerable instability. Labor initially agreed to support a Free Trade government headed by

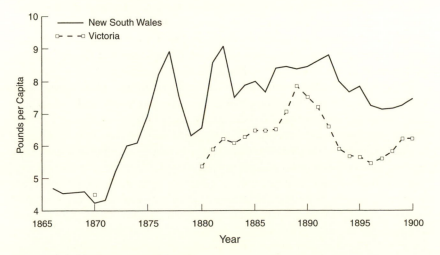

Figure 8.4. Public Revenue, 1866–1900.

Parkes in exchange for a program of "progressive" legislation. A few weeks later, however, the cabinet had to resign when, with the help from some radical Protectionists, Labor members of the legislative assembly (MLAs) insisted upon an eight-hour clause on a Coal Miners' Regulation. With the fall of Parkes, the Protectionist party, led by Dibbs, moved to strike a deal with the Labor caucus on the same terms Parkes had offered before. The alliance proved all but firm. Labor MLAs shared a common program except in the "fiscal issue," in which they were deeply divided between pro–free traders and pro-protectionists in two equal halves. As the economic recession of the early 1890s deepened, and following the proposal for a tariff rise by Dibbs, the Labor parliamentary party formally split into various factions. Mostly relying on the protectionist elements of Labor, Dibbs passed a moderate tariff reform in exchange for a Trades Disputes Conciliation and Arbitration Act and a new electoral law that included reforms demanded by Labor and the most progressive section of the two main parties of the Legislative Assembly. Nevertheless, the depth of the economic recession, the opposition of the legislative council to income taxation for mining, and the handling of the 1892 strike by the government finally alienated the support of Labor and caused the Dibbs cabinet to fall in 1894.

The election of 1894 was confronted by revamped Free Trade and Labor parties. After the Labor parliamentary caucus unraveled in 1891, the trade union movement reinforced its grip on the party. Labor candidates were now required to pledge its abeyance to any of the decisions taken by the party's governing committee. Within the Free Trade party, the party leadership had passed from Parker to Reid, who abandoned the strictly free trade strategy that the party had pursued in the 1880s. To appeal to both Sydney's commercial community and to the lower-middle class and segments of the urban working class, Reid campaigned now on the basis of a two-pronged platform of lower tariffs and progressive taxation (Rickard 1976). The election of July 1894 led to a Legislative Assembly again without a majority: there were fifty-eight Free Traders (a third of them from country districts), forty Protectionists (all elected in rural constituencies), and twenty-seven Labor MLAs (with a third from the countryside).[11]

The new Free Trade government, which encompassed two independent Labor ministers, speedily introduced two bills to establish progressive land and income taxes. Both initiatives met with the strong rejection of the Legislative Council and Reid, in a manner parallel to Asquith's strategy sixteen years later in Britain, opted to embrace a confrontational path with the upper house. After dissolving the Legislative Assembly, Reid presented the new elections of July 1895 as a contest between "democracy and privilege" and promised to reform the Legislative Council. A sweeping victory for the Free Trade party, which now had consolidated its position as a truly radical liberal party, translated into the rapid passage of both direct taxation schemes. Reid's progressivism overcame the initial skepticism with which Labor had greeted the new Free Trade cabinet in 1894 and solidified the collaboration of both parties. This in turn led to the unfolding of an advanced liberal policy regime. Besides low tariffs and direct taxation, Reid introduced a minimum wage in government contracts, regulatory legislation on mining and factory conditions, and an electoral law to reduce to one month the period of residence to qualify for the right to vote. The support of Labor also involved the passage of legislation to extend immigration restrictions to "all coloured races."

The Case of Victoria

Although also divided between Free Traders, Protectionists, and Labor parliamentarians, Victorian politics differed from New South Wales in two counts. First, it lacked the sort of relatively disciplined parties that prevailed in the other colony in the 1890s. Instead, factionalism and a relatively fluid set of coalitions dominated the Legislative Assembly. Second, an independent Labor party remained a weak political force, and unions often resorted to supporting and lobbying liberal candidates directly.

After the first labor candidate successfully contested a by-election in April 1891, the Trades Hall Council decided to launch its own political party, the Progressive Political League (PPL) a month later. Relative to New South Wales, the electoral performance of an independent labor force in the election of April 1892 was disappointing. PPL candidates gathered 20.1 percent of the vote—only 1.7 percent less than their New South Welsh counterpart a year before. But with its vote much more concentrated in the urban areas (the PPL had made no specific appeal to either farmers or miners), it captured only one-tenth of the seats in the Legislative Assembly. In part due to the relative failure of the PPL and in part as a result of a long tradition of political and ideological cooperation going back to the 1860s, Victorian trade unions remained wedded to the Liberal movement. After Labor candidates fared badly in the by-elections of 1893, unions tacitly abandoned independent Labor activity and urged the reorganization and strengthening of the Liberal party. In June 1894 the United Labour and Liberal Party, which encompassed both working-class candidates and radical middle-class members such as Berry and Deakin, replaced the defunct PPL. As put by Rawson, it simply became "a specialized section of the broader liberal movement" (1977: 73). In that institutional context in which unions were still part of the liberal-protectionist coalition and thus harder to attract to another policy regime, a free trade-compensation solution had to be a more unlikely deal than in Sydney.

Precisely at the same time that New South Wales shifted back to a Free Trade government, the election of September 1894 resulted in the defeat of the Patterson government, which had proposed a moderate reduction in tariffs in Victoria, and in the corresponding return of the protectionists, now under Turner. Still, the new composition of the lower house seemed to indicate that a majority was "favorable to some revision of the tariff" (Rickard 1976: 86). Moreover, a report from the Tariff Board, released in May 1895, supported a reduction of what was considered a too-obtrusive tariff.

Reacting to what was reckoned to be an offensive against protection, members from the Protectionist Association and representatives of various industries met in May 1895 and approved a motion in which they supported the introduction of a minimum wage in order to pass the full benefits of protection to workers. In this way, protectionists ensured the support of unions in response to free traders' claims asserting that import duties ultimately drove wages down. As the newspaper *Argus* put it, there was "no reason why the operatives should not get some benefit from the high tariff and advised the labor members that they owed it, as a sacred duty to their constituents to do something tangible for their benefit before the tariff passes out of hand, by inducing the Assembly to apply the minimum wage principle to protected industries" (Rickard 1976: 96).

Fully blessed by the leading protectionist publication, the *Age*, the motion was quickly supported by both the radical liberal Deakin and the Labor member Prendergast in the Legislative Assembly and approved in November of 1895 by forty-nine votes to twenty. To implement the measure, the legislative assembly simply decided to employ the administrative boards that were being set up, in the Factory Act currently in discussion, to supervise the work conditions of women and children in the apparel industry.

The extension of a minimum wage clause to protected manufactures strengthened the liberal coalition. Although the Trades Hall Council tried again to establish an independent working-class party, the United Labor Party (ULP), in May 1896, the ULP was unable to mount a real threat in the elections in the following year. Whereas Liberal candidates received 64 percent of the vote, the ULP obtained 10 percent of the votes, or half of the votes of the PPL in 1892 and the ULLP in 1894. Similar poor results haunted the Labor party until the mid-1900s. It became a stronger force only after Federation occurred (and the support of the New South Wales organization was available). In fact, it was not until 1952 that Labor won a majority of seats in the state lower house.

The decision of 1895 not only reinforced the hegemony of the Liberal party. It sustained the protectionist arrangement of high tariffs even after the Conservative party was returned to office. As a matter of fact, in 1899 a resolution was passed granting either of the two chambers the unilateral right to set up a wage board in any industry. By breaking the potential veto of the more conservative upper house, that decision allowed Victoria to extend the wage board arrangement throughout all of Victorian industry in a systematic manner.

The Protectionist-Redistributive Solution Extended to the Australian Federation

The first years of the Australian commonwealth resembled the unstable, cyclical nature of New South Wales's and Victoria's Legislative Assemblies in the early 1890s. In the election of 1901, the Protectionist party won thirty-two seats, the

Free Trade party twenty-six, and Labor fifteen (two seats were held by independents). The balance of power among the three forces became more even in the election of 1903, with the parties winning 26, 25, and 23 seats respectively. With a Labor party so internally divided between free trade and protectionist wings (respectively concentrated in New South Wales and Victoria) that it decided to delegate any decision over the tariff question to a national referendum, governments succeeded each other at a quick pace.

At the beginning of the Federation, Protectionists controlled the government, with the sporadic support of Labor's, first under Barton and then very briefly under Deakin. The resistance of the latter to extend the arbitration system to public employees caused, however, the withdrawal of Labor's support and the formation of the first Labor cabinet under Watson in April of 1904. Four months later, the Free Trade party formed government under Reid with the support of moderate protectionists. What looked as the growing crystallization of a classical left-right cleavage (around taxation rather than trade) pushed Labor into the arms of radical Protectionists. After considerable maneuvering, Deakin came back to power in June of 1905, leading a coalition of centrist and radical protectionist parliamentarians and the Labor party. Still, the agreement across parties remained tentative. The parliamentary caucus agreed only to "a general support during this Parliament," and Labor organizations outside Parliament, which were adverse to a coalition, forced the party to resolve that "the Federal Labour Party should not enter into any alliance that would extend beyond the then existing Parliament, nor grant immunity at election time" (La Nauze 1965: 403).

In response to complaints of the Australian agricultural implements industry about strong and unfair competition from American and Canadian harvesting machines, the government appointed a Tariff Commission. The commission proved evenly divided, but the chairman's report sustained the view that special protection was required "against invasion and unfair attack" and declared that "American efficiency is 'purchased at the terrible sacrifice of the constitutions and lives of men'" (Greenwood 1955: 216). The government decided to follow those members who had recommended a large increase of import duties. Still, part of the Labor party stood as an obstacle to that solution. Its members, particularly those from New South Wales, had consistently claimed that protection would increase manufacturers' profits rather than workers' wages and that its cost would fall disproportionately on the workers. Direct redistribution through a larger budget, they claimed, was overall a much safer means to boost the latter's standard of living.

To lure Labor, the Deakin government eventually supported the introduction of an excise duty, the equivalent of the tariff on imports, upon agricultural machines manufactured in Australia, which would then be waived when a manufacturer paid wages that conformed to the awards of wage boards or arbitration courts. A year later, the Harvester Judgment from the Court of Conciliation and Arbitration established the obligation of manufacturers to pay a "fair and reasonable wage" to meet "the normal needs of an average employee regarded as a human being living in a civilized community."[12]

This decision simply bolstered the case for a very substantial increase in rates in the 1908 tariff law. By that time, Labor support for high tariffs in exchange for the legal recognition of a wage floor had solidified completely. In reaction to the decision of Australia's High Court to declare unconstitutional major aspects of Deakin's "new protection" legislation on the grounds that it conflicted with states' rights, the Labor party adopted an electoral platform that included the passage of constitutional reforms to ensure effective federal legislation for both arbitration and protection. As the leading Protectionist politician Isaacs had predicted in 1906, "our friends of the Labour party will soon realize that they cannot provide means for paying good honest wages to the workers unless they protect the manufacturers."[13]

Sustaining a wage threshold required uncoupling (parts of) the domestic economy from international markets. Tariffs to protect the domestic industry were stepped up in the interwar period in two phases. Comprehensive tariffs were adopted in 1920–21 to sustain the gains made by the industrial sectors that had grown during World War I. Tariffs were set to "allow the costs associated with Australia's higher labor rates (usually relative to those of the United Kingdom) [. . .] to be recouped [. . .] to protect the most labor-intensive manufacturing industries" (Andersen and Garnaut 1987: 49). With the economic depression from 1927 to 1931, tariffs were again increased. After World War II, the artificial wartime protection resulting from the disruption of commercial flows between 1939 and 1945 was maintained through exchange controls and import licensing.[14]

The use of methods to shape the wage structure significantly lessened any social demands for a large welfare state. In 1949–50, Australia spent only 4.7 percent of its GDP on social security—compared to an average of 8.0 percent in fourteen advanced industrial democracies (Castles 1985). By 1975, tax revenue as a proportion of GDP was 7.5 percentage points below the OECD average in Australia. Still, equality of conditions was higher than in countries with comparable levels of social spending. Based on the Luxembourg Income Study data, Castles and Mitchell estimate the Australian post-tax Gini index of 1980–81 at 0.287—lower than France, the Netherlands, Canada, the United States, and Switzerland. According to Gottschalk and Smeeding (1997), the male workers' earnings in the top decile (of the earning distribution) were about three times larger than the earnings of the lowest decile—compared to a ratio of 3.9 in Sweden and 7.2 in the United States.[15]

OPENNESS AND DOMESTIC COMPENSATION IN EUROPE

The introduction of a laissez-faire trade regime in the first half of the nineteenth century in Britain and its gradual extension to continental Europe in the following decades was achieved without any simultaneous expansion of domestic mechanisms of compensation. Free trade was introduced with the support of commercial and urban interests in Britain and the backing of working class associations (Rogowski 1989; Schonhardt-Bailey 1991). But the triumph of Manchesterian liberalism (the quasi-welfare system structured by the Poor Laws was dismantled around that period) was equally related to the extremely restrictive nature of the franchise. Only one in eight men was entitled to vote after 1833, and about three out of ten after 1868. Moreover, the electoral system was extremely biased against rural areas, which had borne most of the losses of the tariff reform of 1846, and against the urban poor.

The stability of the Cobdenite regime was put into question, however, by two parallel developments at the turn of the century. On the one hand, after the electoral reform of 1884, which equalized the franchise conditions of the rural counties to those already in place in urban boroughs, the British electorate doubled to encompass between two-thirds and four-fifths of the adult male population.[16]

On the other hand, a fall in agricultural prices and, above all, the growth of German competition unnerved British public opinion. Several anti–free trade episodes, such as an early resolution of the National Union of Conservative Associations in 1887 in favor of "fair trade," the "Made in Germany" panic of 1896, and the reimposition of sugar dues, the coal export duty, and the corn duty in the late 1890s and early 1900s preluded a new political realignment on trade policy. Chamberlain's proposals for tariff reform became hegemonic within the Conservative party by 1906. In turn, among Liberals and Labor intellectuals, free trade and state interventionism rapidly mixed in what Howe has termed the "New Liberal" synthesis (1997). Following a spat of works by Adam, Haldane, and the Webbs calling for increased public spending on education, the Liberal League pamphlets of 1902 already defended a much more aggressive stance of the state in the economy to defend Britain's commitment to free trade. Although the Liberal party won in the 1906 landslide election under the banner of free trade, the economic downturn of 1907–08 and stagnant real wages resulted in a marked popular shift to Tariff Reform candidates in several by-elections (Searle 1992). The Liberal government, now headed by Asquith and with Lloyd George in the Treasury, immediately responded by creating an old-age pension program in 1908; raising land taxes through the "People's Budget" and introducing labor exchanges and trade boards the following year; establishing national insurance for sickness, invalidity, and unemployment in 1911; and passing the Miners' Minimum Wage Act of 1912. The combination of free trade and compensation embraced by the Liberal cabinet pushed Conservatives and moderate Liberals into the tariff reform camp. As the Duke of Northumberland, a former opponent of Tariff Reform, wrote to Strachey in the autumn of 1909 in reaction to Lloyd George's fiscal plans, "protection cannot be worse than Socialism (. . .) And as (. . .) Tariff Reform or Socialism are the only possible alternatives at this moment, I am quite prepared to swallow the former."[17] The political debate that emerged at the turn of the twentieth century continued to structure the agenda of the interwar period. The Conservative party led the battle for imperial protection in the 1923 elections and was able, with the growing support of manufacturers and financial interests of the City, to impose its solution in 1931. By contrast, Labor, which had succeeded the Liberals as the progressive alternative, almost unanimously defended free trade.[18] The fiasco of the 1930s policies and the victory of Labor in 1945 eventually brought Britain to the camp of open borders and sizable public intervention.

A similar evolution, with a much faster and radical commitment to the compensation strategy, took place in Scandinavia. As shown by Baldwin for Denmark and partly for Sweden, the basis of universalist compensatory policies were already put in place at the turn of the century (Baldwin 1990). As soon as the Liberal party, sustained by the Danish farming community, secured a strong majority in parliament, all-inclusive, noncontributory, tax-financed pensions were established in the 1890s. The type and size of pensions directly responded to the tradeable character of the farming sector: first, they were "one of the more successful measures tried" to attract labor needed by farmers to keep being competitive "just as competition and falling prices fettered their ability to improve conditions and stem migration" (Baldwin 1990: 75); second, due to the international-prices-taker nature of Danish farming producers, their costs (and benefits) were spread across the whole population. As has been well documented in the literature (Cameron 1978; Katzenstein 1985), the strategy of openness in conjunction with compensatory mechanisms deepened in the 1930s and intensified again in the 1960s and 1970s. A brief set of data will give a sense of the difference in public interventionism by level of openness. In the early 1970s and among OECD nations, public spending in education averaged 5.4 percent of GDP in open economies (those were exports equal 40 percent or more of GDP) and 3.7 percent in closed countries; income maintenance programs were 12.9 percent of GDP and 8.6 percent of GDP respectively; public fixed capital formation was 4.5 percent and 3.7 percent of GDP; subsidies were 2.5 and 1.2 percent respectively; and labor market policies amounted (in 1985) to 1 and 0.5 percent in each set of countries (OECD 1990).

Conclusions

To explain both the political causes of trade policy and the empirical correlation that the literature has noted between free trade and publicly funded compensation mechanisms, this chapter examines the choice of protectionism as one among several strategies that states employ to redistribute income toward sectors hurt by changes in world markets.

In response to changes in the international competitiveness of domestic industries and to the volatility of the world business cycle, national policymakers may embrace two distinct strategies. To insulate domestic actors from internationally induced changes in relative prices, they may choose to close the domestic economy. Conversely, since this "laissez-faire" solution may have substantial distributional consequences, such as lower levels of wefare protection and likely increases in income inequality during economic downturns, they may decide to set up public programs to compensate trade losers to get the latter's political support for an open economy.

Policy-makers choose the level of trade openness partly as a function of the costs of trade and the average level of openness across the world. Ultimately, however, the policy regime in place is the result of a political deal and hence of the incentives and capacity free traders have to commit, in a credible manner, to a compensation package. If free traders offer a compensatory package to entice part of the import-competing sectors, then a free trade solution will be imposed. Conversely, if they do not or if their offer is not credible, the latter will rather support protectionism. The two self-governing colonies of Victoria and New South Wales before the formation of the Australian Commonwealth in 1901 supply us with the closest case to a "laboratory experiment" to test the key role of political institutions and agenda-setting powers. Although both political units were strikingly similar in population size, living conditions, endowments, economic structure, and constitutional arrangements, they followed two divergent trade policies, particularly in the 1890s. In New South Wales the Free Trade party struck a compact with the Labor party to sustain low tariffs in exchange for progressive direct taxation, a battery of industrial regulations, and stable and generous public expenditure. By contrast, in Victoria, protectionist politicians used the strong relationship between their Liberal party and unions to create a "new protection" regime in which workers supported high tariffs in exchange for an arbitrational and tax system that made sure that part of the gains of protection were directly passed onto workers through high wages. In short, the choice of trade regime hinged on the strategic capacity of politicians to organize a particular coalition around one of two equally feasible outcomes.

NOTES

I acknowledge the comments of its participants, particularly Michael Wallerstein and Bruce Western, and of one anonymous referee.

1. In a related idea, in Aukrust's (1977) analysis, the tradeable sector, modeled as an international price-taker, employs public spending to buy the acquiescence of the nontradeable sector to low wage increases, therefore ensuring the overall competitiveness (and survival) of the national economy.

2. For a first attempt to point to domestic compensation under a free trade regime as a mechanism to minimize risks, see Bates, Brock, and Tiefenthaler (1991).

3. Purchasing private insurance is, according to Rodrik, unfeasible due to either conflicts between capital market openness and other objectives of governmental policy or incentive and sovereign-risk problems restricting the range and extent of financial instruments available to governments.

4. Using the Summers-Heston database (which includes 147 nations for the period 1950–90, and about 4500 observations), Adserà and Boix (2001) show too that the volatility of the business cycle (calculated as the standard deviation of changes in the growth rate in five-year periods) increases with trade openness. More specifically, for each logged unit of trade openness, the volatility of the business cycle goes up by 0.6 (and its statistically significant at the 1 percent level). The result is robust to the introduction of control variables such as per capita income, economic structure, and weight of fuel and primary exports.

5. Garrett (2001) shows, however, that at least for the mid 1990s, the relationship breaks down for high-spending countries. Higher levels of trade integration have not led to larger public sectors in the past decade.

6. This in turn implies neglecting the literature on the redistributive consequences of public spending (Esping-Andersen 1990; Holsey and Borcherding 1997).

7. Once the economy is closed, aggregate demand management becomes an effective strategy to minimize the occurrence of recessions. Policymakers can then engage in countercyclical policies to smooth the business cycle.

8. A third outcome is for policymakers to keep the economy open while minimizing public expenditure. Free trade without compensation will be imposed only under two circumstances: there is an absolute majority that gains (with certainty) from free trade; and/or the free traders have been able to exclude the rest of society from the decision-making process. This strategy is modeled and tested in Adserà and Boix (2002).

9. Own estimation is based on data from Patterson (1968).

10. As a matter of fact, the electoral reform of 1893 was passed in New South Wales as a result of a deal between the Protectionist government and the Labor party.

11. This distribution does not distinguish between independent candidates and politicians who ran under the party umbrella.

12. Cited in Castles (1989): 34–35.

13. Cited in Andersen and Garnaut (1987): 46.

14. Extremely similar policies were adopted in New Zealand. There the erection of a strong tariff system to sustain prices in the domestic manufacturing industry in the 1920s and 1930s met with clear success. Whereas export prices fell by 40 percent between 1920 and 1935, real weekly wages of workers only decreased by 5 percent in the same period. For an analysis of that country, see Mabbett (1995).

15. The dispersion of household incomes is, however, much higher in Australia and closer to other English-speaking countries.

16. The proportion of enfranchised adult men varies across authors depending on the age chosen to count men and assumptions about the weight of plural votes in rural counties. For relatively low estimates, see McKibbin, Matthew, and Kay (1990). For high estimates, see Blewett (1972).

17. Cited in Blewett (1972): 79.

18. As late as 1931, 93 percent of Labor candidates supported free trade in their manifestos (Howe 1997: 285).

REFERENCES

Adserà, Alícia, and Carles Boix. 2002. "Trade, Democracy and the Size of the Public Sector." *International Organization,* 56 (2): 229–62.

Alt, James E. 1985. "Political Parties, World Demand, and Unemployment: Domestic and International Sources of Economic Activity." *American Political Science Review* 79: 1016–40.

Alt, James E., Jeffry Frieden, Michael J. Gilligan, Dani Rodrik, and Ronald Rogowski. 1996. "The Political Economy of International Trade: Enduring Puzzles and an Agenda for Inquiry." *Comparative Political Studies* 29: 689–717.

Alt, James E., and Michael J. Gilligan. 1994. "The Political Economy of Trading States: Factor Specificity, Collective Action Problem, and Domestic Political Institutions." *Journal of Political Philosophy* 2 (2): 165–92.

Andersen, Kym, and Ross Garnaut. 1987. *Australian Protectionism: Extent, Causes and Effects.* Sydney: Allen and Unwin.

Aukrust, Odd. 1977. "Inflation in the Open Economy: A Norwegian Model." In L. Krause and W. Salant (eds.), *Worldwide Inflation.* Washington, D.C.: Brookings.

Baldwin, Peter. 1990. *The Politics of Social Solidarity.* New York: Cambridge University Press.

Bates, Robert H., Philip Brock, and Fill Tiefenthaler. 1991. "Risk and Trade Regimes: Another Exploration." *International Organization* 15: 1–18.

Blewett, Neal. 1972. *The Peers, the Parties and the People: The British General Elections of 1910.* Toronto: University of Toronto Press.

Boix, Carles, and Sebastian Rosato. 2001. "A Complete Data Set of Political Regimes, 1800–1999." Manuscript, University of Chicago.

Cameron, David R. 1978. "The Expansion of the Public Economy: A Comparative Analysis." *American Political Science Review* 72: 1243–61.

Castles, Francis G. 1985. *The Working Class and Welfare: Reflections on the Political Development of the Welfare State in Australia and New Zealand, 1890–1980.* London: Allen and Unwin.

———. 1989. "Social Protection by Other Means: Australia's Strategy of Coping with External Vulnerability." Ch. 2 in Francis G. Castles (ed.), *The Comparative History of Public Policy.* New York: Oxford University Press.

Castles, Francis G., and Deborah Mitchell. 1993. "Worlds of Welfare and Families of Nations." Pp. 93–128 in *Families of Nations: Patterns of Public Policy in Western Democracies.* Aldershot, U.K.: Dartmouth.

Deininger, Klaus, and Lyn Squire. 1996. "A New Data Set Measuring Income Inequality." *The World Bank Economic Review* 19 (3): 565–91.

Esping-Andersen, Gøsta. 1990. *The Three Worlds of Welfare Capitalism.* Cambridge: Polity.

Garrett, Geoffrey. 1998. "Governing in the Global Economy: Economic Policy and Market Integration Around the World." Manuscript, Yale University.

———. 2001. "The Distributive Consequences of Globalization." Manuscript, Yale University.

Gollan, Robin. 1960. *Radical and Working-Class Politics.* Melbourne: Melbourne University Press.

Gottschalk, Peter, and Timothy M. Smeeding. 1997. "Cross-National Comparisons of Earnings and Income Inequality." *Journal of Economic Literature* 25 (June): 633–87.

Greenwood, Gordon. 1955. *Australia: A Social and Political History.* Sydney: Angus and Robertson.

Holsey, Cheryl M., and Thomas E. Borcherding. 1997. "Why Does Government's Share of National Income Grow? An Assessment of the Recent Literature on the U.S. Experience." In Dennis C. Mueller (ed.), *Perspectives on Public Choice: Handbook.* New York: Cambridge University Press.

Howe, Anthony. 1997. *Free Trade and Liberal England, 1846–1946.* New York : Oxford University Press.

Katzenstein, Peter. 1985. *Small States in World Markets: Industrial Policy in Europe.* Ithaca: Cornell University Press.

La Nauze, J. A. 1965. *Alfred Deakin.* 2 vols. Carlton, Victoria: Melbourne University Press.

Mabbett, Deborah. 1995. *Trade, Employment, and Welfare: A Comparative Study of Trade and Labour Market Policies in Sweden and New Zealand, 1880–1980.* Oxford: Clarendon.

McKibbin, Ross, Colin Matthew, and John Kay. 1990. "The Franchise Factor in the Rise of the Labour Party." Ch. 3 in Ross McKibbin (ed.), *The Ideologies of Class.* New York: Oxford University Press.

Mitchell, Brian R. 1992. *International Historical Statistics, Europe, 1750–1988.* New York: Stockton.

OECD. 1990. *OECD National Accounts. Main Aggregates. 1960–89,* vol. 1. Paris: OECD.

Patterson, G. D. 1968. *The Tariff in the Australian Colonies, 1856–1900.* Sydney: F. W. Cheshire.

Ray, Debraj. 1998. *Development Economics.* Princeton: Princeton University Press.

Rawson, D. W. 1977. "Victoria." In P. Loveday, A. W. Martin and R. S. Parker (eds.), *The Emergence of the Australian Party System.* Sydney: Hale and Iremonger.

Rickard, John. 1976. *Class and Politics: New South Wales, Victoria and the Early Commonwealth, 1890–1910.* Canberra: Australian National University Press.

Rodrik, Dani. 1995. "What Does the Political Economy Literature on Trade Policy (Not) Tell Us that We Ought to Know." In *Handbook of International Economics,* vol. 3. Amsterdam: North Holland.

———. 1998. "Why Do Open Economies Have Bigger Governments?" *Journal of Political Economy* 106: 997–1032.

Rogowski, Ronald. 1989. *Commerce and Coalitions: How Trade Affects Domestic Political Alignments.* Princeton: Princeton University Press.

Scitovsky, T. 1942. "A Reconsideration of the Theory of Tariffs." *Review of Economic Studies* 9: 89–110.

Schonhardt-Bailey, Cheryl. 1991. "Lessons in Lobbying for Free Trade in 19th-Century Britain: To Concentrate or Not." *American Political Science Review* 85 (March): 37–58.

Searle, Geoffrey R. 1992. *The Liberal Party: Triumph and Disintegration, 1886–1929.* New York: St. Martin's.

CHAPTER 9

Public Opinion, International Economic Integration, and the Welfare State

Kenneth Scheve & Matthew J. Slaughter

IDENTIFYING THE CONSEQUENCES of international economic integration for social insurance and redistributive policymaking involves specifying the economic and political constraints that these policy areas generate for one another. The main questions addressed in this inquiry typically take the form of determining whether increased international flows of goods, services, and factors of production raise the economic costs of the provision of social insurance and redistributive transfers such that political support for these policies is substantially diminished in democratic states. The most common answer to these questions is that yes, economic globalization reduces the capacity or at least political resolve of states to implement generous social insurance and redistributive policies. Dissents to this mainstream view, however, are many. These scholars point to a long tradition of egalitarian policymaking in highly open and internationally competitive economies (e.g., Cameron 1978; Rodrik 1997; Garrett 1998). At the core of most of these dissents is the idea that international economic liberalization generates costs for workers and thus may actually increase political support for social insurance and redistributive policymaking. An obvious strategy for evaluating this dissenting view regarding the supposed opposition of economic globalization and egalitarian policymaking is to evaluate how exposure to international integration may influence public support for both economic integration itself and the social insurance and redistributive policies that are the core of the modern welfare state.

In this chapter, we focus on one aspect of this research agenda and investigate the determinants of public support for the policies that govern the liberalization of flows of goods, services, and factors of production. This analysis is informative for debates about the relationship between globalization and egalitarian redistribution for at least two reasons. First, as is widely recognized, global economic integration is in part determined by policy liberalization—the reduction of impediments to international trade and flows of capital and labor. Any political economy model that seeks to explain policymaking for these areas in democratic states must specify the preferences of citizens in addition to the institutions that aggregate these preferences. To understand the impact of globalization on political support for the welfare state, it is necessary to understand the political bases of support for globalization itself. Second, our analysis emphasizes the importance of labor market concerns in individuals' evaluations of international economic policies and how these concerns may be mitigated in the presence of generous adjustment, insurance, and/or training schemes. We contend that simple conclusions that substantial social insurance and redistributive policies are inconsistent with economic globalization are implausible because political support for liberalism itself depends in part on those very policies.

There are four remaining sections to the chapter. The next section describes the broad patterns of public opinion around the world about international economic integration. Given the importance of labor market concerns evident in this description, the third section briefly reviews the theoretical effects of integration on the level and volatility of wages and employment and the existing empirical evidence evaluating these theories. The fourth section is the main section of the paper, and it examines the determinants of variation across individuals and countries in policy preferences. The final section concludes with a discussion of the implications of this evidence for explanations of variation in economic policymaking, including both those policies that govern the pace of international economic integration and those social insurance and redistributive policies that may alter its consequences for the welfare of workers.

Public Attitudes about International Economic Integration

What do people around the world think about the forces of trade, immigration, and FDI that drive international economic integration? Is there unabashed support? Or resistance? Or is there a more fundamental lack of understanding of the relevant economic issues at hand? In this section, we outline some broad patterns of public opinion around the world about globalization.

The comparative focus of this section draws on a growing body of recent research on preferences around the world over international economic policies. Our earlier work in this literature examined the United States, and others have addressed many other OECD and non-OECD countries as well.[1] The interested reader can note that commonly used cross-country data include the 1995–97 World Values Survey (WVS), a set of surveys designed for cross-national comparisons; and the 1995 International Social Survey Programme (ISSP). U.S.-specific data include the biennial National Election Studies surveys and the quadrennial surveys of the Chicago Council on Foreign Relations (CCFR).

In drawing upon these and other sources, our goal is not to generate an exhaustive catalog of each. Instead, we use them selectively to provide a representative overview of the salient patterns in public opinions about globalization and its constituent forces of trade, immigration, and FDI. We now address each of these in turn, where throughout we enumerate a list of salient facts.

Public Attitudes about Globalization

Fact 1: In many countries—but not all—a plurality or majority of people think that globalization is good for the overall country.

The broadest question one could ask about cross-border integration would invoke the catch-all term "globalization." CCFR (2002a, b) reports responses of seven countries to the question, "Overall do you think globalization is good or bad for the national economy?" The good-bad split ranges from 62 to 22 percent in the Netherlands to 25 to 34 percent in Poland, which is the one country among the seven sampled in which a plurality regards globalization as a net minus, not a plus.[2]

Fact 2: People perceive an asymmetric distribution of the benefits of globalization: more for consumers and corporations but less for workers.

The phrasing of the above question is open to a wide range of interpretations, as globalization encompasses a range of economic and noneconomic topics. That said, some insight on the salient issues can be gleaned from a set of related U.S. questions in CCFR (2002a) that asked whether globalization is good or bad for different constituencies. When given the same good-or-bad choice, majorities of Americans think globalization is good both for "consumers like you" (55 to 27 percent) and for "American companies" (55 to 30 percent).

There is much more ambivalence, however, about the labor-market impacts of globalization. Americans are evenly split (within sampling error) over whether globalization is good or bad for "creating jobs in the U.S." (43 to 41 percent), and a sizable majority thinks that globalization is bad for "job security of American workers" (51 to 32 percent). This widespread concern about labor markets will be seen quite clearly below when we examine the particular modes of global integration of trade, immigration, and FDI. This concern also appears when placed in the context of U.S. foreign policy. An overwhelming 85 percent of Americans state that protecting the jobs of American workers should be a "very important" goal of U.S. foreign policy (with this percentage representing the third highest-ranking goal chosen).

Fact 3: Some evidence suggests that in some countries, support for globalization has waned in recent years.

It is notable that recent surveys (e.g., CCFR, 2002a) suggest that American support for globalization has been waning in recent years. For example, the 52 percent in 2002 who stated that globalization is good for consumers was down from 68 percent in 2000. Similarly, the 85 percent in 2002 who stated job protection should be a "very important" goal for U.S. foreign policy was the highest response rate for this item since it was first asked by CCFR in 1974. Such trends over time might reflect many factors, such as a deepening of globalization in recent years or the deteriorating U.S. macroeconomy and labor market since 2000.

Public Attitudes about Trade

Fact 4: In most countries around the world, a plurality to majority of individuals prefer policy options aimed at more trade restrictions, not freer trade. Thus, the "average" citizen of the world appears to be more of a protectionist than a free-trader.

The most comprehensive comparative data on public attitudes about trade comes from the 1995–97 WVS. For the following question, this wave of the WVS reports responses for fifty-two countries (or intranational regions) around the world:

> Do you think it is better if goods made in other countries can be imported and sold here if people want to buy them, or that there should be stricter limits on selling foreign goods here, to protect the jobs of people in this country.

Of the 65,123 total respondents stating a preference for one of these two options, 64.2 percent chose stricter limits on trade. By country, a similar pattern emerges: in 42 of the 52 countries a majority of respondents stating a preference for one of these two options chose stricter trade limits. Anti-trade sentiments appear to be particularly strong in many countries of North and South America: the United States (73.0%), Peru (83.3%), Mexico (83.5%), Brazil (87.0%), Venezuela (87.9%), and Uruguay (92.6%). Most of the ten "pro-trade" countries were formerly part of the Soviet bloc (Armenia, Azerbaijan, Belarus, Bosnia, Georgia, Serbia, Ukraine), with only two from the OECD (Western Germany and Japan, the country with the highest pro-trade response rate at 71.7 percent).

The WVS question frames the trade issue in an explicit labor-market context. Given the earlier evidence that an—if not *the*—important reservation people express about globalization is its possible labor-market damage, one might worry that the widespread anti-trade sentiment in WVS responses is sensitive to framing. An alternative frame of reference is given by the 1995 ISSP survey. Here, trade protection is considered in the context of the overall economy, rather than the labor-market in particular.

> How much do you agree or disagree with the following statements: (Respondent's country) should limit the import of foreign products in order to protect its national economy.
>
> - Agree strongly
> - Agree
> - Neither agree nor disagree
> - Disagree
> - Disagree strongly

One can count pro-trade opinions as those responding "disagree" or "disagree strongly," and similarly anti-trade opinions as those responding "agree" or "agree strongly." Of the 29,350 total respondents stating a preference, only 22.3 percent were pro-trade while 59.5 percent were anti-trade. As with the WVS evidence, here too in the large majority of countries—21 of 23—a majority of respondents stating a preference for one of these two options chose stricter trade limits. The only two without such a minority are the Netherlands and Japan (with West German opinions, broadly consistent with the WVS evidence, nearly evenly split).

Even with the ISSP evidence, though, one might still worry about question framing. The ISSP question does not offer any rationale for disagreeing with protection as a policy choice. Indeed, the question could be read as though the idea that import limits somehow protect economies is indisputable fact, evidence from the economics profession notwithstanding.

Scheve and Slaughter (2001c) explore the impact of question framing for the case of the United States, thanks to their sample of hundreds of trade-policy survey questions from the 1930s forward. They document two broad categories of trade-policy questions: those that mention both benefits and costs to trade (e.g., the WVS question) and those that do not. For questions in the former category, a plurality to majority of respondents still oppose policies aimed at freer trade. Some of the latter questions elicit more pro-trade responses—especially questions that do not mention policy per se, but rather the general idea of international trade as cross-border commerce. Even with these questions, however, the evidence at best suggests the U.S. public is split on the issue of trade. Thus, while a more systematic examination of framing issues in a cross-section of countries would be of help, for now, our reading of the evidence is that the "average" respondent across countries is skeptical about trade liberalization.

One might also wonder about whether Fact #4 has held consistently over time. U.S. evidence indicates that the split in that country's opinions between freer and more protected trade has existed for about a generation. Scheve and Slaughter (2001c) report time-series evidence from a *Los Angeles Times* survey conducted annually since 1982. Every year, approximately two-thirds of respondents have opted for a policy of trade barriers to protect jobs over a policy of free trade to allow broader consumer variety and lower consumer prices. CCFR (2002a) reports similar time-series stability for a trade-policy question it has asked quadrennially since 1976. Every year, approximately half or slightly more of respondents have opted for a policy of trade barriers to protect jobs over a policy of free trade to lower consumer prices.

Fact 5: Anti-trade opinions do not simply reflect ignorance about the subject. The U.S. evidence is that large majorities of individuals acknowledge that trade generates the benefits that economic theory predicts. Similarly large majorities also worry, however, that trade generates labor market costs in terms of job destruction and lower wages.

Scheve and Slaughter (2001c) document evidence on both components on this fact. Gains from trade that large majorities of Americans acknowledge include lower consumer prices (especially for poor families), wider consumer variety, and sharper competitive and innovative pressures for American firms. Yet a wide swatch of questions reveals deep concerns among consistent pluralities to majorities that trade destroys U.S. jobs and pressures U.S. wages. For detailed questions and discussion, see Scheve and Slaughter (2001c). Note how this U.S. evidence on the perceived distribution of benefits and costs for trade parallels the perceived distribution for globalization noted earlier in Fact 2.

Facts 4 and 5 can be brought together in sharp relief by recent U.S. questions by CCFR and the Program on International Policy Attitudes (PIPA). In 2000 and then again in 2002, PIPA and then CCFR asked the following question:

> Which of the following three positions comes closest to your point of view? A: I favor free trade, and I believe that it IS necessary for the government to have programs to help workers who lose their jobs. B: I favor free trade, and I believe that it is NOT necessary for the government to have programs to help workers who lose their jobs. C: I do not favor free trade.

In 2000 66 percent of Americans chose option A, the policy duo of free trade plus labor-market supports. In 2002 73 percent of Americans chose this option. The response to this particular trade-policy question stands in sharp contrast to the questions discussed for Fact 4. When the policy option of free trade is explicitly linked with policies aimed at ameliorating any adverse labor market impacts, large majorities of Americans opt for free trade.

Public Attitudes about Immigration

Fact 6: In most countries around the world, a plurality to majority of individuals prefer policy options aimed at admitting fewer immigrants, not more. Thus, the "average" citizen of the world appears to be prefer less immigration, not more.

Public opinion about immigration broadly parallels that of trade. As with trade, for comparative evidence we start with the WVS question:

> How about people from other countries coming here to work? Which one of the following do you think the government should do?

- Let anyone come who wants to.
- Let people come as long as there are jobs available.
- Place strict limits on the number of foreigners who can come here.
- Prohibit people coming here from other countries.

We aggregated responses by assigning each a number one through four (in the foregoing order) and then averaging. Of the 64,369 total respondents stating a preference, the average was about 2.42—that is, the "average" response was somewhere between allowing immigrants conditional on job availability and strictly limiting immigrants. We consider this to be lukewarm enthusiasm for immigration, at best. By country, a similar picture emerges: in 47 of the 49 countries the average response was over two.

The WVS question frames the immigration issue in an explicit labor-market context. Indeed, the question seems to presume that immigrants tend to take jobs away from natives. Given the earlier evidence that an—if not *the*—important reservation people express about globalization and trade are the possible labor-market damage, one might worry that the widespread anti-immigration sentiment in WVS responses is sensitive to framing. An alternative frame of reference is given by the 1995 ISSP survey. Here, respondents are asked about changes in existing immigration levels without reference to any particular economic issue.

> Do you think the number of immigrants to (Respondent's country) nowadays should
> be reduced a lot, reduced a little, remain the same as it is, increased a little, or increased
> a lot?

One can count pro-immigration opinions as those responding "increased a little" or "increased a lot," and similarly anti-immigration opinions as those responding "reduced a little" or "reduced a lot." Of the 27,001 total respondents stating a preference, only 7.9 percent were pro-immigration while 61.7 percent were anti-immigration. In all twenty-three countries this anti-immigration group was larger than its pro-immigration counterpart, and the national fraction accounted for by this anti-immigration group was less than half in just three countries: Canada (41.3%), Ireland (21.6%), and Spain (40.0%).

Fact 7: Anti-immigration opinions, like those for trade, appear to have an important labor-market component to them. People acknowledge some benefits from immigration but appear to worry more about costs such as labor-market pressures.

Individuals do acknowledge some economic and social benefits from immigration. For example, the ISSP survey asked whether immigrants make the host country "more open to new ideas and cultures." The average response across all countries was somewhere between neutral and agree. Scheve and Slaughter (2001c) report similar U.S. evidence: for example, 69 percent of Americans agree that "immigrants help improve our country with their different cultures and talents."

But there appears to be widespread concern that immigrants generate social and economic costs. For example, the ISSP survey asked whether immigrants "increase crime rates." The average response across all countries was somewhere between neutral and agree. In terms of economic impacts, the average response was similar to the question of whether immigrants "take jobs away from people who were born in the country." Scheve and Slaughter (2001c) report similar U.S. evidence. Large majorities of Americans think that immigrants take jobs away from natives—with a plurality regularly stating that this outcome is either extremely or very likely. When asked questions about U.S. immigration policy that explicitly raise the potential cost of job competition for natives, large majorities of Americans chose the option of decreasing immigration.

The balance of opinion on immigration, then, looks broadly similar to that for trade. Though people acknowledge benefits, both economic and otherwise, they appear to worry more about costs—especially labor-market costs—such that on balance they opt for policies of less immigration, not more. Consistent with this, the ISSP asked broadly whether "immigrants are generally good for the country's economy." The average response fell between neutral and disagree.

Public Attitudes about FDI

We are unaware of comprehensive comparative evidence on foreign direct investment (FDI) opinions. In Scheve and Slaughter (2001c), we present U.S. evidence, which we briefly summarize. The issue of how this U.S. evidence might be representative of other countries should be treated carefully. Our discussion in this section indicates that many U.S. opinion patterns over trade and immigration that we documented in Scheve and Slaughter (2001c) broadly match patterns elsewhere in the world. That said, to the extent that many other countries have broader histories of inward and outward FDI flows, U.S. opinions over FDI might not generalize as easily.

Fact 8: A majority of Americans want restrictions on both inward and outward foreign direct investment, as Americans acknowledge some economic benefits but seem to worry more about perceived labor-market costs.

On the one hand, a plurality of Americans acknowledge that inward FDI generates economic benefits as foreign firms help invigorate U.S. industry via new technologies and management techniques.

On the other hand, there is significant concern about the labor-market impacts of inward and outward FDI, especially whether it reduces the number of jobs. Across a wide range of questions, a consistent plurality to majority think that FDI in both directions eliminates jobs. This opinion appears more widespread about outward FDI, with the prominent concern that outward FDI entails U.S. firms "exporting" jobs outside the country. Over two-thirds of Americans think that "companies sending jobs overseas" is a "major reason" for "why the economy is not doing better than it is." With inward FDI, there also appears to be concern that inward FDI somehow grants foreigners excessive control over the U.S. economy.

In light of these labor-market and security concerns, one might expect Americans not to support FDI liberalization. This is indeed the case: a majority favors restrictions on FDI.

Summary of Findings: Ambivalence and Variation

Our two-word summary of the opinions collected in this section is "ambivalence" and "variation."

In many countries, pluralities to majorities of citizens acknowledge the many economic benefits of global integration. This belies the idea that globalization is too complex for people to understand. But at the same time, these same pluralities to majorities also vocalize concerns about this process. Particularly salient appear to be concerns about labor-market pressures on wages, employment, and job security. On balance, it appears that the "average" citizen in many countries supports the broad idea of globalization yet at the same time prefers policies aimed at less trade, less immigration, and less FDI. At the very least, it is clear that there is division and therefore substantial concern about further liberalization. Thus, ambivalence is an important feature of the data.

A second important feature is the cross-country variation in opinions. The broad assessments of benefits and costs just described are not uniform in every country. Rather, countries look quite different on many basic questions. It is not the case that in every country the average citizen is against freer trade or immigration. And even within the large groups of anti-liberalization countries, countries vary substantially in how widely these attitudes are held. We examine what accounts for this cross-country variation in the fourth section. But before turning to that analysis, in the next section we briefly outline the possible labor-market impacts of globalization.

THE LABOR-MARKET IMPACTS OF GLOBALIZATION

In this section, we discuss linkages from global economic integration to a few key labor-market outcomes: the level of real and relative wages, and insecurity in terms of the volatility of wages and employment.[3] We have two overall messages to this section: that there are sound reasons in theory that integration can affect labor markets, and that at least some of these links have mattered empirically for some countries in recent decades. As is the case in much of the literature on globalization and labor markets, our discussion in this section presumes the benchmark of relatively flexible labor markets that clear at full employment. In reality, in less flexible labor markets the supply-and-demand forces generated by globalization can have employment as well as wage impacts. This will be considered empirically in the next section.

The Theory of the Impact of Trade on Wages

Standard trade theory predicts that trade's effect on people's current income depends crucially on the degree of intersectoral factor mobility, that is, on the degree of factor specificity. There are two main models to consider. In a Heckscher-Ohlin (HO) framework, where factors can move costlessly across sectors, factor incomes tend to vary by factor type. In contrast, in a Ricardo-Viner (RV) framework, where some or all factors cannot move to other sectors, factor incomes tend to vary by industry of employment. Because factor mobility increases over time, it is often thought the HO model better describes longer time horizons while the RV model better describes shorter ones.[4]

In both models, changes in trade policy affect factor incomes by changing the country's relative product prices. The HO assumption that factors can move cost-lessly across sectors means each factor earns the same return in all industries. Here, trade liberalization tends to raise/lower wages for factors employed rela-tively intensively in sectors whose relative prices are rising/falling (per the Stolper-Samuelson theorem, 1941).

This process works via cross-industry shifts in labor demand. Suppose interna-tional trade changes domestic product prices—for example, because of changes in a country's trade barriers (e.g., the United States eliminates apparel quotas in the Multi-Fiber Arrangement) or because of changes in supply and demand in world markets (e.g., world apparel prices decline as China produces more). Whatever the case, at initial factor prices any industry enjoying a rise in its product price now earns positive profits, while any industry suffering a fall in its price now earns negative profits. Profit-maximizing firms respond by trying to expand out-put in profitable sectors and reduce output in unprofitable sectors. As firms do this, economy-wide demand for factors of production changes. Relative labor de-mand increases for the factors employed relatively intensively in expanding sec-tors and reduces for the factors intensive in the contracting sectors. To restore equilibrium, at fixed labor supply, relative wages must adjust in response to the demand shifts until profit opportunities are arbitraged away.

Note that in the HO framework, it is *not* just people working in traded indus-tries who face wage pressures from international trade. Non-traded workers do too, not directly through international product-market competition, but indi-rectly through domestic labor-market competition. If U.S. trade barriers in ap-parel are removed, it is not just American apparel workers who face wage changes. It is all workers in the American economy competing in the same labor market as these apparel workers—regardless of the industries of these other workers.

Empirical Studies of the Impact of Trade on Wages

Do these linkages from trade to wages seem to matter in the real world? The short answer is, "yes." A comparative analysis of wage changes is clearly beyond the scope of this chapter. We briefly summarize the U.S. experience, both because most academic research in recent years has focused on this case and because its changes have been paralleled in many other countries.

In recent decades, there have been sharply different wage trends for more-skilled and less-skilled Americans. First, the premium earned by more-skilled workers over less-skilled workers has been rising sharply since the late 1970s. Sec-ond, average real-wage growth in the United States has been very sluggish since the early 1970s. And when talking about less-skilled U.S. workers, it is very important to remember that this category, as typically defined by labor economists, constitutes the majority of the U.S. labor force. All this means that *for about twenty-five years less-skilled workers, the majority of the U.S. labor force, have had close to zero or even negative real-wage growth while more-skilled workers have been enjoying real-wage gains.* These patterns differ sharply from earlier decades, when real-wage growth was both faster and enjoyed across all groups with steady and/or declining inequality.[5]

What role has international trade played in these developments? There is a very large academic literature on this subject, with a wide range of conclusions. Taken together, most studies seem to have concluded that technological change favoring skilled workers has been the major force driving up the returns to skill. This "skill-biased" technological change (SBTC), widespread across the majority of U.S. industries, does not appear to be robustly related to various globalization forces.

Most trade economists looking at the role of international trade have organized their data analysis around the Stolper-Samuelson process outlined earlier. For trade to have driven changes in U.S. relative wages via changes in U.S. relative product prices, it would have done so by raising the relative price of less-skill-intensive goods during the 1970s but then lowering the relative price of less-skill-intensive goods since around 1980. Have prices actually moved in this manner? Perhaps. Changes in observed U.S. product prices have not clearly matched up with changes in the skill premium. But when decomposing observed prices into trade-related components, some studies have found evidence of the necessary relative price changes. Most Stolper-Samuelson studies have concluded that trade may have played some role in the rising skill premium, but that it has not been the major force driving wage movements. Other studies using other methods have reached similar conclusions.[6]

Does this U.S. experience apply to other countries? The basic issue for any country is to see if changes in a country's relative product prices related to trade policy (or to some other aspect of trade) correlate in the predicted way with changes in that country's relative wages. In many other countries, Stolper-Samuelson analyses have linked trade with wage changes. For example, Haskel and Slaughter (2001) relate changes in U.K. tariffs with rising U.K. wage inequality. Hanson and Harrison (1999) document that recent increases in Mexican wage inequality coincided with deeper cuts in Mexican tariffs in unskill-intensive industries.

Hanson and Harrison (1999) highlight that this cross-industry pattern of trade liberalization is the opposite of what one would expect if trade protection in a country simply concentrated in its industries that employ relatively intensively its relatively scarce factors *and* if Mexico is poorly endowed with more-skilled labor (i.e., not less-skilled labor) relative to the rest of the world. But while Mexico may be scarce in more-skilled labor relative to the United States, it may be abundant in this factor relative to many lower-income countries in the world such as China.

Mexico's case demonstrates the general point that the expected Stolper-Samuelson cleavages from trade liberalization are likely to be linked with countries' relative endowments of factors or production. Our comparative empirical work in the fourth section returns to this important issue.

The Theory of the Impact of Immigration on Wages

To make the connection between individual factor income and immigration policy, we briefly summarize three models: the HO trade model, the factor-proportions-analysis model, and the area-analysis model.[7] For simplicity we assume just two factors of production, more-skilled and less-skilled labor.

The HO trade model usually assumes interregional factor mobility (as well as intersectoral factor mobility discussed earlier), which means that there are no geographically segmented "local" labor markets. Immigration's wage effects depend on the size of the immigration shock and on whether the country is big enough to have any influence on world product prices.

In the HO framework, immigrant inflows sometimes have *no* wage effects at all. Instead, immigrants are completely absorbed via output-mix changes. With the change in factor supplies available to hire, firms have an incentive to produce more output of those products that employ relatively intensively the now more-abundant factors (per the Rybczynski theorem, 1955). Thanks to trade, these output changes can be absorbed onto world markets, and if the country is too small for this absorption to affect world prices, then its wages do not change either. The long-run nature of the HO model is crucial here, as output-mix changes take time.

In the HO framework, however, immigrant inflows sometimes do change wages. For example, if the country is sufficiently big then its output changes do alter world prices and thus wages (via the Stolper-Samuelson process). Or if the immigration shock is sufficiently big, then firms have an incentive to start up entirely new industries, which means that absorption entails changes in both outputs and wages. In either case, if the immigrant pool is predominantly made up of less-skilled workers, then less-skilled wages fall relative to more-skilled wages.

Like the HO model, the factor-proportions-analysis model also assumes a national labor market. Unlike the HO model, however, this model assumes a single aggregate output sector. This means there can be no output-mix changes to absorb immigrants. Instead, immigrants price themselves into employment via lower wages. Any immigration inflow of, let's assume, less-skilled workers affects national wages as one might expect without output-mix changes: less-skilled immigrants accept lower less-skilled wages to induce firms to hire them. The bigger the immigrant inflow, the bigger the wage changes.

Like the previous model, the area-analysis model also assumes a single output sector. But this model assumes distinct, geographically segmented labor markets within a country. For countries like the United States with lots of internal migration, this assumption is probably inappropriate in the very long run. But it may be realistic over shorter time horizons thanks to frictions such as information and transportation costs that people must incur to move. The more important frictions like these are, the more sensible it is to treat Portland, Maine, and Portland, Oregon, as two distinct labor markets. Given this, economists often analyze "local" labor markets within the United States, usually defined by states, cities, or metropolitan areas (e.g., the Twin Cities of Minneapolis and St. Paul plus surrounding suburbs). Each local market has its own equilibrium wages determined by local supply and local demand.

Empirical Studies of the Impact of Immigration on Wages

There is also a very large literature examining the impact of immigration on native wages in U.S. regions. The standard area-analysis approach is to regress the change in native wages on the change in the stock of immigrants across U.S. metropolitan areas. Most area-analysis studies find that immigration has, at most, a small negative impact on local native wages. Borjas, Freeman, and Katz (1996, 1997) argue that immigration's wage effects should appear nationally rather than in local labor markets. They accordingly work from the factor-proportions perspective, and conclude that greater immigrant inflows have helped pressure the wages of high-school dropouts. Hanson and Slaughter (2002) find evidence that output-mix effects matter for absorbing U.S. immigration flows.[8] Links from immigration to native wages at the national level have also been found outside the United States, for example, Friedberg's (2001) study of the recent immigration surge from Russia into Israel.

The Theory of the Impact of FDI on the Variability of Earnings and Employment

Globalization can help shape labor-market outcomes other than just the level of real and relative wages. Another important issue may be the volatility of wages and employment. The extent of labor-market volatility depends in part on the aggregate shocks influencing firms and their hiring decisions. Greater exposure to the international economy may theoretically increase or decrease these shocks. Labor-market volatility does not, however, depend just on the magnitude of these shocks. For some given level of aggregate shocks, it also depends on the elasticity of labor demand—that is, on how responsive firm's hiring decisions are to changes in wages. Standard models in international trade predict that greater FDI by multinationals can make labor demands more elastic through both the scale and substitution effects.[9] This, in turn, should boost worker insecurity via greater labor-market volatility just described. To see how this works, first consider the idea that greater FDI raises labor-demand elasticities.

Many models predict that FDI and its related international trade make product markets more competitive. Through the scale effect, this should make labor demands more elastic. For example, liberalization of FDI policies can force domestic firms to face heightened foreign competition. Or developments abroad (e.g., capital accumulation via FDI) can be communicated to domestic producers as more-intense foreign competition. In these cases more competitive product markets mean that a given increase in wages, and thus costs, translates into larger declines in output and thus demand for all factors. Different models predict different magnitudes of FDI and/or trade's impact on product-market demand.

The second way through which FDI can increase labor-demand elasticities is through the substitution effect. Suppose that a firm is vertically integrated with a number of production stages. Stages can move abroad either within firms, as multinationals establish foreign affiliates (e.g., Helpman 1984), or at arm's length, by importing the output of those stages from other firms (e.g., Feenstra and Hanson 1997). Globalization of production thus gives firms access to foreign factors of production as well as domestic ones, either directly through foreign affiliates or indirectly through intermediate inputs. This expands the set of factors that firms can substitute toward in response to higher domestic wages beyond just domestic non-labor factors to include foreign factors as well. Thus, greater FDI raises labor-demand elasticities.

How do higher labor-demand elasticities translate into greater labor-market volatility? Visualize equilibrium in a standard competitive labor market drawn as wages against employment. We introduce volatility into the labor market by assuming that the position of the demand schedule is stochastic (in accord with a wide range of empirical evidence). This position depends crucially on product prices and production technologies facing the relevant firms. Movements in prices and technologies trigger movements in labor demand and thus in equilibrium wages and/or employment.

For workers, the critical issue is that volatility in labor-market outcomes depends not just on the volatility of labor-demand shifters such as product prices and production technology. It also depends on the magnitudes of the elasticities of labor supply and demand. If elasticities are assumed to be fixed, then greater labor-market volatility arises if and only if there is greater aggregate volatility in prices or technology. But this is not the only way to generate greater labor-market volatility. It can also be generated from increasing the elasticity of demand for labor, holding fixed the amount of aggregate risk. Higher labor-demand elasticities trigger more-volatile labor-market responses to price or technology shocks to labor demand.[10]

Empirical Studies of the Impact of FDI on the Variability of
Earnings and Employment

In the literature on globalization and labor markets, there are several recent studies indicating that MNEs and FDI influence labor-demand elasticities in the ways just suggested. Using industry-level data for U.S. manufacturing, Slaughter (2001) estimates that demand for production labor became more elastic from 1960 to the early 1990s, and that these increases were correlated with FDI out-flows by U.S.-headquartered multinationals. Using industry-level data for all U.K. manufacturing from 1958 to 1986, Fabbri, Haskel, and Slaughter (2003) estimate increases in labor-demand elasticities for both production and nonproduction labor.

One important margin on which multinationals may affect elasticities is on the extensive margin of plant shutdowns. In response to wage increases, multinationals may be more likely than domestic firms to respond by closing entire plants. Evidence that multinational plants are more likely to close than are domestically owned plants has now been documented for the manufacturing sectors in at least three countries. For the United Kingdom, Fabbri et al. (2003) estimate that multinational plants—again, both U.K.- and foreign-owned—are more likely to shut down than domestic plants are (conditional on a set of operational advantages enjoyed by multinationals that make them less likely to shut down, like being older and larger). Gorg and Strobl (2003) find that foreign-owned plants in Irish manufacturing are more likely to exit. For the United States, Bernard and Jensen (2002) report higher death probabilities for plants owned by firms that hold at least 10 percent of their assets outside the United States.

Does this connection between FDI and elasticities seem to relate to worker insecurity? Scheve and Slaughter (2004) provide one piece of evidence that it does. Their analysis of panel data covering individuals in Great Britain over 1991–99 finds that individual perceptions of economic insecurity are positively correlated with FDI activity in the industries in which individuals work.

More generally, we note that there is now a large body of evidence that labor-market volatility has been rising in many countries, especially in the 1990s, in terms of greater earnings volatility, declining job tenure, and self-reports. Gottschalk and Moffitt (1994) report substantial increases in year-to-year earnings volatility for the United States over the 1970s and 1980s. Looking at the 1990s as well, a symposium issue of the *Journal of Labor Economics* (1999) documented declines in U.S. job stability, especially in the 1990s, for large groups of workers such as those with more tenure. Within that symposium issue, Schmidt's (1999) analysis of individual surveys finds that U.S. workers in the 1990s were more pessimistic about losing their jobs than they were during the 1980s. A wide range of surveys have found evidence of rising U.S. job insecurity over the 1990s relative to earlier decades, despite the ongoing economic expansion (e.g., Bronfenbrenner 2000).

This micro-evidence on FDI, elasticities, and worker insecurity reinforces the point that labor-market volatility does not arise from just aggregate volatility in prices and/or technology. There is ongoing empirical disagreement about whether globalization has played a role in raising aggregate volatility.[11]

Explaining Policy Preferences about International Economic
 Integration

The second section outlined some broad patterns of public opinion around
the world about trade, immigration, and foreign direct investment, emphasiz-
ing the importance of labor market concerns in public attitudes about international economic integration. The third section suggested that there are important theoretical reasons why integration may have substantial consequences for
labor market performance but that these effects should vary across countries according to factor endowments. Further, there is some empirical evidence consistent with these theoretical predictions—though the evidence varies in strength
depending on precisely what link between integration and labor-market performance is in question. In this section, we evaluate empirically the determinants of
differences in public opinion about integration across individuals and across
countries with particular emphasis on how the connections between international economic integration and labor market performance help to account for
this variation.

Theoretical Determinants of Policy Preferences

Why are some individuals more supportive of free trade than others? Why do
some citizens prefer restrictionist immigration policies while others are less concerned with, if not welcoming of, new citizens? It is useful to place answers to
these questions along a number of different dimensions.

First, some explanations emphasize the impact of policy alternatives on aggregate national welfare, while others focus attention on the importance of how policy is expected to affect the individual economic welfare of citizens. In the case of
trade, there is a virtual consensus among academic economists that free trade is
good for national economic welfare and so if this was the only consideration, we
would expect to observe nearly unanimous support in the public for liberalization.[12] As discussed in the previous section, however, it is widely recognized that
while free trade may have aggregate benefits, its distributional consequences generate both winners and losers. This suggests that policy opinions should be expected to be divided along these lines. National and individual welfare considerations are not mutually exclusive, and it is likely that both play a role in opinion
formation. With that said, the data presented in the second section suggest substantial divisions in policy opinions that may be difficult to account for from a
purely national economic welfare framework.

Second, explanations focus more or less attention on economic versus noneconomic considerations that inform individual policy opinions. Economic concerns
include the effects of integration on real and relative wages, the level of unem-

ployment, and the volatility of wages and employment. Further economic considerations include the possible impact of integration on the values of the assets that individuals own as well as national levels of income and growth as discussed earlier. Noneconomic concerns include the possible role individual values and identities might play in informing policy opinions. Again, economic and noneconomic concerns are not mutually exclusive sets of considerations, and there is substantial empirical evidence that both types of factors are important in opinion formation. We will focus attention in this section on political economy approaches that emphasize economic factors but will briefly summarize the evidence in the literature on noneconomic considerations.

A simple political economy model of preference formation focuses attention on how different policy alternatives affect the earnings of individuals in the labor market. As discussed in the previous section, there are a number of different aspects of labor market outcomes that may be affected by international economic integration. For simplicity, we focus on the real and relative income effects described above and limit our discussion to trade and immigration policy.[13]

TRADE POLICY PREFERENCES

For trade policy, recall from the previous section that standard trade theory predicts that trade's effect on people's current income depends crucially on the degree of intersectoral factor mobility, that is, on the degree of factor specificity. Moreover, it is likely that factor mobility varies across countries and across time and thus divisions in the impact of trade liberalization on factor income may vary as well with factor type and industry of employment being better predictors of how liberalization affects worker wages in some countries and at certain times than others.

To demonstrate how different links between policy alternatives and wages might account for differences among individuals in policy opinions, it useful to start with opinion formation in a particular country—the United States. In the HO model with mobile factors, it is usually assumed that protection is received by the sectors that employ relatively intensively the factors with which the country is poorly endowed relative to the rest of the world, because in opening to trade, these factors suffer income declines. In contrast, the factors with which the country is well endowed relative to the rest of the world enjoy income gains in opening to trade. Thus a country's abundant factors support freer trade while its scarce factors oppose it.

Many studies (e.g., Leamer 1984) have documented that the United States is well endowed with more-skilled labor relative to the rest of the world. And the recent U.S. pattern of protection accords with the model's predictions: U.S. tariffs throughout the 1970s and 1980s were higher in less-skill-intensive industries (Haskel and Slaughter 2003). *According to the HO model, U.S.*

more-skilled workers should support freer trade while less-skilled workers should oppose it.

At the opposite extreme from the HO model, the RV model assumes that some or even all factors cannot move across sectors, thanks to mobility barriers such as industry-specific human capital gained through on-the-job experience. These immobile, that is, specific, factors need not earn the same return in all sectors. Instead, income for specific factors is linked to their sector of employment as trade-liberalization-induced changes in relative product prices redistribute income across sectors rather than factors. Sectors whose product prices fall—presumably comparative-disadvantage sectors—realize income losses for their specific factors while sectors whose product prices rise—presumably comparative-advantage sectors—realize income gains for their specific factors. In the RV model trade-policy preferences are determined by sector of employment. *Workers employed in sectors with product prices elevated by trade protection (likely comparative-disadvantage sectors) should oppose trade liberalization while workers employed in sectors with prices lowered by protection should support it.*[14]

IMMIGRATION POLICY PREFERENCES

To make the connection between individual factor income and immigration-policy preferences, we use the three models discussed earlier—the HO trade model, the factor-proportions-analysis model, and the area-analysis model—and again focus our attention initially on the U.S. case. For all three models, we assume U.S. citizens know that current immigrant inflows increase the relative supply of less-skilled workers. This assumption clearly reflects the facts about U.S. immigration in recent decades (e.g., Borjas et al. 1997). It implies that preferences depend on how an immigration-induced shift in U.S. relative labor supply toward less-skilled workers affects factor incomes. For simplicity we assume just two factors of production, more-skilled and less-skilled labor.

The HO model has different predictions about the link between skills and immigration-policy preferences. *If individuals think that immigration does not alter wages, then there should be no link from skills to preferences.* In this case people evaluate immigration based on other considerations. *If individuals think that immigration affects wages, then less-skilled (more-skilled) workers nationwide should prefer policies that lower (raise) immigration inflows.*

In the factor-proportions-analysis model, recall that immigration inflow affects national wages as one might expect without output-mix changes. This model makes a single prediction about the link from skills to immigration-policy preferences. *Less-skilled (more-skilled) workers nationwide should prefer policies to lower (raise) immigration inflows.* Note this prediction can also come from the HO model.

In the area-analysis model, each local market has its own equilibrium wages determined by local supply and local demand. In this framework, how do Americans think about the labor-market impacts of immigration? Well, it depends on where immigrants settle. If there is literally no mobility among local labor markets, then immigrants pressure wages only in the "gateway" communities where they arrive. And it is well documented that in reality, immigrants are indeed concentrated in these gateway communities. In 1990, 75 percent of all immigrants living in the United States were in one of six gateway states: California, Florida, Illinois, New Jersey, New York, and Texas. Borjas et al. (1996) report that in 1992, 60 percent of all U.S. legal immigrants came into California or New York alone; another 20 percent entered the other four gateway states.

What does this framework predict for immigration-policy preferences? *In the area-analysis model less-skilled (more-skilled) workers in gateway communities should prefer policies to lower (raise) immigration inflows. In non-gateway communities there should be no correlation between workers' skills and their preferences.* More generally, with some labor mobility, similarly skilled workers everywhere should share the same preferences, but with a stronger skills-preferences link among gateway workers.

To summarize: trade-policy preferences may cleave along skills and industry of employment; immigration-policy preferences along skills and geography. And different cleavages may hold over different time horizons, as sectoral and/or geographic labor mobility increases over time.

Policy Preferences in the United States

Empirical studies of the determinants of individual trade and immigration policy preferences rely on the analysis of survey data that contain direct measures of individual preferences over policy alternatives. In this section, we report some of the key results of our examination of the 1992, 1994, and 1996 National Election Studies (NES) surveys (Sapiro et al. 1998), each of which is an extensive survey of current political opinions based on an individual-level stratified random sample of the U.S. population. These surveys also report a wealth of respondent information such as educational attainment, occupation, and industry of employment. With this information, we built data sets with several plausible measures of "exposure" to freer trade and immigration across factor types, industries, and many other demographic variables such as age, gender, ideology, and race. Merging this information with the NES surveys yielded individual-level data sets identifying both stated policy preferences and potential trade/immigration exposure through several channels. We then evaluated how these preferences vary with individual characteristics that the theories reviewed in the previous section predict might matter.

Here is a restatement of the NES question about trade-policy preferences.[15]

Some people have suggested placing new limits on foreign imports in order to protect American jobs. Others say that such limits would raise consumer prices and hurt American exports. Do you favor or oppose placing new limits on imports, or haven't you thought much about this?

By coding responses 1 for those individuals favoring protection and 0 for those opposing it, we constructed the variable *Trade Opinion*. This question requires respondents to reveal their general position on the proper direction for U.S. trade policy. Note that the question does not ask what sector(s) would receive import restrictions. We assume that respondent opinions are informed by the belief that import limits will be placed on comparative-disadvantage sectors. This seems more sensible than alternatives such as limits on comparative-advantage sectors, and it allows us to construct measures of factor and industry trade exposure that follow closely from the theory. In 1992 about 67 percent of respondents favored trade restrictions while 33 percent were opposed. In 1996, among those giving an opinion preferences were more evenly divided, with 53 percent supporting restrictions and 47 percent opposed. These marginal rates of opinion are consistent with other survey results.[16]

Here is the NES question about immigration-policy preferences:

> Do you think the number of immigrants from foreign countries who are permitted to come to the United States to live should be increased a little, increased a lot, decreased a little, decreased a lot, or left the same as it is now?

This question requires respondents to reveal their general position on the proper direction for U.S. immigration policy. Note that the question does not ask what skill-mix immigrants would have relative to natives. We assume that respondent opinions are informed by the belief that immigrant inflows would increase the relative supply of less-skilled workers. As discussed in the previous section, this assumption clearly reflects the facts about U.S. immigration in recent decades.[17] We construct the variable *Immigration Opinion* by coding responses 5 for those individuals responding "decreased a lot" down to 1 for those responding "increased a lot." Thus, higher levels of *Immigration Opinion* indicate preferences for more-restrictive policy. The "average" value for *Immigration Opinion* over the three surveys (1992, 1994, 1996) was about 3.8, between the responses "left the same as it is now" and "decreased a little."

We then merged these survey questions with measures of trade and immigration exposure, consistent with the hypotheses outlined in the previous section (see Scheve and Slaughter 2001a, b, c for details about variable construction). To test whether skill levels are a key determinant of policy preferences, for each individual-year observation we constructed two variables measuring skills. One was *Education Years*, recorded in the NES survey as years of education completed. The other was *Occupation Wage*, which was that year's average weekly wage nationwide for the three-digit Census Occupation Code occupation reported for the individual. Educational attainment is a common skills measure; *Occupation Wage* assumes that average national earnings for a given occupation are determined primarily by the skills required for that occupation. According to the HO model, U.S. less-skilled workers are more likely to benefit from trade restrictions and thus are more likely to support new trade barriers.

To test whether sector of employment matters for trade-policy preferences, for each person we constructed two measures of industry trade exposure based on the reported industry of employment coded according to the three-digit 1980 Census Industry Code classification. The first, *Sector Net Export Share*, is the industry's 1992 net exports as a share of output. This variable follows the common assumption that an industry's comparative advantage is reflected in its net exports: industries with positive (negative) net exports are assumed to be comparative-advantage (disadvantage) industries. This variable covers manufacturing, agriculture, and tradable services; for all nontradable services sectors we set this variable equal to zero. The second measure is the industry's 1992 U.S. tariff rate, *Sector Tariff*, constructed as tariff duties collected as a share of customs-value imports. We assume that industries with higher *Sector Tariff* have more of a comparative disadvantage. The tariff data cover all tradable industries in agriculture and manufacturing; for all other sectors we set this variable to zero. For both measures, according to the RV model, workers in industries with greater revealed comparative disadvantages are more likely to support trade protection for these industries.

For both trade policy and immigration policy, our empirical work aims to test how different types of trade and immigration exposure variously defined affect the probability that an individual supports restrictions. Although this analysis is based on the estimation of various logit and ordered probit regression models (see Scheve and Slaughter 2001a, b for details), the main results are summarized intuitively in table 9.1 for trade and table 9.2 for immigration.

The results of our analysis of trade policy opinions strongly support the hypothesis that individuals' skill levels determine trade-policy preferences. Little evidence is found consistent with the hypothesis that industry of employment influences policy preferences. Models 1–4 each include in the original logit model one measure of exposure to trade liberalization based on factor type—the skill level of the respondent—and one measure of exposure based on the respondent's industry of employment. Each column in table 9.1 reports results of a different model. Within each column each row reports the estimated effect on the probability of supporting trade restrictions of increasing that row's variable from one standard deviation below its sample mean to one standard deviation above, holding fixed all other variables at their means. For example, the 1992 results from model 1 indicate that increasing *Occupational Wage* from one standard deviation below its mean ($345 per week) to one standard deviation above its mean ($719 per week) reduces the probability of supporting trade restrictions by 0.139 on average. This change has a standard error of 0.023 and a 90 percent confidence interval of [−0.178, −0.101].

Across all models in table 9.1, higher skills are strongly correlated with lower probabilities of supporting trade restrictions. The mean estimates of probability changes are substantively significant and much larger (in absolute value) than those for the industry measures. They are also precisely estimated: all have 90

TABLE 9.1.
Determinants of Respondent Opinion in the United States on International Trade Restrictions: 1992 Factor-Income Models

Change in Probability of Supporting Trade Restrictions as a Result of a Two-Standard Deviation Increase in the Independent Variable for Each Model

Variables	Model 1	Model 2	Model 3	Model 4
Occupation Wage	-0.139	-0.140		
	(0.023)	(0.022)		
	[-0.178, -0.101]	[-0.175, -0.101]		
Education Years			-0.251	-0.251
			(0.025)	(0.026)
			[-0.293, -0.211]	[-0.293, -0.208]
Sector Tariff	0.014		-0.001	
	(0.017)		(0.004)	
	[-0.013, 0.042]		[-0.006, 0.006]	
Sector Net Export Share		-0.016		0.000
		(0.014)		(0.003)
		[-0.039, 0.007]		[-0.005, 0.005]

Notes: For models 1 through 4, we estimated using multiple imputation with a logit specification the effect of factor and industry exposure to international trade on individuals' trade policy opinions. The parameter estimates from this analysis are reported in Scheve and Slaughter (2001a). Here we interpret those results by presenting the impact of a two standard deviation increase in each independent variable, holding other variables constant, on the probability that the respondent supports trade restrictions. Specifically, each triple of entries in the table begins with the mean effect from 1000 simulations of the change in probability of supporting trade restrictions due to an increase from one-standard deviation below the independent variable's mean to one-standard deviation above, holding all other variables constant at their means. The standard error of this estimate is reported in parentheses. Finally, a 90 percent confidence interval for the probability change is presented in brackets.

TABLE 9.2.
Estimated Effect of Increasing Skill Levels on the Probability of Supporting Immigration
Restrictions in the United States: 1992

Change in Probability of Supporting Immigration Restrictions as a Result of a Two-Standard Deviation Increase in the Independent Variable for Each Model		
Variables	*Model 5*	*Model 6*
Occupation Wage	−0.049 (0.021) [−0.083, −0.013]	
Education Years		−0.102 (0.020) [−0.133, −0.069]

Notes: For models 5 through 6, we estimated using multiple imputation with an ordered probit specification the effect of different measures of skill level on individuals' immigration policy opinions. The parameter estimates from this analysis are reported in Scheve and Slaughter (2001b). Here we interpret those results by presenting the impact of a two-standard deviation increase in each independent variable, holding other variables constant, on the probability that the respondent supports immigration restrictions. Specifically, we simulated the consequences of changing each skill measure from one standard deviation below its mean to one standard deviation above on the probability of supporting immigration restrictions. The mean effect is reported first, with the standard error of this estimate in parentheses followed by a 90 percent confidence interval.

percent confidence intervals strictly less than zero. Similar analyses of the 1996 NES data differ only in that the magnitudes of the effects are even larger.

In contrast, higher industry trade exposure has much more ambiguous effects. In unreported bivariate regressions, greater industry trade exposure is correlated with support for trade restrictions in 1992 but these estimated effects are not statistically significant. Adding the skill measures *Occupational Wage* and *Education Years* as reported in table 9.1 for models 1–4 produces qualitatively similar results (for the *Education Years* measure, the signs are even wrong). The 1996 results are similar though the *Sector Tariff* measure in model 1 is marginally statistically significant in the hypothesized positive direction. But even in this case, the substantive impact is quite small: a two-standard deviation increase in *Sector Tariff* results in just a 0.036 increase in the probability of supporting trade restrictions. Overall, one cannot conclude with a high degree of confidence that individuals employed in relatively trade-exposed sectors are more likely to support trade restrictions, conditional on skill levels.

The key message of the analyses presented in table 9.1 is that in the United States an individual's skill level rather than industry of employment is strongly correlated with the probability of supporting trade restrictions. The effects of skill trade exposure are large and precise; the effects of industry trade exposure are small and uncertain. These results suggest that individuals care about trade policy in a manner consistent with the HO model, and that there is relatively high intersectoral labor mobility in the United States over the time horizons relevant to individuals when evaluating trade policy. It is important to recall that our analysis in no way precludes individuals evaluating both short-run and long-run effects of trade liberalization, where preferences might vary by both factor type and industry of employment.

Table 9.2 reports the summary results for our analysis of this division in public opinion over immigration. The findings strongly support the hypothesis that individuals' skill levels determine immigration-policy preferences. Models 5–6 each include in the original ordered probit model a measure of skill type and a set of control variables including age, race, sex, immigrant status, and ideology. Each column in table 9.2 reports results of a different model. Within each column each row reports the estimated effect on the probability of supporting immigration restrictions (i.e., the probability of supporting a reduction in immigration by either "a lot" or "a little"), of increasing that row's variable from one standard deviation below its sample mean to one standard deviation above, holding fixed all other variables at their means. For 1992, increasing *Occupation Wage* from one standard deviation below its sample mean to one standard deviation above ($325 per week to $699 per week), holding fixed all other regressors at their means, reduces the probability of supporting immigration restrictions by 0.049 on average. This estimated change has a standard error of 0.021 and a 90 percent confidence interval of [−0.083, −0.013]. The 1992 results for *Education Years* are similar. Increasing *Education Years* by two standard deviations (about 10.1 years to 15.7 years), holding fixed all other regressors at their means, reduces the probability of supporting immigration restrictions by 0.102 on average. This estimated change has a standard error of 0.020 and a 90 percent confidence interval of [−0.133, −0.069]. The magnitude of these estimated effects are even larger in unreported results for 1994 and 1996. *Higher skills are strongly and significantly correlated with lower probabilities of supporting immigration restrictions.*

The result that skills correlate with immigration-policy preferences is consistent both with the factor-proportions-analysis model and with an HO model in which immigration affects both wages and output mix. By pooling all regions together, however, we have not tested the area-analysis model. To do this we add to our initial specification an indicator variable for whether the respondent lives in a high-immigration region (see Scheve and Slaughter 2001b for various definitions of what counts as a high-immigration region) and this variable's interaction with the skill measure in each regression. If preferences are consistent with the area-analysis model, then the correlation between skills and preferences should be stronger in gateway communities. These preferences imply a positive coefficient on the high immigration indicator variable and a negative coefficient on its interaction with skills. Our estimates of this model indicate across all years of our data that neither is the high immigration indicator variable significantly positive nor is its interaction with skills significantly negative. *Overall, people in high-immigration*

areas do not have a stronger correlation between skills and immigration-policy prefer-
ences than people elsewhere. This is inconsistent with the area-analysis model.

To summarize, preferences over trade and immigration policy divide strongly
across skills. There is not strong evidence of many other commonly supposed
cleavages. For trade, industry of employment is not systematically related to trade-
policy preferences. Those working in "trade exposed" industries (e.g., textiles and
apparel) are not more likely to oppose freer trade, conditional on skill type. For
immigration, people living in "immigration gateway" communities (e.g., California) are not more or less likely to oppose freer immigration. These results are all
consistent with the importance of labor-market outcomes in determining policy
preferences.[18]

Policy Preferences in Comparative Perspective

These findings can be put into comparative perspective by examining a growing
body of research on the determinants of international economic policy preferences
around the world (Balistreri 1997; Gabel 1998; Scheve 2000; O'Rourke and Sinnott 2001; Baker 2003, forthcoming; Mayda 2002; Mayda and Rodrik 2005;
Beaulieu 2002; Beaulieu, Benarroch, and Gaisford 2002; Hays, Ehrlich, and Peinhardt, forthcoming; Hainmueller and Hiscox, forthcoming). For our purposes,
the key question of interest that is addressed in many of these studies is the extent
to which divisions in public opinion about policy along factor lines—specifically
differences in individual skill levels—are replicated in other countries. In the interest of brevity, we limit our comparative discussion to trade policy preferences.

As discussed in the third section, it is, however, important to be clear that our
theoretical expectation under the HO model is that the direction and magnitude
of the skills cleavage vary across countries according to national skill or human
capital endowments.

The most straightforward way to evaluate these predictions is to reproduce a
figure presented in O'Rourke and Sinnott (2001) and Mayda and Rodrik (2005).
Figure 9.1 plots the marginal effect of skill type on trade opinions in a cross-
section of countries around the world against national skill endowments as measured by the natural log of per capita GDP.[19]

To construct this figure, we used data from the 1995–97 World Values Survey
(WVS) (Inglehart et al. 2000), a set of surveys designed for cross-national comparisons. The first step in the analysis was to construct the dependent variable
similar to the trade opinion measure employed in the U.S. analysis described earlier. As noted in the second section, the World Values Survey includes the following question that measures trade-policy preferences:

> Do you think it is better if 1) goods made in other countries can be imported and sold
> here if people want to buy them or that 2) there should be stricter limits on selling for-
> eign goods here, to protect the jobs of people in this country?

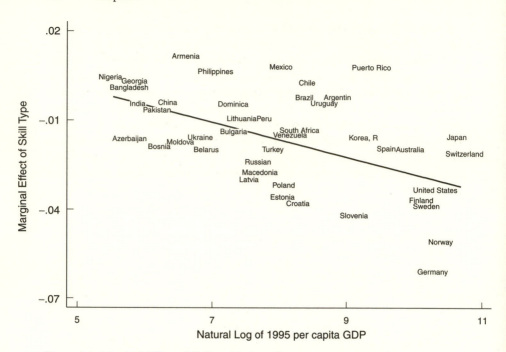

Figure 9.1. Marginal Effect of Skill on Trade Preferences versus National Endowment of Human Capital. Notes: Using data from the World Values Survey, this graph plots the marginal effects of skill type as measured by the slope coefficient of the regression of *Trade Opinion* on *Occupational Skill* against a commonly used measure of national endowment of human capital, the natural log of per capita GDP. There are data points for forty-three countries with all the necessary data available. The ordinary least squares regression estimate of the slope coefficient from the regression of the marginal effect on logged GDP is −.0058 with a robust standard error of 0.0014. The solid line in the graph maps the predicted values for this regression.

By coding responses 1 for those individuals favoring stricter limits and 0 for those who gave the response supportive of trade, we constructed the variable *Trade Opinion*. We then constructed a measure of the skill type of each individual in the surveys. The variable *Occupational Skill* is an 11-point skill measure based on the occupation of each respondent.[20]

Then for each country in our dataset, we regressed the trade measure on the variable *Occupational Skill*.[21] The regression coefficient on the skill measure is an estimate of the marginal effect of skill type on trade-policy opinion. The vertical axis in figure 9.1 is the marginal effect of *Occupational Skill* on trade-policy opinions while the horizontal axis is the natural log of 1995 per capita gross domestic product. This variable is a commonly used measure of each country's relative human capital or skill endowment.[22]

The key result is that the direction and magnitude of the skill-policy preferences correlation varies across countries in a manner generally consistent with the predictions of the HO model. The downward-sloping regression line indicates that as per capita GDP increases, the absolute value of the negative correlation between individual skills and protectionist trade opinion also increases. Consequently, for all the countries in which GDP per capita is roughly equivalent to that in the United States there is a negative and statistically significant correlation between skills and trade-policy opinions. In contrast, at lower levels of per capita GDP, the correlation is sometimes positive and sometimes negative and generally small in magnitude.

To further evaluate the relationship between the marginal effect of skill type on policy opinions and per capita GDP, we regressed the marginal effect measure on the natural log of per capita GDP. The estimated slope coefficient is equal to -0.0058 with a standard error of 0.0014, a statistically significant relationship.[23] Moreover, the natural log of per capita GDP explains nearly 30 percent of the variation in the marginal effect of skill type on trade policy opinions.

For our purposes, the key point in figure 9.1 is that the skills-policy preferences correlation of the United States is also evident in other similarly endowed countries. This is consistent with the claim that individual opinions about international economic policies are substantially influenced by how policy alternatives are expected to affect workers' earnings. At the same time, the evidence in these figures indicates that the magnitude of the skill cleavage in public opinion decreases in countries with lower levels of GDP per capita. This result is again roughly consistent with the prediction of the HO model in that policy liberalization is not expected to advantage skilled workers in countries that are not relatively well endowed with human capital.

The evidence presented in figure 9.1 does raise important questions for how the distributive consequences of trade liberalization in the labor market may influence policy-opinion formation. For example, the HO model predicts that in those countries relatively well endowed with less-skilled workers, the skills-trade-policy-opinion correlation should be in the opposite direction of that observed for countries well endowed with skilled workers. In these countries, the expectation is that less-skilled workers will have more liberal policy preferences than more-skilled workers. In terms of figure 9.1, the theoretical expectation is that in countries with relatively low levels of per capita GDP, the estimated marginal effect of skill type on policy opinions should be positive. In figure 9.1 we do observe an estimated positive effect for some low-income countries, but these estimates are generally not significantly different from zero. While there are a number of possible explanations for this anomaly implicit in the literature (see e.g., Gabel 1998; Beaulieu, Benarroch, and Gaisford 2002; Hiscox 2003; Hainmueller and Hiscox, forthcoming), it is not clear that any of these accounts are likely to be complete replacements for the HO framework, because they do not predict the cross-country variation by national skill endowments in figure 9.1.

Policy Context and Individual Opinion Formation

The previous two sections focused attention on the importance of the impact of policy liberalization on real and relative wages for explaining individual and country variation in trade and immigration policy opinions. In this section, we consider other factors that may influence the links that individuals make between policy alternatives and their individual economic welfare. We focus on the role of two different sets of national-level characteristics that may influence how individuals form opinions about trade policy and thus account for country differences in both the level of and divisions in public support for liberalization: macroeconomic conditions and labor-market policies and institutions.

To evaluate these potential explanations for variation in public opinion about trade, we turn our attention to the 1995 International Social Survey Program (ISSP) dataset, which, like the WVS, is a comparative dataset that elicits individual opinions on trade and immigration policy. To evaluate various arguments about the possible effect of macroeconomic conditions and labor-market policies and institutions, we employ data that is primarily available for relatively wealthy countries—specifically, OECD members. We use the ISSP data in this analysis because it includes more OECD countries than does the WVS data.[24]

In the second section, we noted that public concern about globalization generally and trade liberalization in particular seems to be closely tied to labor-market concerns. Our analysis of the determinants of individual and cross-country variation has so far focused attention on the links among policy alternatives, wage effects, and individual opinion formation. It is these links that are most salient in the academic political economy literature. Nonetheless, given that the public seems attentive to possible links between unemployment and trade liberalization, macroeconomic conditions may influence individuals' overall evaluation of the desirability of trade liberalization or trade protection. Specifically, high levels of unemployment may heighten individual concerns about the employment risks associated with liberal trade policies. This possibility is buttressed by a number of studies that suggest that variation in levels of protection over time and/or regions may be related to variation over time and across regions in macroeconomic conditions, particularly the level of unemployment (Takacs 1981; Cassing, McKeown, and Ochs 1986; Rama 1994; Epstein and O'Halloran 1996).[25]

To assess whether macroeconomic conditions are an important determinant of public opinion about trade, we constructed the variable *Trade Opinion* for the respondents in the ISSP survey.[26] This variable is again a dichotomous variable with individuals giving protectionist responses coded 1 and non-protectionist responses coded 0. We then calculated the average values for each country, *Average Trade Opinion*, to determine an estimate of the level of protectionist opinion. Figure 9.2 plots this variable against unemployment as a percent of the labor force, *Unemployment*, in each country. For the twenty-three countries in the ISSP sample, *Average Trade Opinion* is positively correlated with *Unemployment*.[27] The

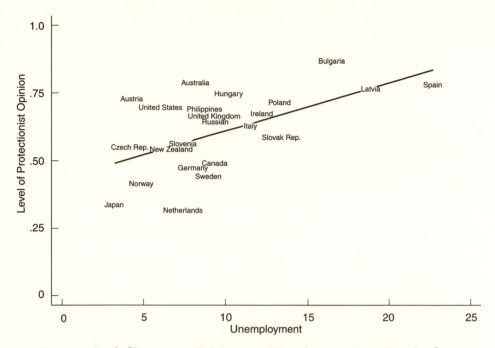

Figure 9.2. Level of Protectionist Opinion versus Unemployment. Notes: Using data from the International Social Survey Program, this graph plots the level of protectionist opinion against unemployment as a percent of the labor force. There are data points for twenty-three countries, or all the countries in the ISSP data. The ordinary least squares regression estimate of the slope coefficient from the regression of the level of protectionist opinion on unemployment is .018 with a robust standard error of 0.005. The solid line in the graph maps the predicted values for this regression.

levels of protectionist opinion are higher in those countries with a greater proportion of their work force unemployed. A bivariate regression of *Average Trade Opinion* on *Unemployment* generates a slope estimate of 0.018 with a standard error of 0.005, thus the positive estimate is significantly different than zero at conventional levels of statistical significance.[28] *The key result is that cross-country variation in trade opinion seems in part a function of the aggregate performance of the labor market as measured by unemployment.* This is consistent both with arguments about the importance of macroeconomic conditions in accounting for trade policies and with the main claim of this chapter that public attitudes toward international economic integration are tightly connected to labor-market concerns.

In the second section, we pointed out that public opinion over trade policy is decidedly less protectionist when policy liberalization is explicitly linked to government adjustment policies for workers (see also Scheve and Slaughter 2001c:

94–96). This characteristic of public opinion resonates with a large literature that links the growth of government to integration with the world economy (Cameron 1978; Katzenstein 1985; Rodrik 1998; Boix 2006). In Rodrik's account, the general argument is that openness to the world economy generates greater risks to workers, which leads them to demand greater levels of public social insurance. Consequently, depending on the supply side of policymaking, including perhaps the impact of economic integration on the state's capacity to provide social insurance, more open economies may have larger public sectors, particularly policies that insure workers against labor market risks, than less-open economies.

An interesting implication of this argument for explaining cross-country variation in public opinion about international economic integration is that the level of public support for workers may have a substantial effect on how individuals view trade. If the risks that workers perceive from integration are largely insured risks or if the adjustment costs that workers perceive from integration are largely subsidized, then individuals are more likely to favor liberalization. Moreover, to the extent that social insurance policies redistribute some of the risks and rewards of integration with the world economy, more generous social insurance policies may mitigate the skill divisions in public opinion over policy liberalization (see Scheve 2000; Scheve and Slaughter 2001c; and Hays, Ehrlich, and Peinhardt forthcoming for previous empirical evidence on these arguments).[29]

Figure 9.3 provides evidence on the first question of whether generous labor-market policies reduce support for protectionism. Since we have already suggested that the evidence is consistent with the idea that increased levels of unemployment raise protectionist sentiments, we control for *Unemployment* in the data presented in figure 9.3. The vertical axis is then composed of residuals from the regression of *Average Trade Opinion* on *Unemployment* and the horizontal axis shows the residuals from the regression of total national spending on labor market programs (unemployment compensation, training, etc.) as percent of GDP, *Labor Spending*, on *Unemployment*. The source for the labor spending data is the OECD, and so the analysis in figure 9.3 includes only sixteen of the original twenty-three countries in the ISSP data.[30]

It is first worth noting that *Unemployment* remains significantly positively correlated with protectionist opinion with the introduction of the *Labor Spending* measure (with or without the natural log of per capita GDP and trade openness). The data in figure 9.3 also offer some modest support for the hypothesis that more generous labor-market policies increase support for freer trade. The partial regression line is downward sloping and the estimated partial regression coefficient on *Labor Spending* is −0.044 with a standard error of 0.015. The observation for Sweden is obviously influential, but, excluding it, the partial regression coefficient is statistically significant at the 0.10 level. The result is also robust to including the natural log of per capita GDP and trade openness as additional control variables.

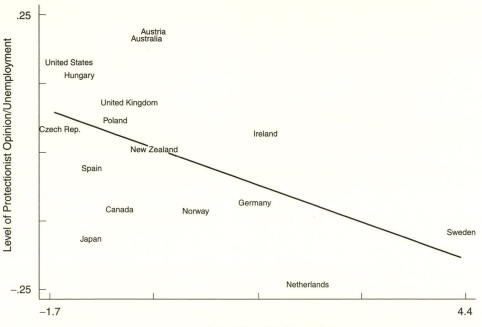

Figure 9.3. Level of Protectionist Opinion versus Labor Spending. Notes: Using data from the International Social Survey Program, this graph plots the level of protectionist opinion, controlling for unemployment, against spending as a percent of GDP on labor market programs, controlling for unemployment. There are data points for sixteen countries with all the necessary data available. The estimate of the partial regression coefficient for labor spending from the regression of the level of protectionist opinion on unemployment and labor spending is −0.044 with a robust standard error of 0.015. The solid line in the graph maps the predicted values for the partial regression.

Given this modest but suggestive evidence for the hypothesis of a link between labor-market policies and protectionist sentiment, we examined a number of other observable implications of the general argument. First, we examined the relationship between the level of protectionist opinion in the WVS and a more-aggregated measure of social insurance spending available for a larger sample of countries—twenty-eight. In this analysis, both the bivariate and partial correlation between spending and protectionist sentiment was negative and statistically significant. Second, returning to the ISSP data, we found a negative and statistically significant bivariate and partial correlation between the OECD's measures of employment protection and the level of protectionist opinion. Employment protection is a very different policy instrument for protecting the welfare of workers from the potential risks of economic openness, but it may have a similar effect of reducing workers' assessments of the risks associated with liberalization.

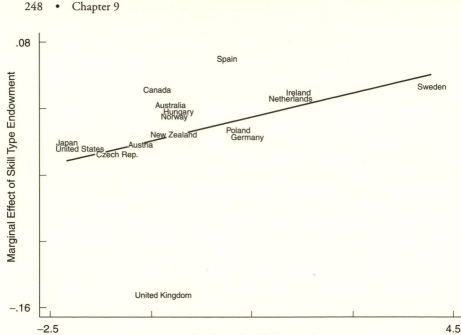

Figure 9.4. Marginal Effect of Skill on Trade Preferences versus Labor Spending. Notes: Using data from the International Social Survey Program, this graph plots the marginal effects of skill type, controlling for the natural log of per capita GDP, against spending as a percent of GDP on labor market programs, controlling for the natural log of per capita GDP. There are data points for sixteen countries with all the necessary data available. The estimate of the partial regression coefficient for labor spending from the regression of the marginal effect on the natural log of per capita GDP and labor spending is 0.012 with a robust standard error of 0.004. The solid line in the graph maps the predicted values for the partial regression.

In total, there is much evidence consistent with the claim that the labor-market policies of governments have a substantial influence on how individuals view the costs and benefits of trade liberalization.

Figure 9.4 provides evidence on our second hypothesized effect of generous labor-market policies: do they mitigate the differences between more- and less-skilled workers in their opinions about trade policy? Since we have already established that the skills-policy preferences correlation varies across countries according to their human capital endowments, the analysis in figure 9.4 controls for the natural log of per capita GDP. The vertical axis in figure 9.4 is equal to the residuals from the regression of the marginal effect of skill type on trade policy opinions on the natural log of per capita GDP. The horizontal axis comprises the residuals from the regression of *Labor Spending* on the natural log of per capita GDP. The positive relationship in this figure between *Labor Spending*, controlling for skill endowments, and the marginal effect of skill type, controlling for endowments, is consistent with the argument that social spending decreases the differences in opinion about trade policy among more- and less-skilled workers. The estimate of the partial regression coefficient for labor spending from the regression of the marginal effect of skill type on trade policy opinions on *Labor Spending* and the natural log of per capita GDP is 0.012 with a standard error of 0.004. This positive estimate is robust to dropping obvious outliers (e.g., United Kingdom or Sweden), and also to adding control variables such as *Unemployment*.[31]

One final national-level characteristic of labor markets that may influence individual opinion formation is the extent of centralized wage bargaining and, more generally, corporatist institutions. Scheve (2000) investigates the argument that because centralized wage bargaining tends to reduce wage inequality (OECD 1997; Wallerstein 1999), the actual distributive consequences of international economic integration will be mitigated in countries with greater centralization, and so skill divisions in public opinion will be lessened as well. This argument resonates with original claims in the comparative political economy literature on the relationship between openness and the welfare state (Cameron 1978; Katzenstein 1985). Scheve (2000) presents evidence consistent with this argument for opinion formation over European regional economic integration using 148 surveys in the 1990s for the fifteen member states of the European Union. An increase in centralization from the United Kingdom's score to the value for Denmark is estimated to decrease the magnitude of skill-integration opinion regression coefficient by 40 percent.

Because comparable measures of wage bargaining centralization are available for a relatively small set of advanced countries, investigating this relationship in the ISSP and WVS data limits the number of observations to between nine and twelve.[32] Not surprisingly, it is not clear in these data that the centralization of wage bargaining significantly attenuates skill divisions in trade-policy opinions. This question, as well as that of the possible influence of other dimensions of corporatism on opinion formation, remains an important question for future research.

One line of this future research might also examine cross-country differences in the endowment of skills, above and beyond measures based on national-level averages. It is well documented that less-skilled workers (e.g., at the fifth or twenty-fifth percentile) within each country can differ quite substantially across countries with similar mean levels of skills. The evidence suggests, for example, that the less-skilled are relatively more-skilled in Nordic countries compared to Anglo-American countries. More-complex measures of national skill endowments might yield additional insight on policy preferences: for example, perhaps less-skilled workers in Nordic countries are less protectionist than their American counterparts because they do not face direct international product-market competition from freer trade with low-wage countries.[33]

Additional Determinants of Policy Preferences

While labor market concerns broadly defined are central to understanding opinion formation, there is also evidence in the literature that noneconomic factors may also play important roles.[34]

For trade policy, both O'Rourke and Sinnott (2001) and Mayda and Rodrik (2005) employ evidence from the ISSP surveys to consider the possible roles of ideas and identities on the formation of individual policy opinions. O'Rourke and Sinnott focus their analysis on evaluating the impact that strong feelings of nationalist identity have on opinions about trade policy. They present evidence that protectionist attitudes are strongly related to nationalist feelings as measured by a group of survey questions identified as measuring patriotism—preference for one's own country—and a group of survey questions identified as measuring chauvinism—an exclusive sense of nationality. They also present strong evidence consistent with the HO model, even when a range of cultural, ideological, and demographic factors are taken into account. Their interpretation is that both nationalist ideologies and economic concerns inform opinions.

As these authors point out, the interpretation of the correlation between nationalist attitudes and policy opinions is problematic. The determinants of nationalist feeling most likely include economic considerations, and so it would be incorrect to attribute all the estimated effect of the nationalism variables to noneconomic considerations. We view this as a reasonable interpretation, but point out that it implies that empirical research posed in the "do economic or noneconomic determinants matter more?" framework may be hopelessly misspecified without serious models of the determinants of nationalist ideologies and other noneconomic factors.[35]

For immigration policy, the starting point of most analyses is noneconomic considerations such as values, identities, and perceptions of the impact of immigration on largely noneconomic issues such as crime or risks of terrorism. Mayda (2002) reports results for the noneconomic determinants of immigration that are representative of the key findings. Individuals with stronger attachments to their national identities, individuals less tolerant of other racial groups, and individuals that value a homogenous culture have more restrictionist immigration opinions.

Summary and Future Research

There is substantial evidence of important links between individual opinions about trade and immigration policy and the likely distributive consequences in the labor market of different policy alternatives. This research raises a number of questions that merit further investigation. First, we noted little evidence that sector of employment is a strong predictor of U.S. opinions about trade. As has been emphasized in the endogenous trade policy literature (e.g., Alt and Gilligan 1994;

Hiscox 2001), factor specificity may vary across individuals, occupations, sectors, time, and countries. Future research that develops measures of intersectoral factor mobility may substantially improve our understanding of variation in opinion formation.[36]

Second, the importance of labor-market institutions for how individuals connect policy alternatives to their interests is not completely clear. For example, by better matching survey data with data on labor-market institutions, it would be possible to evaluate whether the centralization of wage bargaining and other corporatist institutions may mitigate divisions in opinion via redistribution of gains from international economic integration. Finally, only limited attention has been paid to the role of information and elites in influencing how individuals evaluate policy alternatives and their interests. Again, significant cross-country differences in the amount and direction of information regarding the impact of trade on welfare may be important in explaining cross-country variation in opinion.[37]

CONCLUSION

This analysis of public preferences about the policies that regulate international economic integration is essential for constructing explanatory models of policy-making in these issue areas. Political economy models must specify the preferences of all relevant actors as well as the institutions that aggregate these preferences (Rodrik 1995). Characterizing the public's views is an essential element of the task. Only once this specification is made is it possible to identify the importance of many other factors—costs of collective action, properties of electoral systems—that are widely thought to be important determinants of policymaking.

This chapter highlights the importance of labor-market concerns in accounting for individual policy opinions. We contend that this pattern of opinion is informative for debates about the supposed opposition between economic globalization and the modern welfare state. It has long been recognized that protectionism and other restrictionist international economic policies are inefficient instruments for redistributing income and risk. Given that the distributional consequences in the labor market of policy alternatives seem so important in individuals' policy opinions, there is at least the possibility that greater economic openness generates greater demand for social insurance and redistributive spending. If noneconomic considerations dominate opinion formation, then the possibility of side payments to facilitate liberalization is greatly reduced. Our review suggests that the scope for such payments may be quite substantial.

Moreover, there is explicit evidence that political support for international economic liberalization depends on many key features of the modern welfare state. Individual opinions are decidedly more liberal when liberalization is tied to support for workers. Further, countries with more generous labor-market policies have publics with less protectionist opinions and less salient differences in opinion across more- and less-skilled workers. This again suggests that more economic openness generates more demand for social insurance and redistributive spending.

While definitive conclusions, of course, require analyses of opinion formation about welfare state policies and their interaction with the international economic policies discussed here, the evidence presented in this chapter certainly suggests that simple conclusions that substantial social insurance and redistributive policies are inconsistent with economic globalization are implausible because it seems that political support for liberalism itself depends in part on those very policies.

NOTES

For financial support, we thank the National Science Foundation and the Carnegie Corporation's Globalization and Self-Determination Project at the Yale Center for International and Area Studies.

1. Our U.S. studies appear in Scheve and Slaughter (2001a, b, c). Other studies include Balistreri (1997); Gabel (1998); Scheve (2000); O'Rourke and Sinnott (2001); Baker (2003, forthcoming); Mayda (2002); Mayda and Rodrik (2005); Beaulieu (2002); Beaulieu, Benarroch, and Gaisford (2002); Hiscox (2003); Hainmueller and Hiscox (forthcoming); and Hays, Ehrlich, and Peinhardt (forthcoming).

2. The other splits were 52 to 30 percent in the United States, 51 to 30 percent in the United Kingdom, 51 to 31 percent in Italy, 43 to 37 percent in Germany, and 45 to 44 percent in France.

3. The literature on how globalization affects labor markets is far too vast to cover systematically in this section. More thoroughly comprehensive overviews can be found in Johnson and Slaughter (2001) for trade; Hanson, Scheve, Slaughter, and Spilimbergo (2002) for immigration; and Scheve and Slaughter (2004) for FDI. The discussion in this section draws heavily on these earlier works, as well as on the work in Scheve and Slaughter (2001a, b, c).

4. Many studies have examined how an RV short-run equilibrium transforms over time into an HO long-run equilibrium. See, for example, Mussa (1978) and Neary (1978).

5. Obviously, the exact timing and magnitude of wage changes vary somewhat with the data series used. But all series show the same major changes. For more discussion, see, for example, the 1997 and 2000 *Economic Report of the President*, each of which devotes substantial space to labor markets and inequality. Inequality has risen across education, experience, and occupational groups as well as within these groups. These trends also hold even when accounting for the relatively robust wage gains of the late 1990s.

6. Leamer (1998) and Baldwin and Cain (1997) find that U.S. relative product prices fell, not rose, for less-skill-intensive sectors during the 1970s. And these two studies plus Lawrence and Slaughter (1993) and Bhagwati (1991) find no clear trend in U.S. relative product prices during the 1980s. Feenstra and Hanson (1999) decompose U.S. price changes into input-trade-related components and find a non-trivial role for trade in raising inequality. Haskel and Slaughter (2003) apply a similar methodology but decompose U.S. price changes into tariff- and transport cost-related components; they find no strong link from trade-barrier-related price changes to U.S. wages. See Slaughter (2000) for a survey

of these product-price studies. And despite the ambiguous product-price evidence, Leamer (1998) argues greater international trade has played a role. Borjas, Freeman, and Katz (1997) calculates trade's role in rising inequality by calculating changes in U.S. labor supplies "embodied" in flows of U.S. exports and imports. This is a very different methodology from the product-price studies, but they also find only a small role for trade. Surveys of methods and results also appear in Freeman (1995), Richardson (1995), and Johnson and Slaughter (2001).

7. The terms "area analysis" and "factor-proportions analysis" come from Borjas, Freeman, and Katz (1996).

8. Recent immigration papers include Card (2001) from the area-analysis perspective and Borjas et al. (1996, 1997) from the factor-proportions perspective. For surveys see Borjas (1999a, b) and Hanson et al. (2002).

9. This elasticity consists of two parts. One is the substitution effect. It tells, for a given level of output, how much the firm substitutes away from labor toward other factors of production when wages rise. The second is the scale effect. It tells how much labor demand is altered after a wage change thanks to the change in the firm's output. Higher wages imply higher costs and thus, moving along the product-market demand schedule, lower firm output. When wages rise, both the substitution and scale effects reduce the quantity of labor demanded. The firm substitutes away from labor toward other factors, and with higher costs the firm produces less such that it demands less of all factors, including labor.

10. See Scheve and Slaughter (2004) for a mathematical derivation of this point.

11. For example, Rodrik (1997) presents evidence that exposure to external risk, measured by the interaction between trade openness and the standard deviation of a country's terms of trade, is positively correlated with growth volatility. But Iversen and Cusack (2000) present evidence that, at least for advanced economies, there is no correlation between trade- or capital-market openness and volatility in output, earnings, or employment.

12. Note that there is some disagreement in the literature about the contribution of trade liberalization to growth—that is, the dynamic gains to trade. See, for example, Rodriguez and Rodrik (2001).

13. It may be useful to think about the wage effects best describing the consequences of policy change in countries with relatively flexible labor markets. In less flexible labor markets, these effects may be more likely to be observed in employment/unemployment rates.

14. What about the preferences of workers in nontraded industries? Unlike in the HO model, here nontraded workers are insulated from international product-market competition to the extent that domestic nontraded prices, by definition, are not directly affected by trade pressures. But insofar as freer trade raises national income, if income elasticities of demand for nontraded goods are positive then freer trade should raise nontraded prices by raising demand for nontraded goods. So in an RV model workers in nontraded sectors support freer trade, but perhaps less than do comparative-advantage-sector workers because trade policy's effect on nontraded prices works indirectly through nontraded demand. If some factors remain mobile across sectors in the RV model, factor prices are not so clearly linked to product-price changes. Changes in real factor prices for these mobile factors depend on the consumption basket of these mobile factors. In the above discussion we focus only on the specific factors.

15. Note that this trade question was not asked in the 1994 NES survey, so our analyses are limited to 1992 and 1996.

254 • Chapter 9

16. As discussed earlier, marginal responses in the United States to questions on trade and immigration policy do appear to be somewhat sensitive to the question frame. For example, does the question mention any reasons why trade may be good or bad? If so, do those reasons include price effects, wage effects, employment effects, or all three? The key results reported in this section that focus on divisions in public opinion have been replicated across a number of different question frames.

17. We recognize that this assumption abstracts from other interesting facts about the distribution of the skills of U.S. immigrants. For example, Borjas et al. (1997: 7) show that the skill distribution of U.S. immigration has been somewhat bimodal at both the high-skill and low-skill ends of the distribution.

18. These conclusions about the determinants of individual trade and immigration policy preferences are robust to a wide variety of sensitivity tests. These include, for example, inclusion or exclusion of a number of control variables including sex, age, race, immigration status, party identification, ideology, union membership, measures of ethnic and racial tolerance, retrospective evaluations of economic performance, skill mix of the immigrants in the respondent's region, and state unemployment rates. Further, we investigated the impact of possible omitted variables based on the idea of issue linkage—for example, including measures of individual environmental concerns as independent variables in the trade analysis. We also evaluated the possibility that degrees of political awareness might account for the correlation between skill type and opinions, particularly for trade in which one might argue elite messages are predominantly favorable toward freer trade and so more politically aware citizens may be more likely to consume these messages and adopt the mainstream opinion. The main results reported in this section do not depend on the inclusion or exclusion of these regressors. See Scheve and Slaughter (2001a, b, c) for a number of alternative analyses exploring such issues as different measurement strategies for key variables of interest and alternative substantive interpretations of the results, all of which further verify our findings.

19. This measure and all other national level variables unless otherwise noted are from the *World Development Indicators Online* (World Bank 2003).

20. Occupations were coded according to the following rules based on the categories available in the World Values Survey: 1 = agricultural worker; 2 = farmer; 3 = unskilled manual worker; 4 = semi-skilled manual worker; 5 = skilled manual worker; 6 = foreman or supervisor; 7 = non-manual office worker in nonsupervisory role; 8 = supervisory office worker; 9 = professional worker; 10 = employer manager of establishment with less than 10 employees; 11 = employer manager of establishment with 10 or more employees. Since these categories do not necessarily measures differences in skills of equal intervals, it is important to note that the results here are robust to a number of alternative codings of this variable. Further, and perhaps more importantly, the results are robust to employing a measure of skill based on the age that the respondent completed his or her formal education.

21. In alternative specifications, we followed the procedure of regressing the policy measures on *Occupational Skill* and a number of demographic and political control variables. This did not substantively alter the results.

22. Consistent with the literature on trade-policy opinions, the results reported here can be replicated for alternative measures of national factor endowment—for example, GDP per capita, country tertiary enrollment ratio, and country scientists and engineers in research and development per one million persons.

23. This estimate is robust to dropping potentially influential observations. With that said, obviously the comparative evidence presented here is based on small-n cross-sectional analyses and thus some caution should be made with respect to all the inferences made based on this evidence.

24. The ISSP data was not featured in the previous section because overall it has fewer country observations and does not include nearly as many developing countries (thus variation in factor endowments is truncated in the ISSP data). Nonetheless, key results from the analyses of the WVS data can be replicated using the ISSP surveys, which have in fact been the primary dataset used in the literature (O'Rourke and Sinnott 2001; Mayda 2002; Mayda and Rodrik 2005; Beaulieu, Benarroch, and Gaisford 2002).

25. Despite the strong empirical reasons for thinking macroeconomic conditions are an important determinant of trade opinions, we note again that unemployment is not a feature of the standard models of international trade typically employed in the political economy literature. We view the link between unemployment and trade opinions as largely reflecting the differences in the real adjustments costs that workers face when macroeconomic conditions are good and when they are not. See Wallerstein (1987) for a theoretical explanation for the connection between unemployment and the demand for the protection that depends on the existence of collective bargaining.

26. The specific question wording in the ISSP data was "How much do you agree or disagree with the following statements: (R's country) should limit the import of foreign products in order to protect its national economy." The variable *Trade Opinion* was coded so that those respondents giving the "agree" or "agree strongly" responses were coded a 1, while those respondents giving one of the remaining three valid responses were coded a 0.

27. Note that in some studies using the 1995 ISSP data, East and West Germany are treated as separate countries and thus the analyses reported include twenty-four rather than twenty-three countries.

28. This finding is also true if potentially influential observations such as Spain and Latvia are omitted from the analysis. It is also robust to including a number of possible control variables such as the natural log of per capita GDP and trade openness. For the ISSP data the natural log of per capita GDP is negatively correlated with protectionist trade opinions while trade openness is not significantly correlated with average trade opinions.

29. Boix (2006) points out that, of course, both openness and social insurance policies are endogenous and it often may be equally feasible to meet the demands of workers through either protection and/or generous social insurance. This point is surely correct and thus an individual's policy opinions about trade and social insurance may be simultaneously determined. We will return to this possibility in the concluding discussion. The argument pursued in this section requires only that we assume that when individuals form an opinion about trade they take existing government labor market policies as exogenous. Among other considerations, the historical basis of and persistence of cross-national differences in labor market policies makes this a tenable assumption.

30. The main results of this section can be replicated for much more aggregated "subsidies and transfers" data from the World Bank, which allow inclusion of twenty of the original twenty-three observations.

31. A couple of qualifications to figure 9.4 should be kept in mind. First, there is not evidence in this data that employment protection policies also lessen differences in opinion across workers. Second, the correlation is not evident between the more aggregated

measure of spending discussed earlier and the marginal effect of skill type on trade opinions in the WVS data. This may indicate a problem with the argument, simply suggest that the appropriate measure for social insurance spending is that spending targeted for labor-market programs, or reflect the fact that the WVS data is populated mostly by relatively poorer countries for which there is often no skill division in opinion for social insurance spending to attenuate.

32. These numbers are based on using the Golden, Lange, and Wallerstein (2002) measures for centralization. Similar or fewer observations would be available using alternative sources for measures of wage bargaining centralization.

33. We thank an anonymous referee for suggesting the issues presented in this paragraph.

34. There is also evidence in the literature that other economic considerations may be important determinants of opinion formation. For example, Scheve and Slaughter (2001a) argue that asset ownership may also be important for trade-policy preferences and provide evidence that home ownership in geographic regions with a manufacturing mix concentrated in comparatively disadvantaged industries is correlated with support for trade protection. Baker (2003, forthcoming) argues that the consumption gains to trade are critical in understanding support for trade reform. Hanson et al. (2002) argue that the perceived fiscal impact of immigration may play an important role in opinion formation.

35. One other result emphasized in the O'Rourke and Sinnott study is the gender gap in opinion over trade, with women having more protectionist opinions. This result is evident in most other studies (see, e.g., Scheve and Slaughter 2001c). The theoretical basis behind the gender gap has not been developed in the literature. One possibility is simply that labor markets are partially segmented by sex and that women face greater risks in the labor market from trade policy liberalization.

36. Note that one practical task for future research is simply to gather comparative surveys in which the industry of employment of respondents is recorded in detail. To our knowledge, only Scheve and Slaughter (2001a) employ survey data with this information and thus are able to construct reasonable measures of industry exposure (Mayda and Rodrik's (2005) industry results are derived without actually knowing what industry individuals are employed in).

37. See Darden (2002), Busch and Reinhardt (2000), and Hainmueller and Hiscox (forthcoming) for three very different studies on belief formation about trade policy. Note also the importance of exploring low-information rationality perspectives on opinion formation about international economic policies. It is quite likely that individuals gather information about policy alternatives via work experiences, group affiliations, and the media and construct summary evaluations broadly consistent with their interests and values without actually forming complex causal beliefs about the effects of different alternatives.

REFERENCES

Alt, James E., and Michael Gilligan. 1994. "The Political Economy of Trading States: Factor Specificity, Collective Action Problems, and Domestic Political Institutions." *Journal of Political Philosophy* 2 (2): 165–92.

Baker, Andy. 2003. "Why Is Trade Reform so Popular in Latin America?" *World Politics* 55 (April): 423–55.

———. Forthcoming. "Who Wants to Globalize? Consumer Tastes and Labor Markets in a Theory of Trade Policy Preferences." *American Journal of Political Science.*

Baldwin, Robert E., and Glen G. Cain. 1997. "Shifts in U.S. Relative Wages: The Role of Trade, Technology, and Factor Endowments." NBER Working Paper no. 5934.

Balistreri, Edward J. 1997. "The Performance of the Heckscher-Ohlin-Vanek Model in Predicting Endogenous Policy Forces at the Individual Level." *Canadian Journal of Economics* 30 (1) (February): 1–17.

Beaulieu, Eugene. 2002. "Factor or Industry Cleavages in Trade Policy? An Empirical Test of the Stolper-Samuelson Theorem." *Economics and Politics* 14 (2) (July): 99–131.

Beaulieu, Eugene, Michael Benarroch, and James Gaisford. 2002. "Intra-Industry Trade Liberalization: Why Skilled Workers Everywhere Resist Protectionism." Manuscript, University of Calgary.

Bernard, Andrew B., and J. Bradford Jensen. 2002. "The Death of Manufacturing Plants." NBER Working Paper no. 9026.

Bhagwati, Jagdish. 1991. "Free Traders and Free Immigrationists: Strangers or Friends?" Russell Sage Foundation Working Paper.

Boix, Carles. 2006. "Between Redistribution and Trade: The Political Economy of Protectionism and Domestic Compensation." In this volume.

Borjas, George J. 1999a. *Heaven's Door: Immigration Policy and the American Economy.* Princeton: Princeton University Press.

———. 1999b. "The Economic Analysis of Immigration." Pp. 1697–1760 in Orley C. Ashenfelter and David Card (eds.), *Handbook of Labor Economics.* Amsterdam: North-Holland.

Borjas, George J., Richard B. Freeman, and Lawrence F. Katz. 1996. "Searching for the Effect of Immigration on the Labor Market." *American Economic Review* 86 (2): 247–51.

———. 1997. "How Much Do Immigration and Trade Affect Labor Market Outcomes?" *Brookings Papers on Economic Activity* 1: 1–90.

Bronfenbrenner, Kate. 2000. "Uneasy Terrain: The Impact of Capital Mobility on Workers, Wages, and Union Organizing." Working paper, September.

Busch, Marc, and Eric Reinhardt. 2000. "Geography, International Trade, and Political Mobilization." *American Journal of Political Science* 44 (4) (October): 703–19.

Cameron, David. 1978. "The Expansion of the Public Economy." *American Political Science Review* 72: 1243–61.

Card, David. 2001. "Immigrant Inflows, Native Outflows, and the Local Labor Market Impacts of Higher Immigration." *Journal of Labor Economics* 19 (1): 22–64.

Cassing, James, Timothy McKeown, and Jack Ochs. 1986. "The Political Economy of the Tariff Cycle." *American Political Science Review* 80 (3) (September): 843–62.

Chicago Council on Foreign Relations (CCFR). 2002a. *Worldviews 2002: American Public Opinion and Foreign Policy.* Chicago: CCFR.

———. 2002b. *Worldviews 2002: European Public Opinion and Foreign Policy.* Chicago: CCFR.

Darden, Keith. 2002. *Liberalism and Its Rivals.* Manuscript, Yale University.

Economic Report of the President. 1997, 2000. Washington, D.C.: U.S. Government Printing Office.

Epstein, David, and Sharyn O'Halloran. 1996. "The Partisan Paradox and the U.S. Tariff, 1877–1934." *International Organization* 50 (2) (Spring): 301–24.

Fabbri, Francesca, Jonathan E. Haskel, and Matthew J. Slaughter. 2003. "Does Nationality of Ownership Matter for Labor Demands?" *Journal of the European Economics Association* 1 (2/3): 698–707.

Feenstra, Robert C., and Gordon H. Hanson. 1997. "Foreign Direct Investment and Relative Wages: Evidence from Mexico's Maquiladoras." *Journal of International Economics* 42 (May): 371–93.

———. 1999. "The Impact of Outsourcing and High-Technology Capital on Wages." *Quarterly Journal of Economics* (August): 907–40.

Freeman, Richard. 1995. "Are Your Wages Set in Beijing?" *Journal of Economic Perspectives* 9 (3) (Summer): 15–32.

Friedberg, Rachel. 2001. "The Impact of Migration on the Israeli Labor Market." *Quarterly Journal of Economics* 116: 1373–1408.

Gabel, Matthew. 1998. *Interests and Integration: Market Liberalization, Public Opinion, and European Union.* Ann Arbor: University of Michigan Press.

Garrett, Geoffrey. 1998. *Partisan Politics in the Global Economy.* New York: Cambridge University Press.

Golden, Miriam, Peter Lange, and Michael Wallerstein. 2002. "Union Centralization among Advanced Industrial Societies: An Empirical Study." Dataset available at http://www.shelley.polisci.ucla.edu/data. Version dated September 19, 2002.

Gorg, Holger, and Eric Strobl. 2003. "Footloose Multinationals?" *Manchester School* 71 (1): 1–19.

Gottschalk, Peter, and Robert Moffitt. 1994. "The Growth of Earnings Instability in the U.S. Labor Market." *Brookings Papers on Economic Activity* 2: 217–54.

Hainmueller, Jens, and Michael Hiscox. Forthcoming. "Learning to Love Globalization? Education and Individual Attitudes Toward International Trade." *International Organization.*

Hanson, Gordon H., and Ann Harrison. 1999. "Trade Liberalization and Wage Inequality in Mexico." *Industrial and Labor Relations Review* 52: 271–88.

Hanson, Gordon, Kenneth Scheve, Matthew Slaughter, and Antonio Spilimbergo. 2002. "Immigration and the U.S. Economy: Labour-Market Impacts, Illegal Entry, and Policy Choices." Pp. 169–285 in Tito Boeri, Gordon Hanson, and Barry McCormick (eds.), *Immigration Policy and the Welfare System.* London: Oxford University Press.

Hanson, Gordon H., and Matthew J. Slaughter. 2002. "Labor-Market Adjustment in Open Economies: Evidence from U.S. States." *Journal of International Economics* 57 (1): 3–29.

Haskel, Jonathan E., and Matthew J. Slaughter. 2001. "Trade, Technology, and U.K. Wage Inequality." *The Economic Journal* 111 (January): 163–87.

———. 2003. "Have Falling Tariffs and Transportation Costs Raised U.S. Wage Inequality?" *Review of International Economics* 11 (4): 630–50.

Hays, Jude, Sean Ehrlich, and Clint Peinhardt. Forthcoming. "Government Spending and Public Support for Trade in the OECD: An Empirical Test of the Embedded Liberalism Thesis." *International Organization.*

Helpman, Elhanan. 1984. "A Simple Theory of Trade with Multinational Corporations." *Journal of Political Economy* 92: 451–71.

Hiscox, Michael. 2001. *International Trade and Political Conflict: Commerce, Coalitions, and Mobility*. Princeton: Princeton University Press.

———. 2003. "Through a Glass and Darkly: Framing Effects and Individuals' Attitudes toward International Trade." Harvard University Working Paper.

Inglehart, Ronald, et al. 2000. *World Values Surveys and European Values Surveys, 1981–1984, 1990–1993, and 1995–1997*. Computer File, ICPSR Version. Ann Arbor: Institute for Social Research.

International Social Survey Programme (ISSP). 1995. *National Identity*. Archived by Zentralarchiv Für Empirische Sozialforschung, Cologne.

Iversen, Torben, and Thomas Cusack. 2000. "The Causes of Welfare State Expansion." *World Politics* 52 (April): 313–49.

Johnson, George, and Matthew J. Slaughter. 2001. "The Effects of Growing International Trade on the U.S. Labor Market." Pp. 260–306 in Robert Solow and Alan B. Krueger (eds.), *The Roaring Nineties: Can Full Employment Be Sustained?* New York: Russell Sage Foundation.

Katzenstein, Peter. 1985. *Small States in World Markets: Industrial Policy in Europe*. Ithaca: Cornell University Press.

Lawrence, Robert Z., and Matthew J. Slaughter. 1993. "International Trade and American Wages in the 1980s: Giant Sucking Sound or Small Hiccup?" In Martin Neil Baily and Clifford Winston (eds.), *Brookings Papers on Economic Activity: Microeconomics* 2: 161–211.

Leamer, Edward E. 1984. *Sources of International Comparative Advantage*. Cambridge: MIT Press.

———. 1998. "In Search of Stolper-Samuelson Linkages between International Trade and Lower Wages." Pp. 141–202 in Susan M. Collins (ed.), *Imports, Exports, and the American Worker*. Washington, D.C.: Brookings Institution Press.

Mayda, Anna Marie. 2002. "Who Is Against Immigration?: A Cross-Country Investigation of Individual Attitudes toward Immigrants." Harvard University Working Paper.

Mayda, Anna Marie, and Dani Rodrik. 2005. "Why Are Some People (and Countries) More Protectionist than Others?" *European Economic Review* 49 (6) (August): 1393–1430.

Mussa, Michael. 1978. "Dynamic Adjustment in the Heckscher-Ohlin-Samuelson Model." *Journal of Political Economy* 86 (September).

Neary, Peter. 1978. "Short-Run Capital Specificity and the Pure Theory of International Trade." *The Economic Journal* 88 (September): 448–510.

OECD. 1997. "Economic Performance and the Structure of Collective Bargaining," in *OECD Employment Outlook*. Paris: OECD.

O'Rourke, Kevin, and Richard Sinnott. 2001. "The Determinants of Individual Trade Policy Preferences: International Survey Evidence." In S. M. Collins and D. Rodrik (eds.), *Brookings Trade Forum: 2001*. Washington, D.C.: Brookings Institution Press.

Rama, Martin. 1994. "Endogenous Trade Policy: A Time-Series Approach." *Economics and Politics* 6 (November): 215–32.

Richardson, J. David. 1995. "Income Inequality and Trade: How to Think, What to Conclude." *Journal of Economic Perspectives* (summer): 33–55.

Rodriguez, Francisco, and Dani Rodrik. 2001. "Trade Policy and Economic Growth: A Skeptic's Guide to the Cross-National Evidence." In Ben Bernanke and Kenneth Rogoff (eds.), *Macroeconomics Annual 2000*. Cambridge: MIT Press.

Rodrik, D. 1995. "Political Economy of Trade Policy." Pp. 1457–94 in G. Grossman and K. Rogoff (eds.), *Handbook of International Economics*, vol. 3. Amsterdam: Elsevier Science.

———. 1997. *Has Globalization Gone too Far?* Washington, D.C.: Institute for International Economics.

———. 1998. "Why Do More Open Economies Have Bigger Governments?" *Journal of Political Economy* 106 (5): 997–1032.

Rybczynski, T. M. 1955. "Factor Endowments and Relative Commodity Prices." *Economica* 22: 336–41.

Sapiro, Virginia, Steven J. Rosenstone, Warren E. Miller, and the National Election Studies. 1998. "American National Election Studies, 1948–1997." CD-ROM. Ann Arbor: Inter-University Consortium for Political and Social Research.

Scheve, Kenneth F. 2000. "Comparative Context and Public Preferences over Regional Economic Integration." Paper presented at the 2000 Annual Meetings of the American Political Science Association.

Scheve, Kenneth F., and Matthew J. Slaughter. 2001a. "What Determines Individual Trade-Policy Preferences." *Journal of International Economics* 54 (2) (August): 267–92.

———. 2001b. "Labor-Market Competition and Individual Preferences over Immigration Policy." *Review of Economics and Statistics* 83 (1) (February): 133–45.

———. 2001c. *Globalization and the Perceptions of American Workers*. Washington, D.C.: Institute for International Economics.

———. 2004. "Economic Insecurity and the Globalization of Production." *American Journal of Political Science* 48 (4) (October).

Schmidt, Stefanie R. 1999. "Long-Run Trends in Workers' Beliefs about Their Own Job Security: Evidence from the General Social Survey." *Journal of Labor Economics* 17 (4): S127–S141.

Slaughter, Matthew J. 2000. "What Are the Results of Product-Price Studies and What Can We Learn From Their Differences?" Pp. 129–70 in Robert C. Feenstra (ed.), *The Impact of International Trade on Wages*, NBER Conference Volume.

———. 2001. "International Trade and Labor-Demand Elasticities." *Journal of International Economics* 54 (1): 27–56.

Takacs, Wendy. 1981. "Pressures for Protectionism: An Empirical Analysis." *Economic Inquiry* 19 (October): 687–93.

Wallerstein, Michael. 1987. "Unemployment, Collective Bargaining, and the Demand for Protection." *American Journal of Political Science* 31: 729–52.

———. 1999. "Wage-Setting Institutions and Pay Inequality in Advanced Industrial Societies." *American Journal of Political Science* 43: 649–80.

World Bank. 2003. *World Development Indicators Online*. Accessed March 2003 at http://devdata.worldbank.org/dataonline/.

CHAPTER 10

Immigration and Redistribution in a Global Era

Stuart Soroka, Keith Banting & Richard Johnston

DEBATES ABOUT THE IMPACT of globalization on the redistributive capacities of the state have paid remarkably little attention to the most human dimension of the global era, the movement of millions of people around the globe. There are intense debates about whether globalization constrains the room to maneuvre available to nation-states, or tilts the domestic political balance between traditional supporters and opponents of the welfare state. Students of globalization, however, have largely ignored the impact of immigration on the politics of redistribution.

This intellectual divide presumably reflects the fact that immigration has not been part of the international process of economic liberalization in recent decades. Whereas multilateral agreements have facilitated trade and capital flows around the world, the movement of people remains regulated by national laws. Immigration was deliberately left beyond the ambit of trade agreements, and immigration policy continues to reflect the resilience of nation-states and domestic politics (Joppke 1999).[1]

Moreover, national legislation has not become more open in the past twenty years; if anything, politics have driven in the opposite direction. As Dani Rodrik has noted, "[T]he liberalization of trade and capital flows has benefited greatly from the push of political forces. The same forces have been conspicuous by their absence in the case of international labour movements" (2002: 341).

Nevertheless, waves of global economic integration do seem to be linked historically with mass movements of people.[2] The late ninetieth and early twentieth centuries, a period of rapid growth in international trade and foreign investment, witnessed a great migration that brought over twenty-five million people to the United States alone. The current wave of globalization is also accompanied by large-scale migration, and the rate of movement was accelerating in the closing years of the twentieth century. The United Nations estimates that as many as 150 million people live outside the country of their birth—approximately 2.3 percent of the earth's population. Although this percentage has not changed significantly since 1965, there have been important shifts in the nature of the flows in different regions of the world. Migrants have increased as a proportion of the total population throughout Europe, North America, Australia, and New Zealand. By 1998, migrants represented over 20 percent of the population in Australia, New Zealand, and Switzerland; 18 percent in Canada; almost 12 percent in the United States; and close to 10 percent in France, the Netherlands, and Sweden. Equally important, the sources of immigration have shifted, with larger proportions of immigrants to northern countries coming from peripheral regions—such as Turkey in the case of Europe, and Mexico in the case of the United States—and from developing countries of the south. These changes have increased the ethnic, linguistic, and religious diversity of the populations of advanced welfare states, and made multiculturalism a defining feature of the contemporary era.

Immigration has the potential to raise powerful challenges to the political legitimacy of the welfare state. Immigration can unsettle historic conceptions of community, which define those who are "us," recognized members of existing networks of rights and obligations, and those who are "strangers" or "others" whose needs seem less compelling. According to many commentators, the growing presence of newcomers, especially ethnically distinct newcomers, may erode the sense of social solidarity on which welfare states are constructed.

This chapter examines the relationship between immigration and the welfare state, arguing that there is indeed a link between increasing levels of migration and decreasing social welfare expenditures. The chapter begins with a description of existing research, and a review of the various linkages that may exist between social spending and immigration. We then explore the links between these two variables in advanced industrial democracies since 1965 with multivariate analyses at various time scales. These analyses suggest that increasing migration is one way in which globalization may adversely affect social welfare programs, raising important issues about the integration of newcomers into prevailing conceptions of community and social citizenship in Western democracies.

EXISTING RESEARCH

As previously noted, the literature on globalization has yet to come to grips with immigration. Analysts have focused on whether globalization limits the capacity of countries to build and preserve distinctive social contracts that reflect domestic politics and cultures. Although economic integration may not trigger a race to the very bottom, many worry that it creates pressures for convergence toward the more modest level of social protection in the trading system, such as is characteristic of the United States.[3] Others have asked whether globalization weakens social solidarity within countries, eroding the foundations on which the welfare state was built. Over a decade ago, Robert Reich argued that globalization and technological change have increased not only the income gap but also the political gap between highly skilled professionals and unskilled workers, as Reich's "symbolic analysts" retreat physically and politically into gated communities (Reich 1991). Others have argued that economic restructuring has shifted the domestic political balance between capital and labor. This literature, however, has not asked whether immigration patterns are straining social cohesion or disrupting the political coalitions that built the welfare state.

The same gap appears in the literature on the welfare state. The first generation of this research highlighted the role of class structures and alliances, the strength of organized labor, and role of social democratic politics in the rise of the welfare state (Stephens 1979; Korpi 1983; Esping-Anderson 1985). More recent analyses of differences in the levels of social spending have broadened the range of factors to include the level of economic development, the openness of the economy, the size of the elderly population, the relative strength of organized labor, the historical dominance of parties of the left and right, and, in more recent studies, the structure of political institutions. In contrast, immigration and ethnic diversity of populations receive little attention.[4] For example, four recent book-length studies by leading scholars in the field are all silent on these social changes (Hicks 1999; Huber and Stephens 2001; Swank 2002; Esping-Andersen 2002).

Fortunately, other researchers have not been so reticent. The large literature on immigration has explored the interactions between immigration and social programs. Economists in particular have asked whether generous social programs represent a welfare magnet, part of the attractive pull for people from low-income countries. In the case of the United States, George Borjas argues that welfare programs reduce out-migration among immigrants who fail in the U.S. labor market, increasing migrants as a proportion of the total population (Borjas 1999: 114–15). In similar terms, a recent European study concluded that, while the effect is moderate in quantitative terms, generous social benefits in countries like Denmark and the Netherlands seem to attract migrants disproportionately likely to be dependent on welfare (Boeri, Hanson, and McCormick 2002: chapter 3). Economists have also asked whether migrants rely more heavily on social assistance programs than natives in Europe and North America. This was not the case in the 1960s, but recent migrants from low-income countries tend to have lower educational and skill levels relative to the native population and to face greater problems in the labor market. Although the evidence suggests that the long-term net fiscal impact is small, most studies conclude that in the short-term—which is probably more important politically—immigrants in Europe and the United States rely more heavily than natives on social assistance programs, especially in "gateway" cities and regions.[5]

Resentment about migrants' dependency on welfare contributed to a political backlash in a number of jurisdictions, most famously in California during the 1990s, and governments have often responded with policy changes that deny or delay eligibility for welfare programs to immigrants. In the United States, the largest financial savings for the federal government from the welfare reforms introduced by the 1966 Personal Responsibility and Work Opportunity Reconciliation Act resulted from restrictions on immigrant eligibility for social benefits, including Food Stamps, Supplementary Security Income, Medicaid, and public assistance. A similar pattern of requiring immigrants to establish longer periods of residency before qualifying for a variety of means-tested programs has emerged in a number of other countries, including Australia and the United Kingdom

(Banting 1999: 120–21). The Danes have recently moved in the same direction (*Economist* 2003).

The politics of immigration and the welfare state is also charged by the multi-cultural nature of contemporary migration flows. Immigration and ethnic diversity are analytically distinct phenomena. Not all immigration increases the ethnic diversity of host countries; indeed, for two-thirds of the twentieth century, immigration policies in most welfare states were carefully designed to avoid such an outcome. And not all ethnic diversity is the result of recent immigration; in many cases, ethno-linguistic differences predate the formation of the states that now contain them, or reflect population movements centuries old, as in the case of African Americans. Nevertheless, in the past thirty years, immigration has been a source of growing ethnic and racial diversity in most Western countries.

As a result, the politics of the welfare state is increasingly haunted by a difficult question: is there is a tension between ethnic diversity and strong public support for redistribution? Research in a surprisingly diverse set of fields suggests that the answer may be yes. For example, development economists at the World Bank and elsewhere increasingly point to the debilitating consequences of ethnic rivalries and conflicts in explaining the weaker economic and social performance of a number of poorer countries, especially in Africa. While the main focus of this literature is on economic growth, findings also suggest that spending on private as opposed to public education tends to be higher in countries with more linguistic and religious diversity, and transfer payments tend to be lower in countries with high levels of ethnic diversity.[6]

Similar themes can be found in recent discussions about the nature of altruism and reciprocity in experimental economics (Bowles, Fong, and Gintis 2001), and in studies of countries in the developed world. Race has been a long-standing feature in studies of the politics of social policy in the United States. Numerous authors have told the story of the way in which the politics of race contributed to the fracturing of the New Deal coalition. In addition, recent studies have pointed to racial diversity in explaining why Americans "hate welfare" (Gilens 1999), why the United States did not develop a European-style welfare state (Alesina and Glaeser 2004), and why there are significant differences in the level of social expenditures across cities and states within the country (Alesina, Baqir, and Easterly 2001; Hero and Tolbert 1996; Plotnick and Winters 1985). In Europe, a study of European attitudes toward immigrants and their reliance on welfare concludes that opposition is driven less by economic and fiscal concerns than by racial intolerance (Boeri et al. 2002: chapter 5). Sven Steinmo (2003: 44) suggests that the recent Swedish pattern depends on the ethnically homogeneous nature of its population. And political scientists seeking to understand the strength of radical right-wing parties point to a potent cocktail of resentments against racially distinct immigrants and social transfers to them—leading one scholar to worry about the basic political viability of a multicultural welfare state (Kitschelt 1995; but see also Swank and Betz 2003).

In his analysis of nationalism, David Miller has argued that mutual trust facilitates support for social programs, that trust is aided by identification with fellow citizens, and that such identification is easier in societies that nurture a common sense of national identity. By implication, if more diverse societies fail to nurture such a sense of common identity, support for social welfare may be less certain (Miller 1995: 90-99).[7] A particularly intense debate centers on multiculturalism. Here the focus is not on the level of ethnic diversity per se, but on multiculturalist policies that provide public recognition, support, or accommodation of ethnic groups, their identities and their practices, whether in schools, in public rituals, or in public spending. Some critics of such policies insist that they erode the welfare state by diverting time, energy, and money from the politics of redistribution to the politics of recognition, or by eroding trust and solidarity among marginal groups that would otherwise be natural allies, or by leading vulnerable groups to define their problems as a reflection of their culture rather than economic barriers that confront other groups as well (Barry 2001; Gitlin 1995; Wolfe and Klausen 1997).

Such arguments do not go without challenge. Canada represents an interesting test case for such arguments, characterized as it is by the powerful combination of a historic division between English and French-speaking communities, the presence of aboriginal peoples, and one of the very highest immigration rates in the world. Moreover, Canada is widely seen as a leader among countries adopting strong multiculturalism policies. Notwithstanding this complexity, evidence from a national survey designed to plumb the relationships among ethnic diversity, levels of interpersonal trust, and support for social programs finds no evidence that ethnic diversity and multiculturalism erode the welfare state (Soroka, Johnston, and Banting 2004). Similarly, a cross-national analysis of the relationship between multiculturalism policies and social policies finds no evidence that multiculturalism policies systematically erode the welfare state. In general, countries that have adopted strong multiculturalism policies have not had greater difficulties in sustaining their welfare states over the past twenty-five years than other countries (Banting and Kymlicka 2004). This does not preclude the possibility that such tensions do exist in particular places for particular groups of people, however.

Clearly, the debate about globalization and the redistributive state needs to be extended to incorporate the movement, not just of microchips and money, but of people, millions of people who represent the human face of a global era. Given the concern that globalization erodes the capacity of nation-states to sustain ambitious social contracts, a key question is whether immigration affects *political* support for the welfare state? The causal pathway may be direct, in weakening the attitudinal base for welfare programs among the public. Or it may be indirect, in inducing a surge in support for parties of the "New Right." Support for these parties may be driven by anti-immigrant sentiment and not by antipathy to the welfare state. But the parties themselves commonly express such antipathy, and so a New Right groundswell is likely to carry policy consequences beyond resistance to immigration.

A proper test of these propositions requires a fully specified model of demand for social spending. Immigration can affect welfare expenditure in quasi-automatic ways, some increasing proportionate outlays, others decreasing them. Immigration levels themselves can be affected by other factors in welfare supply and demand, and so simple bivariate tests are vulnerable to charges of spuriousness. A properly specified model will also give us some sense not just of *whether* immigration matters but of *how much* it matters, compared to other factors. It should also bring out divergence in effect between the short and long run.

The literature suggests a number of possible pathways or links between immigration and social spending:

A. Increased immigration is associated with *increased* social spending, at least in the short term:

    1. In Europe and the United States, recent immigrants have lower levels of education and training, weaker economic performance, and heavier reliance on unemployment and social assistance benefits than both previous generations of immigrants and natives.

    2. Immigrants tend to be younger on average than natives, altering the demographic profile of the country and raising expenditures on child-related programs, such as child benefits and education.

B. Increased immigration leads to *reduced* social spending:

    1. For the same reason, that immigrants tend to be younger than natives, immigration reduces the share of the population over 65. To the extent that the welfare state is oriented more to the old than the young, immigration reduces demand for social services quasi-automatically, and this alone would create a negative relationship between immigration and social spending. This relationship would be causal, certainly not spurious, but in contrast to the effect in A.2., it is of little political consequence. Its possibility alerts us to the need for a fully specified setup, however. Conceivably, over the full life-cycle the net demographic impact of immigration on the destination country's fiscal position is small and ambiguous.

    2. Most critically, increasing proportions of "new" beneficiaries—who have not been contributors—may lead to a decline in general public support for redistributive policies, whatever the beneficiary group.

    3. Immigration could lead to pressures to reduce the eligibility of immigrants in particular for welfare. If immigrants come to dominate the traditional categories of welfare eligibility, this would reduce the system's overall transfer capacity or limit growth in social expenditures.

    4. Over time, political resistance to high levels of immigration increases support for conservative political parties. In the European context, the vehicle for this protest tends to be radical right-wing parties.[8] Voters supporting such parties may not intend any signal about the welfare state but find themselves inadvertently sending such a signal anyway.

Whatever the predicted direction of impact, all the foregoing place immigration in the causal driver's seat. But immigration levels may also be the consequence of prior differences or changes in social spending:

C. High social spending may lead to increased immigration:

    1. Generous social assistance programs represent a welfare magnet that increases immigration and/or reduces out-migration among migrants who fail in the labor market.

D. High social spending may lead to reduced immigration:

    1. Political reaction to high levels of immigration and immigrant dependency on welfare may also be to tighten immigration policy and reduce immigration levels rather than cut welfare benefits. Traditional supporters of the welfare state, such as labor unions, might prefer reduced economic migration to reduced welfare spending for natives.[9]

This enumeration of competing and often contradictory causal pathways reinforces the need mentioned earlier for a fully specified model. Moreover, because social spending is driven by factors outside any nexus with immigration, control for these factors should help stabilize the estimation and allow immigration-related effects to emerge. Estimation needs to be sensitive to lags and to time scale, to account for the divergence among the foregoing predictions.

MIGRATION AND SOCIAL SPENDING: THE BASIC PATTERN

Table 10.1 presents the data on social spending and immigration for all OECD countries for which data are available.[10] Figure 10.1 presents the basic relationship between the two for the 1970–98 interval, a period of notable gains in overall international migration and striking changes in its sources. By "social spending" is meant total social welfare spending as a proportion of GDP, created by splicing together two OECD series: the 1980–2000 OECD Social Expenditures Database (SOCX), and 1960–80 data from the appendix in OECD, *Social Expenditure, 1960–1990: Problems of Growth and Control.* By "immigration" is meant foreign-born migrant stock as a proportion of the total population. Yearly data are based on UN estimates for 1965, 1975, 1985, 1990, and 2000, with linear interpolation for intervening years.[11] Migrant stock is only one of several possible indicators. Swank and Betz (forthcoming) use inflows of asylum seekers and refugees, for instance. This indicator may be suited to modeling right-wing party support but represents an incomplete measure for our purposes. Others (e.g., Boeri et al. 2002) have used measures of foreign nationals, also an incomplete measure as it is affected by naturalization rates, which vary greatly across countries. Total net migration is a readily available measure, but outflows can (and do) hide considerable

TABLE 10.1.
Levels of Social Welfare Spending and Migrant Stock, 1970 and 1998

Country	Social Wefare Spending, % of GDP		Migrant Stock, % of Population	
	1970	1998	1970	1998
AUL	6.5	17.8	18.7	24.3
AUT	18.9	26.8	2.3	8.7
BEL	15.3	24.5	6.7	8.7
CAN	10.5	18.0	15.3	18.2
DEN	20.8	29.8	2.4	5.4
FIN	13.1	26.5	0.7	2.3
FRA	15.6	28.8	9.8	10.6
FRG	15.4	27.3	3.5	8.4
GRE	9.4	22.7	1.1	4.7
IRE	10.5	15.8	4.2	8.4
ITA	14.7	25.1	1.7	2.8
JPN	4.8	14.7	0.6	1.2
NET	21.6	23.9	2.7	9.5
NOR	14.3	27.0	2.3	6.2
NZL	11.6	21.0	15.2	21.1
SWE	18.7	31.0	6.0	10.8
UKM	14.6	24.7	5.0	6.7
USA	10.2	14.6	5.2	11.5
Average	13.5	23.6	6.2	10.1

inflows in certain countries. The ideal series for our purposes might be total *gross* migration, but the measure is available only for select OECD countries in certain years. Our indicator—change in migrant stock—captures more migrants than the asylum-seekers measure and should be unaffected by naturalization rates.

Table 10.1 shows levels of spending and migrant stock for the countries in our sample in 1970 and 1998. These are the first and last years for which data are available for all countries, but these years also nicely capture the recent period of globalization. Without exception, immigrants claim a larger share of each country's population in 1998 than in 1970. Averaged across the whole set of countries, that share is roughly two-thirds again as large at the end as at the beginning. This has not produced a global reduction in social spending, however, as spending growth has been even more spectacular, typically a near doubling of its share of GDP during the same period. If no country, however, has seen a decline in either indicator, cross-national variation in each is striking. So the question becomes whether the rate at which social spending increases is larger or smaller according to the magnitude of immigration.

At a first cut, in figure 10.1, the answer seems to be clearly yes. The figure plots percentage-point changes in the variables against each other. The largest increases in migrant stock are associated with the smallest increases in social welfare expen-

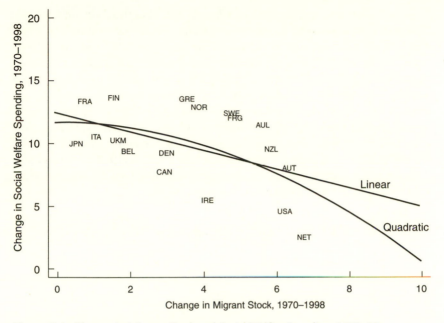

Figure 10.1. Changes in Migrant Stock and Social Welfare Spending, 1970–98.

ditures. The relationship does not appear to be linear, however. A quadratic fit represents the relationship in a simple and powerful way, as further analysis will confirm. By the quadratic relationship in the graph, a country with an average net gain in foreign-born would devote about 1.5 percent less of GDP to social spending than it would have had it closed its borders.[12]

MULTIVARIATE ESTIMATIONS

Figure 10.1 establishes only a starting point, however, as it glosses over all the explanatory considerations and caveats mentioned earlier. Not least, it leaves completely open the direction of causation. A more rigorous test of the relationship will include variables capturing political, economic, and demographic effects on social welfare expenditures, closely modeled on Huber and Stephens (2001), Swank (2002), and Hicks (1999).

Four political variables merit consideration:

- Left-party seats as a percentage of all seats in the governing coalition.
- Christian Democratic party seats as a percentage of all seats in the governing coalition.
- Radical right-wing (RW) party votes as a percentage of all votes.
- Union density, measured as union membership, as a percentage of the employed labor force.

Both Huber and Stephens 2001 and Swank 2002 find that Left and Christian Democratic representation in *government* increase social welfare spending, hence our concentration on seats in the numerator and governing coalition—as opposed to the whole Parliament—seats in the denominator. Radical right-wing parties (not Christian Democratic parties) are represented by their share of the popular vote, not just by seats in governing coalitions (which they rarely are invited to join), or by their seats in the legislature (to partly get around electoral system effects). The supposition is that impact from RW parties is through perceived electoral threat, not through conventional bargaining at cabinet tables (Kitschelt 1997). Inclusion of union density follows Hicks (1999), among others.

Economic and demographic variables are essentially "demand" variables positively linked to increases in social welfare expenditures:

- The percentage of the population below age 16, anticipating that infants will increase health care and day care costs and that school-age children will increase education costs.
- The population of the population over age 64, the most powerful single driver of social spending growth.
- Inflation (year over year change in CPI).
- Unemployment, a key source of short-term flux.
- GDP per capita.
- The percent of females in the labor force, following Huber and Stephens (2001), a driver of child care costs

In all estimations, social spending (as a dependent variable) and immigration are modeled as changes, the current value minus the preceding value. As table 10.1 and figure 10.1 show, levels of spending increased across all countries in our sample during this period, and so it is the magnitude of the increase that matters. As it is spending change that we model, it seems appropriate that it be driven by change rather than level of migrant stock. Other variables are modeled as levels or changes according to the logic of the situation. Huber and Stephens 2001 suggest, for example, that the partisan composition of government has an effect on spending that is cumulative, requiring an extended period to manifest itself, while economic and demographic variables have more concurrent effects. The mix of change and level variables will reflect the time scale for the estimation.[13]

Moreover, the time scale should be allowed to vary. There is an appealing directness to the twenty-eight-year period in figure 10.1, and so we start with an estimation quite like the one implicit in the figure, and we elaborate on it. The number of variables quickly converges on the number of cases, however, and causal priority always remains a nagging issue in what can never get beyond being a cross-sectional estimation. There follows, then, a more ambitious setup: time-series cross-sectional (TSCS) analyses of changes in social welfare spending from 1965 to 2000, using five- to one-year time periods. Successive re-estimations allow us to examine the period over which different variables have (or do not have) an effect on social spending.

Cross-sectional Analysis

Results from the cross-sectional analyses of 1970–98 changes are presented in table 10.2. For these models, migrant stock and social spending are measured in 1970–98 changes, while all other variables are measured as averages over this period. Model 1 examines the simple impact of 1970–98 percentage-point changes in migrant stock and the corresponding changes in social welfare expenditures. The only additional variable is the 1970 level of social spending, included to allow for the possibility that countries initially spending a great deal on social welfare will have less potential for increase than countries that spend comparatively less. Model 2 extends the analysis to all variables with potential impact except union density. The last indicator is missing for three of the eighteen countries, and so we drop it to preserve degrees of freedom; it returns later in the richer TSCS estimations. This saturated estimation creates a baseline for comparison with the TSCS models. Model 3 in table 10.2 presents the results of backward elimination of variables, such that only those that cross at least the 0.10 threshold for statistical significance remain. Each of the models 1 through 3 is estimated separately for linear and quadratic representations of growth in migrant stock.

Table 10.2 confirms the superiority of the quadratic model of immigration effects. The coefficient on the migration variable is always more stable in quadratic form and more variance is explained.[14] Whatever the form of the migration indicator, its impact is utterly independent of the level of social spending in 1970, in the sense that migration coefficients in table 10.1 are essentially identical to those implicit in figure 10.1.[15] Impact from the 1970 spending level variable is negative, as expected, but insignificant.

The direct effect of immigration is largely impervious to control. The value of the coefficient hardly changes as additional variables come and go. The saturated model generates enough multicollinearity to expand the standard error on the immigration coefficient, taking it below the conventional significance threshold, but the trimmed estimation (model 3) renders it even more stable and significant than in the baseline model. The impact remains as before: the typical migration experience lowers the predicted growth in welfare spending by 1.5 points, about 15 percent of the average expenditure change (10.1 percentage points) during the period.

Of the variables that remain, female labor force participation and the percentage of population over age 64 dominate the impact from demography. Left-party seats in governing coalitions dominates among political factors. What all this means is that the impact of immigration is largely unmediated by variables that lie along the potential causal pathways outlined earlier. Immigration does affect the percentage over 64 (table A2) and that percentage does affect welfare spending,

TABLE 10.2.
Modeling Changes in Social Spending: 1970–98

Independent Variables	Dependent Variable: Percentage Point Change in Social Welfare Spending, as a % of GDP_t, 1970–98					
	Model 1	Model 2	Model 3	Model 1	Model 2	Model 3
Δ Migrant Stock	-.724* (.359)	-.721 (.464)	-.724*** (.232)	—	—	—
Δ Migrant Stock²	—	—	—	-.109** (.046)	-.129 (.067)	-.104*** (.030)
Social Spending ('70)	-.040 (.160)	-.336 (.248)	-.411*** (.127)	-.031 (.154)	-.228 (.256)	-.377** (.125)
Left Seats	—	.166* (.071)	.155*** (.040)	—	.180** (.068)	.156*** (.037)
ChristDem Seats	—	-.008 (.073)	—	—	.008 (.070)	—
RW Votes	—	-.096 (.237)	—	—	-.160 (.232)	—
Unemployment	—	.102 (.826)	—	—	-.302 (.865)	—
Inflation	—	.186 (.364)	—	—	.248 (.347)	—

GDP per Capita	—	.112 (.538)	—	—	.308 (.543)	—
Female Labour Force	—	.095 (.092)	.102* (.052)	—	.085 (.087)	.100* (.049)
Population <16	—	−.119 (.436)	—	—	−.047 (.412)	—
Population >64	—	.523 (.563)	.703** (.320)	—	.276 (.569)	.605* (.316)
Constant	12.846*** (2.428)	3.403 (17.338)	2.086 (4.133)	11.976*** (2.207)	1.697 (16.200)	2.113 (3.892)
Observations	18	18	18	18	18	18
R^2	.231	.841	.820	.289	.862	.836

Note: Cells contain OLS regression coefficients with standard errors in parentheses.

*** $p < .01$; ** $p < .05$; * $p < .10$.

but the effect of each on the ultimate dependent variable is independent of the effect of the other. Immigration growth is a factor in support for parties of the new Right (table A2, again), but social spending seems unaffected by the threat posed by such parties.

TSCS Analysis

Cross-sectional estimations have the advantage of being relatively simple and surprisingly robust given the small number of observations. Restricting the estimation to 1970–98 changes is not ideal, however. Effects may be masked or augmented by the long time period. The small number of observations restricts the deployment of potential explanatory and control variables. Accordingly, tables 10.3 and 10.4 present results from time-series cross-sectional (TSCS) analyses. Following Beck and Katz (1995), analyses use panel-corrected standard errors (PCSEs).[16] The sample size in the yearly TSCS analysis varies from 78 to 560, depending on temporal frequency, and so we can afford to be more aggressive about explanatory variables. Some estimations include total union density, which was excluded from cross-sectional analyses. Estimations begin with five-year intervals, where a yearly dataset is collapsed into five-year periods beginning in 1965 and all variables represent their average value over the five-year interval. Political variables are included as levels for each five-year period; all other variables are included as changes from the last five-year period to the current one. For such variables, entries are for $t - 1$ rather than t, on the grounds that budgets for the current period are made in the previous period, and so it should be the last period's government that has an effect on this period's spending (see, e.g., Wlezien 1996; Wlezien and Soroka 2003).[17] The model is then replicated using successively smaller intervals, culminating with a frequency of one year.[18]

Table 10.3 bridges us to the baseline quadratic estimation in table 10.2. In this simple setup, impact from immigration seems unaffected by the temporal frequency.[19] By implication, a one-point change in migrant stock over five years should have roughly the same effect as a one-point change over one year. Relative to the cross-sectional estimation, however, its substantive significance seems reduced. In the yearly model, a one-point change in migrant stock is associated with a .023-point decrease in social spending. In coefficients, this suggests that immigration has a short-term impact only one-fifth to one-quarter as great as its cumulative impact. Put another way, however, the substantive significance of immigration is reduced even more: the average yearly change in migrant stock, +0.124, predicts a 0.003-point decrease in social spending change, less than one percent of the average yearly change in social spending (+0.385).

As in the cross-sectional estimation, the direct impact of immigration shrinks only slightly, if at all, when other variables enter the fray in table 10.4. The first five columns (Model 1) deploy the same countries as table 10.2. The second five

TABLE 10.3.
Modeling Changes in Social Spending: Basic TSCS Models

Independent Variables	Dependent Variable: Percentage Point Change in Social Welfare Spending as a % of GDP$_t$				
	5-year	4-year	3-year	2-year	Yearly
Δ Migrant Stock^2 $_t$	−.024***	−.022***	−.023***	−.023***	−.023***
	(.008)	(.008)	(.007)	(.008)	(.008)
Spending $_{t-1}$	−.076	−.067*	−.059*	−.036*	−.018**
	(.050)	(.039)	(.031)	(.020)	(.009)
Constant	3.506***	2.732***	2.265***	1.469***	.740***
	(.903)	(.715)	(.573)	(.379)	(.178)
Observations	107	160	197	303	593
Number of Countries	18	18	18	18	18
R^2	.116	.105	.088	.058	.029

Note: Cells contain regression coefficients from a time-series cross-sectional analysis using panel-corrected standard errors (in parentheses).

***$p < .01$; **$p < .05$; *$p < .10$.

(Model 2) are of greater substantive interest, as they include the effect of union density (with three fewer countries, however). There is a hint in both models that the impact of immigration is slightly more mediated—its coefficient shrinks—the higher the frequency. The most likely mediating variable is the demography of age: the impact from the percentage under age 16 grows as the estimation's temporal frequency increases.

Immigration is not the only variable to see its effect attenuate as we move from cross-sectional to TSCS setups. As foreshadowed by Huber and Stephens 2001, the effect of the partisan composition of government disappears almost entirely in the shorter-term TSCS models. Only in the five- and three-year models are Left party seats significant, and then only with union density excluded (model 1). As before, neither Christian Democratic seats in government nor right-wing party votes in the electorate have any impact.[20]

The effect of economic and demographic "demand" variables increases in significance as the time period shortens, confirming that these variables have sizeable influence on social spending in the short term. Changes in the unemployment rate are consistently positive and significant; changes in the CPI are positive and usually significant. As in the twenty-eight-year model, the percentage of women in the labor force is positively associated with social spending. So too is union density, in line with previous work.

TABLE 10.4.
Modeling Changes in Social Spending, TSCS Analysis at Various Intervals

Dependent Variable: Percentage Point Change in Social Welfare Spending as a % of GDP $_t$

Independent Variables	Model 1					Model 2				
	5-year	4-year	3-year	2-year	Yearly	5-year	4-year	3-year	2-year	Yearly
Δ Migrant Stock² $_t$	−.022***	−.015**	−.017**	−.015**	−.016**	−.028***	−.028***	−.024**	−.024**	−.021**
	(.006)	(.007)	(.007)	(.006)	(.007)	(.008)	(.011)	(.010)	(.010)	(.010)
Spending $_{t-1}$	−.061	−.044	−.040*	−.023	−.013*	−.057	−.014	−.019	−.007	−.004
	(.042)	(.029)	(.021)	(.015)	(.008)	(.041)	(.030)	(.024)	(.016)	(.008)
Left Party Seats $_{t-1}$	.018**	.006	.007*	.005	.002	.010	.002	.003	.001	.000
	(.008)	(.005)	(.004)	(.003)	(.002)	(.010)	(.007)	(.005)	(.004)	(.002)
ChristDem Party Seats $_{t-1}$	−.003	.002	.004	.003	.003	−.005	−.003	.002	.003	.003
	(.008)	(.007)	(.006)	(.004)	(.002)	(.009)	(.007)	(.005)	(.004)	(.002)
RW Party Votes $_{t-1}$	−.025	−.002	−.001	−.003	.003	−.026	−.008	.004	.002	.010
	(.055)	(.034)	(.024)	(.018)	(.008)	(.064)	(.048)	(.032)	(.023)	(.010)
Δ Unemployment Rate $_t$	.979***	1.009***	1.088***	1.007***	.751***	1.016***	.782***	1.011***	.927***	.720***
	(.192)	(.194)	(.148)	(.133)	(.102)	(.227)	(.197)	(.165)	(.141)	(.109)
12-month Δ CPI $_t$	.039	.105***	.056**	.049***	.032***	.017	.113*	.068	.065**	.047***
	(.042)	(.032)	(.024)	(.018)	(.011)	(.090)	(.059)	(.046)	(.028)	(.014)

ΔGDP per Capita $_t$	-.235 (.166)	-.135 (.125)	-.284** (.132)	-.314*** (.121)	-.475*** (.112)	-.316 (.239)	-.173 (.175)	-.437** (.198)	-.492*** (.170)	-.647*** (.145)
ΔFemale Labour Force $_t$	.170*** (.061)	.131** (.060)	.183*** (.059)	.140*** (.051)	.126*** (.044)	.190* (.098)	.109 (.086)	.188** (.085)	.155** (.068)	.125** (.059)
ΔTotal Union Density $_t$	—	—	—	—	—	.071 (.045)	.072* (.042)	.056 (.037)	.062* (.035)	.065** (.031)
Δ% pop < 16 $_t$	.595*** (.153)	.555*** (.135)	.643*** (.146)	.584*** (.134)	.608*** (.154)	.579*** (.150)	.544*** (.131)	.652*** (.159)	.619*** (.143)	.633*** (.163)
Δ% pop > 64 $_t$	.276 (.254)	.499** (.248)	.329 (.242)	.367 (.261)	.235 (.263)	.018 (.319)	.044 (.330)	-.001 (.348)	.099 (.361)	-.021 (.318)
Constant	3.238*** (1.084)	1.600** (.650)	1.792*** (.549)	1.104*** (.336)	.672*** (.180)	3.872*** (1.374)	1.788** (.763)	1.956*** (.694)	1.133*** (.392)	.618*** (.185)
Observations	102	150	186	285	560	78	104	133	206	414
Number of Countries	18	18	18	18	18	15	15	15	15	15
R²	.487	.516	.560	.488	.339	.462	.400	.509	.469	.377

Note: Cells contain regression coefficients from a time-series cross-sectional analysis using panel-corrected standard errors (in parentheses).

*** $p < .01$; ** $p < .05$; * $p < .10$.

The varying effects of demographic variables across models deserve some explanation. First, the fact that population over age 64 is no longer significant in the TSCS analyses should not be taken at face value. Lagged levels of welfare spending are highly correlated with lagged levels of population over 64. (Population over 64 is the variable that is most highly correlated with levels of welfare spending, in fact; see bivariate correlations in the appendix.) As a consequence, the effect of this population variable likely occurs in these models mainly over the long term via lagged levels of spending. Population under age 16, on the other hand, was not significant in the twenty-eight-year model but is consistently significant in the TSCS analyses. It appears as though this variable has a shorter- rather than longer-term impact.[21]

Discussion and Conclusions

International migration does seem to matter for the size of the welfare state. Although no welfare state has actually shrunk in the face of the accelerating international movement of people, its rate of growth is smaller the more open a society is to immigration. The typical industrial society might spend 16 or 17 percent more than it now does on social services had it kept its foreign-born percentage where it was in 1970.

The effect seems wholly political and wholly through its direct impact on mainstream governing parties. Extensive controls for the impact of international migration on the socio-demographic drivers of welfare demand reduce the measured impact of immigration hardly at all. And although immigration is powerfully implicated in the rise of parties of the New Right, these parties seem to contribute no further pressure on governments to restrain spending growth. In this sense, the New Right parties may be epiphenomenal, products of the same forces that move their political rivals directly.

How seriously should we take these propositions? It is an awkward fact that the biggest apparent effect of immigration is in the estimation with the weakest basis: data from two time points in eighteen countries. It does seem appropriate that estimated cumulative impact is greater for an implicitly low-frequency estimation than for very high-frequency—annual at the extreme—modeling. But we do feel diffident about the point estimate in our simple cross-sectional estimation. Our anxiety is increased only by that estimate's vulnerability to inclusion or exclusion of particular cases. Of the cases we include, the United States and the Netherlands carry a heavy burden. If we tell single-country stories, the United States provides an internally consistent one that requires no reference to external migratory pressure. Gilens (1999) argues that Americans have become more resistant to welfare, in particular to programs for the poor, as welfare policy has come to be increasingly racialized in its media presentations. The racial focus is mainly on

African Americans. We also know, however, that immigrants also figure in that country's discourse. And we can supply no obvious purely domestic story to cover the Netherlands case. An implication of the U.S. and Netherlands role, however, is that modest increments in the foreign-born share carry much less proportionate charge than big ones.[22]

What do the propositions imply? At the theoretical level, they seem to vindicate Miller's (1995) worries about threats to the national basis of the welfare state. Obviously, we cannot replicate the steps in his argument with data as highly aggregated and as lacking in direct indicators of voter sentiment, but suppositionally the evidence points in Miller's direction. At the policy level, the results here highlight a major challenge facing Western democracies. International migration will continue to be a fact of life, not least because of declining replacement rates for industrial work forces. The question is how to combine openness at the global level with social integration at the domestic level. Progress here will depend in part on realistic analyses of the attitudinal dynamics among voters that underpin the tension between immigration and social spending analysed here. Evidence suggests that the attitudinal problem is more among natives than newcomers (Soroka, Johnston, and Banting 2002), and undoubtedly reflects an amalgam of perceived cultural threat and economic cost. Understanding these fears and apprehensions is critical. But progress will also depend on finding ways to incorporate newcomers into national fabrics, to construct new and more inclusive forms of citizenship and national identity that can sustain a sense of social solidarity. How to strengthen the bonds of community in multicultural societies is one of the most compelling questions confronting Western democracies. The debate about multiculturalism policies thus takes on added importance. Such programs are likely to be part of the answer, rather than part of the problem; certainly, the evidence here does not buttress a case against multicultural policies (see also Banting and Kymlicka 2003). But finding the appropriate balance here is crucial. Otherwise, the human component of globalization may increasingly constrain welfare states that seemed fully consolidated two decades ago.

APPENDIX A: DATA SOURCES AND DESCRIPTIVES

Datasets for the twenty-eight-year changes model and the two to five-year models were derived from the yearly TSCS dataset. Accordingly, variables are here described as they were created for the yearly TSCS analysis. As described in the text, these variables were collapsed into two-, three-, four-, and five-year averages for models in table 10.4. For results in table 10.2, spending and migrant stock variables are measured as the total change from 1970 to 1998; all other variables are the mean for this period.

Variables

Spending: Social welfare spending as a proportion of GDP. Data for 1980–2000 are from the OECD Social Expenditures (SOCX) database. Data for 1960–1980 are from the appendix in OECD, *Social expenditure, 1960–1990: Problems of Growth and Control.* Data were missing for Austria (1981–84; 1986–89) and Norway (1981–84; 1986–87), and so are interpolated for these years. The final series are available from 1960–1998, without gaps, for all countries.[23]

Migrant stock: Migrant stock as a proportion of the total population, based on UN estimates, as described in the text. The resulting series are available from 1965 to 2000 for all countries.

Population under 16: Population under 16 as a proportion of the total population. Data are from OECD Health Data 2001. Available from 1960 to 1999 for all countries except Italy (1980–99).

Population over 64: Population over 64 as a proportion of the total population. Data are from OECD Health Data 2001. Available from 1960 to 1999 for all countries except Italy (1980–99).

Female labor force: Female labor force as a percentage of the total female population. Data are from OECD Labor Statistics and OECD Health Data 2001. There are some individual years before 1980 for which data are missing; for the final series, these values are interpolated using linear interpolation. Data begin between 1960 and 1964 for all countries except Netherlands (1971).

Total union density: Total union membership (less self-employed) weighted by the total dependent labor force. Data are from Miriam Golden, Peter Lange, and Michael Wallerstein (2002) "Union Centralization among Advanced Industrial Societies: An Empirical Study." Dataset available at http://www.shelley.polisci.ucla.edu/data. Version dated September 19, 2002.

Unemployment Rate: Data are from OECD Labor Statistics. Data available from 1960–1998 or 1999 for all countries except Italy (1970–99), Japan (1962–99), and Switzerland (1991–99).

GDP per capita: Gross domestic product per capita, in constant U.S. dollars. Data are from OECD Health Data 2001. Data available from 1960 to 2000 for all countries except Denmark (1966–2000).

CPI: 12-month percent change in the Consumer Price Index. Data are from IMF Statistics (available at http://www.imf.org). Available from 1960 to 2001 for all countries.

Left-party seats: Left governing party seats as a proportion of all legislative seats. This variable is drawn from Duane Swank's *Comparative Parties Data Set,* available online at http://www.marquette.edu/polisci/Swank.htm. Available from 1960 to 2000 for all countries.

ChristDem party seats: Christian Democratic governing party seats as a proportion of all legislative seats. Same source as for Left-party seats. Available from 1960 to 2000 for all countries.

RW votes: Right Wing Populist votes as a proportion of all party votes. Same source as for Left-party seats. Available from 1960 to 2000 for all countries.

Descriptives

TSCS analyses are based on data with no gaps, beginning in the first year and ending in the last year as listed in table 10.5.

TABLE 10.5.
Data Availability

Country	Without Union Density			With Union Density		
	N (year)	First Year	Last Year	N (year)	First Year	Last Year
AUL	34	1966	1999	24	1966	1989
AUT	30	1969	1998	28	1969	1996
BEL	33	1966	1998	30	1966	1995
CAN	34	1966	1999	34	1966	1999
DEN	28	1971	1998	27	1971	1997
FIN	33	1966	1998	32	1966	1997
FRA	33	1966	1998	30	1966	1995
FRG	33	1966	1998	32	1966	1997
GRE	24	1975	1998		n/a	
IRE	33	1966	1998		n/a	
ITA	18	1981	1998	17	1981	1997
JPN	33	1966	1998	16	1966	1981
NET	27	1972	1998	26	1972	1997
NOR	33	1966	1998	32	1966	1997
NZL	34	1966	1999		n/a	
SWE	33	1966	1998	32	1966	1997
UKM	33	1966	1998	30	1966	1995
USA	34	1966	1999	24	1966	1989

Note: TSCS analyses are based on data with no gaps, beginning in the first year and ending in the last year as listed above.

TABLE 10.6.
Bivariate Correlations[a]

Variables	1	2	3	4	5	6	7	8	9	10	11
1 Δ Social Spending $_t$	1.000 (672)										
2 Δ Migrant Stock^2 $_{t-1}$	-.075 .067 (593)	1.000 (630)									
3 Left Seats $_{t-1}$	.062 .114 (660)	.041 .306 (621)	1.000 (723)								
4 ChristDem Seats $_{t-1}$	.018 .653 (660)	.044 .272 (621)	-.086 .020 (723)	1.000 (723)							
5 RW Votes $_{t-1}$	-.075 .053 (660)	.199 .000 (621)	.140 .000 (723)	.025 .497 (723)	1.000 (723)						
6 Δ Unemployment Rate $_t$	.445 .000 (660)	-.022 .582 (604)	.011 .776 (673)	-.008 .836 (673)	.002 .951 (673)	1.000 (687)					
7 12-month Δ CPI $_t$	.263 .000 (672)	-.170 .000 (630)	.072 .052 (723)	-.139 .000 (723)	-.194 .000 (723)	.251 .000 (687)	1.000 (756)				

	1	2	3	4	5	6	7	8	9	10	11	12
8 GDP per Capita	**-.357** *.000* (672)	.054 *.177* (629)	.032 *.399* (700)	**-.091** *.016* (700)	**.250** *.000* (700)	**-.290** *.000* (681)	**-.117** *.002* (714)	1.000				
9 Δ Female Labour Force $_t$	.037 *.352* (645)	-.051 *.209* (610)	.028 *.474* (668)	**-.077** *.048* (668)	-.017 *.671* (668)	-.072 *.065* (659)	**.144** *.000* (681)	**.186** *.000* (675)	1.000 (681)			
10 Δ Total Union Density $_t$	**.130** *.004* (504)	**-.157** *.001* (444)	**.158** *.000* (534)	-.010 *.814* (534)	-.033 *.444* (534)	-.015 *.745* (506)	**.130** *.003* (534)	**-.138** *.002* (513)	-.062 *.168* (493)	1.000 (534)		
11 Δ % pop < 16 $_t$	.027 *.493* (652)	**.264** *.000* (597)	.023 *.557* (668)	**.217** *.000* (668)	**.138** *.000* (668)	**-.089** *.021* (677)	**-.255** *.000* (682)	**-.110** *.004* (676)	**-.223** *.000* (653)	-.083 *.064* (498)	1.000 (682)	
12 Δ % pop > 64 $_t$	.009 *.826* (652)	**-.166** *.000* (597)	.063 *.102* (668)	.058 *.133* (668)	-.070 *.073* (668)	-.024 *.538* (677)	.008 *.826* (682)	-.031 *.421* (676)	-.037 *.341* (653)	**.184** *.000* (498)	**-.219** *.000* (682)	1.000 (682)

Notes: Cells contain pairwise bivariate correlation coefficients using all available cases from 1960–2000. Significance levels are in italics; the number of observations is in parentheses. All correlations significant at p < .05 are in bold.

[a]To check for collinearity in the models presented in table 10.3, these correlations were also generated using (a) only cases included in model 1 and (b) only cases included in model 2. Results do not change dramatically.

NOTES

A previous version of this chapter was presented at the Annual meeting of the Canadian Political Science Association, Dalhousie University, Halifax NS, May 29–June 1 2003. This research is made possible by the "Equality, Security, and Community" Major Collaborative Research Initiative, Jon Kesselman, Principal Investigator. Financial Support comes from the Social Sciences and Humanities Research Council of Canada and our respective universities. We are grateful for the encouragement of Michael Wallerstein, Samuel Bowles, Pranab Bardhan, and Donald Forbes. None of these institutions or individuals is responsible for any errors of fact or interpretation.

1. There is a debate about the extent to which national immigration policies are constrained by international human rights regimes. Whatever side of the debate one takes, however, it is clear that such constraints as do exist are less stringent than those in the world of trade and finance. See Joppke (1999) and Soysal (1994).

2. For an argument that if money, goods, and ideas flow effortlessly around the globe, people will have to follow eventually, see Sassen (1998).

3. For recent discussions, see Garrett (1998); Hall and Soskice (2001); and Kitschelt et al. (1999).

4. One early exception was Stephens (1979), which noted that ethnic and linguistic diversity was strongly and negatively correlated with the level of labor organization, which in turn was strongly related to social spending. This early lead, however, did not figure in Stephen's own later work (see Huber and Stephens 2001).

5. See OECD (1997), Borjas (1994, 1999); Boeri et al. (2002). This evidence has sparked proposals in both Europe and the United States for reforms to immigration policy to actively select more highly skilled immigrants, as is done in Canada, where immigrants appear less dependent on social assistance than natives (Baker and Benjamin 1995).

6. See, for example Easterly (2001a, b); Easterly and Levine (1997); James (1987, 1993); Nettle (2000), and Grafton, Knowles, and Owen (2002).

7. See also Steinmo's suggestion that the recent Swedish pattern depends on the ethnically homogeneous nature of its population (Steinmo 2003: 44). Similar themes can be found in recent discussions about the nature of altruism and reciprocity in experimental economics (Bowles, Fong, and Gintis 2001).

8. See Kitschelt (1997) for European cases. The Canadian Reform party (now the Alliance) that broke through in 1993 also exemplifies this kind of reaction.

9. The Canadian model is arguably a variant on this. Canadian immigration policy selects a relatively skilled immigration flow through a points system and by requiring sponsorship agreements for family reunification, such that sponsors guarantee that sponsored immigrants will remain off welfare for ten years.

10. The one exception is Switzerland. Both migration and spending data are available, but the OECD version of the latter presents an inaccurate history of Swiss social welfare spending. In 1990 the OECD added "mandatory private" social spending to their measure of total public social spending, in line with what appears to have been an established belief among Swiss analysts that mandatory private insurance schemes should be regarded as part of the Swiss welfare state. As a consequence, there is a jump in the Swiss social spending series in the early 1990s—a jump that is the product of a change in definition rather than a genuine change in policy. We consequently exclude Switzerland from our analyses. (Its in-

clusion in other studies of social welfare spending such as Huber and Stephens 2001 is facilitated in part by the use of ILO social spending data, which end in the early 1990s, and so are unaffected by this change in definition.) We are grateful to Giuliano Bonoli for advice on the Swiss case.

11. OECD data on migrant stock are available yearly from 1980, but only for some of the countries in our sample and in some cases only intermittently. UN and OECD definitions and sources are slightly different, and so the two sets of data cannot be merged. We rely on the UN data because they are available more consistently, for a greater number of countries, and over a longer time period.

12. A natural anxiety, however, is that the relationship is driven by the extreme cases, the United States and the Netherlands. As it happens, the relationship is not merely dependent on one or the other of these countries. Dropping the United States from the estimation weakens it hardly at all. Dropping the Netherlands, cuts the value of linear and quadratic coefficients by about 30 percent but leaves them significant by a one-tailed test. Cutting both countries does drive the relationship effectively to zero. The two hardly seem like an artifactual pair, however. Just about the only thing they have in common are changes in the variables of central interest.

13. TSCS models in changes were also estimated in levels using a Prais-Winsten estimation to account for serial correlation. There are few differences between the analyses in terms of levels and changes, a testament to the robustness of many of the findings about to be presented.

14. The quartic form was also tested and proved to be slightly less powerful a curvilinear representation than the more accessible quadratic.

15. For instance, the quadratic coefficient in figure 10.1 is -0.742. In table 10.2 it is -0.724.

16. To check for any autocorrelation that might remain after differencing, all regressions were also replicated using a Prais-Winsten estimation accounting for first-order autoregressive processes. In all cases, the estimated ρ, the coefficient indicating serial correlation in disturbances, is small and other results do not change.

17. This is less clear when we are looking at longer intervals than one year, admittedly. Accordingly, these variables were tested at both t and $t-1$.

18. Estimating each model at five- to one-year intervals reveals the different time periods over which different variables have an effect on spending. It also serves as a diagnostic check: Some of our variables are yearly, and some are less frequent. Interpolating the latter to produce yearly series creates one possible difficulty, and averaging yearly data across longer intervals creates another. It is significant, then, that the general trends we observe are consistent across all time periods.

19. The principal effect of increasing the frequency is to bring lagged spending into the realm of statistical significance, but only by shrinking standard errors through sheer multiplication of degrees of freedom.

20. Swank and Betz's (forthcoming) finding that inflows of asylum seekers and refugees are positively associated with right-wing party vote shares is echoed in our TSCS dataset, in a regression (not reported here) of right-wing vote share on changes in migrant stock, unemployment, inflation, and GDP per capita.

21. The effect of population under age 16 is particularly important given the hypothesis that migration increases social spending by altering the demographic profile of a country. Indeed, our data indicate a positive relationship between changes in migrant stock and

changes in the percent of population under 16 (see bivariate correlations in the appendix). Consequently, while the direct effect of changes in migrant stock is clearly negative, the same changes should also push social spending upward by increasing the population under 16. The effect should be very slight, however. While changes in population under 16 have a considerable effect on social spending, migration accounts for a very small proportion of this demographic change.

22. Although the estimated impact of the average increase in the foreign-born percentage hardly seems trivial.

23. The two databases have slightly different expenditure definitions, although both include expenditures on health, pensions, unemployment, and "other" social welfare programs. Values for 1980 are the same in the two databases for some countries, and slightly different for others. Accordingly, the complete 1960–2000 series were created as follows: Data from 1980–2000 are from the new database. Data for 1979 are estimated by taking the percentage difference from 1980 to 1979 in the old database, and applying this same percentage difference to derive the 1979 value from the 1980 value in the new database. This is done repeatedly, back to 1960, so that pre-1980 values in the final series reflect the same percentage changes as in the old database, post-1980 values are identical to those in the new database, and there is no artificial punctuation in 1980. This is a relatively common method of merging expenditure series, used by both HM Treasury (United Kingdom) and Statistics Canada, for instance. The other possible source of primary data on social expenditures is from the ILO. These ILO data have the advantage of consistency from the 1960s to 1993, but are no longer being updated.

REFERENCES

Alesina, Alberto, and Edward Glaeser. 2004. *Fighting Poverty in the US and Europe: A World of Difference.* Oxford: Oxford University Press.

Alesina, Alberto, Reza Baquir, and William Easterly. 2001. "Public Goods and Ethnic Divisions." NBER Working Paper No. 6009.

Baker, Michael, and Dwayne Benjamin. 1995. "The Receipt of Transfer Payments by Immigrants to Canada." *Journal of Human Resources* 30 (4): 650–76.

Banting, Keith. 1999. "Social Citizenship and the Multicultural Welfare State." In Alan Cairns, John Courtney, Peter MacKinnon, Hans Michelmann, and David Smith, eds. *Citizenship, Diversity and Pluralism: Canadian and Comparative Perspectives.* Montreal: McGill-Queen's University Press.

Banting, Keith, and Will Kymlicka. 2004. "Do Multiculturalism Policies Erode the Welfare State?" In Philippe van Parijs, ed., *Cultural Diversity versus Economic Solidarity.* Brussels: Deboeck Université Press.

Barry, Brian. 2001. *Culture and Equality: An Egalitarian Critique of Multiculturalism.* Cambridge: Polity Press.

Beck, Nathaniel, and Jonathan N. Katz. 1995. "What to Do (and Not to Do) with Time-Series Cross-Section Data." *American Political Science Review* 89 (3): 634–47.

Boeri, Tito, Gordon Hanson, and Barry McCormick, eds. 2002. *Immigration Policy and the Welfare System.* Oxford: Oxford University Press.

Borjas, George. 1994. "The Economics of Immigration." *Journal of Economic Literature* 32 (4): 1667–717.

————. 1999. *Heaven's Door: Immigration Policy and the American Economy.* Princeton: Princeton University Press.

Bowles, Samuel, Christina Fong, and Herbert Gintis. 2001. "Reciprocity and the Welfare State." Manuscript.

Easterly, William. 2001a. "Can Institutions Resolve Ethnic Conflict?" *Economic Development and Cultural Change* 49 (4): 687–706.

————. 2001b. *The Elusive Quest for Economic Development: Economists' Adventures and Misadventures in the Tropics.* Cambridge: MIT Press.

Easterly, William, and Ross Levine. 1997. "Africa's Growth Tragedy: Policies and Ethnic Divisions." *Quarterly Journal of Economics* 112: 1203–50.

Economist. 2003. "Special Report: Europe's Minorities," May 10, pp. 22–24.

Esping-Anderson, Gøsta. 1985. *Politics Against Markets: The Social Democratic Road to Power.* Princeton: Princeton University Press.

————. 2002. *Why We Need a New Welfare State.* Oxford: Oxford University Press.

Garrett, Geoffrey. 1998. "Global Markets and National Politics: Collision Course or Virtuous Circle." *International Organization* 52: 787–824.

Gilens, Martin. 1999. *Why Americans Hate Welfare: Race, Media, and the Politics of Antipoverty Policy.* Chicago: University of Chicago Press.

Gitlin, Todd. 1995. *The Twilight of Common Dreams: Why America Is Wracked by Culture Wars.* New York: Metropolitan Books.

Grafton, Quentin, Stephen Knowles, and Dorian Owen. 2002. "Social Divergence and Productivity: Making a Connection." In Andrew Sharpe, France St-Hilaire, and Keith Banting, eds., *The Review of Economic Performance and Social Progress: Towards a Social Understanding of Productivity* Montreal: Institute for Research in Public Policy.

Hall, Peter, and David Soskice, eds. 2001. *Varieties of Capitalism: The Institutional Foundations of Comparative Advantage.* Oxford: Oxford University Press.

Hero, Rodney, and Caroline Tolbert 1996. "A Racial/Ethnic Diversity Interpretation of Politics and Policy in the States of the US." *American Journal of Political Science* 840: 851–71.

Hicks, Alexander 1999. *Social Democracy and Welfare Capitalism.* Ithaca: Cornell University Press.

Huber, Evelyne, and John Stephens. 2001. *Development and Crisis of the Welfare State: Parties and Policies in Global Markets.* Chicago: University of Chicago Press.

James, Estelle. 1987. "The Public/Private Division of Responsibility for Education in International Comparison." *Economics of Education* Review 6 (1): 1–14.

————. 1993. "Why Do Different Countries Choose a Different Public/Private Mix of Education Services?" *Journal of Human Resources* 18 (3): 531–92.

Joppke, Christian. 1999. *Immigration and the Nation-State: The United States, Germany, and Great Britain.* Oxford: Oxford University Press.

Kitschelt, Herbert. 1997. *The Radical Right in Western Europe: A Comparative Analysis.* Ann Arbor: University of Michigan Press.

Kitschelt, Herbert, Peter Lange, Geoffrey Marks, and John Stephens. 1999. *Continuity and Change in Contemporary Capitalism.* Cambridge: Cambridge University Press.

Korpi, Walter. 1983. *The Democratic Class Struggle.* Boston: Routledge and Kegan Paul.

Miller, David. 1995. *On Nationality.* Oxford: Oxford University Press.

Nettle, D. 2000. "Linguistic Fragmentation and the Wealth of Nations." *Economic Development and Cultural Change* 49: 335–48.

OECD 1997. *Trends in International Migration: Annual Report 1996.* Paris: OECD.

Plotnick, Robert, and Richard Winters. 1985. "A Politico-Economic Theory of Income Redistribution." *American Political Science Review* 79: 458–73.

Reich, Robert. 1991. *The Work of Nations: Preparing Ourselves for 21st Century Capitalism.* New York: Random House.

Rodrik, Dani. 2002. "Final Remarks." In Tito Boeri, Gordon Hanson, and Barry McCormick, eds. *Immigration Policy and the Welfare System.* Oxford: Oxford University Press.

Sassen, Saskia 1998. "The *de facto* Transnationalizing of Immigration Policy." In Christian Joppke, ed. *Challenge to the Nation-State: Immigration in Western Europe and the United States.* Oxford: Oxford University Press.

Soroka, Stuart, Richard Johnston, and Keith Banting. 2004. "Ethnicity, Trust and the Welfare State." In Philippe van Parijs, ed. *Cultural Diversity versus Economic Solidarity.* Brussels: Deboeck Université Press.

Soysal, Yasemin. 1994. *Limits of Citizenship.* Chicago: University of Chicago Press.

Steinmo, Sven. 2003. "Bucking the Trend? The Welfare State and the Global Economy: The Swedish Case Up Close." *New Political Economy* 8 (1): 31–48.

Stephens, John. 1979. *The Transition from Capitalism to Socialism.* Urbana: University of Illinois Press.

Swank, Duane. 2002. *Global Capital, Political Institutions and Policy Change in Developed Welfare States.* Cambridge: Cambridge University Press.

Swank, Duane, and Hans-Georg Betz. 2003. "Globalization, the Welfare state, and Right-Wing Populism in Western Europe." *Socio-Economic Review.* 1 (2): 215–45.

Wlezien, Christopher. 1996. "Dynamics of Representation: The Case of U.S. Spending on Defence." *British Journal of Political Science* 26: 81–103.

Wlezien, Christopher, and Stuart Soroka. 2003. "Measures and Models of Budgetary Policy" *Policy Studies Journal* 31: 273–86.

Wolfe, Alan, and Jyette Klausen. 1997. "Identity Politics and the Welfare State." *Social Philosophy and Policy* 14 (2): 213–55.

CHAPTER 11

Economic Integration, Cultural Standardization, and the Politics of Social Insurance

Samuel Bowles & Ugo Pagano

DOES THE FREER MOVEMENT of goods, people, ideas, and money across national boundaries mean that, as Charles Kindleberger (1969: 207) put it, "the nation state is just about through as an economic unit" when it comes to the provision of social insurance and programs of egalitarian redistribution? Surely globalization will not eliminate the conditions—economic insecurity and distributions of income widely thought to be unfair—that initially gave rise to the welfare state. What form will responses to these conditions take in a globally integrated economy?

The thesis we will advance is this. Globalization is an extension of nationalism (not its antithesis) with regard to some aspects of culture and economic structure: like nationalism, it promotes cultural standardization and economic integration. But it does this across national boundaries. And unlike nationalism, globalization does this without providing either the international cultural solidarity or governmental institutions capable of supporting egalitarian redistribution and insurance on a global scale, while weakening the nation-based institutions for the same. In this respect a globalized world may re-create the social structure of the archetypal agrarian empire: a dominant class of cosmopolitans speaking a common language and presiding over a heterogeneous and provincial underclass that speaks a Babel of dialects, with little solidarity across the language groups and weak nationally based instruments of social insurance and egalitarian redistribution.

The politics of social insurance may thus increasingly pit the cosmopolitans against the provincials (not capital against labor, or even the high earners against the low earners, as many of the cosmopolitans are far from rich). The result need not be institutional convergence to a world of uniformly minimalist welfare states, however, for the process of specialization induced by greater integration may support distinct institutional arrangements appropriate to each economy's divergent product mixes. Countries specializing in goods characterized by volatile demand (e.g., capital goods) or requiring high levels of specific skills might be induced by globalization to strengthen their systems of social protection.

It is likely, however, that in many countries the reverse will occur. In these economies, social insurance will be compromised, leaving the provincials increasingly vulnerable to industry- or occupation-specific shocks. Where this occurs, risk reduction may take the form of foregoing specialization in occupation- or industry-specific skills, and maintaining a relatively unspecialized national "portfolio" of sectors and occupations to which one may move if one's own source of livelihood is threatened.

In this case, optimal integration into the global order requires balancing the marginal gains in expected income associated with greater specialization (the gains from trade) against the marginal losses associated with the enhanced risks occasioned by specialization. This optimum will not be achieved by private decision-making, because the availability of a diverse portfolio of sectors and occupations has a public good aspect.

We advance this thesis not as the confirmed result of a coherent model adequately tested empirically, but rather as a research agenda that is not inconsistent with what is known, and worth pursuing in light of the importance of the issues it addresses.

Globalization: The Highest Stage of Nationalism?

Globalization is typically represented by economists as the process of integration of national economies brought about by the reduction in costs of transportation and communication and the removal of impediments to the movement of goods, people, and finance across national borders. But the same processes that have fostered the freer movement of goods, people, and finance are also creating a global culture, that is, a common language and system of meanings among people in many nations.

Ernest Gellner (1983) defined nationalism as a movement seeking congruence between the ethnic community and the political community: "one national state, one national culture!" has been its political motto.[1] Because we are going to claim that globalism is an extension of Gellner's nationalism, we will consider his interpretation in some detail:

> [N]ationalism is a theory of political legitimacy which requires that ethnic boundaries should not cut across political ones and in particular that ethnic boundaries within a given state . . . should not separate the power holders from the rest. (Gellner 1983: 1)

The standardization of language and culture within a nation that nationalism sought and largely accomplished is what made it so radical during its early years, especially by comparison with the structure of the agrarian empires and other agrarian societies that it replaced.

The technological stagnation of agrarian society allowed the endless repetition of the same production process; families passed the same jobs based on the same skills from one generation to the next. Cultural diversity among all except the elite stabilized these roles. It limited both horizontal and vertical mobility and allowed the endless reproduction of the social fabric over time. Cultural diversity—both between the elite and the rest, and among the rest—was both a condition for and a result of societal inertia. It supported the stagnation of society by depriving most of its members of the incentives to seek social mobility. At the same time cultural diversity along both its horizontal and vertical dimensions was favored by the unchanging structure of society.

The rudimentary and geographically confined division of labor in these societies was such that ordinary farmers and craftsmen in one locality had little need to communicate with their counterparts in other localities. Other than the payment of taxes or the transfer of a share of their crops, they had even less need to interact with members of the elite.

But the broadening scope of goods markets and eventually the emergence of labor markets and other capitalist economic institutions radically altered the cultural requirements of economic life. Again, Gellner:

> For the first time in human history, explicit and reasonably precise communication becomes generally, pervasively used and important. In the closed local communities of the agrarian or tribal worlds, when it came to communication, context tone, gesture, personality and situation were everything. (1983: 33)

Communication "by means of written, impersonal, context-free to-whom-it-may-concern type messages" required what Gellner termed "exo-education," that is, childhood socialization by specialists who are not members of one's family or group of close associates. Paradoxically, he wrote,

> [I]ndustrial society may . . . be the most highly specialized society ever: but its educational system is unquestionably the least specialized, the most universally standardized, that has ever existed. (1983: 27)

This was the process that, in Eugen Weber's phrase, turned *Peasants into Frenchmen* (Weber 1976) and villagers into citizens around the world wherever nationalism took hold. In many cases, far from being the expression of a unified culture, states preceded the emergence of a nation. Massimo D'Azeglio (1867), former prime minister of Piedmont, wrote about his country's unification, observing that "Italy has been made. Italy, but not the Italians."

The assimilation of local agrarian idioms and symbols into a standardized national culture would have been resisted more forcefully had it not provided important benefits for those making the transformation. Though Gellner did not stress this, exo-education in a common language and culture is a form of risk reduction, for it gives the exo-educated individual general skills that may be deployed in a variety of pursuits rather than the occupation- or sector-specific skills that were passed on by parents engaged in the forms of endo-education typical of agrarian societies.[2]

To see this, suppose that uncertainty takes the form of the occurrence of either a status quo state, in which the individual continues his current livelihood with income y, or a bad state in which there is no demand for an individual's particular line of work, and he thus must pursue some other livelihood in which he receives $y(1 - s)$ where $s > 0$ is a measure of the degree to which his skills are specific to the initial livelihood. Suppose the status quo occurs with probability $p > \frac{1}{2}$. The individual's expected income is

$$E(y) = py + (1 - p)y(1 - s) \tag{1}$$

and the variance of his realized income is $p(1 - p)(ys)^2$.

The structural and technical dynamism of capitalism arguably lowered the probability of the status quo, increasing the variance of income but exo-education lowered s with the opposite effect. Because of cultural homogenization coupled with the spread of mass exo-education, investments in human capital became more general and (in bad states) more easily deployed in alternative uses. In the process of creative destruction, successful creation was now greatly remunerated while, at the same time, the costs of destruction and failure were substantially decreased by the increased reversibility and liquidity of human skills.

If the emergence of mobility and markets required some minimum degree of cultural homogenization, their development also implied a dramatic further increase in cultural homogenization that, in most cases, caused a deepening of the feelings of national solidarity. Cultural homogenization and social solidarity within large well-defined territories are, thus, two complementary aspects of nationalism. At the same time, they are also substitutes in the sense that they can act as alternative insurance devices against the risk associated to the specialization of skills in a volatile market society (D'Antoni and Pagano 2002).

While the national state originated this self-reinforcing process, it could not be contained forever within the boundaries of national states. Some national states developed a sense of "global mission" and started doing to other languages and traditions what the national state had done to the diverse cultures and dialects that had existed within its boundaries. Included are Britain with its Commonwealth, the Russian Empire in its last manifestation as the Soviet Union, and United States with its federal system, its frontier, and its melting pot of different ethnic groups.

In many cases, national states—especially the non-English speaking ones—now find themselves in opposition to the further advancement of the very process of cultural homogenization that a century earlier had been their main task and, arguably, the fundamental reason for their existence. The former cultural standardizers of the Age of Nationalism have become the victims of standardization on an even grander scale, a historical nemesis that threatens the survival of their own traditions. The energetic defense of the French language by the French state and the ongoing battles within the World Trade Organization about national subsidization of cultural production reflect this development.

COSMOPOLITANS AND PROVINCIALS

This is the sense in which we mean that globalism is the highest stage of nationalism. But the emerging global world order marks a new age, as different from the
nationalisms with which it now contends as from the ancient empires with which
it is inevitably compared.

Globalism is different from the empires that had in the past politically unified
large areas of Europe, Northern India, and even China. The Roman Empire of
antiquity and, after that, the Holy Roman Empire never posed a comparable challenge to cultural diversity. The universal culture and the lingua franca remained
the distinctive mark of the ruling classes. The same could be said with only slightly
less force of the Mughal Empire. In the ancient empires, a modicum of political
unity was accomplished in the absence of cultural unity. Globalization appears
likely to do the opposite.

Modern globalization spreads global culture well beyond a ruling minority.
But while the economic integration and cultural standardization accomplished by
globalization may favor greater political integration, political unity today is mainly
based on the dominance of the United States, on local processes of political integration such as the European Community, and on the limited governance of
some international institutions.

In addition to its lack of well-defined boundaries, the nature of modern globalism is also fundamentally different from nationalism. The political unity of the
national state made possible a distinctive method of risk reduction: cultural homogenization and social protection combined to reduce the risks associated with
specialization in the market economy. Tax and transfer policies that redistributed
income from the lucky to the unlucky decreased risk exposure, while those workers who had acquired job-specific skills were buffered from the vagaries of the labor market by employment safeguards and unemployment insurance. The willingness of the lucky to insure the unlucky even after the dice had been rolled was
enhanced by the feeling that "it could have been me," and thus is itself a product
of cultural homogenization.

Modern globalism not only lacks the international institutions allowing social
protection on a world scale, it also makes the traditional forms of social protection offered by the national state increasingly problematic. The increased mobility of capital and other factors of production owned by the relatively well off has
provided a rationale for shifting taxation away from these factors, thus raising the
cost of policies designed to redistribute income within the nation state.[3] Increasingly competitive goods markets, along with greater mobility of capital and professional labor, has also reduced the scope for trade union bargaining (as Choi's
chapter shows) and in some countries weakened job protection.

Moreover, cultural standardization—the other instrument by which national
economies have traditionally insured their citizens against the risks of market

mobility—is very limited in the internationally integrated economy. Access to the dominant cultural standard—English fluency—is much more unequally distributed on a world scale that the national equivalents within national boundaries—fluency in the national language. The result is a division between those endowed with mobile intellectual assets that are easily redeployed throughout the global economy—the *cosmopolitans*—and those whose skills are less mobile and more specific to the national economy—the *provincials*. The distinction, roughly, is between the skills typical of people working in Silicon Valley and in Detroit, or in Bangalore and in Kanpur.

Cosmopolitians—even those with modest incomes—may prefer to replace social protection with cultural standardization as their preferred form of insurance, withdrawing where possible from the mutual insurance system that characterizes national states. Like financial capital, these workers may become difficult to tax. Their relatively easy exit from a national system of mutual insurance makes it even more difficult to finance the traditional forms of social protection supplied by the national state and worsens the situation of those workers who lack access to the global cultural standard.

The partial cultural standardization associated with modern globalism may thus create a world cosmopolitan elite communicating amongst themselves in a new Latin that cannot be used as a working language by the vast majority of the populations among whom they live. The result would be an information-age equivalent to the old agrarian societies studied by Gellner, presided over by an elite whose high culture unites them around the globe as it separates them from the rest of their own societies, who are in turn separated one from another by the persistence of linguistic and cultural divisions. The fact that many workers of modest incomes will count themselves among the cosmopolitans differentiates modern globalism from the ancient agrarian societies and empires. But, as we will see, this may also exacerbate the challenge facing the nationally based welfare state.

The Politics of Insurance

To show this, we will model the social insurance preferences of a citizenry of identical decreasingly risk-averse individuals. Preferences among citizens are identical but, due to differences in the nature of their income-earning assets, they differ in expected income and risk exposure.[4] If an individual's utility as a function of her income is $U = U(y)$ then the Arrow-Pratt measure of risk aversion is $\lambda = -U''/U'$. If the utility function is less concave at higher levels of income, or $d\lambda/dy < 0$, then *decreasing risk aversion* is said to obtain, meaning that the rich are less risk averse than the poor.[5]

While the concavity of the utility function undoubtedly captures important aspects of behavior in the face of risk, it certainly misses important influences such as aversion to uncertainty, ambiguity, and fear of the unknown. We therefore use a framework in which the concavity of the utility function is but one of many reasons a citizen may wish to avoid risk. The approach captures the Arrow-Pratt logic under appropriate conditions, but is not restricted to it. The basic idea of our framework is that expected income is a "good" and the variance of income is a "bad." We model social insurance as a way of reducing one's exposure to the bad by trading away some of the good.

Suppose the income y of an individual with a given set of assets income varies in response to stochastic shocks according to

$$y = z\sigma + g, \tag{2}$$

where g is expected income and z is a random variable with mean zero and unit standard deviation. Thus, σ is the standard deviation of income, a measure of risk. Then we write the individual's utility function as

$$v = v\{g, \sigma\}. \tag{3}$$

With suitable restrictions on its partial derivatives, this function expresses the individual's positive valuation of higher levels of expected income ($v_g > 0$) and negative valuation of more uncertain income ($v_\sigma \le 0$), without implying that the latter is due solely to the concavity of the function $U(y)$. Because of the particular way we have introduced risk (equation (2)), however, this function is also able to capture the logic of the Arrow-Pratt measure.[6]

The indifference loci representing the preferences of an individual with decreasing risk aversion appear in figure 11.1. They are increasing and convex in σ, flat at the vertical intercept ($v_\sigma = 0$ for $\sigma = 0$), become flatter for increasing g when $\sigma > 0$ and become steeper for increasing σ. The slope of an indifference locus, $-v_\sigma / v_g \equiv \eta(g, \sigma)$, is the marginal rate of substitution between risk and expected income. Thus $\eta(g, \sigma)$ is a measure of the level of risk aversion experienced by an individual faced with a given level of expected income and risk. It is clear that this measure of risk aversion is increasing in the level of risk exposure (movements to the right in figure 11.1) and decreasing in the level of expected income (movements upward in figure 11.1).

Figure 11.1 also indicates the $\{\sigma, g\}$ pairs that may be associated with four classes of citizens demarcated by their income levels and risk exposure.

Now suppose the citizens may tax themselves at a rate t, paying to each citizen an equal share of the proceeds of the tax, $ty^o(1 - w)$, where y^o is mean income and w is the proportional loss in distributed benefits due to administration, deadweight losses, capital flight, or other costs of operating the system. The citizen's post-tax and transfer expected income is now

$$g^t = g(1 - t) + ty^o(1 - w), \tag{4}$$

and its standard deviation, σ^t, is $\sigma(1 - t)$.

Varying t affects both expected income and the standard deviation of income. The effect on expected income (differentiating (4) with respect to t) is

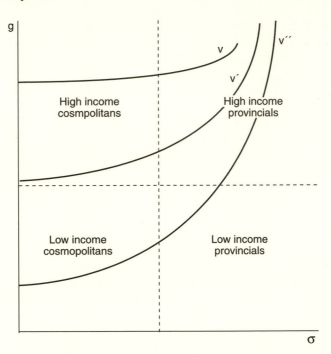

Figure 11.1. Indifference Loci of a Decreasingly Risk Averse Citizenry with a Taxonomy of Citizens According to Their Assets and Associated Expected Income and Risk Exposure.

$-\{g - y^o (1 - w)\}$, and the effect on the standard deviation of income is $-\sigma$. Thus for $\sigma > 0$ this "insurance technology" implies a "price of insurance," ρ, namely the loss in expected income associated with a reduction in risk exposure, or what may be termed the marginal rate of transformation of expected income into risk reduction. This price is just the ratio of the two effects of varying t, and so

$$\rho = \{g - y^o(1 - w)\}/\sigma. \tag{5}$$

The price of insurance is increasing in expected income and declining in risk exposure, as one would expect. If she could unilaterally determine the tax rate, the citizen whose expected income is less than $y^o(1 - w)$ could "purchase" insurance at negative cost (i.e., $\rho < 0$), benefitting from both the risk reduction and the fact that her transfer will exceed her tax payment.

What tax and transfer level would citizens prefer, if they were in position to determine t? A citizen with $g > y^o(1 - w)$ would maximize expected after-tax and transfer utility, $v^t = v\{g^t(t), \sigma^t(t)\}$ by selecting the value of t that equates the price of insurance (the marginal rate of transformation of expected income into risk reduction) to the marginal rate of substitution between risk and expected income, that is, $\rho = \eta$. In figure 11.2 this optimum is point **a** for a person whose assets placed her at **a′**.

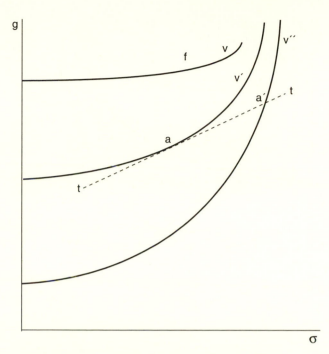

Figure 11.2. A Citizen's Optimal Level of Insurance. Notes: The person with assets which the absence of insurance would yield the outcome at **a'** prefers to purchase insurance at the price indicated by the slope of the "insurance technology" locus, tt.

A person whose assets placed him at point **f**, better off than at point **a'** and less risk exposed, would prefer a tax rate of zero (if he could, he would happily run the tax system in reverse, setting $t < 0$ with all citizens paying a given lump sum in return for a linear subsidy of their earnings, but we will not consider this case). Thus, we can divide the citizenry into two classes: those whose asset position yields a positive optimal tax rate, and those who would prefer no social insurance.

We know that an individual with no risk exposure ($\sigma = 0$) and $g = y^o(1 - w)$ will be indifferent to the choice of t, for it will affect neither his risk exposure nor his expected income. Now consider a person for whom g exceeds $y^o(1 - w)$ by a small amount. If the person is not risk exposed, he will oppose social insurance; but there will be some level of risk exposure that will make him indifferent between no tax and a positive tax rate, namely that for which $\rho = \eta$. The (g, σ) pairs for which $\rho = \eta$ define the "zero tax locus" in figure 11.3. Those whose assets place them above the zero tax locus will oppose social insurance, while those below it will support some level of taxation.

This view of voter preferences receives support from a study by Iversen and Soskice (2001). They estimated the relationship between support for redistributive

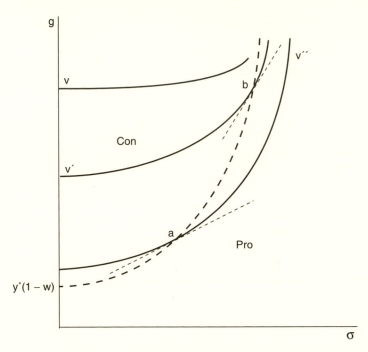

Figure 11.3. Social Insurance: Pro and Con. Notes: Individuals whose assets place them at points a or b favor zero social insurance. Individuals above and to the left of **a** and **b** oppose social insurance. The *zero tax locus*—the heavy dashed line—is the locus of all such points. Thus those above the zero tax locus oppose social insurance; those below it support it.

measures and the degree of specificity of an individual's skills in two social survey data sets in eleven advanced democracies in the late 1990s. Conditioned on other influences on political preferences (income, sex, employment status, party affiliation, and age), the degree of skill specificity is a highly significant determinant of support for redistributive policies, and its effect is equal in size to income (that is, a standard deviation difference in skill specificity is associated with a difference in redistributive preferences equivalent in size to a standardization deviation difference in income).

GLOBALISM VS. THE WELFARE STATE?

Consider three effects of globalism. First, the costs of redistribution may increase. In our model this is just an increase in w, which (from (5)) has the effect of raising the price of insurance, increasing the slope of the tt locus in figure 11.2 and thereby shifting the zero tax locus downward. As a result, more citizens are included in the con rather than the pro classes.

Second, if economic integration raises incomes (as one may expect it to do on average), it will move citizens upward in figure 11.3, reducing the degree of risk aversion and leading to reduced support of the welfare state.

Third, globalism may alter the distribution of citizens in $\{g, \sigma\}$ space. Rodrik (1998), Garrett (1998), and others have suggested that openness may increase support for the welfare state by increasing risk exposure (shifting voters to the right in figure 11.3.) These effects appear to have been at work in a number of countries, including those that pioneered the institutions that we now call the welfare state (Moene and Wallerstein 1995.)[7]

While we believe these effects to be operative in many cases, we have stressed another possible shift in the distribution of citizens: the emergence of a large class of cosmopolitans, including many with middling incomes. To dramatize the importance of this shift (through a bit of exaggeration), consider a "prototype nineteenth-century economy." It is composed of what Alchian and Demsetz (1972) called "classical capitalist firms" whose single owner hires (in a daily spot market) workers with few firm-specific skills (what Marx termed abstract labor). An owner of tangible assets in such a firm is highly risk exposed, as there is a substantial loss in the value of an asset once it is installed—in the modern economy typically well over half of the initial cost (Asplund 2000). By contrast, the workers' job assets—abstract labor—make them much less risk exposed. In this world, the owners would be classed among the high-income provincials in figure 11.1, while the workers would be the low-income cosmopolitans: the distribution of citizens would lie in the "northeast" and "southwest" quadrants. Of course most workers' expected incomes would be such that $g < y^o(1 - w)$, and so most workers and all but the very rich owners would support the welfare state.

This economy is imaginary, but the contrast between it and what may be the emerging global order is striking. Workers now receive substantial job rents, that is, pay far above their next best alternative. These are the result either of workers' firm-specific skills, or of the widespread use by employers of contingent renewal strategies of labor discipline that result in equilibrium wages in excess of workers' reservation wages. And while industrial assets are still highly specific, many of the assets used in the sales and service sectors of the economy (far larger than manufacturing in most advanced economies) are quite general (buildings and computers, for example). Moreover, in contrast to the fictive classical capitalist firm above, ownership of these assets is highly diversified. Both diversification and the more general nature of these assets have the effect of greatly reducing risk exposure. Additionally, there is now a large class of salaried employees whose high level of general skills, including their access to the global cultural standard, greatly reduces their risk exposure. These are the new cosmopolitans.

Figure 11.4 illustrates these shifts. The inner dashed contour indicates a greater density of citizens, and the increasingly "northwest, southeast" array of citizens suggests a new dimension of support and opposition for social insurance, namely the degree of access to the global cultural standard. One cannot rule out a "twin

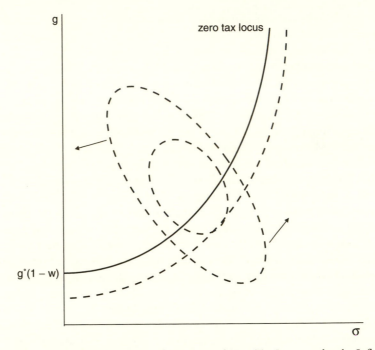

Figure 11.4. Changing Distribution of Citizens and Zero Tax Locus under the Influence of Globalization. Notes: The dashed contours give the distribution of voters. The dashed zero tax locus shows the effect of the increased price of insurance.

peaks" distribution emerging, with a concentration of well-to-do cosmopolitans and less-well-off provincials divided by a ravine of cultural disparity and divergent economic opportunity. To avoid unnecessary simplification, we have deliberately not specified how the national tax rate will be selected. So one cannot predict the effect on the amount of support for social insurance in general.

This is especially the case because the process of economic integration is also one of specialization, the effect of which is that countries will become more distinct in the kinds of skills and other assets that their product mix requires. Suppose there are two goods, grain and plows, and that in the absence of international exchange each of two countries would employ equal numbers of worker-citizens to produce the two goods. The demand for plows, as an investment good, is highly volatile (it is proportional to the *change in the level* of demand for grain), while the demand for grain, a consumption good, is less volatile, depending on the *level* of income and population. Because of the resulting differences in the level of risk exposure, except for the very well paid, those employed producing plows will be supporters of insurance, while except for the poorest, those growing grain will oppose it. Many models of the process electoral competition would predict that the resulting social policy would include some but not very much social insurance.

Following economic integration, however, one country specializes in plow production and the other in grain production. As a result, the voters in Ploughland are now almost uniformly supporters of social insurance, while the citizens of Grainia are equally opposed (unless, of course, openness has increased risk exposure in Grainia sufficiently to offset the reduction in risk associated with specialization in the less volatile good). The result is that economic integration may lead to greater institutional diversity, rather than, as is sometimes predicted, institutional homogenization.

Only slightly less transparent is the case where sectors differ in the importance of specific skills, and integration leads to some countries specializing in producing general-skill goods and others in specific-skill goods. This view is advanced by Hall and Soskice (2001: 38): [N]ational institutional frameworks provide nations with comparative advantage. In the presence of trade, these advantages should give rise to . . . specialization." In turn, according to Hall and Soskice, specialization in those goods for which a country has a comparative advantage is likely to support institutional divergence.

In these cases, the specialization associated with integration may enhance the diversity of 'technology-institutional equilibria' (Pagano 1993). Hall and Soskice have interpreted the differing social policies of the United States and Germany in this light, the German product mix requiring high levels of specific skills, the protection of which through generous unemployment benefits and other forms of job protection is supported by large majorities of the public. The presence of these social protection policies, in turn, allows these specific skill-intensive industries to attract labor and remain viable in international competition.

The presumption that globalism induces institutional convergence is based on a simple, but wrong model. Global competition is represented as a kind of selection pressure operating to force the elimination of inferior designs. But geography and history combine to make specialization advantageous, and given that some institutions are better able to coordinate the production of some goods, while other institutions do better for other goods, the increase in selection pressure may produce divergence rather than convergence (Pagano 2001). It was economic integration—not autarky—that induced the divergence in institutional structure between the sugar-growing islands of the Caribbean on the one hand, and those economies of Central America, such as Costa Rica, whose geography is ill suited to plantation crops.[8] Another example: the importance of family-owned firms in the Italian economy distinguishes it from most of its competitors, and is in turn explained by the fact that due to economic integration, Italy increasingly specializes in those goods for which this form of governance is effective.

To the extent that some nations' policies of social insurance are indeed simply inferior designs, while other nations' lack of social insurance are also simply flawed designs, globalism will increase the pressures for policy convergence. But one cannot say if these forces will be offset by the persistence of distinct institutional arrangements associated with high levels of specialization.

Optimal Specialization?

We have seen that investment in general rather than industry- or occupation-specific skills and assets is a means of reducing risk exposure, and thus may be a substitute for the kinds of social insurance modeled earlier. What may be termed a cosmopolitan risk reduction strategy may become increasingly attractive in those countries in which economic integration creates pressures to reduce the scope of social insurance and job protection. Unless emigration is a feasible option, however, even those with general assets are vulnerable in an economy specialized in the production of a limited range of goods. This is because the protection against adverse price shocks offered by an individual's general assets takes the form of their ability to redeploy these skills in other industries or occupations for which the relevant shocks and prices are substantially uncorrelated. The shock-induced relocation of inputs from one industry to another will generate adverse price effects even when assets being relocated are entirely general. In an economy with a diverse "portfolio" of industries and occupations, however, these effects will be small as long as the adversely affected sectors are small relative to the size of the economy as a whole.

The existence of such a diverse "portfolio" of industries and occupations is, however, a public good in the sense that it provides general risk-reduction benefits that are not accounted for in the individual's utility- or profit-maximizing choices concerning occupational or sectoral location. For this reason, economies guided entirely by private incentives will tend to overspecialize. Global economic integration will exacerbate this market failure *if* it increases risk exposure and reduces the scope of substitute forms of risk reduction such as social insurance.

Conclusion

If we are correct, understanding the impact of globalism on national policies for redistribution and social insurance would be enhanced by greater attention to the degree of specificity of the assets held by people and to the possible emergence of a large class of cosmopolitans with little interest in traditional social insurance policies and weak solidarity with co-resident provincials. It would be valuable to know, as an empirical matter, if among people with similar incomes those with more general education (and hence presumably less specific skills) tend to oppose social insurance. Equally important is the possible divergence of national institutional trajectories as a consequence of more advanced levels of specialization made possible by global integration. Are there empirical cases in which divergence in social insurance policies can be plausibly linked to divergent patterns of specialization following economic integration?

Our approach also suggests some interesting puzzles. Why, for example, are the children of the relatively well off the cosmopolitans, while the children of the less well off tend to become provincials? Given the greater risk aversion of the latter group (parents and children alike), one might have expected the reverse. Of course in most countries, the types of education experienced by the two groups differ, with the cosmopolitans more likely to gain a classical liberal arts education including languages, while the latter acquire occupational skills. But there is a substantial element of choice involved in implementing this difference. Are the general skills of the cosmopolitans complementary with wealth, so that children from the asset-poor families benefit less from learning English, or programming skills, for example, than the children of the well to do? Another intriguing puzzle would be to understand one of the few effective political coalitions across the provincial-cosmopolitan divide, namely the anti-globalization movement in Europe and North America.

NOTES

We have benefitted from the comments of Massimo D'Antoni, Pranab Bardhan, Franco Belli, Marianna Belloc, Michele Di Maio, Michael Wallerstein and Elisabeth Wood. We would like to thank the the Behavioral Sciences Program of the Santa Fe Institute, Russell Sage Foundation, and the PAR funding of the University of Siena for support of this research.

1. Gellner's later works (1999, 1998) recognized the continuity between nationalism and globalism. See also Pagano (2003).

2. The role of schooling in facilitating relationships among non-kin and even strangers is the central argument of Dreeben (1967).

3. We say "has provided the rationale" because the evidence that own-country investment is more sensitive to tax differentials among nations than previously is lacking thus far.

4. We are here following the work of Sinn (1995) and Domar and Musgrave (1944), who modeled the welfare state as a process of redistribution from the lucky to the unlucky rather than from the rich to the poor. Our model is an adaptation of D'Antoni and Pagano (2002). Contrary to compelling evidence of widespread fair-mindedness and concern for the less well off even among higher income earners (e.g., Fong 2001), we assume that our citizens are entirely self-regarding.

5. Evidence that risk aversion is decreasing in income is presented in Saha, Shumway, and Talpaz (1994).

6. The general utility function $U(y)$ can be expressed as a simple two-parameter utility function in this case because the variation in income is generated by what is termed a linear class of disturbances. The technical details are in Bardhan, Bowles, and Gintis (2000), drawing on the earlier work of Meyer (1987) and Sinn (1990).

7. The study by Iversen and Cusack (2000) of the sources of welfare state expansion in the advanced countries finds that technology shocks and structural transformations of the economy unrelated to globalization have larger effects.

8. Ortiz (1963) describes the correspondence between the nature of agricultural crops—tobacco and sugar—and the institutions governing their production in pre-Revolutionary Cuba.

REFERENCES

Alchian, Armen A., and Harold Demsetz. 1972. "Production, Information Costs, and Economic Organization." *American Economic Review* 62 (5): 777–95.

Asplund, Marcus. 2000. "What Fraction of a Capital Investment Is Sunk Costs?" *Journal of Industrial Economics* 48 (3): 287–303.

Bardhan, Pranab, S. Bowles, and H. Gintis. 2000. "Wealth Inequality, Credit Constraints, and Economic Performance." Pp. 541–603 in Anthony Atkinson and François Bourguignon (eds.), *Handbook of Income Distribution.* Dortrecht: North-Holland.

Bardhan, Pranab, S. Bowles, and Michael Wallerstein. 2004. *Globalization and Redistribution.* New York: Russell Sage Foundation.

D'Antoni, M., and Ugo Pagano. 2002. "National Cultures and Social Protection as Alternative Insurance Devices." *Structual Change and Economic Dynamics* 13: 367–86.

D'Azeglio, Massimo. 1867. *I miei ricordi.* Turin: Taparelli.

Domar, Evsey, and Richard A. Musgrave. 1944. "Proportional Income Taxation and Risk-Taking." *Quarterly Journal of Economics* 58: 388–422.

Dreeben, Robert. 1967. *On What Is Learned in School.* Reading, Mass.: Addison-Wesley.

Fong, Christina. 2001. "Social Preferences, Self Interest and the Demand for Redistribution." *Journal of Public Economics* 82 (2): 225–46.

Garrett, Geoffrey. 1998. *Partisan Politics in the Global Economy.* Cambridge: Cambridge University Press.

Gellner, Ernest. 1983. *Nations and Nationalism.* Ithaca: Cornell University Press.

———. 1998. *Nationalism.* London: Phoenix.

———. 1999. "The Coming of Nationalism, and Its Interpretation: The Myths of Nation and Class." Pp. 179–225 in S. Bowles, M. Franzini, and U. Pagano (eds.), *The Politics of Exchange and Economics of Power.* London: Routledge.

Hall, Peter, and David Soskice. 2001. *Varieties of Capitalism: The Institutional Foundations of Comparative Advantage.* Oxford: Oxford University Press.

Iversen, Torben, and Thomas Cusack. 2000. "The Causes of Welfare State Expansion: Deindustrialization or Globalization?" *World Politics* 52: 313–49.

Iversen, Torben, and David Soskice. 2001. "An Asset Theory of Social Policy Preferences." *American Political Science Review* 95 (4): 875–93.

Kindleberger, Charles P. 1969. *American Business Abroad: Six Lectures on Direct Investment.* New Haven: Yale University Press.

Meyer, Jack. 1987. "Two-Moment Decision Models and Expected Utility." *American Economic Review* 77 (3): 421–30.

Moene, Karl Ove, and Michael Wallerstein. 1995. "How Social Democracy Worked: Labor-market Institutions." *Politics and Society* 23: 185–212.

Ortiz, Fernando. 1963. *Contrapunteo Cubano del Tabaco y el Azucar*. Barcelona: Editorial Ariel.

Pagano, Ugo. 1993. "Organizational Equilibria and Institutional Stability." In S. Bowles, H. Gintis, and B. Gustafsson, (eds.), *Markets and Democracy: Participation, Accountability and Efficiency*. Cambridge: Cambridge University Press.

——. 2001. "The Origin of Organizational Species." In Ugo Pagano and Antonio Nicita (eds.), *The Evolution of Economic Diversity*. London: Routledge.

——. 2003. "Nationalism, Development, and Integration: the Political Economy of Ernest Gellner." *Cambridge Journal of Economics* 27: 323–46.

Rodrik, Dani. 1998. "Why Do Open Economies Have Larger Governments?" *Journal of Political Economy* 106 (5): 997–1032.

Saha, Atanu, Richard C. Shumway, and Hovav Talpaz. 1994. "Joint Estimation of Risk Preference Structure and Technology Using Expo-Power Utility." *American Journal of Agricultural Economics* 76 (2): 173–84.

Sinn, H. W. 1990. "Expected Utility, mu-sigma Preferences, and Linear Distribution Classes: A Further Result." *Journal of Risk and Uncertainty* 3: 277–81.

——. 1995. "A Theory of the Welfare State." *Scandinavian Journal of Economics* 95 (4): 495–526.

Weber, Eugen. 1976. *Peasants into Frenchmen: The Modernization of Rural France, 1870–1914*. Stanford: Stanford University Press.

Conclusion

Pranab Bardhan, Samuel Bowles & Michael Wallerstein

HAS THE INCREASED EASE with which goods, capital, and people move across national borders undermined the ability of governments to implement policies that alleviate poverty and provide social insurance? Does globalization raise the costs and compromise the viability of traditional redistributive policies at the level of the nation-state? If so, are there alternatives or modifications of standard social insurance policies that could succeed, both politically and economically, in a world with few controls on the international movement of goods and factors of production?

These are the questions that we posed at the beginning of this volume. Although the conclusions of the individual chapters are nuanced and diverse, it is possible to state a set of key lessons that we believe can be drawn from the set of essays in this volume. We can divide the lessons into four topics: (1) the impact of globalization on the level, security, and inequality of incomes around the world; (2) the impact of globalization on the economic feasibility of egalitarian redistribution policies; (3) the impact of globalization on the political viability of egalitarian redistribution policies; and (4) the impact of policy choices regarding redistribution on the political sustainability of increased international economic integration.

THE IMPACT OF GLOBALIZATION ON INEQUALITY, INSECURITY, AND PROSPERITY

There is a wide gap between the optimistic view of most economists concerning the economic benefits of the removal of controls on the international movement of goods and capital, and the anxiety felt by large numbers of citizens regarding their future in a world without economically meaningful borders. There is little dispute that economic conditions have worsened for many workers in the advanced economies, especially for workers at the bottom of the pay scale, since 1980. Income inequality has grown significantly in the past twenty-five years in many rich and middle countries, including the United States, Britain, Australia, Sweden, Mexico, and Argentina (Gottschalk and Smeeding 1997; Hanson and Harrison 1999). The evidence in the United States indicates than the volatility of income for individual workers over time has grown as the inequality of income between workers has risen (Gottschalk and Moffitt 1994; Scheve and Slaughter 2004). The large continental economies of the European Unions that have not witnessed large increases in income inequality are plagued by persistent high levels of unemployment (Blau and Kahn 2002). Unions are in retreat, with membership in decline and employers aggressively demanding concessions on wages and working hours (Wallerstein and Western 2000). Governments of both the right and left issue warnings that current levels of pension and health care benefits are unsustainable.

Yet most economists writing about trade and inequality argue that the growth of trade and international capital flows relative to national income have had only a minor effect on the distribution of wages and employment in advanced industrial societies, while propelling impressive rates of growth in developing countries that have opened their borders. One often-cited reason for skepticism is that the lion's share of both trade and movements of capital occurs among advanced industrial societies that have similar levels of development and labor costs (Krugman 1994). In addition, the standard approach to understanding the impact of trade on inequality in advanced industrial societies, the Stolper-Samuelson theorem, identifies changes in relative output prices as the driver of changes in the income distribution. Rising imports from less developed countries with large supplies of unskilled labor, the argument goes, cause the relative prices of goods that are produced with relatively large amounts of unskilled labor in rich countries to fall, which in turn depresses the demand for unskilled workers in rich countries. The consequence is either lower wages or higher unemployment (or both) for unskilled workers in advanced industrial societies. That researchers have not found robust evidence that the relative prices of unskilled labor-intensive goods in advanced industrial societies have fallen significantly in the past twenty-five years has been taken as further evidence that trade with less developed countries has had only a small impact on wage inequality (Slaughter 2000). The general, albeit not universal, conclusion is that rising inequality and/or rising unemployment of low-skilled workers in advanced industrial countries is largely a consequence of technical progress or the decline of unions or the decline of the real minimum wage, and that while globalization may have increased inequality, its contribution is relatively minor compared to these other causes.

Researchers in political science and sociology who study social insurance policies among advanced industrial societies in the postwar period have also expressed skepticism regarding the importance of globalization as a constraint on government expenditures. Cameron (1978) demonstrated that the government expenditures as a share of GDP was positively, not negatively, associated with trade openness among advanced industrial countries. Rodrik (1997) found a similar positive relationship between government consumption and trade, both as share of GDP, for a broader set of 115 countries. In general, the studies can be divided into those that argue that the relationship between trade and government expenditures is spurious (Cameron 1978; Iversen and Cusack 2000; Hicks 1999; Huber and Stephens 2001)[1] and those that argue that trade dependence increases the political support for social insurance expenditures to compensate for the risks associated with greater participation in the global economy (Katzenstein 1985; Rodrik

1997; Garrett 1998). Studies of the impact of globalization on tax revenues in general and on taxes on capital in particular have also failed to find significant effects (Swank 2002). In general, the most important problems facing the future of social insurance programs are seen by most researchers as stemming from changes in demographics (the aging of the population), technology (the decline of industrial employment, the rising cost of health), women's participation in the work force (the need for day care), and political opposition to taxes, not international trade or capital mobility.

Many of the contributors to this volume argue, in contrast, that citizens of advanced industrial societies have good reason to be anxious about the consequences of globalization. The chapters by Minsik Choi and by Kenneth Scheve and Matthew Slaughter show that economists have missed the most important mechanisms linking trade with declining wages for unskilled workers by focusing on relative prices in the product market. Choi presents evidence that the increasing ease with which firms can transfer production abroad has increased their bargaining power in wage negotiations with unions and has enabled firms to capture a larger share of the surplus. Scheve and Slaughter argue that both trade and foreign direct investment have increased the degree to which workers in different countries are substitutes in production. The result is to increase the volatility of workers' income in response to fluctuations in consumer demand or in workers' productivity.

While the increase in employers' bargaining power and the increase in the volatility of labor earnings can effect high-income and well as low-income workers, the effects are strongest among the least skilled. The wage premium historically associated with union membership in the United States was greatest for unskilled workers, so the decline of the union wage premium has hurt the unskilled more than others, as Choi documents. And the volatility of earnings is generally higher for low-skilled than for high-skilled workers. Scheve and Slaughter document that opposition to free trade in advanced industrial societies is greatest among the least skilled, and that difference between the attitudes of the high skilled and low skilled are greatest in countries with the least general systems of social insurance.

Claus Offe's chapter advances the view that economic integration within the European Union threatens to destroy the European model of social insurance and labor market regulations. Offe argues that firms' ability to relocate productions where labor taxes and capital taxes are low is undermining the ability of governments and unions to protect workers' incomes. It is not just the taxation of capital that is constrained by the threat of disinvestment. Payroll taxes or costly labor market regulations are equally constrained by firms' readiness to move production to low-tax, less-regulated countries unless workers accept wage reductions of sufficient magnitude to keep the cost of labor from rising. Even the ability of national governments to increase consumption taxes such as the VAT above the levels of neighboring countries in Europe is limited by the fact that a majority of

European residents live within a half-day's drive of a national border. While these constraints are doubtless more important in smaller European nations than in larger and less open economies such as the United States, and while econometric and other evidence for these constraints is surprisingly weak, it is clear that many political actors and policymakers believe the constraints to be operative.

Adam Przeworski and Covadonga Meseguer's chapter in this volume provides a reconciliation of Offe's argument regarding the constraints imposed by globalization and the failure, noted earlier, of researchers to find evidence that governments in more open economies tend to spend less on welfare or to lower the tax burden on capital. Przeworski and Meseguer argue that taxes and spending are jointly determined by voters' support for redistribution taxation and the threat of firms to move their production abroad. While firms' ability to move abroad raises the cost of taxation in countries where taxes are relatively high, globalization may also increase the inequality and insecurity of income, which raises voters' willingness to support redistribution taxation at a given cost. Whether the net effect is to support higher or lower levels of taxation is ambiguous.[2] According to Przeworski and Meseguer, the impact of globalization on taxation is not necessarily observed in lower taxes but rather in governments' inability to raise taxes sufficiently to provide workers full compensation for the increase in inequality and volatility of labor incomes. It may be that, even if social insurance programs have not been dismantled, international economic integration may prevent welfare programs from adequately responding to the increased insecurity of European workers.

The first important lesson is that there is evidence that the international movement of goods, capital, and labor has increased the inequality and/or volatility of labor earnings in advanced industrial societies while constraining governments' ability to tax the winners from globalization to compensate workers for their loss. We don't mean to suggest that globalization is a straightjacket that forces all governments to adopt the same set of market-conforming policies. Nor, as we explain later, do we believe that globalization eliminates all room for egalitarian redistributive policies. It is important not to underestimate, however, the potential impact of globalization on both inequality and income security for workers in rich countries.

In contrast to the impact of globalization in rich countries, Bardhan's contribution to this volume addresses the impact of trade and cross-border flows of capital and labor on the more than one billion people who live on less than one dollar a day (at 1993 prices) in poor and middle-income countries. In the labor market or as self-employed, the very poor suffer from lack of education, ill health, lack of credit, lack of infrastructure, and predation. None of these impediments is due to globalization. To the extent that the Stolper-Samuelson mechanism works, it can work to the advantage of unskilled workers in poor countries. The poor who produce goods for export, such as garment workers in South Asia, would reap large gain from the elimination of the trade restrictions that still exist. Poor farmers in Africa, Asia, and Latin America competing with U.S. and European farmers in global markets are not hurt by free trade but by the agricultural tariffs and pro-duction subsidies paid to farmers in rich countries that allow rich-country farm products to be sold far below their cost of production. Relaxing restrictions on immigration from poor countries would provide large benefits for both those who leave their homes to find higher-paying jobs in rich countries and those who stay behind. Although Bardhan cites special circumstances where increased trade and foreign investment can hurt the poor, his general conclusion is that globaliza-tion can open up opportunities for the enhancement of the well-being of the poor. Some countries take advantage of these opportunities and others do not, largely depending on their domestic political and and economic institutions. The main impediments to poverty alleviation policies, according to Bardhan, are of-ten domestic vested interests, which may sometimes be weakened by the forces of global competition.

The second important lesson is that the free flow of goods, capital, and labor creates opportunities for enhancing the welfare of the poor in poor and middle-income coun-tries. This is perhaps the most compelling reason for an egalitarian to look for ways to help the victims of globalization without restricting international flows of goods and factors of production.

The Economic Feasibility of Redistributive Policies in a Global Economy

Factors of production that can be easily moved across national borders cannot be taxed by national governments in the absence of international coordination in tax policy. Since labor is relatively immobile compared with capital, wage earners end up paying the tax whether taxes are nominally levied against profits or wages. If capital is mobile, any tax that initially reduces the after-tax rate of return on capital causes investment to fall until the rise in the before-tax rate of return on capital compensates investors for the initial loss. In the medium run, capital own-ers earn the same after-tax rate of return as before while wage earners pay the tax in the form of lower wages or lower employment. The same occurs with attempts by governments or unions to improve working conditions or to shorten the work week. While workers might receive immediate gains, in the medium term work-ers will pay for the additional costs imposed on firms in the form of lower wages or lower employment as firms shift their investments to locations where labor costs are less.[3] Layna Mosley's study of the international bond market in this vol-ume documents how bond traders' assessments of the risk of default is reflected in the borrowing costs of developing countries. Mosley's study implies that the cost of default is borne not by international investors, who have priced the risk of de-fault into the cost of capital, but by the country's taxpayers (i.e., the country's work force), who have to pay the higher interest payments on the government debt. The argument can be generalized to include some workers as well. Govern-ments have a limited ability to tax workers who can easily relocate their residence to countries with lower tax rates.

The same logic implies, however, that the expected after-tax return on mobile factors cannot be *increased* in the long run, as Samuel Bowles points out in his contribution to this volume. Government policies that increase workers' productivity may cause profits to rise in the short run, but the higher rate of return will attract capital from abroad until the rate of return on investments falls back to the level that investors can earn in other countries around the globe. If global capital mobility constrains each country's expected after-tax rate of profit to be at the same global level, then in the long run, it is the immobile workers who receive all of the benefits from productivity-enhancing policies. *The third lesson is that free trade and capital mobility increases the effectiveness of redistributive policies that raise workers' productivity while diminishing the effectiveness of redistributive policies that lower the rate of return received by mobile factors of production.*

Bardhan and Bowles list a variety of redistribution policies that simultaneously increase inefficiency and reduce inequality. Land redistribution can have a large impact on agricultural productivity by turning farm workers into owners, with much stronger incentives to care for the soil and to work without supervision. The provision of subsidized credit to individuals too poor to borrow privately except at exorbitant rates can enable the poor to make small investments with a big return. The organization of cooperatives or the cooperation of unions can reduce monitoring costs associated with the employment relationship. Improvements in the quality of basic education and vocational training take time to bear fruit, but the return in terms of both equality and workers' productivity may be large. The case for adopting efficiency-enhancing reforms does not depend on globalization. But the potential gains for immobile workers from productivity-enhancing reforms are larger in an integrated global economy that in a world with closed borders.

Nor does globalization eliminate the ability of governments to provide insurance. The welfare state consists of policies that smooth consumption across an individual's lifespan, increasing a worker's income when unemployed, sick, or retired, and decreasing worker's income when gainfully employed. With perfect capital markets, workers could smooth their consumption through private borrowing in time of need without government help. Given the absence of perfect capital markets, however, the consumption smoothing that can achieved privately is inferior to what the government can provide. In addition, social insurance policies redistribute from individuals who are lucky to those who are unlucky, just as auto insurance redistributes income from those who have not suffered accidents to those who have. Finally, social insurance policies typically employ formulas for the calculation of contributions and benefits that imply redistribution from high-income workers to low-income workers. Capital mobility constrains governments from passing some of the cost of social insurance onto firms. To the extent that high-wage earners become mobile, governments will be forced to reduce the redistribution from high-income workers to low-income workers implicit in current social insurance programs. Globalization does not, however, impair governments' ability to provide insurance as long as workers bear the cost. Even without the ability to pass some the cost onto mobile factors of production, workers can receive large benefits from the insurance provided by social insurance policies. *A fourth lesson, then, is that free trade and capital mobility do not constrain policies that redistribute income among (immobile) wage earners.*

Karl Moene and Michael Wallerstein's contribution to this volume combines lessons three and four in their discussion of social democracy as a strategy of development based on the compression of wage differentials. Applied in the Nordic countries from the 1950s to the 1980s, the unions advocated a large redistribution of income among wage earners, raising the wages at the bottom of the labor market while limiting wage increases at the top of the labor market, without reducing the average rate of return to capital. Moene and Wallerstein suggest that the policy promoted productivity growth as well as equality. In the system of industry-level bargaining that existed prior to the introduction of the policy of wage compression, workers obtained wages though collective bargaining that reflected, in part, the productivity of the industry where they were employed. By reducing the wage premium received by workers in the strongest bargaining positions, the policy of wage compression lowered wage costs and increased investment and employment growth in the most productive firms. Reduced wage inequality promoted economic development, at least initially, in countries exceptionally dependent on international trade. The *economic* feasibility of promoting development by reducing the inequality of wages, Moene and Wallerstein argue, is enhanced, not diminished, by international economic integration.

The Politics of Redistribution in Open Economies

We have a better understanding of the consequences of the free movement of goods and factors of production for the economic feasibility of different types of redistributive policies than we do for their political viability. The determinants of political support for redistributive policies is a vast topic. Here we confine our discussion to the ways that globalization might change the politics of redistribution.

There are five ways in which globalization might affect the political equilibrium with regard to redistributive taxes and transfers. Globalization can affect the costs of redistributive fiscal policies. Globalization can affect the level of risk that voters face in their economic pursuits and hence their support for social insurance. Globalization can affect the distribution of income among voters and hence the income of the voter with median preferences over redistribution. By increasing the competitiveness of markets generally, globalization can enhance the political influence of both labor and capital operating in more competitive and less monopolistic market settings. Finally, by altering voters' beliefs about the importance of such determinants of economic success and failure as hard work or bad luck, or other reasons, globalization can affect the degree to which voters feel solidarity with one another.

We mentioned the first of these effects—the problem of redistribution in "leaky buckets"—in our introduction. The consequence of economic integration is to increase the tax burdens of the vast majority of voters who hold immobile assets. The higher the cost of redistributive fiscal policy, the lower the level of redistribution that voters will support. The effect of an increase in the cost of taxation may be offset, however, by the impact of the effect on globalization on the distribution of income and of income risk. Where globalization increases income inequality and lowers the income of the median voter relative to the mean, a higher level of redistributive fiscal policy will prevail in the political equilibrium for a given cost of taxation.[4] As the analysis of Przeworski and Meseguer demonstrates, the combined net impact of an increase in the cost of taxation and an increase in income inequality on the level of fiscal redistribution can go either way. Similarly, to the extent that globalization increases the riskiness of income for risk averse voters, the increased demand for social insurance at a given cost may offset the effect of the rise in the cost of taxation.

The contribution by Samuel Bowles and Ugo Pagano explores the potential political implications of a split in the work force between what they term the "cosmopolitans" and the "provincials." They speculate that some workers may be increasingly able to reduce their exposure to risk via interindustry or even international mobility while other workers find their income increasing dependent on job-specific skills. Among workers with job-specific skills, the demand for social insurance rises with exposure to greater international competition. In contrast, cosmopolitans may prefer to withdraw from national insurance schemes and find security in their mobility. Thus, according the Bowles and Pagano, globalization may strengthen the support for social insurance among some while weakening the support for social insurance among others.

The aspect of globalization that we have paid least attention to so far is immigration. Relaxing restrictions on immigration from poor to rich countries could have a large effect on global inequality and poverty. Bardhan cites estimates that the global gains from allowing the temporary entry of labor equivalent to 3 percent of the work force in OECD counties would exceed the gains from trade liberalization by 50 percent, and the poor in poor countries would gain the most. But no other aspect of globalization has aroused such strong political opposition in Europe.[5] The rise of right-wing populist parties expressing nationalist and xenophobic sentiments in many European countries indicates the electoral appeal of hostility to non-European immigrants.

Stuart Soroka, Keith Banting, and Richard Johnston in this volume study the impact of immigration on support for the welfare state by comparing changes in social insurance expenditures with changes in the stock of immigrants in advanced industrial societies. They estimate that "the typical industrial society might spend 16 or 17 percent more than it now does on social services had it kept its foreign-born percentage where it was in 1970." Scheve and Slaughter present evidence that voters in advanced industrial societies oppose immigration out of concerns that migrants contribute to crime and take jobs from natives, and there is evidence that immigration has contributed to the decline of real wages for unskilled workers in the United States (Borjas, Freeman, and Katz 1996, 1997). But opposition to immigration because of immigration's economic consequence would not, by itself, reduce popular support for welfare spending. Support for re-distribution policies, however, may depend on more than voters' self-interested comparison of expected benefits and expected costs. Voters may be more willing to provide assistance to others, especially to those who are like themselves but poorer. Immigration may erode a sense of community that sustains voters' will-ingness to help others and may undermine voters' trust that those receiving help are deserving of help. *The fifth lesson, then, is that the aspect of globalization that may have the greatest impact of the politics of redistribution within advanced industrial societies is the growth of immigration.*

So far, we have discussed the variety of ways in which globalization might affect the politics of redistributive fiscal policy. We understand even less about the ways in which globalization promotes or hinders the adoption of the sort of efficiency-enhancing policies discussed by Bardhan, Bowles, and Moene and Wallerstein. For egalitarians, the lack of understanding of the political conditions that made efficiency-enhancing reforms feasible is an embarrassing lacuna in our knowledge.[6]

Until now we have written as if globalization was an exogenous phenomenon to which countries respond. But the reduction of trade barriers and the removal of restrictions of international capital flows are themselves policy choices. Thus, it is important to ask, not only how globalization affects the politics of redistribu-tion but also how redistribution affects the politics of liberalization. This is the question studied by the comparison by Carles Boix of two Australian provinces, Victoria and New South Wales, in the second half of the nineteenth century. In both provinces, the main divide following the granting of home rule by the British was protectionism versus free trade, with labor as the swing group. In New South Wales, the outcome was a coalition of free traders and labor that com-bined low tariffs with relatively high levels of public spending in a classic social democratic fashion. In contrast, in Victoria and eventually in the Australian Commonwealth as a whole, the outcome was an alliance of protectionist interests and labor in which the unions obtained a share of the rents from protection by means of regulated wages in protected industries. Boix's essay is concerned with the party strategies that explained the divergence path of the two provinces. Here we want to focus on the fundamental observation that in a political context where labor was pivotal, the reduction of trade barriers was impossible without an increase in redistribution via taxes and government spending.

Offe makes the same point with respect to contemporary European politics. Offe interprets the rise of the populist, anti-immigrant, and anti-European parties throughout Europe as a response to popular resistance to the erosion of national systems of protection (as advocated by supporters of liberalization) without a viable replacement at the level of the European Union (as advocated by social democrats, so far without much success). As Offe writes, "[I]t is . . . widely felt by political elites that to maintain popular support for both the deepening of ('ever closer') European integration and the widening of its scope ('Eastern Enlargement'), Europe must present itself to its citizens as a credible project of social security and protection, and certainly not as a threat to established social status rights." Scheve and Slaughter find, in a comparison of surveys conducted in advanced industrial societies, that the greatest support for free trade is found in countries where social spending is highest (and where unemployment is lowest). In addition, Scheve and Slaughter find that the divergence in views regarding protectionism between high-skill and low-skill workers is least in countries where social insurance programs are most generous.

Scheve and Slaughter conclude their chapter with the observation that "simple conclusions that substantial social insurance and redistributive policies are inconsistent with economic globalization are implausible because it seems that political support for liberalism itself depends in part on those very policies." Or, to paraphrase Boix, public spending may be the quid pro quo of free trade. Globalization is not an inexorable process, but a consequence of policy choices that can be reversed. The economic gains from the free movements of goods and capital may be politically irrelevant in the absence of a political mechanism that can at least partially compensate the losers for their losses. *Thus, our final lesson is that whether the process of globalization continues or whether it is reversed may depend on governments' success in redistributing income and providing protection against the risks inherent in specialized production for global markets.*

Redistributive policies that are compatible with international openness are needed both to protect the poor, the vulnerable, and the unlucky in an increasingly global economic environment as well as to protect the economic gains that economic openness allows. Our hope, in publishing this work, is that we may contribute in a small way to a world at once more integrated and also more secure and more bountiful for the least well off.

NOTES

1. Here "spurious" can mean either that no causal relationship exists or that the impact of trade dependence is indirect, a cause of something else, such as corporatist institutions, that is a direct cause of high levels of social insurance expenditures.

2. See Rodrik (1997), Swank and Steinmo (2002), and Basinger and Hallerberg (2004) for parallel arguments that tax policy is subject to countervailing international and domestic pressures.

3. One qualification to the inability to tax capital with capital mobility stems from the fact that investments are no longer mobile once buildings are constructed and machinery

is installed. Thus, it is possible to design a tax system that taxes the returns on old capital without affected firms' return on new investment, for example by combining a tax on profits with a 100 percent depreciation allowance in the first year of new plant and equipment (Wallerstein and Przeworski 1995).

4. Note that greater income inequality can reduce the demand for redistributive social insurance if insurance is a normal good. As the median voter becomes poorer, the price of social insurance to the median voter declines, but so does her demand for social insurance. Which effect will dominate depends on the details of how contributions and benefits are calculated (Moene and Wallerstein 2003).

5. The comparable issue in the United States would be racial conflict, which one might describe as a legacy of an earlier period of globalization.

6. If the reforms made everyone better off, it would be hard to explain why governments have not already taken action. The real question concerns the political obstacles that block productivity-enhancing reforms that leave some groups worse off. What prevents the losers from being compensated from the increased income received by the winners? A plausible answer is that the potential gainers cannot credibly commit to compensating the losers.

REFERENCES

Basinger, Scott J., and Mark Hallerberg. 2004. "Remodeling the Competition for Capital: How Domestic Politics Erases the Race to the Bottom." *American Political Science Review* 98 (2): 261–76.

Blau, Francine D., and Lawrence M. Kahn. 2002. *At Home and Abroad: U.S. Labor Market Performance in International Perspective*. New York: Russell Sage Foundation.

Borjas, George J., Richard B. Freeman, and Lawrence F. Katz. 1996. "Searching for the Effect of Immigration on the Labor Market." *American Economic Review* 86 (2): 247–51.

———. 1997. "How Much Do Immigration and Trade Affect Labor Market Outcomes?" *Brookings Papers on Economic Activity* 1: 1–90.

Cameron, David. 1978. "The Expansion of the Public Economy." *American Political Science Review* 72: 1243–61.

Garrett, Geoffrey. 1998. *Partisan Politics in the Global Economy*. Cambridge: Cambridge University Press.

Gottschalk, Peter, and Robert Moffitt. 1994. "The Growth of Earnings Instability in the U.S. Labor Market." *Brookings Papers on Economic Activity* 2: 217–72.

Gottschalk, Peter, and Timothy Smeeding. 1997. Cross-National Comparisons of Earnings and Income Inequality. *Journal of Economic Literature*, 35 (2): 633–87.

Hanson, Gordon H., and Ann Harrison. 1999. "Trade Liberalization and Wage Inequality in Mexico." *Industrial and Labor Relations Review* 52: 271–88.

Hicks, Alexander. 1999. *Social Democracy and Welfare Capitalism: A Century of Income Security Politics*. Ithaca: Cornell University Press.

Huber, Evelyne, and John D. Stephens. 2001. *Development and Crisis of the Welfare State: Parties and Polities in Global Markets*. Chicago: University of Chicago Press.

Iversen, Torben, and Thomas Cusack. 2000. "The Causes of Welfare State Expansion." *World Politics* 52: 313–49.

Katzenstein, Peter. 1985. *Small States in World Markets: Industrial Policy in Europe.* Ithaca: Cornell University Press.

Krugman, Paul. 1994. *Peddling Prosperity.* New York: Norton.

Moene, Karl O., and Michael Wallerstein. 2003. "Earnings Inequality and Welfare Spending: A Disaggregated Analysis." *World Politics,* 55 (4): 485–517.

Rodrik, Dani. 1997. *Has Globalization Gone too Far?* Washington, D.C.: Institute for International Economics.

Scheve, Kenneth F., and Matthew J. Slaughter. 2004. "Economic Insecurity and the Globalization of Production." *American Journal of Political Science* 48 (4).

Slaughter, Matthew J. 2000. "What Are the Results of Product-Price Studies and What Can We Learn from Their Differences?" In *The Impact of International Trade on Wages,* vol. 129–70, edited by Robert C. Feenstra. Cambridge: National Bureau of Economic Research Conference.

Swank, Duane. 2002. *Global Capital, Political Institutions, and Policy Change in Developed Welfare States.* Cambridge: Cambridge University Press.

Swank, Duane, and Sven Steimo. 2002. "The New Political Economy of Taxation in Advanced Capitalist Democracies." *American Journal of Political Science* 48 (3): 642–55.

Wallerstein, Michael, and Adam Przeworski. 1995. "Capital Taxation with Open Borders." *Review of International Political Economy,* 2 (3): 425–45.

Wallerstein, Michael, and Bruce Western. 2000. "Unions in Decline? What Has Changed and Why?" *Annual Review of Political Science,* 3: 377–77.

Index

Adserà, Alícia, 196–97, 214nn4 and 8
Africa, 15; and drugs for AIDS patients, 27.
　See also specific African countries
Aides, Alberto F., 166n11
Alchain, Armen A., 299
Allan, James P., 112n4
Allen, Steven G., 80, 83n18
Andersen, Kym, 201
area-analysis model, 228–29
Argentina, 95, 306
Attanasio, O., 19n9
Aubert, C., 28n1
Aukrust, Odd, 213n1
Australia, 194, 198, 213, 263, 306, 314; and
　the Victorian "fiscal" model, 208–10
Autor, D., 82n5
average-member Nash equilibrium model, 174

Baker, Andy, 256n34
Baldwin, Peter, 212
Baldwin, Robert E., 252n6
Bangladesh, 30n15
Banting, Keith, 313–14
Barbados, 136
Barcelona European Council (2002), 34
Bardhan, Pranab, 7, 28n1, 133, 141n6,
　143n20, 303n6, 309–10, 311, 313, 314
bargaining channel, 65
Bashkar, V., 141n7
Basinger, Scott J., 315n2
Bates, Robert H., 213n2
Bayesian learning, 179
Beck, Nathaniel, 274
Belgium, 162
Benabou, R., 183
Bernard, Andrew B., 19, 231
Bertola, G., 172n2
Besley, T., 186
Betz, Hans-Georg, 267, 285n20
Bhagwati, Jagdish, 252n6
Birdsall, N., 141n6
Bjørgum, Jorunn, 166n7
Blanchflower, David G., 68, 141n7
Blau, Francine D., 166n9
Blewett, Neal, 214n16

Bobbio, N., 184
Boix, Carles, 9–10, 196–97, 214nn4 and 8,
　255n29, 314
bond market, and national policy choices, 7,
　87–90; convergence, divergence, and
　economic globalization and, 90–92; default
　risk, information, and financial market
　influences and, 92–93, 310; developed versus
　developing nations and, 95–97; financial
　market influence in the developed world, 97;
　financial market influence in emerging
　markets, 97–98; interview and survey
　evidence concerning the importance of de-
　fault risk, 98–103; quantitative evidence: —
　correlates of interest rates, 103–8; —variation
　in government policies, 103; investment risk
　and economization and, 94–95
Borjas, George J., 229, 253nn6, 7, and 8,
　254n17, 263
Bossi, Umberto, 48
Bowles, Samuel, 8–9, 133, 138, 141nn6 and 7,
　143n20, 303n6, 311, 313, 314
Boyer, Robert, 141n7
Branting, Hjalmar, 184
Brazil, 29n8, 112n4, 148, 152, 220; left parties
　in, 88, 89–90
Brehm, John, 114n51
Bresser Pereira, L. C., 188n13
Brock, Philip, 213n2
Brooks, Sarah M., 112n16
Bureau of Economic Analysis (BEA), 79–80
Busch, Marc, 256n37

Cain, Glen G., 252n6
Calvo, Guillermo A., 113n22
Cameron, David R., 177, 192, 194, 195, 307
Canada, 265; immigration policy of, 284nn5
　and 9
Canadian Reform Party, 284n8
capital markets, 90
capital mobility, 4–5, 49, 92–93, 126–30, 163,
　178, 293–94, 311, 315–16n3; increase of,
　68, 188n4; and trade, 178–82. *See also* capital
　mobility, and threat effects of on wage
　bargaining

Europeanness, 35; distinctive features of, 34
"exo-education," 291, 292

Fabbri, Francesca, 231
factor mobility, 225–26
factor price equalization theorem, 3, 64
Fajnzylber, P., 29n10
Fearon, James D., 113n32
Feenstra, Robert C., 66, 252n6
Feldstein, M., 141n7
Feleciano, Z. M., 19
Fini, Gianfranco, 48
Fitch-IBCA, 102
foreign direct investment (FDI), 82n3; impact
  on variability of earnings and employment,
  229–31; public attitudes about, 224. See also
  capital mobility, and threat effects of on wage
  bargaining
Fortuyn, Pim, 48
France, 150
Franzini, M., 141n6
free trade: and compensation, 194–97; public
  support for, 10
Freeman, Richard B., 65, 79, 166n9, 229,
  253nn6 and 7
Friedberg, Rachel, 229
Frisch, Ragnar, 148, 149

Galor, Oded, 143n24
Garnaut, Ross, 201
Garrett, Geoffrey, 177, 178, 196, 214n5, 299
Gaston, Noel, 66, 80
Gellner, Ernest, 290, 291, 294, 303n1
Germany, 162, 211, 301; left parties in, 89–90
Gilens, Martin, 278
Gintis, H., 133, 141n6, 143n20, 303n6
Glaeser, Edward L., 166n11
global specialization, 11
globalization, 27–28, 121, 217, 219, 222, 225,
  229–30, 262, 279; aspects of, 13; contributors to, 3; and control over short-term capital
  flows, 14; and convergence, 90–92; and
  cultural protection, 14; definition of, 2–3;
  and democracy, 169–70, 183–87; and
  divergence, 90–92; effect on taxation, 308–9;
  effect on wages, 6–7; and egalitarian
  redistribution, 2, 121–26, 139–41; and the
  elasticity of relative labor demand, 82n1;
  versus European integration, 39–41;
  globalization eras, 3; impact on inequality,
  insecurity, and prosperity, 306–10; and

intercountry differences in economic independence, 175–78; modern, 293–94; and
  policy choices, 8; public attitudes about,
  219–20; and redistributive capacities of the
  state, 261; and redistributive policies that
  enhance efficiency, 7–8; and reduction of
  inequalities, 3; and Third World poverty, 6,
  13–27. See also labor market impacts of
  globalization; nationalism; welfare state,
  European, effects of globalization on
Glyn, A., 141n7
Goldberg, P. K., 19, 29n9
Golden, Miriam, 166n8
Gordon, David M., 4, 141n7
Gorg, Holger, 231
Gottschalk, Peter, 210, 231
government expenditures, 129–30, 143n18
Great Britain. See United Kingdom
gross domestic product (GDP), 196, 268–69,
  307; per capita, 243, 248–49, 255n28. See
  also Norway, GDP of; Sweden, GDP of
Grossman, Sanford J., 112n19
Growth, Competitiveness, and Employment
  (Delors), 42, 53

Hagen, Carl, 48
Haider, Jorg, 48
Hainmueller, Jens, 256n37
Hall, Peter, 301
Hallerberg, Mark, 315n2
Hanson, Gordon H., 66, 227, 229, 252nn3 and
  6, 256n34
Harkins, Tom, 30n15
Harris, John R., 166n11
Harrison, Ann, 19, 26, 227
Harrison, G. W., 19–20
Haskel, Jonathan E., 227, 252n6
Heckscher-Ohlin (HO) framework/model,
  225–26, 228, 233, 234, 240, 241, 243, 250
Hibbs, Douglas A., 155, 166n9, 187n2
Hicks, Alexander, 269, 270
Hiscox, Michael, 256n37
Howe, Anthony, 211
Huber, Evelyne, 269–70, 275

immigration, 240–41, 250, 264, 284n1,
  313–14; and alleviation of world poverty, 14;
  effect of increases in, 266–67; "immigration
  gateway" communities, 241; impact on social
  insurance expenditures, 9; impact on wages,
  228–29; number of people living outside the